Risk Analysis and Portfolio Modelling

Risk Analysis and Portfolio Modelling

Special Issue Editors

David Allen

Elisa Luciano

MDPI • Basel • Beijing • Wuhan • Barcelona • Belgrade

Special Issue Editors
David Allen
University of Sydney
Australia

Elisa Luciano
University of Torino
Italy

Editorial Office
MDPI
St. Alban-Anlage 66
4052 Basel, Switzerland

This is a reprint of articles from the Special Issue published online in the open access journal *Journal of Risk and Financial Management* (ISSN 1911-8074) from 2018 to 2019 (available at: https://www.mdpi.com/journal/jrfm/special_issues/risk_analysis).

For citation purposes, cite each article independently as indicated on the article page online and as indicated below:

LastName, A.A.; LastName, B.B.; LastName, C.C. Article Title. *Journal Name* **Year**, *Article Number*, Page Range.

ISBN 978-3-03921-624-6 (Pbk)
ISBN 978-3-03921-625-3 (PDF)

Contents

About the Special Issue Editors

David Allen is currently an Honorary Professor, in the School of Mathematics and Statistics, at the University of Sydney, Australia; an Honorary Professor, in the School of Business and Law, Edith Cowan University, Joondalup, Western Australia; and an Honorary Chair Professor, in the Department of Finance, Asia University, Taiwan. Prior to retirement in 2013, he held Finance Chairs successively at Curtin and Edith Cowan Universities in Western Australia. He has a Ph.D in Finance from the University of Western Australia and an M.Phil in the History of Economic Thought from Leicester University, England.

He is a Fellow of the Modelling and Simulation Society of Australia and New Zealand and the International Engineering and Technology Institute. His research interests include financial economics, financial econometrics, market microstructure, risk modeling, and portfolio analysis. He has published five books in finance and economics, the most recent in (2017), which featured the use of R in economics and finance research. His research output includes over 150 papers and chapters in books, on a diverse range of topics, which have been published in economics, finance, statistics, and operational research journals.

Elisa Luciano is currently a Professor of Finance at the University of Torino; the Scientific Director of LTI@Unito, a think tank on long-term investors; a Fellow of Collegio Carlo Alberto; and has been a Visiting Scholar at the Wharton School, Cornell University, INSEAD, and the University of Zurich.

She is an expert in asset allocation, asset pricing, insurance, and risk management. She has published around 100 articles in academic journals, including the Journal of Finance and the Review of Financial Studies. She has published also for MIT Press.

She belongs to the EIOPA Occupational Pensions Stakeholder Group and is in the top 2% of SSRN Authors, and the top 8% of women economists according to REPEC-IDEAS.

Journal of
Risk and Financial Management

MDPI

Editorial

Risk Analysis and Portfolio Modelling

David Edmund Allen [1,2,3,*] **and Elisa Luciano** [4]

1 School of Mathematics and Statistics, University of Sydney, Sydney, NSW 2006, Australia
2 Department of Finance, Asia University, Wufeng 41354, Taiwan
3 School of Business and Law, Edith Cowan University, Joondalup, WA 6027, Australia
4 Department of Economics and Statistics, University of Torino, I-10134 Torino, Italy; elisa.luciano@unito.it
* Correspondence: profallen2007@gmail.com

Received: 18 September 2019; Accepted: 18 September 2019; Published: 21 September 2019

Abstract: Financial risk measurement is a challenging task because both the types of risk and their measurement techniques evolve quickly. This book collects a number of novel contributions for the measurement of financial risk, which addresses partially explored risks or risk takers in a wide variety of empirical contexts.

Keywords: risk analysis; portfolio analysis; risk attribution

---

In a special issue of the *Journal of Risk and Financial Management*, there was a call for contributions within the broad topic of portfolio analysis. This topic includes any novel, theoretical, or empirical research application in the area of portfolio analysis. This book collects a number of novel contributions for the measurement of financial risk, which address partially explored risks or risk takers in a wide variety of empirical contexts. Financial risk measurement is a challenging task because both the types of risk and their measurement techniques evolve quickly.

The more theoretical contributions in the book include an adjusted present value (APV) model of capital allocation for decentralized businesses. Further, it includes an integration of communication regarding theoretic models and portfolio theory. At the opposite end of the spectrum, this collection includes a study that details the links between insider trading and institutional holdings in the context of United States (US) equity issues (SEOs).

A number of issues relating to portfolio risk and performance are addressed in this volume. Apart from the construction of novel portfolio performance benchmarks, these include various aspects of default rates, probability of loss, and loss distributions on small enterprise loans. Further, value-at-risk (VaR) is examined in the context of crop insurance programs, as is herding in smart beta investments and determinants of sovereign risk premiums. There are two contributions regarding real estate markets that include the analysis of links between real estate and stock markets, plus the analysis of risk in Sweden housing market segments.

Turnbull (2018) considers a theory of capital allocation for decentralized businesses, considering the costs associated with risk capital. He derives an APV expression for making investment decisions that incorporates a time varying profile of risk capital. This differs from a top-down approach, in which, in the case of a bank, senior management decides on the optimal buffer size and the allocation to individual businesses within the bank make up its component activities. Managers who run sub-units of said business would presumably prefer a situation where the determination of a project's risk capital depended on project characteristics under their remit, not the characteristics of the bank as a whole. This is because they are concerned about risks over which they have some control. Turnbull derives an expression for the APV of a business by aggregating across the individual projects within a business. The associated difficulty is that this means there is no simple benchmark, such as risk adjusted rate of return on capital (RAROC), with which to compare the relative performance of different projects in the same company.

Using U.S. data, Wu and Yang (2018) analyze the impact of insider trades and institutional holdings on seasoned equity offerings (SEOs). They report that insider transactions have a significant impact on institutional holdings in SEOs. They suggest that institutional holdings change in the same direction as insider transactions. They interpret this as evidence that both insiders and institutional investors have similar SEO information sources. They also report a link between insider transactions and the long-term performance of SEO firms, which have greater explanatory power than institutional holdings.

Frahm and Huber (2019) propose a new performance measure that can be used to compare a strategy with a specified benchmark and develop the basic statistical properties of its maximum likelihood estimator in a Brownian motion framework. They adopt outperformance probability as a measure of portfolio performance and investigate whether mutual funds are able to beat the S&P 500 or the Russell 1000. They report that most mutual funds are able to beat the market, but not at standard levels of significance. Further, Frahm and Huber suggest that a performance metric should refer to differential returns when comparing a strategy with a given benchmark and should not compare both the strategy and the benchmark with a money market account. This is a standard feature of asset pricing-based performance metrics, which are linear and include the return on a risk-free asset. The authors suggest that this explains why mutual funds often appear to underperform in the market. This conclusion, they assert, is fallacious.

The best known performance measure is the Sharpe ratio, which divides the expected excess return on investment by the standard deviation of the excess return. Most other performance measures found in the literature are based on the same principle—they divide the return on investment by its risk, where the precise meaning of "return" and "risk" differ from one performance measure to another. Indeed, asset pricing is currently in a state of confusion. Cochrane (2011) complained about a "zoo" of factors that compete to explain risk–return relationships. Each different factor model will produce a different performance metric.

Frahm and Huber term the new metric the outperformance probability (OP), a concept which differs from customary return-to-risk measures. Their metric compares some strategies with a specified benchmark, which do not necessarily need to include a money market account. Their measure is based on a probability and is not determined in terms of specific holding periods. Furthermore, the holding period of the investor is consider to be random. This enabled them to compute the performance of an investment opportunity for arbitrary liquidity preferences.

Bedin et al. (2019) investigate the default probability, recovery rates, and loss distribution of a portfolio of securitized loans granted to Italian small and medium enterprises (SMEs). The authors use loan level data information provided by the European DataWarehouse platform, employing a logistic regression to estimate the company default probability. The analysis includes loan-level default probabilities and recovery rates used to estimate the loss distribution of the underlying assets. They report that bank securitized loans are less risky than an average bank lending to small and medium enterprises. This analysis provides novel information about the risks of asset backed securities (ABS) when structured in portfolios featuring loans to small to medium enterprises (SMEs).

Ramsey and Goodwin (2019) consider VaR and models of dependence in the U.S. Federal Crop Insurance Program. This is a complex issue because the program consists of policies across a wide range of crops, plans, and locations. Outcomes are affected by weather and other latent variables such as pests. This creates a complex dependency structure. The computation of VaR is an important issue because a standard reinsurance agreement (SRA) allows a portion of the risk to be transferred to the federal government. VaR is typically expressed as a probable maximum loss (PML) or as a return in the form of a loss in a given period.

Ramsey and Goodwin (2019) estimate the VaR of a hypothetical portfolio of crop insurance policies in which the marginal distributions are permitted to follow an arbitrary distribution. Given that any joint distribution can be decomposed into a marginal distribution and a copula function, they apply bounds to the VaR via the rearrangement algorithm (Embrechts et al. 2013). They report that there is a large degree of model risk related to the assumed dependence structure.

Krkoska and Schenk-Hoppé (2019) analyze herding in smart beta investment products and posit that the herding of investors is a major risk factor typically ignored in statistical approaches to portfolio modelling and risk management. Smart beta investment products involve the application of factor models, such as the ubiquitous Fama–French three-factor model, as an investment screening tool. The authors review the literature and suggest potential analytical approaches.

Mpapalika and Malikane (2019) examine the determinants of sovereign risk premiums in African countries using a fixed effects panel data approach. They report that public debt to GDP ratio, GDP growth, inflation rate, foreign exchange reserves, commodity price, and market sentiment are significant determinants at 5% and 10% levels. A feature of their sample is that a country's risk premium is an important factor in determining the choice between foreign currency borrowing and local currency borrowing. The stability of macroeconomic factors plays an important role in influencing the sovereign risk premium.

Liow et al. (2019) applies a wavelet analysis to explore the relationship between securitized real estate and local stock markets across five developed markets. The advantage of wavelet analysis is that it facilitates the decomposition of a time series into components of different frequency or duration. A standard time series analysis has a constant interval in finance applications, as exemplified by daily, weekly, or monthly data. Their approach permits the analysis of correlations at different frequencies. The authors report that securitized real estate markets appear to lead stock markets in the short-term, whereas stock markets tend to lead securitized real estate markets in the long-term, and to a lesser degree in the medium-term.

Arici et al. (2019) propose a communication theoretic interpretation of modern portfolio theory that includes short sales, leverage, and transaction costs. Thus, their paper posits a connection between portfolio optimization and matched filter theory, providing a means of incorporating the aforementioned market features.

Using the owner-occupied apartment market segment of the Swedish market in Stockholm, Wilhelmsson and Zhao (2018) analyze the risks from housing apartments in different housing market segments. They analyze risk in this market from the lender's perspective, focusing on credit risk and market risk; they suggest that both can be reduced by diversification. They analyze diversification across a number of criteria, including geographical dispersion and ownership characteristics, using a variety of methods including beta analysis, hedonic pricing, and analytical hierarchy processing. Their results suggest that both larger apartments and more recently built apartments experience higher price volatility. They suggest that older apartments with just one room are more likely to experience risk reduction benefits in the context of a housing portfolio.

Sajjad and Zakaria (2018) examine the relationship between credit rating scales and debt maturity choices using a sample of non-financial listed Asian companies rated by Standard and Poor's rating agency. The non-financial companies are chosen from eight selected Asian regions: Japan, South Korea, Singapore, China, Hong Kong, Indonesia, Malaysia, and India. Moreover, Sajjad and Zakaria apply a generalized linear model (GLM) and pool an ordinary least square (OLS) in their analysis. Their results suggest that companies with high and low ratings have a shorter debt maturity whilst companies with medium ratings have a longer debt maturity structure. There is a negative association between liquidity and longer debt maturity structures.

This volume includes a wide variety of theoretical and empirical contributions that address a wide range of issues and topics related to risk analysis, portfolio analysis, and risk attribution.

Funding: Financial support from the Italian ministry of Education, University and Research (MIUR), Dipartimenti di eccellenza, grant 2018-2022, is gratefully ackowledged.

Conflicts of Interest: The authors declare no conflict of interest.

References

Arici, Giorgio, Marco Dalai, Riccardo Leonardi, and Arnaldo Spalvieri. 2019. A Communication Theoretic Interpretation of Modern Portfolio Theory Including Short Sales, Leverage and Transaction Costs. *Journal of Risk and Financial Management* 12: 4. [CrossRef]

Bedin, Andrea, Monica Billio, Michele Costola, and Loriana Pelizzon. 2019. Credit Scoring in SME Asset-Backed Securities: An Italian Case Study. *Journal of Risk and Financial Management* 12: 89. [CrossRef]

Cochrane, John H. 2011. Presidential address: Discount rates. *The Journal of Finance* 66: 1047–108. [CrossRef]

Embrechts, Paul, Puccetti Giovanni, and Rüschendorf Ludger. 2013. Model uncertainty and VaR aggregation. *Journal of Banking and Finance* 37: 2750–64. [CrossRef]

Frahm, Gabriel, and Ferdinand Huber. 2019. The Outperformance Probability of Mutual Funds. *Journal of Risk and Financial Management* 12: 108. [CrossRef]

Krkoska, Eduard, and Klaus R. Schenk-Hoppé. 2019. Herding in Smart-Beta Investment Products. *Journal of Risk and Financial Management* 12: 47. [CrossRef]

Liow, Kim H., Xiaoxia Zhou, Qiang Li, and Yuting Huang. 2019. Time–Scale Relationship between Securitized Real Estate and Local Stock Markets: Some Wavelet Evidence. *Journal of Risk and Financial Management* 12: 16. [CrossRef]

Mpapalika, Jane, and Christopher Malikane. 2019. The Determinants of Sovereign Risk Premium in African Countries. *Journal of Risk and Financial Management* 12: 29. [CrossRef]

Ramsey, A. Ford, and Barry K. Goodwin. 2019. Value-at-Risk and Models of Dependence in the U.S. Federal Crop Insurance Program. *Journal of Risk and Financial Management* 12: 65. [CrossRef]

Sajjad, Faiza, and Muhammad Zakaria. 2018. Credit Ratings and Liquidity Risk for the Optimization of Debt Maturity Structure. *Journal of Risk and Financial Management* 11: 24. [CrossRef]

Turnbull, Stuart M. 2018. Capital Allocation in Decentralized Businesses. *Journal of Risk and Financial Management* 11: 82. [CrossRef]

Wilhelmsson, Mats, and Jianyu Zhao. 2018. Risk Assessment of Housing Market Segments: The Lender's Perspective. *Journal of Risk and Financial Management* 11: 69. [CrossRef]

Wu, Ching-Chih, and Tung-Hsiao Yang. 2018. Insider Trading and Institutional Holdings in Seasoned Equity Offerings. *Journal of Risk and Financial Management* 11: 53. [CrossRef]

Journal of
Risk and Financial Management

MDPI

Article

Capital Allocation in Decentralized Businesses

Stuart M. Turnbull

Bauer College of Business, University of Houston, TX 77004, USA; stuartmturnbull@gmail.com

Received: 23 October 2018; Accepted: 22 November 2018; Published: 26 November 2018

Abstract: This paper described a theory of capital allocation for decentralized businesses, taking into account the costs associated with risk capital. We derive an adjusted present value expression for making investment decisions, that incorporates the time varying profile of risk capital. We discuss the implications for business performance measurement.

Keywords: risk capital; capital allocation; decentralization; performance measurement; RAROC

1. Introduction

The credit worthiness of a bank is a major concern to its management, trading partners, creditors and bank regulators. The lower the credit worthiness, the greater will be the agency and monitoring costs, resulting in increased credit spreads and lower credit ratings. It will also increase the need to provide larger collateral. Steps to increase the credit worthiness will lower these costs while increasing the opportunity cost of holding a protective buffer.

Senior management must decide on the optimal size of a buffer to hold and the allocation to individual businesses within the bank.[1] Erel et al. (2015) (EMR) take a top-down approach to asset and risk capital allocation subject to constraints on the default put to liability ratio and the total amount of risk capital. First, they consider the bank as a whole and then as a multi business. A centralized approach is assumed, with senior management determining the optimal asset allocation for each business. They show that the sum of the product of each asset value of a business and its marginal default put value equals the default value of the bank as a whole. They derive the optimal asset and risk capital allocation to the individual businesses. The model is a single period and debt used to fund investments is assumed to be default free.

For many large multi-business banks, senior management delegate the responsibility of running the businesses to the business managers, subject to various constraints. Individual businesses are held accountable for the risk capital allocated to the business and managers are judged on how well they run the individual businesses. Consequently, managers would prefer performance metrics to be based on factors for which they have direct control. For example, the determination of risk capital for a project should depend on the characteristics of the project and not the characteristics of the bank, as in Erel et al. (2015). The maturity of the debt used to finance a project should be similar to the expected maturity of the project and not the average maturity of the bank's debt.[2] The question of how to allocate capital internally is a question faced by all banks. In this paper, we assume decentralized management, unlike Erel et al. (2015), who assume centralized management.

A manager of a business decides on the asset allocation to maximize the present value of investments, subject to constraints set by senior management. First, there is a limit to the total

[1] For reviews of extant work on capital allocation, see Bhatia (2009), Matten (2000) and Crouhy et al. (1999). Bajaj et al. (2018) provide a review of the types of methodologies employed by different financial institutions.

[2] This issue does not arise in Erel et al. (2015), as it is a single period model and bonds are assumed to be pari passu if default occurs.

amount of risk capital that a business can employ. Second, there is a limit on the credit risk for each business. The determination of the default put option depends on the characteristics of the business and not the rest of the bank. This implies that we no longer have the aggregation result given in EMR; the sum of the value of the default puts for all the businesses will be greater than the default put for the bank, giving rise to what is termed "the portfolio effect". This is not surprising, given the work of Merton (1973) and Merton and Perold (1993). We show how the credit risk limit assigned to individual businesses by senior management can be set such that the portfolio effect is zero.

With decentralization come issues of setting bonuses for business managers, senior management must determine the relative performance of the different businesses. We show how to determine the adjusted present value of each business. Simple performance measures such as the risk adjusted rate of return on capital (RAROC) do not correctly adjust for credit and market risk (see Wilson (1992), Froot and Stein (1998), Crouhy et al. (1999) and Erel et al. (2015) and the errors can be large, see Demine (1998)). We discuss alternative measures.

Section 2 of the paper provides some basic definitions, drawing on the work of Erel et al. (2015). Section 3 extends the Erel et al. (2015) model to decentralized management. Section 4 examines business performance and conclusions are given in Section 5.

2. Top-Down Planning

In this section, we briefly describe the Erel et al. (2015) model. Risk capital has been defined as a buffer to absorb unexpected losses and provide confidence to investors and depositors—see Bhatia (2009). It is the amount needed to cover the potential diminution in the value of assets and other exposures over a given time period using some metric as a risk measure. The expected risk capital requirements will vary over the life of a project. For example, the risk capital for a foreign currency swap will increase as its maturity declines. The amount of risk capital is determined internally by the company, using a risk measure such as the value-at-risk (VaR) or expected shortfall.[3] This definition updates the definition given in (Matten 2000, p. 33). Economic capital is defined as

$$\text{Economic Capital} = \text{Risk Capital} + \text{Goodwill}.$$

Instead of using VaR or expected shortfall, Merton and Perold (1993) (MP) introduce a different definition of risk. Risk capital is defined as the cost of buying insurance (default put), so the debt of the firm is default free. If default occurs, the default put pays bondholders. It is assumed that there is no counterparty risk associated with the seller of the insurance. This definition is used by Erel et al. (2015), who consider the issue of capital allocation for a firm with different businesses in a single period model. They show how tax and other costs of risk capital should be allocated to the individual businesses.

The market value of debt, D, can be written as

$$D = L - P, \tag{1}$$

where L denotes the default free value of liabilities and P the value of the put option with strike price equal to the face value plus coupon payment. The term P is a measure of the dollar cost arising from the risk of default and financial distress. We assume that goodwill is zero, a similar assumption is made in Erel et al. (2015). Merton and Perold (1993) define the risk capital C as

$$C = A - L, \tag{2}$$

3 Artzner et al. (1999) show that expected short fall is a coherent risk measure.

where A represents the market value of the assets. The risk capital is a measure of the cushion between the assets of the firm and amount of liabilities arising from issuing debt. The larger the risk capital, the greater is the credit worthiness. The risk capital ratio is defined as $c = C/A$, where

$$c = 1 - \frac{L}{A}. \tag{3}$$

The value of the put option is given by

$$P = \int_{z \in Z} [LR_L - AR_A]\pi(z)dz = \int_{z \in Z} A[(1-c)R_L - R_A]\pi(z)dz,$$

where Z is the set of states for which the revenues are insufficient to meet obligations—more formally defined as $Z = \{z; (1-c)R_L - R_A(z) > 0\}$ and $\pi(z)$ is the pricing kernel. If $R_A(z)$ is assumed to have a mean μ_A and standard deviation σ_A, then we can write $R_A(z) = \mu_A + \sigma_A z$, where z has zero mean and unit variance. This does not imply that z is normally distributed. It is assumed that μ_A and σ_A do not depend on A, and a similar assumption is implicitly made in EMR. Note

$$A(1-c)R_L - AR_A(z) > 0 \quad \Leftrightarrow \quad \tfrac{(1-c)R_L - \mu_A}{\sigma_A} > z.$$

Let $U \equiv \frac{(1-c)R_L - \mu_A}{\sigma_A}$; then,

$$P = A \int_{-\infty}^{U} [(1-c)R_L - (\mu_A + \sigma_A z)]\pi(z)dz. \tag{4}$$

The default put option is a function of the level of assets, the risk capital ratio c and U. The marginal put value is

$$p = \frac{\partial P_j}{\partial A} = \int_{-\infty}^{U} [(1-c)R_L - (\mu_A + \sigma_A z)]\pi(z)dz \tag{5}$$

assuming that μ_A and σ_A are not functions of the asset level A. The above expression implies $P = Ap$. Note that the marginal put value depends on the risk capital ratio, c, given U, implying $p = p(c; U)$.

The term P/L can be interpreted as a measure of the credit risk of the business. For a given level of liabilities, the lower the value of the put option, the lower is the credit risk. We assume the bank sets a limit, α, on the default put to liability ratio

$$q = \frac{P}{L} \leq \alpha, \tag{6}$$

where q is a measure of the credit risk of the bank. The lower the level of α, then the lower is the credit risk of the bank and the greater is the credit worthiness. Most banks are prepared to accept a positive amount of default risk; no large American banks have a triple A credit rating.

2.1. Top Down Planning

The net present value of the bank's assets

$$NPV(A, q) = \int_A npv(y, q)dy,$$

where $npv(y, q)$ denotes the marginal net present value. It is assumed to be a function of the credit risk, q. There are additional costs imposed on the bank as it alters its asset mix—first are the costs associated with the risky debt used to finance investments due to default and financial distress, as measured by the value of the default put P. The value of the put option will depend on the amount of the assets and the risk capital. Second, there are costs from holding risk capital, τC. Holding risk capital imposes an implicit opportunity cost, as the capital could be employed to generate additional income. Here, we assume that τ is positive. It is not uncommon for τ to be set equal to the required rate of return on equity. The bank is assumed to maximize the net present value of allocation of assets subject to the constraint of maintaining a given level of credit quality. The bank places a restraint on the level of credit risk it is prepared to accept. Expression (6) can be written in the form

$$P \leq \alpha A(1-c).$$

2.2. Allocation to Individual Businesses

We assume the bank has N internal businesses. The assets in business j are denoted by A_j and the face value of debt liabilities attributed to the business by L_j. The total return at the end of the period is given by $R_{A,j}A_j$ and total debt payments $R_{L,j}L_j$.[4] For the bank,

$$R_A A \equiv \textstyle\sum_{j=1}^{N} R_{A,j}A_j \quad \text{and} \quad R_L L \equiv \sum_{j=1}^{N} R_{L,j}L_j,$$

where

$$A = \textstyle\sum_{j=1}^{N} A_j \quad \text{and} \quad L = \sum_{j=1}^{N} L_j. \tag{7}$$

The value of the default put for the bank can be expressed in the form

$$P = \int_{-\infty}^{U} \sum_{j=1}^{N} A_j[(1-c_j)R_{L,j} - R_{A,j}]\pi(z)dz, \tag{8}$$

where $c_j = C_j/A_j, = (1 - L_j/A_j), j = 1, \ldots, N$. The contribution by the j business to the default put is described by:

$$p_j = \frac{\partial P_j}{\partial A_j} = \int_{-\infty}^{U} [(1-c_j)R_{L,j} - R_{A,j}]\pi(z)dz, \tag{9}$$

implying that the marginal contribution to the put option is a function of U and c_j: $p_j = p_j(U, c_j)$. Given that the range of integration U does not explicitly depend on the individual business, then we have the additivity result first derived by Erel et al. (2015) (EMR):

$$P = \sum_{j=1}^{N} A_j p_j. \tag{10}$$

EMR assumes that senior management directly determines the size of the individual businesses, subject to constraints on the aggregate credit risk

$$\sum_{j=1}^{N} A_j p_j \leq \alpha \sum_{j=1}^{N} A_j(1-c_j)$$

and the amount of risk capital

$$\sum_{j=1}^{N} c_j A_j < \bar{C}. \tag{11}$$

[4] It should be remembered that while specifying possibly different funding rates for each business, given the assumptions in the Erel et al. (2015) model - single period and pari passu if default risk, all the rates will be equal.

In the capital allocation program, different amounts of risk capital will be assigned to the different businesses, given the constraint that the total risk capital for the bank is $\bar{C}$. The capital allocation program facing management can be expressed in the form

$$\begin{aligned} V(A,c) &= \max_{\{A_k,c_k\}}\{\textstyle\sum_{k=1}^{N}\int_{A_k} npv_k(y,q)dy - \tau c_k A_k - wA_k p_k \\ &\quad +\lambda[\alpha(1-c_k)A_k - p_k A_k]\} + \kappa[\bar{C} - \textstyle\sum_{k=1}^{N} c_k A_k], \end{aligned} \tag{12}$$

where the decision variables are the assets allocated to each business $\{A_k\}$, and the risk capital $\{C_k\}$; λ and κ are Lagrangian coefficients.

3. Decentralized Management

At the senior management level, the central planning system helps to determine the amount of risk capital to allocate to the individual businesses within the bank. However, to encourage entrepreneurship at the business level, operating decisions are left to the business managers, subject to various constraints. Each business is treated as having its own balance sheet. Usually, business managers try to match borrowing requirements to the average duration of the business assets. The business borrows an amount L_j from the bank and the cost of borrowing is determined by the current yield on the bank's debt for a specified maturity. Let $R_{L,j}$ denote the borrowing rate for the j th business. By definition, the risk capital of the business is $C_j = A_j - L_j$. The cash flow at the end of the period is $A_j R_{A,j} - L_j R_{L,j}$.

The value of the default put option to the business is

$$P_j = \int_{z\in Z_j} A_j[(1-c_j)R_{L,j} - R_{A,j}]\pi(z)dz,$$

where $c_j = C_j/A_j$, the capital ratio for the business, Z_j is the set of states for which the revenues are insufficient to meet obligations—more formally defined as $Z_j = \{z; (1-c_j)R_{L,j} - R_{A,j}(z) > 0\}$ and $\pi(z)$ is the pricing kernel. Note that the definition for Z_j is business specific, unlike the definition for Z that referenced the conditions for the whole bank. This difference implies that we will no longer have the additivity result (10). The business wants its risk capital to depend only on the operations of the business. It does not want is risk capital being directly influenced by other businesses within the bank. The strike price of the put option depends on the duration of the business's liabilities, $R_{L,j}$, and the magnitude of its debt, L_j.

If $R_{A,j}(z)$ is assumed to have a mean $\mu_{A,j}$ and standard deviation $\sigma_{A,j}$, then we can write $R_{A,j}(z) = \mu_{A,j} + \sigma_{A,j}z$, where z has zero mean and unit variance. It is assumed that $\mu_{A,j}$ and $\sigma_{A,j}$ do not depend on A_j. Let $U_j \equiv \frac{(1-c_j)R_{L,j}-\mu_{A,j}}{\sigma_{A,j}}$, then

$$P_j = A_j \int_{-\infty}^{U_j} [(1-c_j)R_{L,j} - R_{A,j}]\pi(z)dz. \tag{13}$$

The upper limit of integration depends on the characteristics of the business, unlike the upper limit of integration in expression (4) that depends on the cash flows of the whole bank.

The marginal contribution to the default put is

$$p_j = \frac{\partial P_j}{\partial A_j} = \int_{-\infty}^{U_j} [(1-c_j)R_{L,j} - R_{A,j}]\pi(z)dz, \tag{14}$$

implying that the marginal contribution to the put option is a function of c_j and U_j: $p_j = p_j(c_j, U_j)$. The greater the capital ratio c_j, the lower is the value of the default put option.

Senior management is assumed to impose a common limit, α_B, for the credit risk applied to all businesses:

$$q_j = \frac{P_j}{L_j} \leq \alpha_B. \tag{15}$$

In general, this rate may differ from the rate used by the bank for central planning.

The business wants to pick an asset level A_j to maximize the net present value. There are also constraints—first, the constraint on credit risk, written in the form

$$p_j A_j \leq \alpha_B (1 - c_j) A_j, \tag{16}$$

second the risk capital for the business can not exceed the limit imposed by the senior management

$$c_j A_j \leq \bar{C}_j,$$

where $\bar{C}_j$ denotes the amount of risk capital assigned to the business.

The optimization facing the business is described by

$$\begin{aligned} V_j(A,c) &= \max_{A_j,c_j} \int npv_j(A_j,q_j)dA_j - \tau c_j A_j - w p_j A_j \\ &\quad + \lambda_j[\alpha_B(1-c_j)A_j - p_j A_j] + \kappa_j(\bar{C}_j - c_j A_j), \end{aligned} \tag{17}$$

where $npv_j(A_j, q_j)$ denotes the marginal net present value, $and \lambda_j$ and κ_j are the Lagrangians arising from the two constraints. One way to interpret this specification is the business picks an asset class(es) with credit risk, q_j. Different businesses will have different inherent credit risks and different returns. The greater the credit risk, the larger are the costs associated with risky debt. Ex ante, the business hopes to offset these costs with higher returns. The business must decide on the appropriate asset class and level of investment. It is instructive to compare the above objective function with the top-down objective represented by expression (12). The obvious difference is that the top-down approach considers the asset allocation for all businesses and the constraints refer to the bank as a whole, while (17) is at the business level. The Lagrangian coefficients λ_j and κ_j and the value of the default put P_j are business specific.

The first order condition for the asset level is given by

$$\begin{aligned} \frac{\partial V_j}{\partial A_j} &= npv_j(A_j,q_j) + \frac{\partial q_j}{\partial A_j} A_j \frac{\partial}{\partial q_j} npv_j(A_j,q_j) \\ &\quad -(\tau+\kappa_j)c_j - w p_j + \lambda_j[\alpha_B(1-c_j) - p_j] \\ &= 0, \end{aligned}$$

where, following Erel et al. (2015), we have used the assumption $\frac{\partial q_j}{\partial A_j}\frac{\partial}{\partial q_j}\int(npv_j(A_j,q_j)dA_j = \frac{\partial q_j}{\partial A_j}A_j\frac{\partial}{\partial q_j}npv_j(A_j,q_j)$. Now $\frac{\partial q_j}{\partial A_j} = \frac{\partial q_j}{\partial c_j}\frac{\partial c_j}{\partial A_j}$ and at the optimum, changes in the risk capital ratio do not affect the credit quality, $\frac{\partial q_j}{\partial c_j} = 0$. Therefore, we have

$$\frac{\partial V_j}{\partial A_j} = npv_j(A_j,q_j) - (\tau+\kappa_j)c_j - w p_j + \lambda_j[\alpha_B(1-c_j) - p_j] = 0. \tag{18}$$

For the amount of risk capital, we can write, after simplification,

$$\frac{\partial V_j}{\partial c_j} = -[(\tau+\kappa_j) + w\frac{\partial p_j}{\partial c_j} + \lambda_j(\alpha_B + \frac{\partial p_j}{\partial c_j})]A_j = 0. \tag{19}$$

For the constraints, the Kuhn–Tucker conditions are

$$\frac{\partial V_j}{\partial \lambda_j} = A_j[\alpha_B(1-c_j) - p_j]\lambda_j = 0.$$

If the constraint is binding, $\lambda_j > 0$, then the optimal risk capital ratio for business j is determined by solving the equation

$$\alpha_B(1-c_j^*) = p_j(U_j, c_j^*) \tag{20}$$

so that $c_j^* = c_j(U_j, \alpha_B)$. For the risk capital constraint,

$$\frac{\partial V_j}{\partial \kappa_j} = (\bar{C}_j - c_j A_j)\kappa_j = 0. \tag{21}$$

We can solve the above four numbered equations to determine the optimum values for A_j^* and c_j^* and the Lagrangians λ_j and κ_j.

Aggregation

Each individual business determines its own level of asset investment $\{A_j\}$ and risk capital $\{C_j\}$. This will differ from the asset allocation determined by the bank in a top-down approach for at least three reasons. First, the bank uses the distribution generated by the aggregated cash flows. Second, in the top-down approach, the strike price of the default put is given by the aggregated level of debt payments. Third, the level of credit risk, q, is determined at the aggregate level.

The sum of the business put options is given

$$\sum_j P_j = \alpha_B \sum (A_j - C_j).$$

At the aggregate level, the total level of debt payments is $A(1-c)R_L = \sum_j A_j(1-c_j)R_{L,j}$ and the total cash flow generated by the individual businesses is given by $AR_A = \sum A_j R_{A,j}$, which defines the return R_A with mean μ_{BU} and standard deviation σ_{BU}. We can write $R_A = \mu_{BU} + \sigma_{BU} z$, where z has zero mean and unit variance. Given the individual business decisions, the value of the default put option for the bank is

$$P = \int_{-\infty}^{U_{BU}} [A(1-c)R_L - AR_A]^+ \pi(z) dz, \tag{22}$$

where $U_{BU} = \frac{(1-c)R_L - \mu_A}{\sigma_A}$. We continue to assume that the only uncertainty is with respect to the aggregate rate of return from the different businesses. Note the upper limit of integration in the above expression is U_{BU}, while, in expression (13), the upper limit of integration is U_j and, consequently, we do not have the top-down aggregation result (10). From Merton and Perold (1993), we know that the sum of the individual business put options is greater than the put option on the bank, $\sum_j P_j \geq P$. The difference is often called the "portfolio effect".

One of the consequences of decentralization is businesses pick, subject to constraints, the asset level $\{A_j\}$, risk capital $\{C_j\}$ and credit risk $\{q_j\}$. The individual businesses can have a lower degree of credit worthiness than the bank. By aggregating across the businesses and assuming that returns are not perfectly correlated, the value of the default put for the bank is lower than the sum for the individual businesses. The actual value of α_B is set by senior management and involves a trade-off between return and the impact on the bank's credit worthiness. What is required is a way to measure the relative performance of the different businesses.

4. Business Performance

The need to employ risk capital affects the determination of the value of investment projects and business performance metrics. Each project a business undertakes affects the credit risk of the business and management of the business wants to determine the trade-off between how the project enhances the value of the business and the associated credit risk. We start the analysis by considering a business undertaking a project and will discuss some of the many practical issues that arise. We do not consider the implications of corporate taxation at the business level. It is quite difficult for businesses to determine the effective tax rate, as senior management at the bank level has flexibility in adjusting when certain cash flows are recorded. To reduce agency problems at the business level, taxation is usually ignored when comparing business performance.

The initial implicit price per share of equity is $\bar{S}_0$ and the number of shares h_0, so that the implicit value of equity in the business is $\bar{S}_0 \times h_0$, reflecting current projects. When a business undertakes a new project, the investment is assumed to be financed with debt. The cost of the debt financing reflects the credit risk of the bank and the maturity of the project. We will denote the interest rate for the project as R_d, where d denotes the expected duration of the project. For each project, the business is required to assign risk capital to the project, so that it does not adversely affect the credit worthiness of the bank. Let $\{C_0, C_1, \ldots, C_{n-1}\}$ denote the required risk capital for the project. Note that the risk capital in general changes over the life of the project. Some projects initially require little risk capital, such as foreign exchange swaps. The business uses a bank approved risk metric to estimate the required risk capital. The implicit assumption is that risk capital is financed by equity. The actual determination of the required risk capital is far from easy. There is an array of different approaches: value at risk, expected shortfall or estimating the value of implicit default put options, each with advantages and disadvantages when used for actual estimation arising from issues of data availability and underlying model assumptions.

In practice, the bank allocates a certain amount of risk capital to a business and charges the business for the use of the capital. The cost is often specified as the required rate of return on equity, denoted by the symbol k. The business to partially off set the cost of risk capital assumes it can invest in default free assets of the life of the project. We denote the rate of interest as r and, for the sake of simplicity, assume it is constant. At time i, the business has risk capital C_{i-1} and the net cost of risk capital is $C_{i-1} \times (k - r)$.

At the end of the i period, the risk capital changes from C_{i-1} to C_i. The risk capital is financed via equity. We employ the following convention by calling the change $(C_i - C_{i-1})$ a cash inflow, recognizing that the change could be negative implying that shares are implicitly repurchased.

When a business undertakes a project, it is possible for the project to be prematurely terminated: the business may decide to cut losses or to take profits. To concentrate the focus on establishing a framework for judging the performance of a business within a bank, we ignore the possibility of premature termination.

At the maturity of the project, the cash flow before tax generated by the project is

$$Z_n \equiv F_n - I_0(1 + R_d) + C_{n-1} \times (-\bar{k}),$$

where the term F_n represents the cash flow when the project is matures, I_0 is the initial outlay to finance the project and $\bar{k} = k - r$. Again, for simplicity, we assume there is only one initial outlay. This assumption can be dropped, though it adds complexity without adding additional insight. The second term, $I_0(1 + R_d)$, represents the repayment of principal and interest from the business to the bank. As the project terminates, $C_n \equiv 0$ and the remaining capital C_{n-1} is used to repurchase equity. Note that the terminal cash flow Z_n may be negative. The business records the loss, with the bank acting as lender of last resort.

At time $n-1$, the market value of the business's equity project is

$$(h_{n-1}+m_{n-1})S_{n-1} = PV_{n-1}(B_n) + PV_{n-1}(Z_n) - PV_{n-1}(C_n - C_{n-1}|n],$$

where B_n is the cash flow generated by existing projects within the business. The last term on the right side represents the present value at time $t = n-1$ of the issuance of equity to finance the change in risk capital at $t = n$. Note that $C_n = 0$, as the project has matured. To simplify the analysis, we assume that the risk capital for the existing projects is constant. Financing the change in required risk capital implies issuing or repurchasing equity

$$m_{n-1}S_{n-1} = C_{n-1} - C_{n-2}$$

so that the total value of the equity of the business is

$$\begin{aligned} h_{n-1}S_{n-1} &= PV_{n-1}(B_n) + PV_{n-1}(F_n) - PV_{n-1}[I_0(1+R_d)] \\ &\quad + PV_{n-1}(C_{n-1} \times (1-\bar{k})|n] - C_{n-1} + C_{n-2}. \end{aligned}$$

At time $n-1$, the cash flow for the project is

$$Z_{n-1} \equiv F_{n-1} - I_0 \times R_d + C_{n-2} \times (-\bar{k}).$$

At time $n-2$, the investment in risk capital is given by

$$m_{n-2}S_{n-2} = C_{n-2} - C_{n-3}.$$

Hence,

$$\begin{aligned} h_{n-2}S_{n-2} &= PV_{n-2}(B_n) + PV_{n-2}(B_{n-1}) \\ &\quad + PV_{n-2}[F_n - I_0(1+R_d)|n] + PV_{n-2}[F_{n-1} - I_0 \times R_d|n-1] \\ &\quad + PV_{n-2}[C_{n-1}(1-\bar{k})|n] - PV_{n-2}[C_{n-1}|n-1] \\ &\quad + PV_{n-2}[C_{n-2} \times (1-\bar{k})|n-1] - PV_{n-2}[C_{n-2} - C_{n-3}|n-2]. \end{aligned}$$

Repeating this analysis and simplifying gives

$$h_0S_0 = \sum_{j=1}^{n} PV_0(B_j) + \sum_{j=1}^{n} PV_0(F_j - I_j) + \sum_{j=1}^{n} PV_0(C_{j-1} \times (1-\bar{k})|j] - \sum_{j=0}^{n-1} PV_0(C_j|j),$$

where $C_{-1} \equiv 0$, as $m_0S_0 = C_0$, $C_n \equiv 0$, and I_j is the debt payment at time j. Before the new project is undertaken, we have

$$h_0\bar{S}_0 = \sum_{j=1}^{n} PV_0(B_j)$$

so that

$$h_0(S_0 - \bar{S}_0) = \sum_{j=1}^{n} PV_0(F_j) - \sum_{j=1}^{n} PV_0(I_j) + \sum_{j=1}^{n} PV_0(C_{j-1} \times (1-\bar{k})|j] - \sum_{j=0}^{n-1} PV_0(C_j|j). \quad (23)$$

The above expression represents the adjusted present value of the project. The first two terms on the right side represent the net present value of the project, ignoring the costs arising from risk capital. The first term on the right side is the present value of the project's cash flows. The discount rate used in determining the present value represents the risk of the project's cash flows and in general this differs from the bank's required rate of return on equity or weighted average cost of capital.[5] The second term is the present value of the debt funding payments. The last set of terms arise because the project affects the credit worthiness of the bank and represents the present value of the costs from risk capital.

4.1. Return on Capital for a Project

The return on the project over the first period is given by

$$\begin{aligned}&\{F_1 - I_0 \times R_d + C_0 \times (1-\bar{k}) - C_1 \\ &+ \textstyle\sum_{j=2}^{n} PV_1(F_j) - \sum_{j=2}^{n} PV_1(I_j) \\ &+ \textstyle\sum_{j=2}^{n} PV_1(C_{j-1} \times (1-\bar{k})|j+1] - \sum_{j=1}^{n-1} PV_1(C_j|j)]\}/m_0S_0,\end{aligned} \tag{24}$$

where $m_0S_0 = C_0$, the initial risk capital. This expression with the denominator being the initial risk capital looks similar to the definition of the risk adjusted rate of return on capital (RAROC)—see Chapter 9 in Matten (2000) and Turnbull (2009). The attraction of a measure like RAROC is that it is simple and it is claimed that it can be used to compare the performance of different businesses, on a risk adjusted basis. However, it is well known that this is incorrect as it cannot accommodate projects with different systematic risk. Different projects will have different expected rates of return. There is no single rate of return, such as the required rate of return on equity, to provide a benchmark. Management must use its own judgement when ranking projects.

For many types of derivatives, such as forward contracts and foreign exchange swaps, the initial of risk capital is small. Consequently, a RAROC type of measure, which is myopic in nature, tends to be relatively large. The above expression (24) takes into account the changing risk capital profile and avoids the limitations of the traditional measure.

4.2. Return on Capital for a Business

Expression (24) can be re-interpreted to provide the expected rate of return on a business by first aggregating cash flows in the numerator and second aggregating across the change in the required risk capital for all projects in the business. Management can determine the adjusted present value for projects within a business and rank projects on the basis of the adjusted present value per unit of investment, APV_j/A_j. However, the issue of an appropriate benchmark remains. The required rate of return on equity is a common benchmark. But this is generally inappropriate, as businesses are influenced by different risk factors, implying different systematic risk.[6] The errors introduced by employing a fixed benchmark are well known—see (Brealey et al. 2014, chp. 19). Senior management must judge the relative performance of the different businesses, while recognizing the deficiencies of the performance metrics.

5. Conclusions

When determining bonuses for the managers of the individual businesses within the bank, senior management must attempt to judge the relative performance of the different businesses. Consequently, business managers want performance measures that depend on factors under their control. For example, funding costs should reflect the average duration of the assets of the business and risk capital assigned to projects within the business to depend on the assets within the business ignoring the rest of the bank. This paper addresses some of the issues that arise from decentralized management.

We extend the analysis of EMR by allowing individual businesses to make their own asset allocations subject to constraints on the total amount of risk capital and credit risk of the business. Relaxing the assumptions of EMR implies that we no longer have the aggregation result that the risk

---

5 See (Brealey et al. 2014, chp. 19).

6 The systematic risk of the different businesses could be calculated and the capital market line used as a benchmark.

capital allocations based on marginal default values add up exactly. The break-down of this result is to be expected, given the work of Merton and Perold (1993).

Each project has its own risk capital requirements. Risk capital is not free and consequently it is important to determine how the time profile of required risk capital affects the adjusted present value of a project. We derive an expression for the adjusted present value of a project that considers the time profile of risk capital. This necessitates determining the present value of the risky cash flows, as well as the funding costs and the present value of the risk capital costs. From there, we derive an expression for expected rate of return for a project. However, there is no simple benchmark, such as risk adjusted rate of return on capital (RAROC) with which to compare relative performance.

We derive an expression for the adjusted present value of a business by aggregating across the individual projects within a business. Senior managers of a bank need to rank the relative performance of the bank's businesses. There is no simple way to do this, given the absence of a benchmark. Management can rank the businesses using the ratio of the adjusted present value to asset size $\{APV_j/A_j\}$, as suggested by Erel et al. (2015). While this ratio is a percentage measure and useful in comparing large versus small businesses, it does not address the issue that projects have different risk profiles, even with risk capital. It suffers from similar limitations as RAROC.

Business managers can take steps to alter the risk profile of a project by undertaking hedging and entering into collateral agreements. While these activities alter the risk profile, quantifying the impact for over-the-counter contracts can be challenging, especially in stressed financial conditions.

Funding: This research received no external funding.

Conflicts of Interest: The author declares no conflict of interest.

References

Artzner, Philippe, Freddy Delbaen, Jean-Marc Eber, and David Heath. 1999. Coherent Measures of Risk. *Mathematical Finance* 9: 203–28. [CrossRef]

Bhatia, Mohan. 2009. *An Introduction to Economic Capital*. Risk Books. London: Incisive Financial Publishing.

Bajaj, Rasna, Andrew Binmore, Rupak Dasgupta, and Quynh-Anh Vo. 2018. Banks' Internal Capital Markets: How Do Banks Allocate Capital Internally? *Bank of England Quarterly Bulletin* 58: 1–9.

Brealey, Richard A., Stewart C. Myers, and Franklin Allen. 2014. *Principles of Corporate Finance*, 11 ed. Irwin: McGraw-Hill.

Crouhy, Michel, Stuart M. Turnbull, and Lee M. Wakeman. 1999. Measuring Risk Adjusted Performance. *Journal of Risk* 2: 5–35. [CrossRef]

Demine, Jean. 1998. Pitfalls in the Application of RAROC in Loan Management. *Arbitrageur* 1: 21–27.

Erel, Isil, Stewart C. Myers, and James A. Read. 2015. A Theory of Risk Capital. *Journal of Financial Economics* 118: 620–35. [CrossRef]

Froot, Kenneth A., and Jeremy C. Stein. 1998. Risk Management, Capital Budgeting and Capital Structure Policy for Financial Institutions: An Integrated Approach. *Journal Of Financial Economics* 47: 55–82. [CrossRef]

Matten, Chris. 2000. *Managing Bank Capital: Capital Allocation and Performance Measurement*, 2nd ed. New York: John Wiley & Sons.

Merton, Robert C. 1973. Theory of Rational Option Pricing. *Bell Journal of Economics and Management Science* 4: 141–83. [CrossRef]

Merton, Robert C., and Andre Perold. 1993. Theory of Risk Capital in Financial Firms. *Journal of Applied Corporate Finance* 6: 16–32. [CrossRef]

Turnbull, Stuart M. 2009. *Risk Adjusted Return on Capital (RAROC), Encyclopedia of Quantitative Finance*. West Sussex: Wiley & Sons.

Wilson, Thomas. 1992. RAROC Remodelled. *Risk* 5: 112–19.

Journal of
Risk and Financial Management

MDPI

Article

Insider Trading and Institutional Holdings in Seasoned Equity Offerings

Ching-Chih Wu * and Tung-Hsiao Yang

Department of Finance, National Chung-Hsing University, Taichung City 40227, Taiwan; tyang1@nchu.edu.tw
* Correspondence: ccwu886@gmail.com

Received: 21 August 2018; Accepted: 6 September 2018; Published: 10 September 2018

Abstract: We investigate three issues about the impact of insider trades and institutional holdings on seasoned equity offerings (SEOs). First, we test how insider trades affect the trading behavior of institutional investors in SEOs. Second, we test whose trading behavior, either insiders or institutional investors, has greater explanatory power for the performance of SEO firms after issuing new stocks. Third, we analyze the industry-wide spillover effects of insider trades and institutional holdings. Empirically, we find that insiders and institutional investors of SEO firms may utilize similar information in their transactions because insider trades induce similar trading behavior for institutional investors. In addition, insider trades, relative to institutional holdings, have greater explanatory power for SEO firm's long-term performance. Finally, compared with insider trades, institutional holdings have a more significant spillover effect in the industry of SEO firms.

Keywords: insider trade; institutional holding; spillover effect; contagion effect

1. Introduction

Information asymmetry exists in financial markets around the world. Some investors have information advantage relative to others and normally they would take advantage of these information sources to benefit themselves (Akerlof 1970; Chiang and Venkatesh 1988; Marquardt and Wiedman 1998; Noe 1999; Aboody and Lev 2000; Dell'Ariccia and Marquez 2004; Eleswarapu et al. 2004)[1]. Even though the existing evidence supports weak form or semi-strong form market efficiency, it is not uncommon to find some investors have a better investment performance than others due to the information advantage. For example, insiders and institutional investors are two types of investors that may have information advantages over other outside or retail investors (Frankel and Li 2004; Huson and MacKinnon 2003; Baik et al. 2010; Jiang 2010). In general, these two parties may share the same information sources and researchers utilize their trading behavior to forecast the firm's performance after seasoned equity offerings (SEOs) (Piotroski and Roulstone 2004; Wahal and McConnell 2000; Ferreira and Matos 2008; Aggarwal et al. 2011).

In this study, we follow the previous literature by using the SEOs to analyze the trading behavior of insiders and institutional investors (see Chemmanur et al. 2009; Griffin et al. 2012; Harjoto and Garen 2005). In addition, we also extend our research to the spillover effect of these two types of investors in the industries. (Bradley and Yuan 2013; Hameed et al. 2015; Benveniste et al. 2002; Benveniste et al. 2003; Slovin et al. 1992; Hsu et al. 2010).

There are three research questions in this study. First, we test how insider trades affect the trading behavior of institutional investors in the SEOs. Some researchers, such as Piotroski and Roulstone

[1] The accounting performance is also hard to predict, such as earning or sales. de Bruijn and Franses (2018) show that the earning forecast is still unreliable.

(2004), find that insider and institutional trading influences the firms' information environment, but how the asset prices change depends on each group's relative information advantage. In addition, Luo (2005) finds that managers of merging companies appear to extract information from the market reaction of institutional investors and later consider it in closing the deal. The author concludes that firms held by short-term institutional investors have a weaker bargaining position in acquisitions. Weaker monitoring from short-term institutional investors could allow managers to proceed with value-reducing acquisitions. In contrast, Griffin et al. (2012) cannot find supportive evidence to show that institutional investors trade on the information from investment bank connections through takeover advising, initial public offering (IPO) and SEO underwriting, or lending relationships. Therefore, there is a research gap in the information flow between insiders and institutional investors. We fill in this gap and shed light on this issue by utilizing the seasoned equity offerings and test how insider trades affect the institutional holding of these SEO firms.

Second, due to the different characteristics of information sources, we test whose trading behavior, either insiders or institutional investors, has greater explanatory power for long-term performance after SEOs. We measure the insider trades and the institutional holdings before and after the SEOs and analyze the impact of the trading behavior of both groups on the long-term performance, which is measured by buy-and-hold excess returns. This analysis contributes to the related literature of understanding the prediction power of informed traders on a firm's market performance after SEOs.

Third, we analyze the industry-wide spillover effect of insider trades and institutional holdings. In the SEOs, the insiders or institutional investors may signal some private information through their trading behaviors. How do insiders and institutional investors of other firms in the same industry react to these signals? There are two different types of the spillover effect in the literature: contagion effect and competitive effect. Some studies find contagion effect in mergers and acquisitions (M&As), such as Song and Walkling (2000) and Shahrur and Venkateswaran (2009) who analyzed the rival firms of the target and acquiring firms respectively. Others support the competitive effect. For example, Hsu et al. (2010) analyzed the rivals of IPO firms and Erwin and Miller (1998) analyzed the rivals of firms with share repurchases. Bradley and Yuan (2013) show that rival firms react significantly positively (0.26%) to primary SEO announcements, indicative of a competitive effect, but negatively (−0.35%) to secondary share announcements, which is evidence of a contagion effect. Based on the existing evidence, we extend our analysis to the spillover effect of insider trades and institutional holdings on the institutional holdings of matching firms in the SEOs. The analysis helps to understand how insider trades and institutional holdings affect the reaction of institutional investors of firms in the same industry.

There are many other factors that would affect the trading behavior of insiders and institutional investors, such as macro-level conditions, or industrial and firm characteristics. In the regression analyses of the SEOs, we control these factors and focus on the previous three issues. The main contribution of the study is to comprehensively analyze the reaction of insiders and institutional investors in the seasoned equity offerings. In addition, through the analysis of spillover effect for the SEOs, we can find how insiders and institutional investors of firms in the same industry react in the SEOs.

The remainder of this paper is organized as follows. Section 2 briefly summarizes the relevant literature and develops our research hypotheses. In Section 3 we describe the methodology and data collection. Section 4 reports the results of the empirical analysis, while Section 5 concludes.

2. Literature Review and Research Hypotheses

Many studies have examined the trading behavior of insiders and institutional investors and both groups have information advantages relative to other outside and retail investors. There is limited research on the interaction between insiders and institutional investors. Frankel and Li (2004) find that analyst following is negatively related to the profitability of insider trades and has a negative impact on insider purchases. This implies that any process of information disclosure reduces the information asymmetry and further changes the trading behavior of informed traders. Based on the result, we suspect that informed traders, including insiders and institutional investors, adjust their stock holdings in the SEOs once they observe the other group's move.

Piotroski and Roulstone (2004) test how much firm-specific, market-level, and industry-level information is impounded into the firm's stock price. In their research, they find that different informed participants change the information environment and the stock price reflects different information conveyed by different participants. In addition, Griffin et al. (2012) show neither brokerage house clients nor the brokerage houses themselves trade on inside information through the brokerage house associated with the information of M&As, IPOs, and SEOs. From their results, we are interested in testing how the different informed investors change their holdings after observing the trading of other informed investors.

In contrast, Bodnaruk et al. (2009) find that funds affiliated with takeover bidder advisors take positions in target firms before the announcement. Jegadeesh and Tang (2010) also find profitable trading through target advisors. Therefore, we expect that institutional investors may utilize information from insiders by observing insider trading behavior. We test how the insider trades affect institutional holdings after SEOs. The first research hypothesis is as follows.

Hypothesis 1. *Insider trading should have a substantial impact on institutional holdings after SEOs. Therefore, the trading behavior of insiders and institutional investors should be very similar around SEOs.*

The existing literature shows that insiders and institutional investors play an important role in the firm's strategic decision. For example, Wahal and McConnell (2000) find a positive relation between industry-adjusted expenditures for property, plant, and equipment (PP&E) and research and development (R&D) and the fraction of shares owned by institutional investors. In addition, the informed traders may also utilize their information advantage to benefit themselves in their trading. Baik et al. (2010) find that both the level of and change in local institutional ownership predict future stock returns, particularly for firms with high information asymmetry. Gaspar et al. (2005) also show that both target firms and acquiring firms with short-term institutional investors have worse merging benefits relative to those with long-term institutional investors.

As per insiders, Darrough and Rangan (2005) document a positive association between discretionary current accruals in the offering year and managerial selling, suggesting that selling managers manipulate accruals. Therefore, we expect that both insider trading and the change in institutional holdings have certain explanatory power for the firm's performance. The unanswered question is which groups of investors has greater explanatory power than the other. This is our second research question and we construct the second research hypothesis based on it as follows.

Hypothesis 2. *Insider trades and institutional investors have significant explanatory power for the firm's performance after the SEOs.*

An SEO is a crucial corporate event and, therefore, the firm conveys certain important information to the public. Before or after the announcement the firm's insiders and institutional investors may adjust their holdings based on their perception of this event. The counterparties of the non-SEO firms may also adjust their position on the Non-SEO firms to reflect their perception of the effect of this event on the non-SEO firms. This is the spillover effect of the trading behavior of insiders and institutional investors. The spillover effect exists in many different aspects, such as merger waves (Harford 2005), new equity offerings (Benveniste et al. 2002; Benveniste et al. 2003), fraudulent financial reporting (Beatty et al. 2013), or accounting restatements (Gleason et al. 2008).

There are two competing hypotheses about the spillover effect: contagion effect and competitive effect. The 'contagion effect' implies that rival firms would have a similar response to the information with the event firms. For example, Jorion and Zhang (2007) find strong intra-industry contagion effects in the event of filing Chapter 11 bankruptcies. In contrast, the 'competitive effect' suggests that the rival firms would have the opposite effect on the news. For instance, Erwin and Miller (1998) show that open market repurchase announcements have a negative effect on rivals in the same industry with the event firms. Jorion and Zhang (2007) find strong intra-industry competition effects in the event of filing Chapter 7 bankruptcies. In sum, different corporate events may show a different type of spillover effect, and sometimes both effects may exist simultaneously.

Our research contributes to the related literature by analyzing the spillover effect of insider trading and the changes in institutional holdings between SEO firms and non-SEO firms. To the best of our knowledge, this is the first paper to analyze the spillover effect comprehensively in the SEOs. We construct their research hypothesis as follows:

Hypothesis 3. *There exists spillover effect of insider trading and institutional holdings of SEO firms on non-SEO firms in the same industry.*

3. Methodology and Data Collection

3.1. Sample Selection and Variables

We need to collect the sample firms of SEOs in this research. All these samples are in the Thomson Financial Securities Data Corporation (SDC) New Issue database and we collect a sample covering the period from 1990 to 2010 and trace their returns up to 2013. The event firm's CUSIP can be matched with the Center for Research in Securities Prices (CRSP) data. To test SEOs, we collect the sample firms based on this event. To be included in our sample, the observations must meet the following criteria:

1. The SEOs must be of common stocks of firms (share codes 10 and 11) listed on NYSE, AMEX, and NASDAQ. American depository receipts (ADRs), real estate investment trusts (REITs), closed-end mutual funds, and partnership are eliminated from the sample.
2. We exclude non-underwritten offerings, rights offerings, standby offerings, shelf offerings, pure secondary offerings, and unit offerings (equity issue with warrants). In addition, SEOs with an offer price below $5 are dropped since many of them involve price manipulation (See Yang et al. 2016, and Hsu et al. 2016).
3. As in other previous studies, we exclude SEOs of the financial and regulated utility industries (SIC codes 6000–6999 and 4900–4999 respectively) since firms in these industries have to meet regulatory requirements in making the strategic decisions. Also, accounting items of these two industries are distinct from those of other industries.
4. A firm included in the M&As and stock splits events type of sample cannot be in the SEOs type within the three years before and after the corporate event since the long-run performance may arise from the M&As and stock splits events rather than the SEO event of the sampling.

We collect daily returns and number of shares outstanding of the sample firms and daily market indices (CRSP VW and EW) from the CRSP database. Annual accounting data of firm-specific variables are collected from the Compustat database. We collect monthly insider trading data from the Thomson CDA Investment database, and quarterly institutional equity holdings from the Thomson CDA Spectrum database, which are from institutional investors' 13-f filings. We use the institutional codes in the CDA Spectrum database to identify the types of the institutional investors.[2]

We summarize the firm characteristics in Table 1.

[2] Institutional investors with more than $100 million in equities must report their equity ownership to the SEC in quarterly 13-f filings. The CDA Spectrum classifies institutional investors of five types: bank (trust departments), insurance companies, investment companies (mutual funds and closed-end funds), independent investment advisors (principally pension fund advisors), and others (miscellaneous institutions such as endowment funds or public pension funds).

Table 1. Summary statistics for firm characteristics.

Statistics	SIZE	Book-to-Market (BM)	Runup	Buy and Hold Abnormal Return (BHAR)	Over-	Debt
		Ratio	(3 months)	(3 years)	Investment	Ratio
Mean	1468.35	0.298	0.185	−0.170	0.023	0.215
Median	315.86	0.249	0.092	−0.428	0.002	0.128
Std	7112.81	0.332	0.584	1.293	0.159	0.259
Q1	134.04	0.121	−0.087	−0.843	−0.052	0.004
Q3	749.06	0.410	0.306	0.190	0.078	0.351

This table provides summary statistics of SEO firms from 1990 to 2010 and the number of the company of SEOs is 1,400. The variables are defined as follows. Size is the natural log of the firm's market capitalization. BM ratio is the book-to-market ratio. Runup is the buy and hold abnormal return in three months before the SEOs. BHAR is the buy and hold abnormal return for three years after the SEOs. Over-investment is the capital expenditure over the expected level based on the estimation model in Richardson (2006). Debt ratio is the ratio of long-term debt to total assets.

From Table 1, we find that the long-term market performance, however, is poor in the SEO events, which is also consistent with the existing empirical evidence. Finally, the investment level is also above the expected level, which implies that these firms have aggressive investment strategies.

3.2. Relative Measures

We need measures to represent the characteristics of institutional holding, insider trading, and long-term market performance in the empirical tests. Hence, we summarize these measures as follows.

3.2.1. Institutional Holding

To measure the institutional holding, we use the number of shares held by institutions divided by the number of shares outstanding to calculate the percentage of institutional holdings.

3.2.2. Insider Trading

Previous studies measure insider trading in various ways. Gombola et al. (1997) and Gombola et al. (1999) observe the monthly number of insider transactions, number of shares, and dollar value around SEOs. Rozeff and Zaman (1998) employ insider trading deflated by trading volume (number of shares traded by insider over number of shares traded in the market) to investigate the direction of insider trades along the value/glamour spectrum. Lakonishok and Lee (2001) use the ratio of net insider trading (number of insider purchases minus number of insider sales) to total insider transactions over the past few months to examine the market reaction to insider trades. We use the number of net selling shares (number of shares sold minus number of shares bought) over the number of shares outstanding to measure the behavior of insider trading.

In order to capture the asymmetric reaction of insider trading, we decompose net selling into two components and create two variables to represent it. One is pnsh, the meaning of positive net selling when net selling is greater than zero and the other variable is nnsh, meaning of negative net selling when net selling is less than or equal to zero.

3.2.3. Long-Term Market Performance

We calculate buy-and-hold abnormal returns of a portfolio as follows:

$$BHARs_p = \frac{1}{N}\sum_{j=1}^{N}\left[\prod_{t=1}^{T}(1+R_{j,t}) - \prod_{t=1}^{T}(1+R_{bench,t})\right] \quad (1)$$

where $R_{j,t}$ and $R_{bench,t}$, respectively, denote firm j's returns and benchmark returns on day t, and N is the number of firms. We calculate return from the announcement date for these events and set a month to have 21 trading days. If the firm is delisted, returns are compounding until the delist date.

Finally, the Compustat database provides all the accounting data we need for capturing the firm characteristics. Following previous studies, we add firm characteristic variables in the regression analyses, which include over-investment (overinv), the MB ratio (mb), the firm size (size), the debt ratio (dr). We also control for year and industrial fixed effects in our regression analyses. Finally, to alleviate the effect of outliers in the following analysis, we winsorize all independent variables at 1% level.

3.2.4. Empirical Models

There are two parts to the empirical analyses in this study. First is the basic summary statistics for insider trading and the institutional holdings. We summarize the insider trades and the institutional holdings in the different time period before and after the SEOs. In the univariate analysis, we expect to observe the basic statistics of these two measures and check the systematic pattern of these two measures. Second, we perform the multivariate analysis by running the regressions of the level of institutional holdings and long-term market performance of SEO firms. In addition, we also apply the regression analysis on the spillover effect and check how the non-SEO firms react to the trading of insiders and institutional investors of SEO firms.

To test the first hypothesis, we summarize the basic statistics for the change of institutional holdings with respect to different insider trading in SEOs and check the statistics of the change of institutional holdings. We would get the primary results by checking the statistics. To check the robustness of our results, in the multivariate regression analyses, we run the regression of the institutional holdings on insider trades and control for all firm characteristics. The empirical model is as follows:

$$\begin{aligned} &institutional \quad holding \\ &\quad = \alpha + \beta_1 \text{pnsh} + \beta_2 \text{nnsh} + \beta_3 overinv + \beta_4 mb + \beta_5 size + \beta_6 dr \\ &\quad + \beta_6 Runup + \varepsilon_{inst}, \end{aligned} \tag{2}$$

where pnsh denote the positive insider net selling, nnsh is the negative insider net selling. In addition, we also control for industrial and year dummies in regression analyses.

Next, we measure the long-term market performance by three-year buy-and-hold abnormal return after SEOs and compare insider trading and the institutional holdings in the SEOs. We sort the long-term market reaction based on BHAR of different time periods and then summarize the statistics of the insider trading and the change of institutional holdings and analyze the pattern of these statistics. As in our previous analyses, we also perform the multivariate analysis of the long-term market reactions. The empirical model is:

$$\begin{aligned} BHAR(0,t) = \quad & \alpha + \beta_1\, \varepsilon_{inst} + \beta_2 \text{pnsh} + \beta_3 \text{nnsh} + \beta_4 overinv + \beta_5 mb + \beta_6 size \\ & + \beta_7 dr + \beta_8 Runup + \varepsilon, \end{aligned} \tag{3}$$

where ε_{inst} is the residual of the institutional holding in the previous regression of institutional holdings. Based on the result of the first hypothesis testing, there may have endogenous problems because the insider trading may affect the change of institutional holdings. To alleviate the endogenous problem, we utilize two-stage least square in the regression analyses.

Finally, we test the spillover effect of insider trading and the change of institutional holding. To measure the spillover effect, we measure the insider trading and the change of institutional holdings for non-SEO firms. In the analysis of summary statistics, we check the basic statistics of insider trading and the change of institutional holdings for non-SEO firms. If there exists a spillover effect, then we would observe the consistent pattern of insider trading and the change of institutional holdings between event firms and rival firms in the same industry. In addition, we perform the multivariate regression analysis and the empirical models are follows:

$$\text{mholding} = \alpha \quad +\beta_1\text{pnsh} + \beta_2\text{nnsh} + \beta_3 overinv + \beta_4 mb + \beta_5 size + \beta_6 dr \\ +\beta_6 Runup + \varepsilon, \tag{4}$$

$$\text{mholding} = \alpha \quad +\beta_1\,\varepsilon_{inst} + \beta_2\text{pnsh} + \beta_3\text{nnsh} + \beta_4 overinv + \beta_5 mb + \beta_6 size \\ +\beta_7 dr + \beta_8 Runup + \varepsilon, \tag{5}$$

where mholding is the institutional holdings of non-SEO firms. If the spillover effect exists, then we expect that the coefficients of β_1 and β_2 in Equation (4) and of β_1, β_2 and β_3 in Equation (5) would be significant.

4. Empirical Results

We analyze the institutional holdings before and after SEOs. The institutional holdings of four quarters before and after the events are summarized in Table 2.

Table 2. The median and mean of institutional holding.

Quarter	Median	Mean
−4	0.325	0.368
−3	0.323	0.373
−2	0.339	0.381
−1	0.364	0.400
1	0.524	0.518
2	0.534	0.524
3	0.529	0.526
4	0.532	0.527

The median of institutional holdings is calculated on a quarterly basis which is the frequency in the database. The effective date of each event is in Quarter 1 and the first quarter before the effective date is Quarter −1. The number of the company of SEOs is 1,284 in Quarter 1.

From the results in Table 2, we find that the institutional investors increase their holdings substantially after SEOs, which implies that institutional investors do change their holdings after SEOs. Whether these changes are correlated with firms' operational performance is a key question about the information source of the information advantage for institutional investors. We summarize the operational performance in Table 3.

Table 3. The operational performance of sample firms.

Variable		Year						
		−3	−2	−1	0	1	2	3
EBIT/Sales	Median	0.099	0.099	0.112	0.122	0.110	0.106	0.107
	Mean	0.023	0.027	0.035	0.045	0.038	0.032	0.030
ROA	Median	−0.013	−0.046	−0.056	−0.016	−0.040	−0.050	−0.012
	Mean	−0.060	−0.048	−0.026	0.000	−0.021	−0.030	−0.040

We measure the firm's operational performance from EBIT/Sales and ROA. EBIT is the earnings before interest and taxes, ROA is the return on assets. The effective date is in year 0 and the median and mean of both measures are under annual basis. We collect the data for three years before and after the SEO events.

We find that the operational performance does not have an obvious improvement after the SEO events. The EBIT/sales improves in the current year of SEOs but gets back to the original level in the first year after SEOs. These results imply that institutional investors may not rely on the operational performance to adjust their holding of these sample firms.

Next, we check the change of holding of insiders. This may be another information source for institutional investors. We summarize the change of insider transactions in Table 4.

Table 4. The median and mean of insider transaction.

Period	Median			Mean		
	Sell	Purchase	Net Sell	Sell	Purchase	Net Sell
(−6, −3)	0.0002	0.0001	0.0000	0.0022	0.0008	0.0013
(−6, −2)	0.0003	0.0001	0.0000	0.0025	0.0009	0.0016
(−6, −1)	0.0003	0.0001	0.0001	0.0027	0.0010	0.0017
(−6, 1)	0.0027	0.0002	0.0018	0.0173	0.0014	0.0158
(−6, 2)	0.0027	0.0002	0.0016	0.0172	0.0015	0.0158
(−6, 3)	0.0027	0.0002	0.0016	0.0172	0.0015	0.0156
(−6, 6)	0.0030	0.0004	0.0016	0.0175	0.0019	0.0156
(−6, 12)	0.0038	0.0006	0.0018	0.0208	0.0024	0.0183
(−6, 24)	0.0047	0.0011	0.0023	0.0222	0.0035	0.0188
(−1, 1)	0.0025	0.0000	0.0020	0.0183	0.0009	0.0174

We report the median and mean cumulative insider trading from month −6 to month t relative to the SEO events. The number of observation is 1128. All numbers are a percentage of outstanding shares of all sample firms. Net sell is the difference between insider sell and insider purchase.

From Table 4, we find that insiders are in general reduce their holding before and after this event which implies that they do not expect better results after this specific event for the SEO firms. Even though the net sell increases before SEOs, the net sell substantially increases after the effective month. Based on these results, we suspect that insiders are pessimistic about the SEO events.

To analyze whether the insider transactions have a significant impact on the adjustment of institutional holding, we regress the institutional holdings on the net sell of insider transaction and control for other firm characteristics. The results are summarized in Table 5.

Table 5. The impact of insider trades on institutional holding.

Variables	(1)	(2)	(3)
pnsh	−7.042 ***	−5.669 ***	−8.088 ***
	(0.003)	(0.010)	(0.001)
nnsh	−15.163 **	−15.042 **	−1.255
	(0.026)	(0.037)	(0.837)
Over-investment	−0.004	−0.003	−0.049
	(0.917)	(0.947)	(0.281)
Market-to-book (MB) ratio	0.095 **	0.060	0.012
	(0.016)	(0.200)	(0.811)
size	0.124 ***	0.108 ***	0.112 ***
	(0.000)	(0.000)	(0.000)
Debt ratio	0.212 ***	0.210 ***	0.173 **
	(0.000)	(0.000)	(0.020)
Runup	−0.002	−0.011	−0.007
	(0.845)	(0.283)	(0.540)
Constant	−0.346 ***	−0.295 **	−0.274 *
	(0.000)	(0.027)	(0.075)
Year dummy	No	Yes	Yes
Industry dummy	No	No	Yes
Adjusted R-squared	0.395	0.404	0.463

We suspect that there is an asymmetrical impact of insider transaction on institutional holding, and therefore we create the variables of pnsh and nnsh from insider net sell of SEOs. Pnsh denotes the positive net sell of insider transactions when net sell is greater than zero, nnsh is the negative insider net sell of insider transactions when net sell is less than or equal to zero, and net sell is the difference between insider sell and insider purchase. The other variables of SEOs are defined as follows. MB ratio is the market-to-book ratio. Size is the natural log of the firm's market capitalization. Debt ratio is the ratio of long-term debt to total assets. Runup is the buy and hold abnormal return in three months before SEOs. Over-investment is the capital expenditure over the expected level based on the estimation model in Richardson (2006). The numbers in parentheses are robust p-values. ***, **, * represent the significance under 1%, 5%, 10% level respectively.

The results in Table 5 support our expectation that the insider transactions have a significant impact on the adjustment of institutional holdings. Among the SEO events, institutional holdings decrease with the positive net sell of insider transaction. On the other hand, institutional holdings increase with the negative net sell of insider transaction. This result implies that insiders and institutional investors have the same point of views regarding SEOs.

Next, we analyse the impact of institutional investors or insider transaction on the firm's long-term market performance. The regression result is summarized in Table 6.

Table 6. The long-term performance of sample firms.

Variables	(1)	(2)	(3)
ε_{inst}	0.069	0.181	0.176
	(0.892)	(0.745)	(0.753)
pnsh	−24.589 **	−19.172 **	−6.108
	(0.010)	(0.039)	(0.632)
nnsh	22.318	−13.780	−61.112
	(0.545)	(0.743)	(0.359)
Over-investment	0.081	−0.126	−0.230
	(0.755)	(0.772)	(0.634)
MB ratio	0.153	−0.022	−0.199
	(0.542)	(0.955)	(0.727)
size	0.097	0.082	0.139
	(0.250)	(0.407)	(0.295)
Debt ratio	0.639	0.337	−0.047
	(0.183)	(0.549)	(0.934)
Runup	−0.052	−0.076	−0.104
	(0.401)	(0.197)	(0.165)
Constant	−0.849 *	−0.535	−0.413
	(0.068)	(0.377)	(0.585)
Year dummy	No	Yes	Yes
Industry dummy	No	No	Yes
Adjusted R-squared	0.019	0.024	0.159

The variables are defined as follows. The ε_{inst} is the residuals of institutional holding in the regression analysis in Table 5. Pnsh denotes the positive net sell of insider transaction of SEOs when net sell is greater than zero, nnsh is the negative insider net sell of insider transaction when net sell is less than or equal to zero, and net sell is the difference between insider sell and insider purchase of SEOs. MB ratio is the market-to-book ratio. Size is the natural log of the firm's market capitalization. Debt ratio is the ratio of long-term debt to total assets. Runup is the buy and hold abnormal return in three months before SEOs. Over-investment is the capital expenditure over the expected level based on the estimation model in Richardson (2006). The numbers in parentheses are robust p-values. ***, **, * represent the significance under 1%, 5%, 10% level, respectively.

From Table 6, we find that insider transactions have more explanatory power than institutional holding in the SEO firms. The pnsh is significant with BAHR (3 years), but nnsh is not. In sum, we conclude that insider transactions have strong explanatory power to the long-term market performance while positive net sell of insider transactions regarding the SEOs. In contrast, the negative net sell of insider transactions is not.

Next, we check the change of holding of insiders of the matching firms. This may be another information source for institutional investors of the matching firms. We summary the change of insider transactions of the matching firms in Table 7.

Table 7. The median and mean of insider transaction of the matching firms.

Period	Median			Mean		
	Sell	**Purchase**	**Net Sell**	**Sell**	**Purchase**	**Net Sell**
(−6, −3)	0.0001	0.0000	0.0000	0.0031	0.0005	0.0026
(−6, −2)	0.0001	0.0001	0.0000	0.0039	0.0006	0.0033
(−6, −1)	0.0001	0.0001	0.0000	0.0035	0.0007	0.0029
(−6, 1)	0.0002	0.0001	0.0000	0.0047	0.0009	0.0038
(−6, 2)	0.0002	0.0001	0.0000	0.0047	0.0010	0.0037
(−6, 3)	0.0003	0.0001	0.0000	0.0048	0.0011	0.0037
(−6, 6)	0.0004	0.0002	0.0000	0.0047	0.0014	0.0034
(−6, 12)	0.0007	0.0003	0.0000	0.0058	0.0022	0.0036
(−6, 24)	0.0012	0.0007	0.0001	0.0080	0.0048	0.0032
(−1, 1)	0.0001	0.0000	0.0000	0.0035	0.0007	0.0028

We report the median and mean cumulative insider trading from month −6 to month t relative to the firms separately based on the matching firms of SEOs. All numbers are a percentage of outstanding shares of matching firms. Net sell is the difference between insider sell and insider purchase of the matching firms.

From Table 7, we find that insiders of the matching firms are in general reduce their holding before and after this event which implies that they do not expect better results after this specific event for the SEO firms.

Furthermore, we analyze the impact of insider transactions of SEOs on the institutional holding of the matching firms. The regression result is summarized in Table 8.

Table 8. The spillover effect of insider trades of SEOs.

Variables	**(1)**	**(2)**	**(3)**
pnsh	−0.995 ***	−0.933 **	−0.889 **
	(0.004)	(0.012)	(0.024)
nnsh	−9.311 **	−8.963 *	−8.777 *
	(0.026)	(0.053)	(0.073)
Over-investment	−0.009	−0.019	0.002
	(0.876)	(0.736)	(0.973)
MB ratio	0.090 ***	0.049 **	0.047 *
	(0.000)	(0.014)	(0.065)
size	0.055 ***	0.046 ***	0.052 ***
	(0.000)	(0.000)	(0.000)
Debt ratio	0.084 **	0.051	0.077 *
	(0.024)	(0.190)	(0.071)
Runup	0.031 ***	0.030 ***	0.032 ***
	(0.003)	(0.001)	(0.001)
Constant	0.058	0.097 *	0.058
	(0.119)	(0.097)	(0.370)
Year dummy	No	Yes	Yes
Industry dummy	No	No	Yes
Adjusted R-squared	0.135	0.191	0.229

We suspect that there is an asymmetrical impact of insider transactions of SEOs on the institutional holding of matching firms, and therefore we create the variables of pnsh and nnsh from insider net sell of SEOs. Pnsh denotes the positive net sell of insider transaction of SEOs when net sell is greater than zero; nnsh is the negative insider net sell of insider transaction when net sell is less than or equal to zero; and net sell is the difference between insider sell and insider purchase of SEOs. The other variables of matching firms are defined as follows. MB ratio is the market-to-book ratio. Size is the natural log of the firm's market capitalization. Debt ratio is the ratio of long-term debt to total assets. Runup is the buy and hold abnormal return in three months before SEOs. Over-investment is the capital expenditure over the expected level based on the estimation model in Richardson (2006). The numbers in parentheses are robust p-values. ***, **, * represent the significance under 1%, 5%, 10% level respectively.

The results in Table 8 support our expectation that the insider transactions of SEOs have a significant impact on the adjustment of institutional holdings of matching firms. Among the SEO events, the institutional holdings of matching firms decrease with the positive net sell of insider transactions of SEOs. On the other hand, the institutional holdings of matching firms increase with the negative net sell of insider transactions of SEOs. This result implies that institutional investors of matching firms and insiders of SEOs have the same point of views regarding SEOs.

Finally, we analyze the impact of the institutional holding of SEOs on the institutional holding of matching firms. The regression result is summarized in Table 9.

Table 9. The spillover effect of insider trades and institutional holding of SEOs.

Variables	(1)	(2)	(3)	(4)
Iholding	0.306 ***	0.231 ***	0.206 ***	
	(0.000)	(0.000)	(0.000)	
ε_{minst}				0.207 ***
				(0.000)
pnsh				0.170
				(0.321)
nnsh				−0.630
				(0.808)
Over-investment	0.024	0.008	0.029	0.021
	(0.655)	(0.882)	(0.617)	(0.719)
MB ratio	0.066 ***	0.041 *	0.036	0.044
	(0.000)	(0.055)	(0.204)	(0.112)
size	0.029 ***	0.028 ***	0.037 ***	0.053 ***
	(0.000)	(0.000)	(0.000)	(0.000)
Debt ratio	0.070 *	0.051	0.067	0.081 *
	(0.067)	(0.192)	(0.118)	(0.055)
Runup	0.035 ***	0.033 ***	0.035 ***	0.034 ***
	(0.000)	(0.000)	(0.000)	(0.000)
Constant	0.089 **	0.126 *	0.085	0.060
	(0.014)	(0.051)	(0.223)	(0.387)
Year dummy	No	Yes	Yes	Yes
Industry dummy	No	No	Yes	Yes
Adjusted R-squared	0.189	0.222	0.250	0.249

The variables of shares holding are defined as follows. Iholding denotes the institutional holdings of SEOs. The ε_{minst} is the residuals of the institutional holding of matching firms in the regression analysis in Table 8. Pnsh denotes the positive net sell of insider transactions of SEOs when the net sell is greater than zero; nnsh is the negative insider net sell of insider transaction when net sell is less than or equal to zero; and net sell is the difference between insider sell and insider purchase of SEOs. The other variables are defined as follows. MB ratio is the market-to-book ratio. Size is the natural log of the firm's market capitalization. Debt ratio is the ratio of long-term debt to total assets. Runup is the buy and hold abnormal return in three months before SEOs. Over-investment is the capital expenditure over the expected level based on the estimation model in Richardson (2006). The numbers in parentheses are robust p-values. ***, **, * represent the significance under 1%, 5%, 10% level respectively.

From Table 9, we find that the institutional holdings of SEOs have a significant impact on the adjustment of institutional holdings of matching firms. Among the SEO events, the institutional holdings of matching firms increase or decrease in the same direction as the institutional holdings of SEOs. This result implies that institutional investors of matching firms and SEOs have the same point of views regarding SEOs.

5. Conclusions

In this study, we analyze three questions about the interaction between insider trades and institutional holdings in the major corporate SEO events. First, we test how insider trades affect the trading behavior of institutional investors in the SEOs. Second, due to the different characteristics of information sources, we test whose trading behavior, either insiders or institutional investors, has greater explanatory power for the performance of SEO firms after issuing new stocks. Third, in the SEOs, the insiders or institutional investors may signal some private information through their trading behaviors. How insiders and institutional investors of other non-SEO firms in the same industry react to these signals?

The empirical results show that the insider transactions have a significant impact on the institutional holdings. In the SEOs, institutional holdings change in the same direction as insider transactions. This result implies that insiders and institutional investors may have a similar point of view regarding the SEOs. Second, we find that insider transaction has greater explanatory power than institutional holdings for the long-term performance of the SEO firms after issuing new stocks. In sum, we conclude that institutional investors share similar information sources relative to insiders regarding the SEOs. In addition, the insider transaction has more explanatory power than institutional investors in the long-term market performance. Finally, among the SEO events, we also find that the institutional holdings of non-SEO firms change in the same direction with the insider trades and institutional holdings of SEO firms. This result implies that there exist spillover effects of insider trading and institutional holdings on those of non-SEO firms in the SEOs.

The main contribution of the research is to comprehensively analyze the reaction of insiders and institutional investors in the SEOs. In addition, through the analysis of the spillover effect of the SEOs, we can find how institutional investors of non-SEO firms react to the signals conveyed by insiders and institutional investors of SEO firms.

Author Contributions: C.-C.W. and T.-H.Y. conceived and designed the ideas. C.-C. collected the data and estimated the models. C.-C. and T.-H. analyzed the data and discussed the empirical results. C.-C. and T.-H. revised the paper.

Acknowledgments: We thank Jieran Wu and two anonymous reviewers for helpful comments.

Conflicts of Interest: The authors declare no conflict of interest.

References

Aboody, David, and Baruch Lev. 2000. Information asymmetry, R&D, and insider gains. *The Journal of Finance* 55: 2747–66.

Akerlof, George A. 1970. The market for lemons: Quality uncertainty and the market mechanism. *Quarterly Journal of Economics* 84: 488–500. [CrossRef]

Aggarwal, Reena, Isil Erel, Miguel Ferreira, and Pedro Matos. 2011. Does governance travel around the world? Evidence from institutional investors. *Journal of Financial Economics* 100: 154–81. [CrossRef]

Baik, Bok, Jun-Koo Kang, and Jin-Mo Kim. 2010. Local institutional investors, information asymmetries, and equity returns. *Journal of Financial Economics* 97: 81–106. [CrossRef]

Beatty, Anne, Scott Liao, and Jeff Jiewei Yu. 2013. The spillover effect of fraudulent financial reporting on peer firms' investments. *Journal of Accounting and Economics* 55: 183–205. [CrossRef]

Benveniste, Lawrence M., Walid Y. Busaba, and William J. Wilhelm Jr. 2002. Information externalities and the role of underwriters in primary equity markets. *Journal of Financial Intermediation* 11: 61–86. [CrossRef]

Benveniste, Lawrence M., Alexander Ljungqvist, William J. Wilhelm Jr., and Xiaoyun Yu. 2003. Evidence of information spillovers in the production of investment banking services. *The Journal of Finance* 58: 577–608. [CrossRef]

Bodnaruk, Andriy, Massimo Massa, and Andrei Simonov. 2009. Investment banks as insiders and the market for corporate control. *Review of Financial Studies* 22: 4989–5026. [CrossRef]

Bradley, Daniel, and Xiaojing Yuan. 2013. Information spillovers around seasoned equity offerings. *Journal of Corporate Finance* 21: 106–18. [CrossRef]

de Bruijn, Bert, and Philip Franses. 2018. How informative are earnings forecasts? *Journal of Risk and Financial Management* 11: 36. [CrossRef]

Chemmanur, Thomas J., Shan He, and Gang Hu. 2009. The role of institutional investors in seasoned equity offerings. *Journal of Financial Economics* 94: 384–411. [CrossRef]

Chiang, Raymond, and P. C. Venkatesh. 1988. Insider holdings and perceptions of information asymmetry: A note. *The Journal of Finance* 43: 1041–48. [CrossRef]

Darrough, Masako, and Srinivasan Rangan. 2005. Do insiders manipulate earnings when they sell their shares in an initial public offering? *Journal of Accounting Research* 43: 1–33. [CrossRef]

Dell'Ariccia, Giovanni, and Robert Marquez. 2004. Information and bank credit allocation. *Journal of Financial Economics* 72: 185–214. [CrossRef]

Eleswarapu, Venkat R., Rex Thompson, and Kumar Venkataraman. 2004. The impact of Regulation Fair Disclosure: Trading costs and information asymmetry. *Journal of Financial and Quantitative Analysis* 39: 209–25. [CrossRef]

Erwin, Gayle R., and James M. Miller. 1998. The intra-industry effects of open market share repurchases: Contagion or competitive? *Journal of Financial Research* 21: 389–406. [CrossRef]

Ferreira, Miguel A., and Pedro Matos. 2008. The colors of investors' money: The role of institutional investors around the world. *Journal of Financial Economics* 88: 499–533. [CrossRef]

Frankel, Richard, and Xu Li. 2004. Characteristics of a firm's information environment and the information asymmetry between insiders and outsiders. *Journal of Accounting and Economics* 37: 229–59. [CrossRef]

Gaspar, José-Miguel, Massimo Massa, and Pedro Matos. 2005. Shareholder investment horizons and the market for corporate control. *Journal of Financial Economics* 76: 135–65. [CrossRef]

Gleason, Cristi A., Nicole Thorne Jenkins, and W. Bruce Johnson. 2008. The contagion effects of accounting restatements. *The Accounting Review* 83: 83–110. [CrossRef]

Gombola, Michael, Lee Hei Wai, and Liu Feng-Ying. 1997. Evidence of selling by managers after seasoned equity offering announcements. *Financial Management* 26: 37–53. [CrossRef]

Gombola, Michael J., Hei Wai Lee, and Feng-Ying Liu. 1999. Further evidence on insider selling prior to seasoned equity offering announcements: The role of growth opportunities. *Journal of Business Finance & Accounting* 26: 621–49.

Griffin, John M., Tao Shu, and Selim Topaloglu. 2012. Examining the dark side of financial markets: Do institutions trade on information from investment bank connections? *Review of Financial Studies* 25: 2155–88. [CrossRef]

Hameed, Allaudeen, Randall Morck, Jianfeng Shen, and Bernard Yeung. 2015. Information, analysts, and stock return comovement. *Review of Financial Studies* 28: 3153–87. [CrossRef]

Harford, Jarrad. 2005. What drives merger waves? *Journal of Financial Economics* 77: 529–60. [CrossRef]

Harjoto, Maretno, and John Garen. 2005. Inside ownership beyond the IPO: The evolution of corporate ownership concentration. *Journal of Corporate Finance* 11: 661–79. [CrossRef]

Hsu, Hung-Chia, Adam V. Reed, and Jörg Rocholl. 2010. The new game in town: Competitive effects of IPOs. *The Journal of Finance* 65: 495–528. [CrossRef]

Hsu, Junming, Tung-Hsiao Yang, and Po-Shen Sung. 2016. SEO firms' lottery-like characteristics, institutional ownership, and long-run performance. *Journal of Business Research* 69: 2160–66. [CrossRef]

Huson, Mark R., and Gregory MacKinnon. 2003. Corporate spinoffs and information asymmetry between investors. *Journal of Corporate Finance* 9: 481–503. [CrossRef]

Jegadeesh, Narasimhan, and Yue Tang. 2010. Institutional Trades around Takeover Announcements: Skill vs. Inside Information. *SSRN Electronic Journal*. Available online: https://papers.ssrn.com/sol3/papers.cfm?abstract_id=1568859# (accessed on 9 September 2018). [CrossRef]

Jiang, Hao. 2010. Institutional investors, intangible information, and the book-to-market effect. *Journal of Financial Economics* 96: 98–126. [CrossRef]

Jorion, Philippe, and Gaiyan Zhang. 2007. Good and bad credit contagion: Evidence from credit default swaps. *Journal of Financial Economics* 84: 860–83. [CrossRef]

Lakonishok, Josef, and Inmoo Lee. 2001. Are insider trades informative? *Review of Financial Studies* 14: 79–111. [CrossRef]

Luo, Yuanzhi. 2005. Do insiders learn from outsiders? Evidence from mergers and acquisitions. *The Journal of Finance* 60: 1951–82. [CrossRef]

Marquardt, Carol A., and Christine I. Wiedman. 1998. Voluntary disclosure, information asymmetry, and insider selling through secondary equity offerings. *Contemporary Accounting Research* 15: 505–37. [CrossRef]

Noe, Christopher F. 1999. Voluntary disclosures and insider transactions. *Journal of Accounting and Economics* 27: 305–26. [CrossRef]

Piotroski, Joseph D., and Darren T. Roulstone. 2004. The influence of analysts, institutional investors, and insiders on the incorporation of market, industry, and firm-specific information into stock prices. *The Accounting Review* 79: 1119–51. [CrossRef]

Richardson, Scott. 2006. Over-investment of free cash flow. *Review of Accounting Studies* 11: 159–89. [CrossRef]

Rozeff, Michael S., and Mir A. Zaman. 1998. Overreaction and insider trading: Evidence from growth and value portfolios. *The Journal of Finance* 53: 701–16. [CrossRef]

Shahrur, Husayn, and Anand Venkateswaran. 2009. Industry prospects and acquirer returns in diversifying takeovers. *Journal of Financial Research* 32: 23–51. [CrossRef]

Slovin, Myron B., Marie E. Sushka, and John A. Polonchek. 1992. Informational externalities of seasoned equity issues: Differences between banks and industrial firms. *Journal of Financial Economics* 32: 87–101. [CrossRef]

Song, Moon H., and Ralph A. Walkling. 2000. Abnormal returns to rivals of acquisition targets: A test of the acquisition probability hypothesis'. *Journal of Financial Economics* 55: 143–71. [CrossRef]

Wahal, Sunil, and John J. McConnell. 2000. Do institutional investors exacerbate managerial myopia? *Journal of Corporate Finance* 6: 307–29. [CrossRef]

Yang, Tung-Hsiao, Junming Hsu, and Wen-Ben Yang. 2016. Firm's motives behind SEOs, earnings management, and performance. *International Review of Economics and Finance* 43: 160–69. [CrossRef]

Journal of
Risk and Financial Management

MDPI

Article

The Outperformance Probability of Mutual Funds

Gabriel Frahm * and Ferdinand Huber

Chair of Applied Stochastics and Risk Management, Department of Mathematics and Statistics, Helmut Schmidt University, 22043 Hamburg, Germany

* Correspondence: frahm@hsu-hh.de

Received: 5 May 2019; Accepted: 19 June 2019; Published: 26 June 2019

Abstract: We propose the outperformance probability as a new performance measure, which can be used in order to compare a strategy with a specified benchmark, and develop the basic statistical properties of its maximum-likelihood estimator in a Brownian-motion framework. The given results are used to investigate the question of whether mutual funds are able to beat the S&P 500 or the Russell 1000. Most mutual funds that are taken into consideration are, in fact, able to beat the market. We argue that one should refer to differential returns when comparing a strategy with a given benchmark and not compare both the strategy and the benchmark with the money-market account. This explains why mutual funds often appear to underperform the market, but this conclusion is fallacious.

Keywords: exchange traded funds; inverse coefficient of variation; mutual funds; outperformance probability; performance measurement; Sharpe ratio

JEL Classification: G11; G19

---

1. Motivation

The total value of assets under management in open-end funds was 46.7 trillion US dollars at the end of 2018 (ICI 2019). Nowadays, investors and investment advisors have access to an abundant number of performance measures in order to compare investment vehicles with each other. Most performance measures are based on the seminal work of Jensen (1968); Lintner (1965); Mossin (1966); Sharpe (1964 1966); Treynor (1961). The best-known performance measure is the Sharpe ratio, which divides the expected excess return on investment by the standard deviation of the excess return. Most other performance measures that can be found in the literature are based on the same principle, i.e., they divide the return on investment by its risk, where the precise meaning of "return" and "risk" differs from one performance measure to another. A typical example is the expected excess return to value at risk, which goes back to Alexander and Baptista (2003) as well as Dowd (2000). Other examples are the conditional Sharpe ratio, in which case one chooses the expected shortfall, the tail conditional expectation, or similar downside risk measures as a denominator (Baweja et al. 2015; Chow and Lai 2015). The number of possible combinations of numerators and denominators is practically unbounded. Depending on whether one chooses either the expected excess return or the first higher partial moment as a numerator and some lower partial moment, drawdown measure, or some value-at-risk measure as a denominator, the resulting performance measure is called Omega (Keating and Shadwick 2002), Sortino ratio (Sortino et al. 1999), Calmar ratio (Young 1991), Sterling ratio (Kestner 1996), or Burke ratio (Burke 1994), etc. A nice overview of those performance measures can be found in Table 1 of Eling and Schuhmacher (2006). However, it is evident that any list of return-to-risk measures must be far from exhaustive.

In this work, we propose a new performance measure called *outperformance probability* (OP). It differs in many aspects from return-to-risk measures:

1. The OP compares some strategy with a specified benchmark, which need not necessarily be the money-market account.
2. It is a probability. Thus, it is easy to understand also for a nonacademic audience, more precisely, for people who are not educated in statistics or probability theory.
3. The holding period of the investor is considered random. This enables us to compute the performance of an investment opportunity for arbitrary liquidity preferences.

Ad 1: Most financial studies that make use of performance measures compare, e.g., the Sharpe ratio of some strategy, according to Sharpe (1966), with the Sharpe ratio of a benchmark. The Sharpe ratios measure the outperformance both of the strategy and of the benchmark with respect to the money-market account, i.e., the riskless asset. Hence, one needs to calculate *two* performance measures to evaluate the given strategy. By contrast, our approach is based on the idea of analyzing differential returns, not necessarily excess returns.[1] This idea goes back to Sharpe (1994). To be more precise, since we do not use the money market as an anchor point, we need only *one* measure in order to compare two different investment opportunities. We will see that this sheds a completely different light on the question of whether or not one should prefer actively managed funds to passively managed funds. This fundamental question is still discussed in the finance literature and it is a commonplace that most fund managers are not able to beat their benchmarks after accounting for all management fees and agency costs. We will come back to this point in Section 3.1. However, our empirical study reveals that most actively managed funds, in fact, are able to outperform their benchmarks. The reason for this observation might be explained as follows: The difference between the performance of two investment opportunities is not the same as the performance of one investment opportunity compared to another. Simply put, in general, performance measures are not linear. Let R_S be the return on some strategy, R_B be the return on a benchmark, and r be the risk-free interest rate after some holding period. Further, let π be any performance measure. Hence, the performance of the strategy with respect to the money-market account is $\pi(R_S - r)$, whereas $\pi(R_B - r)$ is the corresponding performance of the benchmark. Now, the problem is that, in general,

$$\pi(R_S - r) - \pi(R_B - r) \neq \pi\big((R_S - r) - (R_B - r)\big) = \pi(R_S - R_B)\,.$$

We suggest to calculate $\pi(R_S - R_B)$ in order to understand whether or not the strategy is better than its benchmark and not to compare $\pi(R_S - r)$ with $\pi(R_B - r)$. By comparing $\pi(R_S - r)$ with $\pi(R_B - r)$, one investigates the question of which of the two investment opportunities is better able to outperform the *money-market account*. However, the fact that one investment opportunity is better able to outperform the riskless asset than another investment opportunity does *not* imply that the first investment opportunity outperforms the second one. This observation is crucial and we will provide an analytical example in Section 2.4.

Ad 2: We do not claim that the OP is more practicable than other performance measures. Indeed, given the computational capacities that are nowadays available, it is quite easy to compute any other performance measure as well. Instead, we refer to a social problem that is frequently discussed in statistical literacy, namely that a major part of our population has no clear understanding of basic statistics. Hence, most people cannot comprehend the precise meaning of "expected value," "standard deviation," or "variance," etc. Presumably, everybody of us knows that it is hard to explain the difference between the sample mean and the expected value to the layman. The same holds true regarding the empirical variance, sample variance, and population variance, etc. Further, our own experience shows that, at the beginning of their studies, many finance students have problems to understand the distinction between an ex-ante and an ex-post performance measure, which can be

[1] Each excess return is a differential return but not vice versa.

attributed to the fact that they are struggling with statistics and probability theory.[2] Thus, we are especially concerned about the problem of *financial* literacy, not only regarding an academic audience. According to the OECD (2016), the "overall levels of financial literacy, indicated by combining scores on knowledge, attitudes and behaviour are relatively low" in all 30 countries that participated in the OECD study. More precisely, it is reported that "only 42% of adults across all participating countries and economies are aware of the additional benefits of interest compounding on savings" and that "only 58% could compute a percentage to calculate a simple interest on savings." Moreover, "only about two in three adults [...] were aware that it is possible to reduce investment risk by buying a range of different stocks" and, in some countries, "no more than half of respondents understood the financial concept of diversification." The OECD study reveals a very low level of numeracy: Many people even are not able to calculate the balance of an account after an interest payment of 2%. Similar results can be found in the comprehensive review article by Lusardi and Mitchell (2013). For example, many people cannot say whether single stocks or mutual funds are more risky.[3] In the light of these findings, we conclude that it is clearly impossible for most people in our population to comprehend the core message of a return-to-risk measure. The OP is a probability and thus it can be much better understood by a nonacademic audience—at least in an intuitive way. Hence, it might help bridging theory and practice.

Ad 3: Performance measures usually presume a fixed holding period. It is well-known that a given performance ratio cannot be extended to other holding periods without making any simplifying—and sometimes quite problematic—assumptions, which are frequently discussed in the literature see, e.g., Lin and Chou (2003); Lo (2002); Sharpe (1994). For example, suppose that the value process $\{S_t\}_{t\geq 0}$ of some asset follows a geometric Brownian motion with drift coefficient $\mu \in \mathbb{R}$ and diffusion coefficient $\sigma > 0$.[4] We may assume without loss of generality that the instantaneous risk-free interest rate per year is zero. Hence, the (excess) return on the asset at time $T > 0$ is given by

$$R = \exp\left(\left(\mu - \frac{\sigma^2}{2}\right) T + \sigma W_T\right) - 1,$$

which means that the expected return is $\mathbf{E}(R) = e^{\mu T} - 1$. Further, the variance of the return amounts to $\mathbf{Var}(R) = \left(e^{\sigma^2 T} - 1\right) e^{2\mu T}$. We conclude that the Sharpe ratio of the strategy is

$$\text{Sh} = \frac{1 - e^{-\mu T}}{\sqrt{e^{\sigma^2 T} - 1}}.$$

Figure 1 depicts the Sharpe ratio of two different assets depending on the holding period T. Asset 1 possesses the parameters $\mu_1 = 0.1$ and $\sigma_1 = 0.2$, whereas Asset 2 has the parameters $\mu_2 = 0.2$ and $\sigma_2 = 0.3$. We can see that the Sharpe ratio is essentially determined by the time of liquidation. Interestingly, the Sharpe ratio is not linear and even not monotonic in time. If we use the Sharpe ratio as a performance measure, it can happen that we prefer Asset 1 for shorter holding periods but Asset 2 for longer holding periods.[5] Hence, the optimal choice between Asset 1 and Asset 2 heavily depends on the investment horizon. That is, in order to give a clear recommendation, we must know the holding period of the investor. However, most investors do not liquidate their strategies after a fixed period of time. More precisely, the time of liquidation is not known to them in advance, which means that it represents a random variable. We take the individual liquidity preference of the investor into

2 It is a matter of fact that some students do not understand even the distinction between parameter and estimator after attending a statistics course.

3 According to Lusardi and Mitchell (2013, pp. 15–16), we can expect that a large number of people cannot understand the question at all because they are unfamiliar with stocks, bonds, and mutual funds.

4 From now on, we will omit the subscript "$t \geq 0$" for notational convenience.

5 In the given example, the critical time point is, approximately, $T = 5$ years.

account by specifying a holding-time distribution. Our approach is time-continuous, whereas most other performance measures are based on a one-period model. This clearly distinguishes the OP from other performance measures and we think that this is one of our main contributions to the literature.

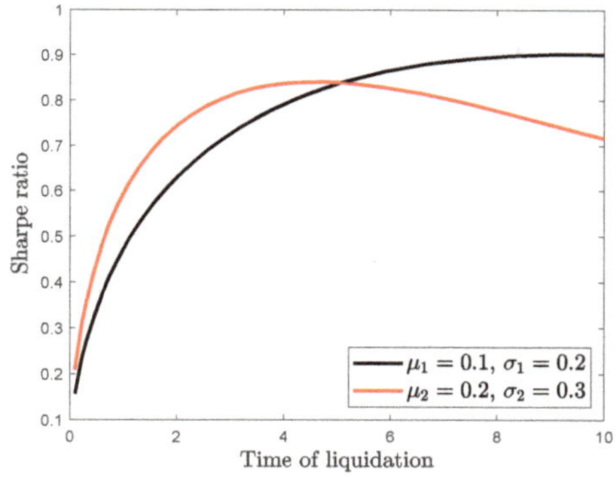

Figure 1. Sharpe ratios as a function of time.

In order to test the OP of different trading strategies, we selected 10 actively managed mutual funds that try to beat the S&P 500 or the Russell 1000 stock-market index. We decided to choose these funds because they focus on growth stocks in the US, have a large amount of assets under management, and their issuers enjoy a good reputation. The question of whether or not it is worth investing in actively managed funds at all is essential because if they do not outperform their benchmarks, market participants might be better advised to buy exchange traded funds (ETFs). More precisely, they should prefer so-called index ETFs, which aim at tracking a stock-market index. Analogously, if it turns out that the mutual funds are not able to outperform the bond market, it could be better to buy some US treasury-bond ETFs.[6] Further, it could happen that the money-market account is preferable and, in the worst case, it is even better to refrain from financial markets at all.

What are the merits of the OP compared to other performance measures?

1. The first one is conceptual:
   (a) A simple thought experiment reveals that comparing two performance measures with one another, where each one compares an investment opportunity with the money-market account, can lead to completely different conclusions than evaluating only one performance measure that compares the given investment opportunities without taking the money-market account into consideration at all. The former comparison refers to the question of which of the two investment opportunities is better able to outperform the money-market account, whereas the latter comparison refers to the question of whether the first investment opportunity is able to outperform the second. In general, performance measures are not linear and so the former comparison does not imply the latter, i.e., an investment opportunity that is better able to produce excess returns than another investment opportunity need not be better than the other.
   (b) Most performance measures presume that the holding period of the investor is fixed. This assumption is clearly violated in real-life because investors usually do not know, in advance, when they will liquidate all their assets. We solve this problem by incorporating any holding-time distribution, which specifies the individual liquidity preference of the

6 The reason why we focus on ETFs is discussed in Section 3.1.

investor. It can be either discrete or continuous and it can have a finite or infinite right endpoint. Any fixed holding period can be considered a special case, which means that we can treat one-period models, too.

2. The second one is empirical:

    (a) The natural logarithm of the assets under management of the mutual funds that are taken into consideration are highly correlated with their inverse coefficient of variation (ICV). The ICV is a return-to-risk measure, which is based on differential log-returns but not (necessarily) on excess log-returns, and in the Brownian-motion framework it is the main ingredient of the OP. This means that capital allocation and relative performance are strongly connected to one another, which suggests that market participants take differential (log-)returns *implicitly* into account when making their investment decisions.

    (b) We emphasize our results by comparing the p-values of the differences between the Sharpe ratios of all mutual funds and the Sharpe ratios of the given benchmarks. The p-values indicate that it is hard to distinguish between the former and the latter Sharpe ratios. For this reason, we cannot say that any fund is better than the benchmark by comparing two Sharpe ratios with one another. A completely different picture evolves when considering the p-values of the ICVs of all funds with respect to their benchmarks. Those p-values are much lower and *economically* significant, i.e., it turns out that most funds are able to beat their benchmarks.

The rest of this work is organized as follows: In Section 2 we present and discuss the OP. To be more precise, Section 2.1 contains our basic assumptions and our general definition of the OP. In Section 2.2 we investigate its theoretical properties, whereas in Section 2.3 we derive the statistical properties of our maximum-likelihood (ML) estimator for the OP. Section 2.4 contains a general discussion of the OP compared to other performance measures. Further, Section 3 contains the empirical part of this work, in which we investigate the question of whether or not mutual funds are able to beat their benchmarks. More precisely, in Section 3.1 we discuss some general observations related to the performance of mutual funds and index ETFs, whereas Section 3.2 contains our empirical results for different holding-time distributions. Our conclusion is given in Section 4.

2. The Outperformance Probability

2.1. Basic Assumptions and Definition

Let $\{S_t\}$ be the value process of some trading strategy and $\{B_t\}$ be the value process of a benchmark. We implicitly assume that $\{S_t\}$ and $\{B_t\}$ are, almost surely, positive. The strategy starts at time $t = 0$ and stops at some *random* time $T > 0$. Hence, T can be considered the time of liquidation and is referred to as the holding period. Throughout this work, time is measured in years. Moreover, we suppose that $S_0 = B_0 = 1$ without loss of generality.

Definition 1 (Outperformance probability). *The OP is defined as* $\Pi = \mathrm{P}(S_T > B_T)$.

Hence, Π is the probability that the value of the strategy will be greater than the value of the benchmark when the investor liquidates his strategy. The time of liquidation, T, is considered a random variable and so the law of total probability leads us to

$$\Pi = \mathbf{E}_T\Big[\mathrm{P}\big(S_t > B_t \mid T = t\big)\Big].$$

The performance measure Π ranges between 0 and 1. In the case that $\Pi = 1$, the strategy is always better than the benchmark, where "always" means "with probability 1," i.e., almost surely. This can be considered a limiting case, which usually does not appear in real life because otherwise the investor would have a weak arbitrage opportunity (Frahm 2016).[7] By contrast, if we have that $\Pi = 0$, the benchmark turns out to be always *at least as good* as the strategy, which does not mean that the benchmark is always *better*.[8] More generally, if the strategy outperforms its benchmark with probability Π, the benchmark outperforms the strategy with probability *less than or equal to* $1 - \Pi$. Therefore, the OP is not symmetric. Finally, if Π is near 0.5, there is no clear recommendation in favor or against the strategy. However, if a fund manager claims to be better than the benchmark, we should expect Π to be greater than 0.5.

We make the basic assumption that the time of liquidation does not depend on whether or not the strategy outperforms the benchmark, viz.

$$\mathrm{P}(S_t > B_t \,|\, T = t) = \mathrm{P}(S_t > B_t), \qquad \forall\, t \geq 0 .$$

Put another way, the decision of the investor whether or not to terminate the strategy at time t does not depend on its performance relative to the benchmark. It follows that

$$\Pi = \mathbf{E}_T\Big[\mathrm{P}(S_T > B_T)\Big] = \int_0^\infty \mathrm{P}(S_t > B_t)\, dF(t),$$

where F represents the cumulative distribution function of the holding period T.

2.2. Theoretical Properties

In this work, we rely on the standard model of financial mathematics, i.e., we suppose that $\{S_t\}$ and $\{B_t\}$ follow a 2-dimensional geometric Brownian motion. This means that the stochastic processes obey the stochastic differential equations

$$\frac{dS_t}{S_t} = \mu_S\, dt + \sigma_S\, dW_{St} \qquad \text{and} \qquad \frac{dB_t}{B_t} = \mu_B\, dt + \sigma_B\, dW_{Bt}\,,$$

where $\mathbf{E}(dW_{St} dW_{Bt}) = \rho dt$ with $-1 \leq \rho \leq 1$. It follows that

$$\begin{bmatrix} \log(S_t) \\ \log(B_t) \end{bmatrix} \sim \mathcal{N}(\gamma t, \Sigma t)\,, \qquad \forall\, t \geq 0,$$

with

$$\gamma = \begin{bmatrix} \gamma_S \\ \gamma_B \end{bmatrix} = \begin{bmatrix} \mu_S - \sigma_S^2/2 \\ \mu_B - \sigma_B^2/2 \end{bmatrix} \qquad \text{and} \qquad \Sigma = \begin{bmatrix} \sigma_S^2 & \sigma_S\sigma_B\rho \\ \sigma_B\sigma_S\rho & \sigma_B^2 \end{bmatrix}.$$

The numbers γ_S and γ_B are called the growth rates of $\{S_t\}$ and $\{B_t\}$, respectively (Frahm 2016). Thus, we have that

$$X := \log\left(\frac{S_1}{B_1}\right) \sim \mathcal{N}\left(\mu_S - \mu_B - \frac{\sigma_S^2 - \sigma_B^2}{2}, \sigma_S^2 + \sigma_B^2 - 2\sigma_S\sigma_B\rho\right).$$

Hence, the random variable X represents the *relative* log-return on the strategy with respect to its benchmark after the first period of time. We implicitly assume that

$$\sigma_S^2 + \sigma_B^2 - 2\sigma_S\sigma_B\rho > 0$$

[7] More precisely, the strategy would *dominate* the benchmark in the sense of Merton (1973).
[8] $\mathrm{P}(X > Y) = 0$ does not imply that $\mathrm{P}(X < Y) = 1$ but $\mathrm{P}(X \leq Y) = 1$.

in order to avoid the case in which X is degenerate, i.e., constant with probability 1. In our Brownian-motion framework, this happens if and only if $\Pi \in \{0,1\}$.

It follows that

$$P(S_t > B_t) = P(X > 0) = \Phi\left(\sqrt{t} \cdot \frac{\mu_S - \mu_B - (\sigma_S^2 - \sigma_B^2)/2}{\sqrt{\sigma_S^2 + \sigma_B^2 - 2\sigma_S\sigma_B\rho}}\right),$$

where Φ is the cumulative distribution function of the standard normal distribution. This leads us to

$$\Pi = \int_0^\infty \Phi\left(\sqrt{t} \cdot \frac{\mu_S - \mu_B - (\sigma_S^2 - \sigma_B^2)/2}{\sqrt{\sigma_S^2 + \sigma_B^2 - 2\sigma_S\sigma_B\rho}}\right) dF(t),$$

which demonstrates that the OP essentially depends on the diffusion coefficient σ_S and not only on the drift coefficient μ_S of the considered strategy.

For example, if we choose the money-market account as a benchmark, we obtain $\mu_B = r$ and $\sigma_B = 0$, where r is the instantaneous risk-free interest rate per year. In this standard case, the OP amounts to

$$\Pi = \int_0^\infty \Phi\left(\sqrt{t} \cdot \frac{\mu_S - r - \sigma_S^2/2}{\sigma_S}\right) dF(t).$$

In general, the benchmark is risky and we can see that the inverse coefficient of variation of the strategy with respect to its benchmark, i.e.,

$$\mathrm{ICV} := \frac{\mathbf{E}(X)}{\mathbf{Std}(X)} = \frac{\mu_S - \mu_B - (\sigma_S^2 - \sigma_B^2)/2}{\sqrt{\sigma_S^2 + \sigma_B^2 - 2\sigma_S\sigma_B\rho}},$$

plays a crucial role when calculating the OP. Note that the ICV refers to the *differential* log-return $X = \log(S_1) - \log(B_1)$, not to the excess log-return $\log(S_1) - r$.

Now, we are ready for our first theorem. Its proof has already been given throughout the previous explanations and so it can be skipped.

Theorem 1 (Outperformance probability)**.** *Under the aforementioned assumptions, the OP is given by*

$$\Pi = \int_0^\infty \Phi\left(\sqrt{t}\,\mathrm{ICV}\right) dF(t). \tag{1}$$

Hence, Π is strictly increasing in ICV. This means that the higher the ICV the higher the OP.[9] However, under the given assumptions, the OP can never be 0 or 1.

For example, suppose that the holding period is *fixed* and equal to $T > 0$. In this case, the OP simply amounts to $\Pi = \Phi(\sqrt{T}\,\mathrm{ICV})$. By contrast, if the holding period is uniformly distributed between 0 and $M > 0$, we obtain

$$\Pi = \frac{1}{M}\int_0^M \Phi\left(\sqrt{t}\,\mathrm{ICV}\right) dt.$$

Further, if the holding period is exponentially distributed with parameter $\lambda > 0$, we have that

$$\Pi = \lambda \int_0^\infty \Phi\left(\sqrt{t}\,\mathrm{ICV}\right) e^{-\lambda t} dt,$$

9 Thus, if a strategy has a higher OP than another strategy, given some holding-time distribution, the same holds true for any other holding-time distribution.

and if we assume that T has a Weibull distribution with parameters $\kappa > 0$ and $\gamma > 0$, we obtain

$$\Pi = \frac{\kappa}{\gamma} \int_0^\infty \Phi\left(\sqrt{t}\,\mathrm{ICV}\right) \left(\frac{t}{\gamma}\right)^{\kappa-1} e^{-(t/\gamma)^\kappa} dt\,.$$

Note that for $\kappa = 1$ and $\gamma = \lambda^{-1}$, the Weibull distribution turns into an exponential distribution with parameter λ. It is evident that the spectrum of possibilities to capture the distribution of T is almost infinite. In this work, we restrict to the aforementioned holding-time distributions. Obviously, F need not be continuous or even differentiable. The first holding-time distribution, which asserts that T is a constant, is deterministic, which poses no problem at all, too.

Figure 2 depicts the densities of the uniform, exponential, and Weibull distribution for different parameterizations. We have chosen all parameters such that the mean holding period equals 5 years. Moreover, Figure 3 contains some curves that quantify the OP depending on the ICV. On the left-hand side we can see how Π depends on ICV if the holding period T is considered a constant, which is the usual assumption in the finance literature, whereas on the right-hand side it is assumed that T is uniformly distributed between 0 and M, i.e., the maximum number of years that the investor maintains the given strategy.

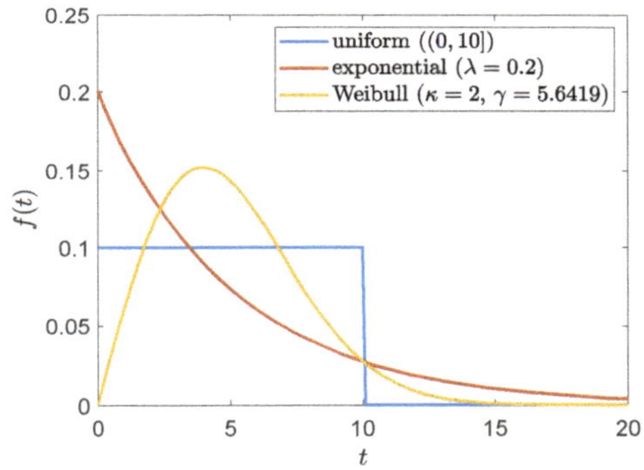

Figure 2. Holding-time distributions with mean 5.

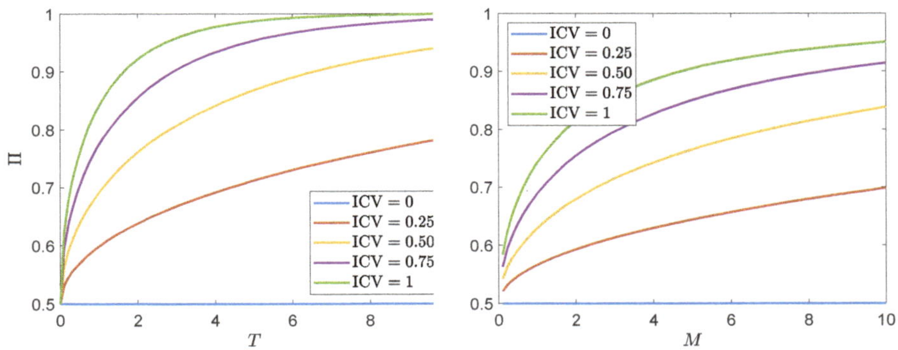

Figure 3. Outperformance probability (OP) depending on the inverse coefficient of variation (ICV) and the (maximal) holding period. On the **left-hand** side, the holding period T is considered fixed, whereas on the **right-hand** side, T is supposed to be uniformly distributed between 0 and M years.

2.3. Statistical Inference

Here, we propose a parametric estimator for Π, based on the assumption that the value processes $\{S_t\}$ and $\{B_t\}$ follow a 2-dimensional geometric Brownian motion. Let

$$X_t = \log\left(\frac{S_t}{S_{t-\Delta}}\right) - \log\left(\frac{B_t}{B_{t-\Delta}}\right), \qquad t = \Delta, 2\Delta, \ldots, n\Delta,$$

be the difference between the log-return on the strategy and the log-return on the benchmark at time t. The period between $t-\Delta$ and t, i.e., $\Delta > 0$, is fixed. Throughout this work, we assume that one year consists of 252 trading days and so we have that $\Delta = 1/252$.

The ML-estimator for the ICV is

$$\widehat{\mathrm{ICV}}_n = \frac{1}{\sqrt{\Delta}} \frac{\frac{1}{n}\sum_{t=\Delta}^{n\Delta} X_t}{\sqrt{\frac{1}{n}\sum_{t=\Delta}^{n\Delta}\left(X_t - \frac{1}{n}\sum_{t=\Delta}^{n\Delta} X_t\right)^2}}.$$

Our first proposition asserts that the ML-estimator for the ICV is strongly consistent.

Proposition 1. *We have that*

$$\widehat{\mathrm{ICV}}_n \xrightarrow{\text{a.s.}} \mathrm{ICV}, \qquad n \longrightarrow \infty.$$

Proof. The strong law of large numbers implies that

$$\frac{1}{n}\sum_{t=\Delta}^{n\Delta} X_t \xrightarrow{\text{a.s.}} \gamma_S - \gamma_B \qquad \text{and} \qquad \frac{1}{n}\sum_{t=\Delta}^{n\Delta}\left(X_t - \frac{1}{n}\sum_{t=\Delta}^{n\Delta} X_t\right)^2 \xrightarrow{\text{a.s.}} \sigma_S^2 + \sigma_B^2 - 2\sigma_S\sigma_B\rho$$

as $n \to \infty$. Hence, the continuous mapping theorem immediately reveals that $\widehat{\mathrm{ICV}}_n$ converges almost surely to ICV as the number of observations, n, grows to infinity. □

The next proposition refers to the asymptotic distribution of $\sqrt{n}(\widehat{\mathrm{ICV}}_n - \mathrm{ICV})$.

Proposition 2. *We have that*

$$\sqrt{n}(\widehat{\mathrm{ICV}}_n - \mathrm{ICV}) \xrightarrow{\text{d}} \mathcal{N}\left(0, \frac{1}{\Delta} + \frac{\mathrm{ICV}^2}{2}\right), \qquad n \longrightarrow \infty.$$

Proof. The ICV can be treated like a Sharpe ratio and thus $1 + \mathrm{ICV}^2/2$ is the asymptotic variance of $\sqrt{n}(\widehat{\mathrm{ICV}}_n - \mathrm{ICV})$ in the case that $\Delta = 1$ (Frahm 2018, p. 6). □

Hence, provided that the sample size n is large, the standard error of $\widehat{\mathrm{ICV}}_n$ is

$$\mathbf{Std}(\widehat{\mathrm{ICV}}_n) \approx \sqrt{\frac{1}{n\Delta} + \frac{\mathrm{ICV}^2}{2n}}.$$

Our empirical study in Section 3 reveals that the ICV does not exceed 1 and, since the sample size n is large, we can ignore the term $\mathrm{ICV}^2/(2n)$.[10] Note also that $m := n\Delta$ corresponds to the sample length measured in years. Thus, we obtain the following nice rule of thumb:

$$\mathbf{Std}(\widehat{\mathrm{ICV}}_n) \approx \frac{1}{\sqrt{m}}. \tag{2}$$

[10] This term can be attributed to the estimation error regarding the standard deviation of X (Frahm 2018).

The ML-estimator for Π is obtained, in the usual way, by substituting ICV with $\widehat{\mathrm{ICV}}_n$.

Definition 2 (ML-estimator). *The ML-estimator for Π is given by*

$$\widehat{\Pi}_n = \int_0^\infty \Phi\left(\sqrt{t}\,\widehat{\mathrm{ICV}}_n\right) dF(t).$$

The following theorem asserts that $\widehat{\Pi}_n$ is strongly consistent.

Theorem 2. *We have that*

$$\widehat{\Pi}_n \xrightarrow{\text{a.s.}} \Pi, \qquad n \longrightarrow \infty.$$

Proof. From Proposition 1 we already know that $\widehat{\mathrm{ICV}}_n$ converges almost surely to ICV as $n \to \infty$. According to Equation (1), we have that

$$\Pi\colon \mathrm{ICV} \longmapsto \int_0^\infty \Phi\left(\sqrt{t}\,\mathrm{ICV}\right) dF(t)$$

and it is clear that Π is continuous in ICV. Hence, the continuous mapping theorem reveals that $\widehat{\Pi}_n$ converges almost surely to Π as the number of observations, n, grows to infinity. □

The next theorem provides the asymptotic distribution of $\sqrt{n}(\widehat{\Pi}_n - \Pi)$, which can be used in order to calculate confidence intervals or conduct hypotheses tests. For this purpose, we need only assume that the expected value of $\sqrt{T}$ is finite.[11] In fact, in most practical applications we even have that $\mathbf{E}(T) < \infty$, which holds true also for all holding-time distributions that are considered in this work. Hence, the moment condition is always satisfied.

Theorem 3. *Assume that $\mathbf{E}(\sqrt{T}\,) < \infty$. We have that*

$$\sqrt{n}\,(\widehat{\Pi}_n - \Pi) \xrightarrow{\text{d}} \mathcal{N}(0,\sigma^2), \qquad n \longrightarrow \infty,$$

with

$$\sigma^2 = \left(\int_0^\infty \sqrt{t}\,\phi\left(\sqrt{t}\,\mathrm{ICV}\right) dF(t)\right)^2 \left(\frac{1}{\Delta} + \frac{\mathrm{ICV}^2}{2}\right),$$

where ϕ is the probability density function of the standard normal distribution.

Proof. Note that

$$0 \le \frac{\Phi(\sqrt{t}\,x_1) - \Phi(\sqrt{t}\,x_0)}{x_1 - x_0} \le \left.\frac{d\Phi(\sqrt{t}\,x)}{dx}\right|_{x=0} = \sqrt{t}\,\phi(0)$$

for all $x_0 < x_1$ and $t \ge 0$. Further, we have that

$$\int_0^\infty \sqrt{t}\,\phi(0)\,dF(t) = \phi(0)\mathbf{E}(\sqrt{T}\,) < \infty.$$

Thus, we can apply the dominated convergence theorem, i.e.,

$$\frac{d\Pi(\mathrm{ICV})}{d\mathrm{ICV}} = \frac{d}{d\mathrm{ICV}} \int_0^\infty \Phi\left(\sqrt{t}\,\mathrm{ICV}\right) dF(t) = \int_0^\infty \sqrt{t}\,\phi\left(\sqrt{t}\,\mathrm{ICV}\right) dF(t).$$

11 This is true whenever $\mathbf{E}(T^k) < \infty$ for any $k \ge \frac{1}{2}$.

Now, by applying the delta method and using Proposition 2, we obtain

$$\sqrt{n}\left(\widehat{\Pi}_n - \Pi\right) \xrightarrow{\text{d}} \left(\int_0^\infty \sqrt{t}\,\phi\left(\sqrt{t}\,\text{ICV}\right) dF(t)\right) \mathcal{N}\left(0, \frac{1}{\Delta} + \frac{\text{ICV}^2}{2}\right), \qquad n \longrightarrow \infty,$$

which leads us to the desired result. □

Hence, provided that n is sufficiently large, we can apply Theorem 3 in order to approximate the standard error of $\widehat{\Pi}_n$ by

$$\mathbf{Std}\left(\widehat{\Pi}_n\right) \approx \frac{1}{\sqrt{m}} \int_0^\infty \sqrt{t}\,\phi\left(\sqrt{t}\,\widehat{\text{ICV}}_n\right) dF(t).$$

Figure 4 quantifies the standard error of $\widehat{\Pi}_n$ as a function of m, i.e., the years of observation, for different ICVs. Note that $\mathbf{Std}\left(\widehat{\Pi}_n\right)$ is an even function of ICV and so we may focus on ICV ≥ 0. On the left-hand side it is assumed that T equals 5 years, whereas on the right-hand side T is supposed to be uniformly distributed between 0 and 10 years. Obviously, the specific choice of the holding-time distribution is not essential for the standard errors. They are high even if the sample length, m, is big. This is a typical problem of performance measurement (Frahm 2018). Further, we can see that the standard error of the ML-estimator essentially depends on the ICV. To be more precise, the higher the ICV the lower the standard error.

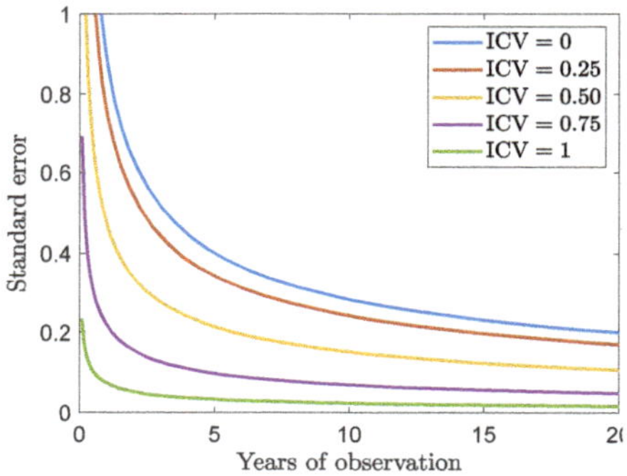

Figure 4. Standard error of $\widehat{\Pi}_n$ depending on the ICV. On the **left-hand** side, the holding period T is considered fixed and is equal to 5 years, whereas on the **right-hand** side, T is supposed to be uniformly distributed between 0 and 10 years.

A typical null hypothesis is $H_0\colon \Pi \leq \Pi_0 \in (0,1)$, which can be tested by means of the p-value

$$p_n = \Phi\left(-\frac{\widehat{\Pi}_n - \Pi_0}{\mathbf{Std}\left(\widehat{\Pi}_n\right)}\right).$$

More precisely, given some significance level α, H_0 can be rejected if and only if $p_n < \alpha$, in which case Π turns out to be significantly larger than Π_0.

2.4. Discussion

Classical performance measures are based on the Capital Asset Pricing Model (CAPM). The most prominent performance measures are the Sharpe ratio (Sharpe 1966), the Treynor ratio (Treynor 1961), and Jensen's Alpha (Jensen 1968). Let R be the discrete return on some strategy after a predefined period of time. Further, let r be the discrete risk-free interest rate after the given holding period and R_M be the return on the market portfolio.

Consider the linear regression equation

$$R - r = \alpha + \beta(R_M - r) + \varepsilon,$$

where α is the Alpha, β is the Beta, and ε represents the unsystematic risk of the strategy. Further, let σ_ε^2 be the variance of ε.

An actively managed fund aims at beating its benchmark. Let us suppose that the benchmark is the market portfolio. If the fund manager performs a strategy with $\beta = 1$, we have that

$$R - r = \alpha + (R_M - r) + \varepsilon$$

and so we obtain the differential return $R - R_M = \alpha + \varepsilon$. Hence, if we want to know whether or not the fund is able to beat the market portfolio, we should analyze the differential return $R - R_M$ and not the excess return $R - r$. More precisely, we should calculate the *generalized* Sharpe ratio according to Sharpe (1994), i.e.,

$$\text{Sh}^{1994} = \frac{\mathbf{E}(R - R_M)}{\mathbf{Std}(R - R_M)} = \frac{\alpha}{\sigma_\varepsilon},$$

and not the *ordinary* Sharpe ratio (Sharpe 1966), i.e.,

$$\text{Sh}^{1966} = \frac{\mathbf{E}(R) - r}{\mathbf{Std}(R)},$$

which is based on the CAPM (Lintner 1965; Mossin 1966; Sharpe 1964).

What happens if the fund's Beta does not equal 1? In this case we should compare the fund with a benchmark strategy that possesses the Beta of the fund. Let β be the proportion of equity that is invested in the market portfolio and $1 - \beta$ be the proportion of equity that is deposited in the money market. The corresponding (benchmark) return is thus

$$R_B = \beta R_M + (1 - \beta)r = r + \beta(R_M - r).$$

Hence, we obtain the differential return $R - R_B = \alpha + \varepsilon$, which leads us to the same result as before, i.e., $\text{Sh}^{1994} = \alpha/\sigma_\varepsilon$.

Why is it so important to consider differential returns instead of excess returns if we want to understand whether or not a given strategy is able to outperform its benchmark? The most simple illustration goes like this: Consider two random variables X and Y. The probability that X is positive is $\text{P}(X > 0)$ and the probability that Y is positive is $\text{P}(Y > 0)$. Suppose that we want to know the probability that X exceeds Y. Then we would calculate $\text{P}(X > Y) = \text{P}(X - Y > 0)$ but not $\text{P}(X > 0) - \text{P}(Y > 0)$ and the same holds true for performance measurement.

This means that in order to judge whether or not a strategy is able to outperform its benchmark we should not compare one ordinary Sharpe ratio with another. Ordinary Sharpe ratios are calculated on the basis of excess returns and so they answer the question of how good a given investment opportunity is able to beat the *money-market account*. Analogously, by comparing $\text{P}(X > 0)$ with $\text{P}(Y > 0)$ we answer the question of whether it is more probable that X or that Y exceeds 0. However, in performance measurement we want to know whether or not a strategy is able to outperform its benchmark, which is a completely different question and it has nothing to do with the money-market account. Analogously, we have to calculate the probability that X exceeds Y and not compare $\text{P}(X > 0)$ with $\text{P}(Y > 0)$.

This shall be illustrated, in financial terms, by a simple thought experiment. Suppose, for the sake of simplicity but without loss of generality, that the risk-free interest rate is zero. Further, let us assume that the return on some mutual fund is $R = R_M + \varepsilon$, where ε is a positive random variable that is uncorrelated with R_M.[12] Hence, the fund *always* yields a better return than the market portfolio and so it is clearly preferable. The ordinary Sharpe ratio of the market portfolio is

$$\mathrm{Sh}_M^{1966} = \frac{\mu_M}{\sigma_M},$$

where $\mu_M > 0$ is the expected return on the market portfolio and $\sigma_M > 0$ represents the standard deviation of the return on the market portfolio. Thus, we have that $\mathrm{Sh}_M^{1966} > 0$. By contrast, the ordinary Sharpe ratio of the strategy is

$$\mathrm{Sh}_S^{1966} = \frac{\mu_M + \mu_\varepsilon}{\sqrt{\sigma_M^2 + \sigma_\varepsilon^2}},$$

where $\mu_\varepsilon > 0$ is the expected value and $\sigma_\varepsilon^2 > 0$ is the variance of ε. We conclude that also Sh_S^{1966} is positive.

Now, depending on μ_ε and σ_ε^2, we can construct situations in which the fund appears to be better than the market portfolio and other situations in which it appears to be worse. To be more precise, we can find a positive random variable ε with a fixed expectation and an arbitrarily high variance. For example, suppose that $\varepsilon = \gamma + \delta\xi$, where $\gamma, \delta > 0$ and ξ is a random variable such that $\mathrm{P}(\xi = 0) = 1 - p$ and $\mathrm{P}(\xi = 1/p) = p > 0$. Hence, we have that $\mathbf{E}(\varepsilon) = \gamma + \delta$ and $\mathbf{Var}(\varepsilon) = \delta^2(1-p)/p$, which means that $\mathrm{Sh}_S^{1966} \searrow 0$ as $p \searrow 0$. Put another way, it holds that $\mathrm{Sh}_S^{1966} < \mathrm{Sh}_M^{1966}$ if we make p sufficiently low. Nonetheless, the OP of the fund is

$$\Pi = \mathrm{P}(R > R_M) = \mathrm{P}(\varepsilon > 0) = 1,$$

which means that the fund outperforms the market portfolio almost surely! It is evident that in such a case every rational investor should prefer the fund.

Why do we come to such a misleading conclusion by comparing the two ordinary Sharpe ratios with one another? The reason is that we analyze the marginal distributions of R and R_M instead of analyzing their joint distribution. In fact, since ε is positive, it is better for the investor to have a large variance σ_ε^2, not a small one. Thus, it makes no sense to penalize the expected return on the fund by σ_ε^2, but this is precisely what we do when we calculate Sh_S^{1966}. However, it is worth noting that, in this particular case, it makes no sense either to calculate the generalized Sharpe ratio

$$\mathrm{Sh}_S^{1994} = \frac{\mathbf{E}(R - R_M)}{\mathbf{Std}(R - R_M)} = \frac{\mu_\varepsilon}{\sigma_\varepsilon}.$$

The problem is that ε is positive, which means that σ_ε is the wrong risk measure in that context.[13] However, irrespective of the parameters μ_ε and σ_ε, we always have that $\Pi = 1$, which clearly indicates that the fund is better than its benchmark. We could imagine plenty of other examples that are less striking, but the overall conclusion remains the same: One should use differential (log-)returns instead of excess (log-)returns when comparing some strategy with a benchmark.

The main goal of this work is to provide a performance measure that is better understandable for a nonacademic audience. The OP is based on the ICV, which compares the log-return on the strategy with the log-return on the benchmark. Thus, it is compatible with Sharpe's (Sharpe 1994) principal argument and so we hope that it can serve its purpose in the finance industry. Most investors want to know whether they can beat a risky benchmark, not the money-market account. It is worth emphasizing that the OP is based on a continuous-time model and we do not make any use of capital market theory. For this reason, the OP cannot be compared with performance measures that are based

[12] This is not a linear regression equation because $\mathbf{E}(\varepsilon) > 0$.

[13] This kind of situation cannot happen in our Brownian-motion framework.

on a one-period model without making any simplifying assumption and thus sacrificing the merits of continuous-time finance. This holds true, in particular, for the classical performance measures mentioned above. The reason why we use log-returns instead of discrete returns is because our model is time-continuous. More precisely, it is build on the standard assumption that the value processes follow a geometric Brownian motion. It is worth noting that return-to-risk measures can change essentially when substituting log-returns with discrete returns or vice versa—even if we work with daily asset (log-)returns.

The classical performance measures are based on the CAPM and so they are vulnerable to a model misspecification. On the contrary, the OP is not based on any capital-market model—it is a probabilistic measure. Thus, it is model-independent although we assume that the value processes of the strategy and of the benchmark follow a 2-dimensional geometric Brownian motion. This assumption is made only for statistical reasons and it has nothing to do with the OP itself (see Definition 1). Hence, it is possible to find nonparametric estimators for the OP, which are not based on any parametric model regarding the value processes of the strategy and of the benchmark. We plan to investigate such kind of estimators in the future.

Nonetheless, in this work we deal with the ML-estimator for Π and this estimator is not unimpeachable:

- It is based on a parametric model, namely the geometric Brownian motion. While this model is standard in financial mathematics, we may doubt that value processes follow a geometric Brownian motion in real life. The assumption that log-returns are independent and identically normally distributed contradicts the stylized facts of empirical finance.
- We assume that the time of liquidation does not depend on whether or not the strategy outperforms the benchmark. This assumption might be violated, for example, if investors suffer from the disposition effect, i.e., if they tend to sell winners too early and ride losers too long (Shefrin and Statman 1985).
- Also the holding-time distribution follows a parametric model, which can either be true or false, too. Indeed, we have to choose some model for T but need not necessarily know its parameters. However, in order to estimate the parameters of F, we would need appropriate data and then the statistical properties of the ML-estimator might change essentially.

The reader might ask whether we want to suggest a better alternative to return-to-risk measures from a pure theoretical perspective or to provide a more illustrative performance measure for the asset-management industry. The answer is that we aim at *both*. However, it is worth emphasizing that we do not try to convince the audience that return-to-risk measures are useless or fallacious *per se*. In fact, the OP itself is based on a return-to-risk measure, namely the ICV, and we will see that this is the most important ingredient of the OP. The question is whether one should use *two* return-to-risk measures or just *one* in order to compare a strategy with some benchmark. We decidedly propagate the latter approach and refer to the arguments raised by Sharpe (1994). Simply put, performance measures are not linear and so the difference between the performance of two investment opportunities is not the same as the performance of the first investment opportunity compared to the second. Our own return-to-risk measure is the ICV and we transform the ICV into a *probability* by treating the time of liquidation stochastic. This is done in order to account for the individual liquidity preference of the investor and, especially, for a better practical understanding.

3. Empirical Investigation

3.1. General Observations

Actively managed funds usually aim at beating some benchmark, typically a stock-market index. Our financial markets and computer technology provide many possibilities in order to pursue that target. For example, we could think about stock picking, market timing, portfolio optimization, technical analysis, fundamental analysis, time-series analysis, high-frequency trading, algorithmic trading, etc. The list of opportunities is virtually endless, but the problem is that most sophisticated trading strategies produce high transaction costs and other expenses like management fees and agency costs. The principal question is whether or not actively managed funds are able to beat their benchmarks after taking all expenses into account.

Jensen (1968) reports that the 115 (open-end) mutual funds that he considered in his study, which covers the period from 1945 to 1964, "were *on average* not able to predict security prices well enough to outperform a buy-the-market-and-hold policy." He states also that "there is very little evidence that any *individual* fund was able to do significantly better than that which we expected from mere random chance." By contrast, Ippolito (1989) investigated 143 mutual funds over the period from 1965 to 1984 and finds that "mutual funds, net of all fees and expenses, except load charges, outperformed index funds on a risk-adjusted basis." This is in contrast to many other studies, but he emphasizes that "the industry alpha, though significantly positive, is not sufficiently large to overcome the load charges that characterize the majority of funds in the sample." Hence, after taking sales charges or commissions into account, the Alpha of mutual funds disappears. Further, Grinblatt and Titman (1989) considered the sample period from 1974 to 1984. They write that "superior performance may in fact exist, particularly among aggressive-growth and growth funds and those funds with the smallest net asset values." However, "these funds also have the highest expenses so that their actual returns, net of all expenses, do not exhibit abnormal performance." Hence, they come to the conclusion that "investors cannot take advantage of the superior abilities of these portfolio managers by purchasing shares in their mutual funds." Finally, Fama and French (2010) considered the period from 1984 to 2006 and they conclude that "fund investors in aggregate realize net returns that underperform three-factor, and four-factor benchmarks by about the costs in expense ratios," which means that "if there are fund managers with enough skill to produce benchmark-adjusted expected returns that cover costs, their tracks are hidden in the aggregate results by the performance of managers with insufficient skill." To sum up, it seems to be better for the market participants to track a stock-market index or to choose the market portfolio.

There exists a large number of passively managed ETFs on the market, which aim at replicating a specific stock-market index like the S&P 500 or the Russell 1000. Elton et al. (1996) vividly explain why it makes sense to compare actively managed funds with index ETFs, and not with stock-market indices, in order to analyze whether or not fund managers are able to beat the market:

> *"The recent increase in the number and types of index funds that are available to individual investors makes this a matter of practical as well as theoretical significance. Numerous index funds, which track the Standard and Poor's (S&P) 500 Index or various small-stock, bond, value, growth, or international indexes, are now widely available to individual investors. [...] Given that there are sufficient index funds to span most investors' risk choices, that the index funds are available at low cost, and that the low cost of index funds means that a combination of index funds is likely to outperform an active fund of similar risk, the question is, why select an actively managed fund?"*

Before the first index ETF, i.e., the SPDR S&P 500 ETF (SPY), came up in 1993, authors had to think about how a private investor would replicate a stock index by himself. That is, they had to take all transaction costs, exchange fees, taxes, time and effort, etc., into account. Index ETFs solved that problem all at once. There are no loading charges and, except for minor broker fees and very low transaction costs, private investors do not have to care about anything in order to track a stock index. Many index funds are very liquid and their tracking error seems to be very small. Thus, it is clear why investors usually are not able or willing to replicate a stock-market index by themselves, which is the reason why we treat index ETFs as benchmarks in this work.

Compared to actively managed funds, index ETFs have much lower expense ratios, but their performance might be worse. In order to clarify whether or not the additional costs of an actively managed fund are overcompensated by a better performance, we compare 10 mutual funds with index ETFs. Most of the funds contain US large-cap stocks and have 1 to 60 billion US dollars of assets under management. In any case, they try to outperform the S&P 500 or the Russell 1000. Hence, our first benchmark is the SPDR S&P 500 ETF. This is almost equivalent to the S&P 500 total return stock index, which serves as a proxy for the overall US stock market. The second benchmark is the iShares Russell 1000 Growth ETF (IWF). That ETF seeks to track the Russell 1000, which is composed of large- and mid-cap US equities exhibiting growth characteristics. In order to reflect the US mid-term treasury-bond market, we chose the iShares 7–10 Year Treasury Bond ETF (IEF). This ETF is composed of US treasury bonds with remaining maturities between 7 and 10 years, including only AAA-rated securities. Our next benchmark is the US money-market account, based on the London Inter-bank Offered Rate (LIBOR) for overnight US-dollar deposits. Our last benchmark is cash, without any interest or risk, i.e., "keeping the money under the mattress." In this special case, the OP quantifies the probability that the final value of the strategy exceeds its initial value, i.e., $\Pi = \mathrm{P}(S_T > 1)$. Hence, to outperform cash just means to generate a positive return, which is the least one should expect when investing money.

Our empirical analysis is based on daily price observations from 2 January 2003, to 31 December 2018. Hence, we take also the financial crisis 2008 into account. The length of that history amounts to $n = 4027$ trading days. All ETFs and mutual funds, together with their symbols, their estimated drift coefficients ($\hat{\mu}$), diffusion coefficients ($\hat{\sigma}$), growth rates ($\hat{\gamma}$), expense ratios (ER), and their assets under management (AUM) are presented in Table 1. It is separated into two parts: The first part shows the benchmarks, whereas the second part contains the mutual funds. We can see that the expense ratios of the mutual funds are up to 90 basis points higher compared to the S&P 500 ETF (SPY). On average, investors pay 67 basis points more for a mutual fund compared to the S&P 500 ETF and 56 basis points more compared to the Russell 1000 ETF (IWF). MSEGX possesses the highest drift coefficient and growth rate,[14] whereas FKGRX has the lowest volatility, i.e., diffusion coefficient, among all mutual funds. PINDX has the lowest drift coefficient and growth rate but the second highest volatility. While the stock-index ETFs are hard to distinguish according to $\hat{\mu}$ and $\hat{\sigma}$, it should be noted that the Russell 1000 ETF has a slightly higher estimated growth rate, $\hat{\gamma}$, compared to the S&P 500 ETF.

Table 1. Basic characteristics of the benchmarks and funds that are taken into consideration, i.e., the estimated drift coefficients ($\hat{\mu}$), diffusion coefficients ($\hat{\sigma}$), growth rates ($\hat{\gamma}$) as well as their expense ratios (ER) and assets under management (AUM).

Benchmark/Fund	Symbol	$\hat{\mu}$	$\hat{\sigma}$	$\hat{\gamma}$	ER (%)	AUM (bn $)
SPDR S&P 500 ETF	SPY	0.0995	0.1815	0.0830	0.09	264.06
iShares Russell 1000 Growth ETF	IWF	0.1064	0.1774	0.0906	0.20	44.44
iShares 7–10 Year Treasury Bond ETF	IEF	0.0465	0.0656	0.0444	0.15	13.31
Money market	–	0.0100	0.0007	0.0100	–	–
Cash	–	0	0	0	–	–
Fidelity Blue Chip Growth	FBGRX	0.1135	0.1919	0.0951	0.72	26.89
T. Rowe Price Blue Chip Growth	TRBCX	0.1200	0.1974	0.1005	0.70	60.37
Franklin Growth A	FKGRX	0.1064	0.1708	0.0918	0.84	14.96
JPMorgan Large Cap Growth A	OLGAX	0.1105	0.1900	0.0924	0.94	15.15
Vanguard Morgan Growth	VMRGX	0.1094	0.1889	0.0915	0.37	14.79
Morgan Stanley Institutional Growth A	MSEGX	0.1299	0.2164	0.1064	0.89	6.93
BlackRock Capital Appreciation	MAFGX	0.1060	0.1931	0.0873	0.76	3.13
AllianzGI Focused Growth Fund Admin	PGFAX	0.1129	0.1942	0.0940	0.99	1.02
Goldman Sachs Large Cap Growth Insights	GCGIX	0.1015	0.1829	0.0848	0.53	2.16
Pioneer Disciplined Growth A	PINDX	0.0993	0.2077	0.0777	0.87	1.22
∅		0.1110	0.1933	0.0922	0.76	14.66

[14] It holds that $\mathbf{E}(S_T) = e^{\mu_S T}$ and so the drift coefficient μ_S can be considered the internal rate of return on the fund.

However, the quantities $\hat{\mu}$, $\hat{\sigma}$, and $\hat{\gamma}$ are subject to estimation errors and it is well-known that the estimation errors regarding μ and γ are much higher than those regarding σ. Even if we work with daily observations, they cannot be neglected. Hence, Table 1 gives no clear recommendation in favor or against the mutual funds if we compare the quantities of the index ETFs and the mutual funds with each other. On average, the annualized drifts, volatilities, and growth rates of the mutual funds are close to those of the S&P 500 ETF and the Russell 1000 ETF. Does the overall picture change if we evaluate the ordinary Sharpe ratios of the mutual funds?

Table 2 contains the ordinary and the generalized Sharpe ratios of all mutual funds, on an annualized basis, with respect to our two stock-market benchmarks and the bond market. We can see that 9 out of all 10 mutual funds have an ordinary Sharpe ratio that is greater than the (ordinary) Sharpe ratio of the S&P 500 ETF. However, 7 mutual funds possess a Sharpe ratio that is lower than the Sharpe ratio of the Russell 1000 ETF. Hence, we could believe that most fund managers are not able to beat that benchmark. Moreover, except for FKGRX, all funds are inferior to the US treasury-bond ETF. This would suggest that it is better to refrain from the stock market at all and to prefer mid-term US treasury bonds. This conclusion is fallacious.

Table 2. Ordinary vs. generalized Sharpe ratios (annualized).

Symbol	Ordinary	Generalized		
		SPY	**IWF**	**IEF**
SPY	0.4933	–	–	–
IWF	0.5433	–	–	–
IEF	0.5579	–	–	–
FBGRX	0.5396	0.2480	0.1608	0.2970
TRBCX	0.5576	0.3570	0.2854	0.3187
FKGRX	0.5649	0.1433	0.0020	0.2914
OLGAX	0.5292	0.1568	0.0788	0.2874
VMRGX	0.5264	0.1954	0.0801	0.2824
MSEGX	0.5544	0.3304	0.2903	0.3366
MAFGX	0.4973	0.1014	−0.0074	0.2628
PGFAX	0.5304	0.2185	0.1338	0.2921
GCGIX	0.5007	0.0436	−0.1372	0.2541
PINDX	0.4302	−0.0028	−0.1008	0.2198
⌀	0.5231	0.1792	0.0786	0.2842

Indeed, the overall picture changes completely when we consider the generalized Sharpe ratios. In fact, 9 out of all 10 mutual funds have a positive Sharpe ratio with respect to the S&P 500 ETF, which means that almost all funds were able to beat this benchmark. Moreover, 7 funds have a positive Sharpe ratio with respect to the Russell 1000 ETF and so the majority of the funds have beaten also that benchmark. Finally, since all Sharpe ratios with respect to the US treasury-bond ETF are positive, it is always better to prefer stocks to bonds. Hence, the given results are entirely different and our conclusion turns into the opposite!

The estimated ICV of a fund tells us how the fund manager performed against some benchmark and, according to Equation (1), it essentially determines the (estimated) OP. Table 3 contains the ICVs of the 10 mutual funds with respect to our 5 benchmarks. This table confirms our latter results. This means that 9 out of all 10 mutual funds, in fact, were able to outperform the S&P 500 ETF. Further, 7 funds outperformed the Russell 1000 ETF. The (uniformly) worst performer is PINDX, which is never preferable compared to the index ETFs. The best performer with respect to the index ETFs is TRBCX, whose track record is extraordinarily good. We conclude that most funds are preferable compared to the index ETFs, which was not clear to us after inspecting the ordinary Sharpe ratios in Table 2. It is worth noting that all mutual funds perform much better if we compare them with the S&P 500 ETF rather than the Russell 1000 ETF. Table 3 reveals also that mutual funds are clearly superior to bonds, the money market, and cash.

Table 3. ICVs of the mutual funds with respect to the benchmarks. The standard errors can be approximated by $1/\sqrt{m} = 0.2502$ (see Equation (2)).

Symbol	**Benchmark**				
	SPY	**IWF**	**IEF**	**LIBOR**	**Cash**
FBGRX	0.2133	0.1002	0.2245	0.4429	0.4947
TRBCX	0.3038	0.2066	0.2432	0.4584	0.5088
FKGRX	0.1825	0.0279	0.2307	0.4790	0.5373
OLGAX	0.1339	0.0346	0.2156	0.4335	0.4858
VMRGX	0.1677	0.0239	0.2115	0.4312	0.4839
MSEGX	0.2539	0.1950	0.2503	0.4454	0.4913
MAFGX	0.0669	−0.0638	0.1896	0.4001	0.4516
PGFAX	0.1790	0.0699	0.2182	0.4326	0.4838
GCGIX	0.0378	−0.1656	0.1865	0.4088	0.4632
PINDX	−0.0747	−0.1845	0.1387	0.3259	0.3738
⌀	0.1464	0.0244	0.2109	0.4258	0.4774

Clearly, TRBCX is the best performer among all mutual funds and so it is evident why it has, by far, the largest amount of assets under management (over 60 billion US dollars). Figure 5 plots the ICV of each mutual fund, both with respect to the S&P 500 and with respect to the Russell 1000, against the natural logarithm of its assets under management. It turns out that the ICV of a fund is highly correlated with the log-amount of assets under management. To be more precise, the correlation between ICV and log(AUM) amounts to 71.22% if we refer to the S&P 500 and to 65.67% if we refer to the Russell 1000. However, we can observe two outliers, namely MSEGX and PGFAX, which performed well between 2003 and 2018 compared to their assets under management.

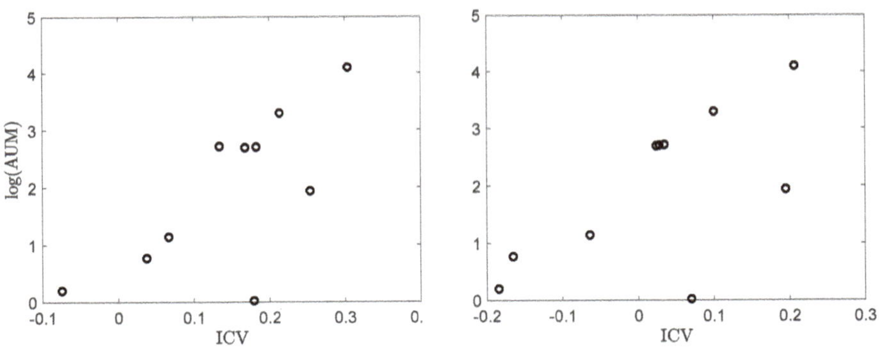

Figure 5. ICV against the natural logarithm of the assets under management of the mutual funds with respect to the S&P 500 (**left**) and the Russell 1000 (**right**).

Our results demonstrate that it is highly important to consider *differential* returns and not excess returns if we want to compare some strategy with a specified benchmark. By comparing the ordinary Sharpe ratio of some strategy with the ordinary Sharpe ratio of a given benchmark (see Table 1) one checks which of the two is better able to outperform the *money-market account*. However, this is not what we want to know when we try to understand whether or not a strategy is able to outperform its *benchmark*. For this purpose we have to calculate the generalized Sharpe ratios in Table 2 (Sharpe 1994) or the ICVs in Table 3.

Our arguments shall be clarified also from a statistical point of view: Let $\widehat{\mathrm{Sh}}_{Sn}$ be the empirical estimator for the annualized Sharpe ratio of the strategy and $\widehat{\mathrm{Sh}}_{Bn}$ be the empirical estimator for the annualized Sharpe ratio of the benchmark. Further, let $\Delta\mathrm{Sh} := \mathrm{Sh}_S - \mathrm{Sh}_B$ be the difference between the annualized Sharpe ratio of the strategy, Sh_S, and the annualized Sharpe ratio of the benchmark, i.e., Sh_B. Then one uses the test statistic $\Delta\widehat{\mathrm{Sh}}_n := \widehat{\mathrm{Sh}}_{Sn} - \widehat{\mathrm{Sh}}_{Bn}$ in order to test the null hypothesis $H_0\colon \Delta\mathrm{Sh} \leq 0$. Our results are presented on the right-hand side of Table 4, which contains also the corresponding p-values for H_0 in parentheses. By contrast, the left-hand side of Table 4 contains the estimated ICVs and their corresponding p-values for the null hypothesis $H_0\colon \mathrm{ICV} \leq 0$.[15] We can see that most p-values on the left-hand side are smaller than those on the right-hand side. This holds true in particular when we compare the funds with the Russell 1000 ETF and the US treasury-bond ETF. Hence, using the ICV instead of comparing two Sharpe ratios with one another in order to test whether a strategy outperforms its benchmark leads to results that are more significant in an *economic* sense. To be more precise, in the majority of cases, the estimated ICVs are positive and their p-values are low enough in order to conclude that most fund managers are able to beat their benchmarks. However, the given results are still insignificant in a *statistical* sense.

Table 4. Test statistics $\widehat{\mathrm{ICV}}_n$ and $\Delta\widehat{\mathrm{Sh}}_n$ together with their corresponding p-values (in parentheses) for the null hypotheses $H_0\colon \mathrm{ICV} \leq 0$ and $H_0\colon \Delta\mathrm{Sh} \leq 0$, respectively.

Symbol	$\widehat{\mathrm{ICV}}_n$			$\Delta\widehat{\mathrm{Sh}}_n$		
	SPY	**IWF**	**IEF**	**SPY**	**IWF**	**IEF**
FBGRX	0.2133 (0.1970)	0.1002 (0.3444)	0.2245 (0.1848)	0.0463 (0.2908)	−0.0183 (0.5168)	−0.0038 (0.5233)
TRBCX	0.3038 (0.1123)	0.2066 (0.2044)	0.2432 (0.1654)	0.0643 (0.2193)	−0.0003 (0.5003)	0.0142 (0.4149)
FKGRX	0.1825 (0.2329)	0.0279 (0.4556)	0.2307 (0.1782)	0.0717 (0.1756)	0.0071 (0.4935)	0.0216 (0.3822)
OLGAX	0.1339 (0.2963)	0.0346 (0.4450)	0.2156 (0.1944)	0.0360 (0.3664)	−0.0286 (0.5264)	−0.0141 (0.5706)
VMRGX	0.1677 (0.2513)	0.0239 (0.4619)	0.2115 (0.1989)	0.0331 (0.3315)	−0.0315 (0.5289)	−0.0170 (0.6200)
MSEGX	0.2539 (0.1550)	0.1950 (0.2178)	0.2503 (0.1585)	0.0611 (0.3071)	−0.0035 (0.5032)	0.0110 (0.4575)
MAFGX	0.0669 (0.3946)	−0.0638 (0.6006)	0.1896 (0.2243)	0.0040 (0.4829)	−0.0606 (0.5556)	−0.0460 (0.7294)
PGFAX	0.1790 (0.2371)	0.0699 (0.3899)	0.2182 (0.1915)	0.0371 (0.3403)	−0.0275 (0.5252)	−0.0130 (0.5728)
GCGIX	0.0378 (0.4400)	−0.1656 (0.7460)	0.1865 (0.2280)	0.0074 (0.4587)	−0.0571 (0.5524)	−0.0426 (0.7818)
PINDX	−0.0747 (0.6173)	−0.1845 (0.7696)	0.1387 (0.2897)	−0.0631 (0.7481)	−0.1277 (0.6165)	−0.1131 (0.8875)

3.2. Empirical Results

In this section, we present our estimates of the OPs for different holding-time distributions. More precisely, we consider a fixed, a uniformly distributed, an exponentially distributed, and a Weibull distributed holding period. In order to make the results comparable, we chose the parameters such that the mean holding period equals 5 years for each holding-time distribution.

Our principal question is whether or not actively managed funds are able to beat their benchmarks, which can be answered in a very simple way by estimating their OPs. In the case that $\Pi \leq 0.5$, we can

[15] All p-values have been computed by using the asymptotic results reported by Frahm (2018).

say that the fund manager is not able to beat the specified benchmark.[16] Then it makes not much sense for an investor to buy the fund share because, with probability greater or equal to 50%, the benchmark performs at least as good as the mutual fund. Hence, our null hypothesis is $H_0\colon \Pi \leq 0.5$. Of course, we have to take estimation errors into account and so we report the estimated OPs along with their standard errors and p-values.

3.2.1. Fixed Holding Period

Let us begin by considering the holding period $T > 0$ fixed. In this case, the ML-estimator for the OP is simply $\widehat{\Pi}_n = \Phi(\sqrt{T}\,\widehat{\mathrm{ICV}}_n)$. Further, its standard error is, approximately,

$$\mathbf{Std}(\widehat{\Pi}_n) \approx \sqrt{\frac{T}{m}}\,\phi(\sqrt{T}\,\widehat{\mathrm{ICV}}_n).$$

Table 5 contains the results if we assume that the holding period equals 5 years. We can see that 9 out of the 10 mutual funds that are taken into consideration are able to outperform the S&P 500 and 7 funds can outperform the Russell 1000. In fact, this follows also from Table 3 because the OP is greater than 0.5 if and only if ICV > 0. Nonetheless, Table 5 provides some additional information. It reveals that the OPs typically range between 0.5 and 0.7 with regard to the index ETFs. An apparent exception is the T. Rowe Price Blue Chip Growth Fund (TRBCX), which has a tremendous OP of 0.7515 with respect to the S&P 500. The worst fund is the Pioneer Disciplined Growth Fund (PINDX), which underperforms both the S&P 500 and the Russell 1000 with a quite small OP of 0.4337 and 0.3400, respectively.

Despite the fact that most funds outperform their stock-market benchmarks, the results are not statistically significant. All p-values that are related to the index ETFs exceed $\alpha = 0.05$. Only TRBCX comes very close to α with a p-value of 0.0779, given that we use the S&P 500 ETF as a benchmark. Of course, this does not mean that we have that $\Pi \leq 0.5$ for any fund. Performance measurement is very susceptible to estimation risk (Frahm 2018) and thus, in that context, we cannot expect to obtain statistically significant results. Nevertheless, we may say that the results are, at least, economically significant. This was surprising to us, since in the finance community it is usually asserted that fund managers, in general, do not better than their benchmarks. This was already discussed in Section 3.1.

All mutual funds outperform the bond market, but these results are not significant either. However, most funds at least outperform the money-market account and cash on a significance level of $\alpha = 0.01$, which can be seen by the p-values at the end of Table 5. The corresponding OPs usually exceed 0.8, which means that the probability of generating some excess return or of making *any* profit at the time of liquidation is greater than 80%. Once again, an exception is PINDX, whose OPs with respect to the money-market account and cash are lower than 80%.

[16] Note that this is precisely the case in which we have that ICV ≤ 0.

Table 5. Results in the case that T equals 5 years.

Fund	SPY			IWF			IEF			LIBOR			Cash		
	OP	Std	p	OP	Std	p	OP	Std	p	OP	Std	p	OP	Std	p
FBGRX	0.6833	0.1992	0.1788	0.5886	0.2176	0.3419	0.6921	0.1967	0.1644	0.8390	0.1367	0.0066	0.8657	0.1210	0.0013
TRBCX	0.7515	0.1772	0.0779	0.6780	0.2006	0.1874	0.7068	0.1925	0.1414	0.8473	0.1320	0.0042	0.8724	0.1168	0.0007
FKGRX	0.6584	0.2053	0.2203	0.5249	0.2227	0.4555	0.6970	0.1954	0.1566	0.8580	0.1257	0.0022	0.8852	0.1084	0.0002
OLGAX	0.6176	0.2134	0.2907	0.5308	0.2225	0.4449	0.6851	0.1987	0.1758	0.8338	0.1395	0.0084	0.8613	0.1237	0.0017
VMRGX	0.6462	0.2080	0.2411	0.5213	0.2228	0.4619	0.6819	0.1995	0.1810	0.8325	0.1402	0.0088	0.8604	0.1243	0.0019
MSEGX	0.7149	0.1899	0.1289	0.6686	0.2029	0.2030	0.7122	0.1908	0.1331	0.8403	0.1359	0.0061	0.8640	0.1220	0.0014
MAFGX	0.5595	0.2207	0.3938	0.4433	0.2209	0.6013	0.6642	0.2040	0.2105	0.8145	0.1496	0.0177	0.8437	0.1340	0.0052
PGFAX	0.6556	0.2060	0.2251	0.5621	0.2204	0.3890	0.6872	0.1981	0.1723	0.8333	0.1398	0.0085	0.8603	0.1243	0.0019
GCGIX	0.5336	0.2224	0.4399	0.3556	0.2084	0.7558	0.6617	0.2046	0.2147	0.8196	0.1470	0.0148	0.8498	0.1305	0.0037
PINDX	0.4337	0.2201	0.6184	0.3400	0.2050	0.7825	0.6217	0.2127	0.2835	0.7669	0.1711	0.0594	0.7984	0.1574	0.0290
⌀	0.6254	0.2062	0.2815	0.5213	0.2144	0.4623	0.6810	0.1993	0.1833	0.8285	0.1417	0.0137	0.8561	0.1263	0.0047

3.2.2. Uniformly Distributed Holding Period

Now, we assume that the investor has a holding period that is uniformly distributed between 0 and M years. The ML-estimator for Π is

$$\widehat{\Pi}_n = \frac{1}{M}\int_0^M \Phi\left(\sqrt{t}\,\widehat{\mathrm{ICV}}_n\right) dt$$

and its standard error can be approximated by

$$\mathbf{Std}(\widehat{\Pi}_n) \approx \frac{1}{\sqrt{m}}\frac{1}{M}\int_0^M \sqrt{t}\,\phi\left(\sqrt{t}\,\widehat{\mathrm{ICV}}_n\right) dt.$$

Table 6 contains the results if we assume that the holding period is uniformly distributed between 0 and 10 years. As we can see, the given results are not essentially different compared to those in Table 5. However, it is conspicuous that the OPs are slightly lower. The same effect can be observed also in Figure 3 if we compare the OPs on the left-hand side for $T = 5$ with the OPs on the right-hand side for $M = 10$. The reason is that liquidating a strategy with a positive ICV prematurely lowers the OP. The problem is that later liquidations cannot compensate for earlier ones if the strategy is profitable compared to its benchmark, i.e., ICV > 0.

While the OPs in Table 6 are slightly lower compared to those in Table 5, we can verify that all funds are still better than the bond market. The majority of funds are even significantly better than the money-market account and cash on a level of 1%. To sum up, *in general*, it is preferable to invest in mutual funds also if the holding period of the investor is uniformly distributed. However, there are noticeable differences regarding the performance of the mutual funds, which means that investors should be aware that some funds perform much better than others. The question of whether or not the estimated OP of a fund is a *persistent* performance measure is not answered in this study. If it *is* persistent, i.e., if it can be used as an ex-ante and not only as an ex-post performance measure, investors should clearly prefer funds with a high estimated OP.

Table 6. Results in the case that T is uniformly distributed between 0 and 10 years.

Fund	SPY			IWF			IEF			LIBOR			Cash		
	OP	Std	p	OP	Std	p	OP	Std	p	OP	Std	p	OP	Std	p
FBGRX	0.6716	0.1839	0.1754	0.5834	0.2042	0.3414	0.6798	0.1813	0.1607	0.8124	0.1208	0.0049	0.8359	0.1064	0.0008
TRBCX	0.7341	0.1607	0.0726	0.6667	0.1854	0.1843	0.6932	0.1767	0.1371	0.8197	0.1164	0.0030	0.8418	0.1027	0.0004
FKGRX	0.6485	0.1906	0.2179	0.5235	0.2099	0.4555	0.6842	0.1798	0.1528	0.8291	0.1107	0.0015	0.8531	0.0952	0.0001
OLGAX	0.6106	0.1994	0.2896	0.5291	0.2096	0.4449	0.6733	0.1834	0.1723	0.8078	0.1235	0.0063	0.8321	0.1088	0.0011
VMRGX	0.6372	0.1935	0.2392	0.5201	0.2100	0.4619	0.6703	0.1843	0.1777	0.8067	0.1241	0.0067	0.8312	0.1094	0.0012
MSEGX	0.7007	0.1740	0.1244	0.6580	0.1879	0.2002	0.6982	0.1749	0.1286	0.8136	0.1201	0.0045	0.8345	0.1073	0.0009
MAFGX	0.5560	0.2076	0.3937	0.4466	0.2078	0.6014	0.6539	0.1891	0.2078	0.7906	0.1331	0.0145	0.8165	0.1184	0.0037
PGFAX	0.6459	0.1913	0.2228	0.5585	0.2073	0.3888	0.6752	0.1827	0.1688	0.8073	0.1237	0.0065	0.8312	0.1094	0.0012
GCGIX	0.5317	0.2095	0.4399	0.3645	0.1939	0.7577	0.6516	0.1897	0.2122	0.7952	0.1306	0.0119	0.8219	0.1151	0.0026
PINDX	0.4376	0.2069	0.6186	0.3499	0.1902	0.7850	0.6144	0.1987	0.2823	0.7480	0.1545	0.0542	0.7763	0.1407	0.0248
⌀	0.6174	0.1917	0.2794	0.5200	0.2006	0.4621	0.6694	0.1841	0.1800	0.8030	0.1258	0.0114	0.8274	0.1113	0.0037

3.2.3. Exponentially Distributed Holding Period

In this section, we discuss the results that are obtained by assuming that the holding period is exponentially distributed. This distributional assumption might be considered more realistic than a fixed or a uniformly distributed holding period. It assigns a high probability to early liquidations and a low probability to late ones. The exponential distribution has no finite right endpoint, which means that T is unbounded above. Hence, this distribution allows for large holding periods. However, the survival probability $\mathrm{P}(T > t)$ decreases exponentially with t.

The ML-estimator for the OP is

$$\widehat{\Pi}_n = \lambda \int_0^\infty \Phi\left(\sqrt{t}\,\widehat{\mathrm{ICV}}_n\right) e^{-\lambda t} dt\,,$$

where $\lambda > 0$ is the parameter of the exponential distribution. The standard error of the ML-estimator can be approximated by

$$\mathbf{Std}\left(\widehat{\Pi}_n\right) \approx \frac{\lambda}{\sqrt{m}} \int_0^\infty \sqrt{t}\, e^{-\lambda t} \phi\left(\sqrt{t}\,\widehat{\mathrm{ICV}}_n\right) dt.$$

We set the parameter λ to 0.2, which means that the mean holding period equals 5 years. The results are given by Table 7. As we can see, the OPs are, once again, slightly lower than those in Table 6 and thus also lower than those in Table 5. The reason is that the exponential distribution assigns earlier liquidations a substantially higher probability than later ones (see Figure 2). The overall conclusion does not differ compared to our previous findings, but it is worth noting that the standard errors and thus also the p-values are somewhat lower than in Tables 5 and 6. Now, we have a p-value of 0.0675 for TRBCX against the S&P 500 ETF, which comes very close to the significance level of 5%. In any case, the mutual funds still outperform the bond market and the riskless investments, i.e., the money market and cash.

Table 7. Results in the case that T is exponentially distributed with $\lambda = 0.2$.

Fund	SPY			IWF			IEF			LIBOR			Cash		
	OP	Std	p	OP	Std	p	OP	Std	p	OP	Std	p	OP	Std	p
FBGRX	0.6598	0.1683	0.1712	0.5782	0.1905	0.3407	0.6672	0.1655	0.1562	0.7868	0.1087	0.0042	0.8081	0.0966	0.0007
TRBCX	0.7165	0.1449	0.0675	0.6553	0.1699	0.1803	0.6795	0.1608	0.1322	0.7934	0.1050	0.0026	0.8134	0.0936	0.0004
FKGRX	0.6386	0.1754	0.2147	0.5221	0.1972	0.4555	0.6713	0.1640	0.1481	0.8019	0.1002	0.0013	0.8237	0.0875	0.0001
OLGAX	0.6035	0.1852	0.2881	0.5273	0.1969	0.4448	0.6613	0.1677	0.1681	0.7827	0.1110	0.0054	0.8046	0.0986	0.0010
VMRGX	0.6281	0.1786	0.2365	0.5189	0.1973	0.4619	0.6586	0.1687	0.1735	0.7817	0.1115	0.0058	0.8038	0.0991	0.0011
MSEGX	0.6863	0.1580	0.1193	0.6473	0.1726	0.1966	0.6840	0.1590	0.1236	0.7879	0.1081	0.0039	0.8067	0.0974	0.0008
MAFGX	0.5526	0.1945	0.3934	0.4498	0.1948	0.6016	0.6436	0.1738	0.2044	0.7673	0.1194	0.0126	0.7905	0.1066	0.0032
PGFAX	0.6362	0.1762	0.2197	0.5550	0.1942	0.3886	0.6631	0.1671	0.1645	0.7823	0.1112	0.0056	0.8038	0.0991	0.0011
GCGIX	0.5298	0.1967	0.4398	0.3734	0.1790	0.7603	0.6414	0.1745	0.2089	0.7714	0.1172	0.0103	0.7954	0.1039	0.0022
PINDX	0.4414	0.1937	0.6189	0.3600	0.1750	0.7882	0.6071	0.1843	0.2806	0.7290	0.1389	0.0496	0.7544	0.1262	0.0219
⌀	0.6093	0.1771	0.2769	0.5187	0.1867	0.4618	0.6577	0.1685	0.1760	0.7784	0.1131	0.0101	0.8004	0.1009	0.0033

3.2.4. Weibull Distributed Holding Period

Finally, we report the results that are obtained by assuming that the holding period is Weibull distributed. The Weibull distribution generalizes the exponential distribution and allows us to consider unimodal holding-time distributions with mode greater than 0 (see Figure 2). The corresponding ML-estimator for the OP is

$$\widehat{\Pi}_n = \frac{\kappa}{\gamma} \int_0^{\infty} \Phi\left(\sqrt{t}\,\widehat{\mathrm{ICV}}_n\right) \left(\frac{t}{\gamma}\right)^{\kappa-1} e^{-(t/\gamma)^{\kappa}} dt$$

and its standard error can be approximated by

$$\mathbf{Std}(\widehat{\Pi}_n) \approx \frac{\kappa\gamma^{-\kappa}}{\sqrt{m}} \int_0^{\infty} t^{\kappa-\frac{1}{2}} e^{-(t/\gamma)^{\kappa}} \phi\left(\sqrt{t}\,\widehat{\mathrm{ICV}}_n\right) dt.$$

In our empirical study, the parameters of the Weibull distribution are $\kappa = 2$ and $\gamma = 5.6419$. Once again, this leads us to a mean holding period of 5 years. The results are contained in Table 8. Now, we can observe that the OPs are close to those that are obtained with respect to the index ETFs by assuming that $T = 5$ is fixed (see Table 5). However, the OPs with respect to the US treasury-bond ETF, the money-market account, and to cash are slightly lower than in Table 5 but still higher than in Tables 6 and 7. Nonetheless, we can see that the given results are not very much driven by our specific assumption about the distribution of the holding period. It turns out that the OP is essentially determined by the ICV, not by the holding-time distribution, provided that the considered holding-time distributions have the same mean.

Table 8. Results in the case that T is Weibull distributed with $\kappa = 2$ and $\gamma = 5.6419$.

Fund	SPY			IWF			IEF			LIBOR			Cash		
	OP	**Std**	p	**OP**	**Std**	p	**OP**	**Std**	p	**OP**	**Std**	p	**OP**	**Std**	p
FBGRX	0.6756	0.1890	0.1764	0.5852	0.2088	0.3415	0.6840	0.1864	0.1619	0.8215	0.1266	0.0056	0.8462	0.1121	0.0010
TRBCX	0.7400	0.1662	0.0744	0.6706	0.1905	0.1853	0.6978	0.1820	0.1385	0.8292	0.1222	0.0035	0.8524	0.1083	0.0006
FKGRX	0.6519	0.1955	0.2186	0.5240	0.2144	0.4555	0.6886	0.1850	0.1540	0.8391	0.1165	0.0018	0.8643	0.1008	0.0001
OLGAX	0.6130	0.2042	0.2899	0.5297	0.2141	0.4449	0.6773	0.1885	0.1734	0.8167	0.1293	0.0072	0.8422	0.1146	0.0014
VMRGX	0.6403	0.1984	0.2398	0.5205	0.2145	0.4619	0.6743	0.1894	0.1787	0.8155	0.1300	0.0076	0.8413	0.1151	0.0015
MSEGX	0.7055	0.1793	0.1259	0.6617	0.1930	0.2011	0.7029	0.1802	0.1301	0.8227	0.1259	0.0052	0.8447	0.1131	0.0012
MAFGX	0.5572	0.2121	0.3937	0.4454	0.2124	0.6014	0.6574	0.1941	0.2086	0.7988	0.1389	0.0158	0.8258	0.1242	0.0043
PGFAX	0.6492	0.1962	0.2235	0.5598	0.2119	0.3889	0.6793	0.1879	0.1699	0.8162	0.1296	0.0073	0.8413	0.1151	0.0015
GCGIX	0.5324	0.2140	0.4399	0.3614	0.1988	0.7571	0.6551	0.1947	0.2129	0.8035	0.1364	0.0130	0.8315	0.1209	0.0031
PINDX	0.4362	0.2115	0.6185	0.3465	0.1951	0.7842	0.6170	0.2034	0.2827	0.7544	0.1601	0.0560	0.7838	0.1465	0.0264
⌀	0.6201	0.1966	0.2801	0.5205	0.2053	0.4622	0.6734	0.1892	0.1811	0.8118	0.1316	0.0123	0.8374	0.1171	0.0041

4. Conclusions

We propose the OP as a new performance measure, especially for a nonacademic audience. It differs in many aspects from return-to-risk measures: (i) The OP compares some strategy with a specified benchmark, not necessarily with the money-market account. (ii) It is easy to understand for people who are not educated in statistics or probability theory. (iii) The holding period of the investor is considered random. In our Brownian-motion framework, the OP is essentially determined by the ICV, i.e., the expected annual relative log-return on the strategy with respect to its benchmark divided by the standard deviation of that log-return. By contrast, the choice of the holding-time distribution seems to be secondary, provided that the mean holding period is the same for all distributions.

The ML-estimator for the OP is strongly consistent and, if the square root of the holding period has a finite expectation, it is also asymptotically normally distributed under the usual standardization. The moment condition is very mild and allows us to take almost any holding-time distribution into consideration. Our asymptotic results enable us to calculate confidence intervals or to conduct hypotheses tests. The basic null hypothesis is that the OP does not exceed 50%, which means that the strategy does not outperform its benchmark. Our empirical results reveal that most mutual funds, in fact, are able to beat their benchmarks, although the results are not statistically significant. Nonetheless, they are economically significant. This might be surprising because it is a commonplace in the finance literature that most fund managers cannot beat the market. However, the crucial point is that one should refer to differential returns when comparing some strategy with a given benchmark, not to excess returns.

The best performer is the T. Rowe Price Blue Chip Growth Fund, whereas the worst one is the Pioneer Disciplined Growth Fund. It is evident that market participants prefer to invest their money in those funds that have a high ICV with respect to the S&P 500 or the Russell 1000. More precisely, the ICV with respect to any index ETF is highly correlated with the log-amount of assets under management of the mutual fund. This means that relative performance and capital allocation are strongly connected to one another, which suggests that market participants take differential returns implicitly into account when making their investment decisions.

Author Contributions: G.F. developed the theoretical part, whereas both authors are responsible for the empirical part of this work.

Funding: This research received no external funding.

Acknowledgments: We would like to thank Philipp Adämmer and Alexander Jonen for our helpful discussions on the manuscript.

Conflicts of Interest: The authors declare no conflict of interest.

References

Alexander, Gordon J., and Alexandre M. Baptista. 2003. Portfolio performance evaluation using value at risk. *Journal of Portfolio Management* 29: 93–102. [CrossRef]

Baweja, Meena, Ratnesh R. Saxena, and Deepak Sehgal. 2015. Portfolio optimization using conditional Sharpe ratio. *International Letters of Chemistry, Physics and Astronomy* 53: 130–36. [CrossRef]

Burke, Gibbons. 1994. A sharper Sharpe ratio. *Futures* 23: 56.

Chow, Victor, and Christine W. Lai. 2015. Conditional Sharpe ratios. *Finance Research Letters* 12: 117–33. [CrossRef]

Dowd, Kevin. Adjusting for risk: An improved Sharpe ratio. *International Review of Economics and Finance* 9: 209–22. [CrossRef]

Eling, Martin, and Frank Schuhmacher. 2006. Hat die Wahl des Performancemaßes einen Einfluss auf die Beurteilung von Hedgefonds-Indizes? *Kredit und Kapital* 39: 419–54.

Elton, Edwin J., Martin J. Gruber, and Christopher R. Blake. 1996. The persistence of risk-adjusted mutual fund performance. *Journal of Business* 69: 133–57.

Fama, Eugene F., and Kenneth R. French. 2010. Luck versus skill in the cross-section of mutual fund returns. *Journal of Finance* 65: 1915–47.

Frahm, Gabriel. 2016. Pricing and valuation under the real-world measure. *International Journal of Theoretical and Applied Finance* 19. [CrossRef]

Frahm, Gabriel. 2018. An intersection-union test for the Sharpe ratio. *Risks* 6. [CrossRef]

Grinblatt, Mark, and Sheridan Titman. 1989. Mutual fund performance: An analysis of quarterly portfolio holdings. *Journal of Business* 62: 393–416. [CrossRef]

ICI. 2019. Worldwide Regulated Open-End Fund Assets and Flows, Fourth Quarter 2018. Available online: https://www.iciglobal.org/iciglobal/research/stats/ww/ci.ww_q4_18.global (accessed on 6 April 2019). [CrossRef]

Ippolito, Richard A. 1989. Efficiency with costly information: A study of mutual fund performance, 1965–1984. *Quarterly Journal of Economics* 104: 1–23. [CrossRef]

Jensen, Michael C. 1968. The performance of mutual funds in the period 1945–1964. *Journal of Finance* 23: 389–416. [CrossRef]

Keating, Con, and William F. Shadwick. 2002. A universal performance measure. *Journal of Performance Measurement* 6: 59–84.

Kestner, Lars N. 1996. Getting a handle on true performance. *Futures* 25: 44–46.

Lin, Mei-Chen, and Pin-Huang Chou. 2003. The pitfall of using Sharpe ratio. *Finance Letters* 1: 84–89. [CrossRef]

Lintner, John. 1965. The valuation of risky assets and the selection of risky investments in stock portfolios and capital budgets. *Review of Economics and Statistics* 47: 13–37.

Lo, Andrew W. 2002. The statistics of Sharpe ratios. *Financial Analysts Journal* 58: 36–52. [CrossRef]

Lusardi, Annamaria, and Olivia S. Mitchell. 2013. *The Economic Importance of Financial Literacy: Theory and Evidence*. Technical Report. Cambridge: National Bureau of Economic Research.

Merton, Robert C. 1973. Theory of rational option pricing. *Bell Journal of Economics and Management Science* 4: 141–83.

Mossin, Jan. 1966. Equilibrium in a capital asset market. *Econometrica* 34: 768–83. [CrossRef]

OECD. 2016. *OECD/INFE International Survey of Adult Financial Literacy Competencies*. Technical Report. Paris: OECD. [CrossRef]

Sharpe, William F. 1964 Capital asset prices: A theory of market equilibrium under conditions of risk. *Journal of Finance* 19: 425–42. [CrossRef]

Sharpe, William F. 1966. Mutual fund performance. *Journal of Business* 39: 119–38.

Sharpe, William F. 1994. The Sharpe ratio. *Journal of Portfolio Management* 21: 49–58. [CrossRef]

Shefrin, Hersh, and Meir Statman. 1985. The disposition to sell winners too early and ride losers too long: Theory and evidence. *Journal of Finance* 40: 777–90. [CrossRef]

Sortino, Frank, Robert Van Der Meer, and Auke Plantinga. 1999. The Dutch triangle. *Journal of Portfolio Management* 26: 50–58. [CrossRef]

Treynor, Jack L. 1961. Market value, time, and risk. Available online: https://dx.doi.org/10.2139/ssrn.2600356 (accessed on 25 June 2019).

Young, Terry W. 1991. Calmar ratio: A smoother tool. *Futures* 20: 1. [CrossRef]

Journal of
Risk and Financial Management

MDPI

Article

Credit Scoring in SME Asset-Backed Securities: An Italian Case Study

Andrea Bedin [1], Monica Billio [2,*], Michele Costola [1] and Loriana Pelizzon [1,2]

[1] Research Center SAFE, Goethe University, 60323 Frankfurt am Main, Germany; bedin@safe.uni-frankfurt.de (A.B.); costola@safe.uni-frankfurt.de (M.C.); pelizzon@safe.uni-frankfurt.de (L.P.)

[2] Department of Economics, Ca' Foscari University of Venice, 30121 Venice, Italy

* Correspondence: billio@unive.it

Received: 31 March 2019; Accepted: 13 May 2019; Published: 17 May 2019

Abstract: We investigate the default probability, recovery rates and loss distribution of a portfolio of securitised loans granted to Italian small and medium enterprises (SMEs). To this end, we use loan level data information provided by the European DataWarehouse platform and employ a logistic regression to estimate the company default probability. We include loan-level default probabilities and recovery rates to estimate the loss distribution of the underlying assets. We find that bank securitised loans are less risky, compared to the average bank lending to small and medium enterprises.

Keywords: credit scoring; probability of default; small and medium enterprises; asset-backed securities

1. Introduction

The global financial crisis (GFC) exacerbated the need for greater accountability in evaluating structured securities and thus has required authorities to implement policies aimed at increasing the level of transparency in the asset-backed securities (ABS) framework. In fact, ABS represents a monetary policy instrument which has been largely used by the European Central Bank (ECB) after the financial crisis. On this ground, in 2010 the ECB issued the ABS Loan-Level Initiative which defines the minimum information requirement at loan level for the acceptance of ABS instruments as collateral in the credit operations part of the Eurosystem. This new regulation is based on a specific template[1] and provides market participants with more timely and standardised information about the underlying loans and the corresponding performance.

After the GFC, a large amount of ABS issued by banks has been used as collateral in repurchase agreement operation (repo) via the ABS Loan Level Initiative in order to receive liquidity. A repo represents a contract where a cash holder agrees to purchase an asset and re-sell it at a predetermined price at a future date or in the occurrence of a particular contingency. One of the main advantages of repo is the guarantee offered to the lender since the credit risk is covered by the collateral in the case of the borrower's default.

To collect, validate and make available the loan-level data for ABS, in 2012 the Eurosystem designated the European DataWarehouse (ED) as the European securitisation repository for ABS data. As stated on the website, the main purpose of the ED is to provide transparency and confidence in the ABS market.

The ED was founded by 17 market participants (large corporations, organizations and banks) and started to operate in the market in January 2013. To be eligible for repurchase agreement transactions

[1] The list of the ECB templates is available at https://www.ecb.europa.eu/paym/coll/loanlevel/transmission/html/index.en.html.

with the ECB, securitisations have to meet solvency requirements: for instance, if the default rates in the pool of underlying assets reach a given level, the ABS is withdrawn as collateral. Clearly, this repository allows for new research related to ABS providing more detailed information at loan level.

In this paper, we consider the credit scoring in ABS of small and medium enterprises (SMEs) by using a database of loan-level data provided by ED. The aim of our analysis is to compare the riskiness of securitised loans with the average of bank lending in the SME market in terms of probability of default.

We consider the SME market since it plays an important role in the European economy. In fact, SMEs constitute 99% of the total number of companies, they are responsible for 67% of jobs and generate about 85% of new jobs in the Euro area (Hopkin et al. 2014). SMEs are largely reliant on bank-related lending (i.e., credit lines, bank loans and leasing) and, despite their positive growth, they still suffer from credit tightening since lending remains below the pre-crisis level in contrast to large corporates. Furthermore, SMEs do not have easy access to alternative channels such as the securitisation one (Dietsch et al. 2016). In this respect, ECB intended to provide credit to the Eurozone's economy in favour of the lending channel by using the excess of liquidity of the banking system[2] due to the Asset-Backed Purchase Program (ABSPP) to ease the borrowing conditions for households and firms. Consequently, securitisation represents an interesting credit channel for SMEs to be investigated in a risk portfolio framework. In particular, SMEs play even a more important role in Italy than the in the rest of the European Union. The share of SME value added is 67% compared to an EU average of 57% and the share of SME employment is 79%. Therefore, the ABS of Italian SMEs represents an interesting case to be investigated since Italy is the third largest economy in the Eurozone.

In this regard, we collect the exposures of Italian SMEs and define as defaulted those loans that are in arrears for more than 90 days. We define the 90-day threshold according to article 178 of Regulation (EU) No 575/2013 (European Parliament 2013), which specifies the definition of a default of an obligor that is used for the IRB Approach[3]. We exploit the informational content of the variables included in the ECB template and compute a score for each company to measure the probability of default of a firm. Then, we analyse a sample of 106,257 borrowers of SMEs and we estimate the probability of default (PD) at individual level through a logistic regression based on the information included in the dataset. The estimated PD allows us to have a comparison between the average PD in the securitised portfolio and the average PD in the bank lending for SMEs.

The variables included in the analysis, which will be presented in Section 3, are: (i) interest rate index; (ii) business type; (iii) Basel segment; (iv) seniority; (v) interest rate type; (vi) nace industry code; (vii) number of collateral securing the loan; (viii) weighted average life; (ix) maturity date; (x) payment ratio; (xi) loan to value and (xii) geographic region. Using the recovery rate provided by banks, we estimate the loss distribution of a global portfolio composed by 20,000 loans at different cut-off date using *CREDITRISK*$^{+TM}$ model proposed by Credit Suisse First Boston (CSFB 1997).

---

2 The ECB and the national central banks of the Eurosystem have been lending unlimited amounts of capital to the bank system as a response to the financial crisis. For more information see: https://www.ecb.europa.eu/explainers/tell-me-more/html/excess_liquidity.en.html.

3 A default shall be considered to have occurred with regard to a particular obligor when either or both of the following have taken place: (a) the institution considers that the obligor is unlikely to pay its credit obligations to the institution, the parent undertaking or any of its subsidiaries in full, without recourse by the institution to actions such as realising security; (b) the obligor is past due more than 90 days on any material credit obligation to the institution, the parent undertaking or any of its subsidiaries. Relevant authorities may replace the 90 days with 180 days for exposures secured by residential or SME commercial real estate in the retail exposure class (as well as exposures to public sector entities).

Our findings show that the default rates for securitised loans are lower than the average bank lending for the Italian SMEs' exposures, in accordance with the studies conducted on the Italian market by CRIF Ratings[4] (Caprara et al. 2015).

The remaining of the paper is structured as follows. Section 2 provides a literature review about SMEs and default estimates while Section 3 illustrates the empirical analysis and our findings. Finally Section 4 concludes the paper.

2. Literature Review

According to Van Gestel et al. (2003), the default of a firm occurs when it experiences sustained and prolonged losses or when it becomes insolvent having the weight of liabilities disproportionately large with respect to its total assets. Different methods have been developed in literature to predict company bankruptcy. From 1967 to 1980, multivariate discriminant analysis (MDA) has been one of the main techniques used in risk assessment. Altman (1968) was the first to implement this technique on a sample of sixty-six manufacturing corporations. The author used a set of financial and economic ratios for bankruptcy prediction and showed that 95 percent of all firms in the defaulted and non-defaulted groups were correctly assigned to their actual group of classification. Aftewards, he applied the same technique to bankruptcy prediction for saving and loan associations and commercial banks (Altman 1977; Sinkey 1975; Stuhr and Van Wicklen 1974). Beaver (1968) showed that illiquid asset measures predict failure better than liquid asset measures; Blum (1974) tested discriminant analysis on a sample of 115 failed and 115 non failed firms showing that the model can distinguish defaulting firms correctly with an accuracy of 94 percent. Using the same approach, Deakin (1972) and Edmister (1972) focused on default prediction with financial ratios. The main limitations that affect MDA are linearity and indipendence among the variables (Karels and Prakash 1987). Barnes (1982) explored the importance of non-normality in the statistical distribution of financial ratios and shows that where financial ratios are inputs to certain statistical models (Regression Analysis and Multiple Discriminant Analysis) normality is irrelevant. Hamer (1983) compared a linear discriminant model, a quadratic discriminant model and a logit model demonstrating that the performance of the linear discriminant analysis and the logit model are equivalent. Other approaches focus on logistic regression. Martin (1977) described the first application of a logit analysis to bank early warning problems and Chesser (1974) applied a logit model to predict non-compliance by commercial loan customers. These statistical techniques share the same idea of dividing defaulted and non-defaulted firms as a dependent variable attempting to explain the classification as a function of several independent variables. eference Ohlson (1980) used a logit approach to test financial ratios as predictors of corporate failures and identified four basic factors as significant in affecting the probability of default: (i) size of the company; (ii) measures of the financial structure; (iii) measures of performance; (iv) measures of current liquidity. Odom and Sharda (1990) compared the discriminant analysis technique with the neural network approach and discovered that the neural network was able to better predict bankruptcy, taking into account the ratios used by Altman (1968). Tam and Kiang (1992) presented a new approach to bank bankruptcy prediction using neural networks, stating that it can be a supplement to a rule-based expert system in real-time applications. Wilson and Sharda (1994) showed that the neural network outperformed the discriminant analysis in predicting accuracy both bankrupt and non-bankrupt firms while Zhang et al. (1999) compared artificial neural networks (ANNs) with logistic regression showing in a sample of 220 firms that ANNs perform better than logistic regression models in default prediction. Kim and Sohn (2010) and Min and Lee (2005) used support vector machines (SVM) to predict SMEs default and show that this model provides better prediction results

4 CRIF Ratings is an Italian credit rating agency authorized to assign ratings to non-financial companies based in the European Union. The agency is subject to supervision by the ESMA (European Securities and Markets Authority) and has been recognized as an ECAI (External Credit Assessment Institution).

compared to neural networks and logistic regression. Van Gestel et al. (2003) analyzed linear and non-linear classifiers and demonstrated that better classification performance were obtained using Least Square Support Vector Machine (LS-SVM). LS-SVM are a modified version of SVMs resulting into a set of linear equations instead of a QP problem. Cortes and Vapnik (1995) constructed a new type of learning machine, the so-called support-vector network, that maps the input vectors in an high dimensional feature space Z through some non-linear mapping chosen a priori and in this space a linear decision surface is constructed with special properties. Bryant (1997) examined the usefulness of an artificial intelligence method, case based reasoning (CBR), to predict corporate bankruptcy in order to show that the CBR is not more accurate than the Ohlson (1980) logit model, which attains a much higher accuracy rate and appears to be more stable over time. Also Buta (1994), Jo et al. (1997) and Park and Han (2002) applied it successfully to default prediction thanks to their ability of identifying a non-linear and non-parametric relationship. In this paper, we make use of the logistic regression since it provides a clear economic interpretation of the indicators that have an influence on the default probability of a firm.

3. Empirical Analysis

In this section, we analyze at loan level a SME ABS portfolio issued by an Italian bank during 2011 and 2012. We carry out the analysis by following the loans included in the sample at different pool cut-off dates, from 2014 to 2016, close to or coinciding with the semester. However, it is not possible to track all loans in the various periods due to the revolving nature of the operations which allows the SPV to purchase other loans during the life of the operation.

We examine those variables that may lead to the definition of a system for measuring the risk of a single counterpart that are included in the ECB template. In particular we select: (i) interest rate index (field AS84 of the ECB SMEs template); (ii) business type (AS18); (iii) Basel segment (AS22); (iv) seniority (AS26); (v) interest rate type (AS83); (vi) nace industry code (AS42); (vii) number of collateral securing the loan (CS28); (viii) weighted average life (AS61); (ix) maturity date (AS51); (x) payment ratio; (xi) loan to value (LTV) and (xii) geographic region (AS17). We compute payment ratio as the ratio between the installment and the outstanding amount and loan to value as the ratio between the outstanding loan amount and the collateral value. Interest rate index includes: (1) 1 month LIBOR; (2) 1 month EURIBOR; (3) 3 month LIBOR; (4) 3 month EURIBOR; (5) 6 month LIBOR; (6) 6 month EURIBOR; (7) 12 month LIBOR; (8) 12 month EURIBOR; (9) BoE Base Rate; (10) ECB Base Rate; (11) Standard Variable Rate; (12) Other. Business type assumes: (1) Public Company; (2) Limited Company; (3) Partnership (4); Individual; (5) Other. Basel segment is restricted to (1) Corporate and (2) SME treated as Corporate. Seniority can be: (1) Senior Secured; (2) Senior Unsecured; (3) Junior (4); Junior Unsecured; (5) Other. Interest rate type is divided in: (1) Floating rate loan (for life); (2) Floating rate loan linked to Libor, Euribor, BoE reverting to the Bank's SVR, ECB reverting to Bank's SVR; (3) Fixed rate loan (for life); (4) Fixed with future periodic resets; (5) Fixed rate loan with compulsory future witch to floating; (6) Capped; (7) Discount; (8) Switch Optionality; (9) Borrower Swapped; (10) Other. Nace Industry Code corresponds to the European statistical classification of economic activities. Number of collateral securing the loan represents the total number of collateral pieces securing the loan. Weighted Average Life is the Weighted Average Life (taking into account the amortization type and maturity date) at cut-off date. Maturity date represents the year and month of loan maturity. Finally the geographic region describes where the obligor is located based on the Nomenclature of Territorial Units for Statistics (NUTS). Given the NUTS code we group the different locations into North, Center and South of Italy[5].

[5] The complete list of fields definitions and criteria can be found at https://www.ecb.europa.eu/paym/coll/loanlevel/shared/files/RMBS_Taxonomy.zip?bc2bf6081ec990e724c34c634cf36f20.

The final panel dataset used for the counterparties' analysis contains 106,257 observations. Table 1 shows the number of non-defaulted and defaulted loans for each pool cut-off date.

Table 1. The table shows the amount of non-defaulted and defaulted exposures for each pool cut-off date. We observe that the average default rate per each reference date remains constant and is equal to 2.84% over the entire sample. We account only for the loans that are active in the pool cut-off date and include the loans that defaulted between two pool cut-off dates. In the case of the first report date, we consider the defaults that occurred from 2011, the date of securitization of the pool, until the first half of 2014, due to missing information on the performance of the securitized pool prior to this date. We analyze in total 106,257 loans granted to SMEs.

Pool Cut-Off Date	Non-Defaulted	Defaulted	% Default	Tot.
2014H1	31,930	904	2.75	32,834
2014H2	26,851	813	2.94	27,664
2015H1	21,724	679	3.03	22,403
2015H2	12,651	372	2.86	13,023
2016H1	10,076	257	2.49	10,333
Tot.	103,232	3025	2.84	106,257

In the process of computing a riskiness score for each borrower, we consider the default date to take into account only the loans that are either not defaulted or that are defaulted between two pool cut-off dates (prior to the pool cut-off date in the case of 2014H1). In the considered sample, the observed defaulted loans are equal to 2.84% of the total number of exposures (Table 1).

We analyze a total of 159,641 guarantees related to 117,326 loans. For the score and the associated default probability, we group the individual loan information together to associate it with a total of 106,257 borrowers over five pool cut-off dates (Table 2). In order to move from the level of individual loans to the level of individual companies, we calculate the average for all loans coming from the same counterparty, otherwise we retain the most common value for the borrower.

Table 2. The table shows the amount of collaterals, loans and borrowers included in the sample for each pool cut-off date. The dataset links together borrower, loan and collateral. In total 159,641 collaterals are associated with 117,326 loans belonging to 106,257 companies.

Pool Cut-Off Date	Collateral Database	Loan Database	Borrower Database
2014H1	53,418	36,812	32,834
2014H2	45,694	30,774	27,664
2015H1	34,583	24,640	22,403
2015H2	14,472	14,000	13,023
2016H1	11,474	11,100	10,333
Tot.	159,641	117,326	106,257

We analyze the variables included in the ECB template individually through the univariate selection analysis which allows to measure the impact of each variable on loan's riskiness. We group each variable's observations according to a binning process in order to: (i) reduce the impact of outliers in the regression; (ii) better understand the impact of the variable on the credit risk through the study of the Weight of Evidence (WOE); (iii) study the variable according to a strategic purpose.

Operators suggest taking the WOE as a reference to test the model predictivity (Siddiqi 2017), a measure of separation between *goods* (non-defaulted) and *bads* (defaulted), which calculates the difference between the portion of solvents and insolvents in each group of the same variable. Specifically, the Weight of Evidence value for a group consisting of n observations is computed as:

$$\textbf{Weight of Evidence} \quad W_i = \left[\ln \frac{DistrGood}{DistrBad}\right] * 100 \tag{1}$$

and could be written as:

$$W_i = \ln\left(\frac{N_i}{\sum N} \Big/ \frac{P_i}{\sum P}\right) \tag{2}$$

The value of WOE will be zero if the odds of *DistrGood*/*DistrBad* is equal to one. If the *DistrBad* in a group is greater than the *DistrGood*, the odds ratio will be less than one and the WOE will be a negative number; if the number of Goods is greater than the *DistrBad* in a group, the WOE value will be a positive number.

To create a predictive and robust model we use a Monotonous Adjacent Pooling Algorithm (MAPA), proposed by Thomas et al. (2002). This technique is a pooling routine utilized for reducing the impact of statistical noise. An interval with all observed values is split in smaller sub-intervals, bins or groups, each of them gets assigned the central value characterizing this interval (Mironchyk and Tchistiakov 2017). Pooling algorithms are useful for coarse classing when individual's characteristics are represented in the model. There are three types of pooling algorithm: (i) non-adjacent, for categorical variable; (ii) adjacent, for numeric, ordinal and discrete characteristics; and (iii) monotone adjacent, when a monotonic relationship is supposed with respect to the target variable. While non-adjacent algorithms do not require any assumptions about the ordering of classes, adjacent pooling algorithms require that only contiguous attributes can be grouped together, which applies to ordinal, discrete and continuous characteristic (Anderson 2007). In this context, MAPA is a supervised algorithm that allows us to divide each numerical variable into different classes according to a monotone WOE trend, either increasing or decreasing depending from the variable considered. For categorical variables we maintain the original classification, as presented in the ECB template. The starting point for the MAPA application is the calculation of the cumulative default rate (bad rate) for each score level:

$$Cumulative\ Bad\ Rate_{k,v} = \frac{\sum\limits_{i=V_{k-1}+1}^{v} B_i}{\sum\limits_{i=V_{k-1}+1}^{v} (B_i + G_i)} \tag{3}$$

where G and B are the good (non-defaulted) and bad (defaulted) counts, V is a vector containing the series of score breaks being determined; v is a score above the last score break; and i and k are indices for each score and score break respectively. We calculate cumulative bad rates for all scores above the last breakpoint, and we identify the score with the highest cumulative bad rate; this score is assigned to the vector as shown in Equation (4).

$$MAPA_{k,v} = max\{v | C_{k,v} = max\{C_{k,v}\}\}, \quad \forall v > V_{k-1} \tag{4}$$

with C representing the cumulative bad rate. This iterative process terminates when the maximum cumulative bad rate is the one associated with the highest possible score. To test the model predictivity together with the WOE we use a further measure: the Information Value (IV). The Information Value is widely used in credit scoring (Hand and Henley 1997; Zeng 2013) and indicates the predictive power of a variable in comparison to a response variable, such as borrower default. Its formulation is expressed by the formula:

$$IV = \sum_{i=1}^{n}(DistrGood_i - DistrBad_i) * \ln \frac{DistrGood_i}{DistrBad_i} \tag{5}$$

where *Distr* refers to the proportion of *Goods* or *Bads* in the respective group expressed as relative proportions of the total number of Goods and Bads and can be rewritten by inserting the WOE as follows:

$$\sum_{i=1}^{n}\left[\left(\frac{N_i}{\Sigma(N)}-\frac{P_i}{\Sigma(P)}\right)*WOE_i\right] \tag{6}$$

with N representing the non-defaulted loans (Negative to default status), P the defaulted (Positive to default), the WOE is calculated on the i-th characteristic and n corresponds to the total number of characteristics analyzed, as shown in Equations (1) and (2). As stated in Siddiqi (2017), there is no precise rule of discrimination of the variables through the information value. It is common practice among operators to follow an approximate rule that consists in considering these factors: (i) an IV smaller than 0.02 shows an unpredictable variable; (ii) from 0.02 to 0.1 power is weak; (iii) from 0.1 to 0.3 average; (iv) above 0.3 strong. Table 3 shows the indication of the information value for each variable within the dataset in the first pool cut-off date.

Table 3. The table shows the information value computed for each variable included in the sample. We report the statistic associated to the variable for each pool cut-off date. Since not all the variables inserted in the regression can be considered strong predictors of borrower's default we decide to insert in the regression those variables that have a IV superior to 0.01, in the lack of other, better information.

Variable	2014H1	2014H2	2015H1	2015H2	2016H1
Interest Rate Index	0.04	0.08	0.01	0.00	0.00
Business Type	0.02	0.05	0.02	0.03	0.02
Basel Segment	0.00	0.01	0.00	0.00	0.01
Seniority	0.09	0.08	0.02	0.12	0.29
Interest Rate Type	0.00	0.00	0.00	0.00	0.00
Nace Code	0.05	0.01	0.01	0.01	0.07
Number of Collateral	0.00	0.00	0.03	0.00	0.00
Weighted Average Life	0.26	0.27	0.22	0.16	0.37
Maturity	0.00	0.08	0.00	0.08	0.00
Payment ratio	0.11	0.08	0.14	0.09	0.10
Loan To Value	0.10	0.08	0.07	0.06	0.11
Geographic Region	0.01	0.00	0.02	0.01	0.03

According to Siddiqi (2017), logistic regression is a common technique used to develop scorecards in most financial industry applications, where the predicted variable is binary. Logistic regression uses a set of predictor characteristics to predict the likelihood of a defined outcome, such as borrower's default in our study. The equation for the logit transformation is described as:

$$Logit(p_i) = \beta_0 + \sum_{j=1}^{k}\beta_j x_j + e \tag{7}$$

where p_i represent the posterior probability of the "event" given different input variables for the i-th borrower; x are input variables; β_0 corresponds to the intercept of the regression line; β_j are parameters and k is the total number of parameters.

The result $logit(p_i)$ in the equation represents a logarithmic transformation of the output, i.e., $log(p[event]/p[nonevent])$, necessary to linearize posterior probability and limit outcome of estimated probabilities in the model between 0 and 1. The parameters $\beta_1 \ldots \beta_k$ measure the rate of change in the model as the value of the independent variable varies unitary. Independent variables must be standardized to be made as independent as possible from the input unit or proceed by replacing the value of the characteristic with the WOE for each class created for the variable. The final formulation becomes:

$$Logit(p_i) = \beta_0 + \sum_{j=1}^{k} \beta_j WOE_j(i) + e \tag{8}$$

The regression is made on a cross sectional data for each pool cut-off date. We measure the impact of the variables on credit risk through the WOE. If we consider the LTV when the ratio between the outstanding loan amount and collateral value increases, the default rate increases as well while the WOE decreases. This indicates that an increment in the LTV is a sign of a deterioration in the creditworthiness of the borrower. The relation is reported in Table 4.

Table 4. The table shows per each LTV class (column 1) the amount of non-defaulted loans (column 2), defaulted loans (column 3); probability, computed as the ratio between non-defaulted and defaulted (column 4) and Weight of Evidence (column 5). As we can see the application of the MAPA algorithm allows to cut the variable into classes with a monotone WOE. The table confirms the relation between LTV and WOE. We show that as the LTV increases the WOE decreases as well as the probability (odds ratio) meaning that the borrower is riskier. For each computed class we associate a score, meaning that a borrower with a lower LTV, i.e., in the third class (0.333–0.608) is associated with a score higher (less risky) compared to a borrower in the fourth class. For sake of space we report the results only for the third pool cut-off date but the same considerations could also be carried out for the other report dates.

LoanToValue 2015H1	Non-Defaulted	Defaulted	Probability	WOE
0–0.285	3383	67	50.49	0.35
0.285–0.333	1523	31	49.12	0.33
0.333–0.608	3531	89	39.67	0.11
0.608–0.769	3357	95	35.33	0.002
0.769–1	2074	77	26.93	−0.26
1–inf	2904	117	24.82	−0.35
Tot.	16,772	476	35.23	

We report in Equation (9) the obtained regression for the first pool cut-off date, for sake of space we include only the first regression. The output of the other pool cut-off date regression is reported in Appendix A. It should be noted that not all the variables included in the sample are considered significant. The LTV due to a high number of missing values, even if predictive according to the criteria of the information value, has not been included in the regression:

$$\begin{aligned} default\ 2014\ H1 = {} & \beta_0 + \beta_1 WeightedAverageLife + \beta_2 Payment\_Ratio \\ & + \beta_3 Seniority + \beta_4 Code\_Nace \\ & + \beta_5 Geographic\_Region + \beta_6 InterestRateIndex + e \end{aligned} \tag{9}$$

Table 5 reports the coefficients of the considered variables along with the significance level, marked by *** at 1% confidence level and by ** at 5%.

Table 5. We illustrate in the table the coefficient and the significance of the variables included in the regression. We denote by *** the significance level of 1%, with ** the level of 5%. The table reports the number of observations, Chi^2-statistic vs. constant model and p-value.

Variable	**2014H1**	**2014H2**	**2015H1**	**2015H2**	**2016H1**
	Coefficient	Coefficient	Coefficient	Coefficient	Coefficient
(int.)	3.550 ***	3.481 ***	3.456 ***	3.523 ***	3.652 ***
InterestRateIndex	0.698 ***				
Seniority	1.489 ***	1.493 ***	0.598	1.325 ***	0.944 ***
Code_Nace	1.048 ***	0.952 ***	0.798 **	0.927 **	0.947 ***
WeightedAverageLife	1.007 ***	0.953 ***	1.168 ***	0.912 ***	0.798 ***
Payment_Ratio	2.456 ***	2.296 ***	1.482 ***	2.300 ***	2.253 ***
Geographic_Region	1.675 ***	1.405 ***	1.432 ***		0.903 ***
Observations	32,834	27,664	22,403	13,023	10,333
Chi^2-statistic vs. constant model	670	541	373	190	222
p-value	0.000	0.000	0.000	0.000	0.000

Figure 1a indicates the default probability associated with each score level for the first pool cut-off date. In the Appendix A we report the relationship for the other pool cut-off dates. We choose a score scale ranging from 500 (worst counterparties) to 800 points (best counterparties). We can see that as the score decreases, the associated default probability increases.

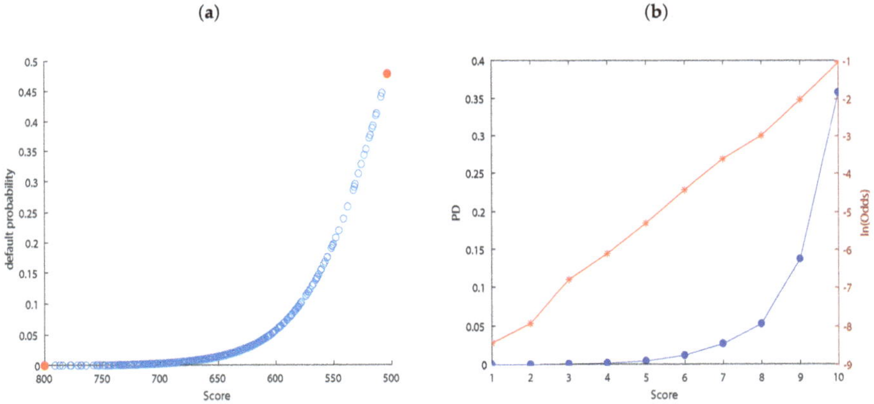

Figure 1. Panel (**a**) illustrates the relationship between score and PD. For each company we compute a score based on the logistic regression output that is an indication of individual PD. Panel (**b**) shows the master scale. This is an indicator of the counterparty's riskiness level. For its creation, we follow the approach presented by Siddiqi (2017). The default probability is linearized through the calculation of the natural logarithm, then the vector of the logarithms of the PD is divided into 10 equal-sized classes and the logarithms of the cut-offs of each class is converted to identify the cut-offs to be associated with each scoring class with an exponential function.

Validation statistics have the double purpose of measuring: (i) the power of the model, i.e., the ability to identify the dependence between the variables and the outputs produced and (ii) the divergence from the real results. We use Kolmogorov-Smirnov (KS) curve and Receiver Operating Characteristic (ROC) curve to measure model prediction capacity.

Kolmogorov-Smirnov (KS) The KS coefficient according to Mays and Lynas (2004) is the most widely used statistic within the United States for measuring the predictive power of rating systems.

The Kolmogorov-Smirnov curve plots the cumulative distribution of non-defaulted and defaulted against the score, showing the percentage of non-defaulted and defaulted below a given score threshold, identifying it as the point of greatest divergence. According to Mays and Lynas (2004), KS values should be in the range 20%–70%. The goodness of the model should be highly questioned when values are below the lower bound. Value above the upper bound should be also considered with caution because they are 'probably too good to be true'. The Kolmogorov-Smirnov statistic for a given cumulative distribution function $F(x)$ is:

$$D_n = sup_x |F_n(x) - F(x)| \tag{10}$$

where sup_x is the supremum of the set of distances. The results on the dataset are included in Figure 2 and show values within the threshold for the first pool cut-off date. In the first report date with a 623 points score the KS value is 23.8%. The statistics for the other pool cut-off dates are reported in Appendix A.

Lorenz curve and Gini coefficient In credit scoring, the Lorenz curve is used to analyze the model's ability to distinguish between "good" (non-defaulted) and "bad" (defaulted), showing the cumulative percentage of defaulted and non-defaulted on the axes of the graph (Müller and Rönz 2000). When a model has no predictive capacity, there is perfect equality. The Gini Coefficient is widely used in Europe (Řezáč and Řezáč 2011), is derived from the Lorenz curve and calculates the area between the curve and diagonal in the Lorenz curve.

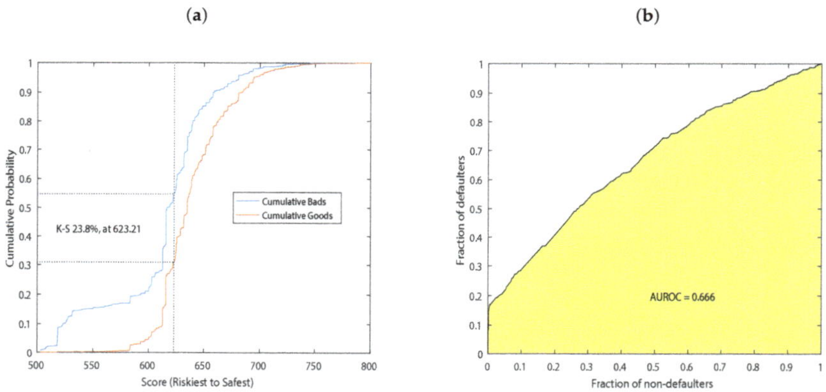

Figure 2. Panel (**a**) illustrates the Kolmogorov-Smirnov curve and the associated statistics for the first pool cut-off date. We show that the KS statistic associated to a score of 623.21 is 23.8%. Panel (**b**) reports the ROC curve and the AUROC value for the first report date. Table 6 reports AUROC, KS statistic and KS score for the entire sample.

Gini coefficient The Gini coefficient is computed as:

$$D = 1 - \sum_{i=1}^{n} ((cpY_i - cpY_{i-1})(cpX_i + cpX_{i-1})) \tag{11}$$

where cpY is the cumulative percentage of defaulters and cpX is the cumulative percentage of non-defaulters. The result is a coefficient that measures the separation between the curve and the diagonal. Gini's coefficient is a statistic used to understand how well the model can distinguish between "good" and "bad".

This measure has the following limitations: (i) can be increased by increasing the range of indeterminates, i.e., who is neither "good" nor "bad" and (ii) is sensitive to the definition of the categories of variables both in terms of numbers and types. Operators' experience, according to Anderson (2007), suggests that the level of the Gini coefficient should range between 30% and 50%, in order to have a satisfactory model.

Receiver Operating Characteristic (ROC) As reported by Satchel and Xia (2008), among the methodologies for assessing discriminatory power described in the literature the most popular one is the ROC curve and its summary index known as the area under the ROC (AUROC) curve. The ROC curve is created by plotting the true positive rate (TPR) against the false positive rate (FPR) at various threshold settings. The true-positive rate is also known as sensitivity and the false-positive rate is also known as the specificity. Specificity represents the ability to identify true negatives and can be calculated as 1 minus the specificity. The ROC therefore results from:

$$\textbf{ROC} \quad X = Pr[S_{FP} \leq S_{Cut\ off}] \quad \text{and} \quad Y = Pr[S_{TP} \leq S_{Cut\ off}] \tag{12}$$

The curve is concave only when the relationship p_i^+/p_i^- has a monotonous relationship with the event being studied. When the curve goes below the diagonal, the model is making a mistake in the prediction for both false positive and false negative but a reversal of the sign could correct it. This is very similar to the Gini coefficient, except that it represents the area under the ROC curve (AUROC), as opposed to measuring the part of the curve above it. The commonly used formula for the AUROC, as reported in (Anderson 2007, p. 207) is:

$$\textbf{AUROC} \quad c_{P,N} = Pr[S_{TP} < S_{TN}] + 0.5Pr[S_{TP} = S_{TN}] \tag{13}$$

and shows that the area below the curve is equal to the probability that the score of a true positive (defaulted, S_{TP}) is less than that of a true negative (non-defaulted, S_{TN}), plus 50% of the probability that the two scores are equal. A 50% value of AUROC implies that the model is making nothing more than a random guess. Table 6 shows the values of the statistics for the analyzed pool cut-off dates.

Table 6. The table reports Kolmogorov-Smirnov statistic, KS score and the area under the ROC curve for the analyzed pool cut-off dates. We can observe that the statistics differs over the sample, due to the different loans included in the pool that changed over the period.

Statistics	2014H1	2014H2	2015H1	2015H2	2016H1
Area under ROC curve	0.66	0.62	0.62	0.60	0.68
KS statistic	0.23	0.18	0.18	0.15	0.27
KS score	623.21	621.4	636.43	545.84	632.18

Once the predictive ability of the model is tested, it is possible to calculate the probability of default for classes of counterparties. In this respect, we create a master scale to associate a default probability to each score. As stated in Siddiqi (2017), a common approach is to have discrete scores scaled logarithmically. In our analysis, we set the target score to 500 with the odds doubling every 50 points which is commonly used in practice (Refaat 2011). The way to define the rating classes is through the creation of a cut-off defined with classes extension. Using the relationship between logarithm and exponential function it is possible to create the ranges for each rating class. The default probability vector by counterparty is linearized through the calculation of their natural logarithm, then this is divided into 10 equal classes and the logarithms of the cut-off of each class have been converted to identify the cut-off to be associated with each scoring class with an exponential function. With this procedure we calculate an average default probability for each range created (Figure 1b).

We validate the results obtained in the logistic regression with an out of sample analysis. In our analysis the validation has been performed by following directly Siddiqi (2017) which illustrated the standard procedure adopted in credit scoring. The industry norm is to use a random 70% (or 80%) of the development sample for building the model, while the remaining sample is kept for validation. When the scorecard is being developed on a small sample as in our case, it is preferred to use all the samples and validate the model on randomly selected samples of 50–80% length. Accordingly, we decided to use the second approach by selecting an out of sample of 50% of the total observations. We proceed as in the in-sample to analyze the statistics of separation and divergence for the *out of sample*, we report the statistics in Table 7. We observe that statistics do not differ substantially between the *out of sample* and the whole sample.

Table 7. The table reports Kolmogorov-Smirnov statistic, KS score and the area under the ROC curve for the out-of-sample. We can observe that the statistics differs over the sample, due to the different loans included in the pool that changed over the period.

Statistics	2014H1	2014H2	2015H1	2015H2	2016H1
Area under ROC curve	0.68	0.62	0.62	0.63	0.68
KS statistic	0.27	0.17	0.17	0.18	0.27
KS score	610.76	654.45	662.80	673.09	628.56

We carry out the analysis of the portfolio composition in all the pool cut-off dates analyzed. The revolving nature of the ABS may cause the composition of the portfolio under study to vary, even significantly. In general, the classes that include most of the counterparties are the central classes, as can be seen in Figure 3b. It is clear that the counterparties included in the ABS have an intermediate rating. For sake of completeness we report in Table 8 the actual default frequency in the sample per each rating class.

(**a**) (**b**)

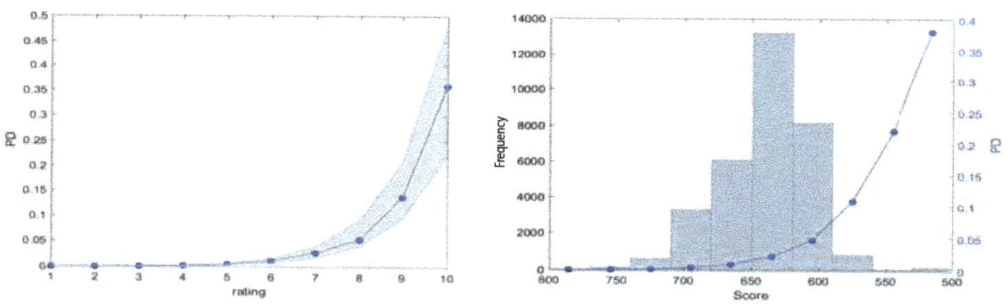

Figure 3. Panel (**a**) reports the final master scale obtained for the first pool cut-off date. To create the master scale we linearize the PD vector through the calculation of the natural logarithm, then this is divided into 10 equal classes and we convert the log of the cut-off of each class in order to identify the cut-off to be associated with each score with the exponential function. Panel (**b**) confirms the frequency of borrowers for each class. In the right y-axis we indicate the default probability associated for each class and in the left y-axis is indicated the frequency of the loans.

Table 8. The table indicates rating (column 1 and 6), amount of non-defaulted exposures (column 2), amount of defaulted loans (column 3), sample default frequency (column 4) and total loan amount in the first pool cut-off date. Column 7 reports the default probability derived from the logistic regression and column 8 reports the actual frequency of default and is equal to column 4. What we can observe is that the model is able to compute the cut-offs in a way that the default frequencies are monotone increasing from A-rated to L-rated. We report the statistics for the entire sample in Appendix A.

Rating 2014H1	Non-Defaulted	Defaulted	pd_actual (%)	Total		pd_estimate	pd_actual
A	4	0	0.00	4	A	0.02	0.00
B	30	0	0.00	30	B	0.04	0.00
C	298	3	1.00	301	C	0.11	1.00
D	707	9	1.26	716	D	0.23	1.26
E	3452	46	1.32	3498	E	0.52	1.32
F	7169	103	1.42	7272	F	1.23	1.42
G	15,264	415	2.65	15,679	G	2.78	2.65
H	4810	174	3.49	4984	H	5.34	3.49
I	134	19	12.42	153	I	13.77	12.42
L	62	135	68.53	197	L	35.87	68.53

To estimate the recovery rate of a default exposure it is necessary to have information regarding the market value of the collateral, the administrative costs incurred for the credit recovery process and the cumulative recoveries. Since those data are not available in the dataset, we analyze the recovery rates starting directly from the data provided by the banks in the template under "AS37" with the name of "*Bank internal Loss Given Default (LGD) estimate*" which estimates the LGD of the exposure in normal economic conditions. The RR of the loan was calculated by applying the equation: $RR(\%) = 100\% - LGD(\%)$.

The average recovery rate through all the collaterals related to one loan calculated by the bank is different depending on the level of protection offered, as evidenced by Figure 4.

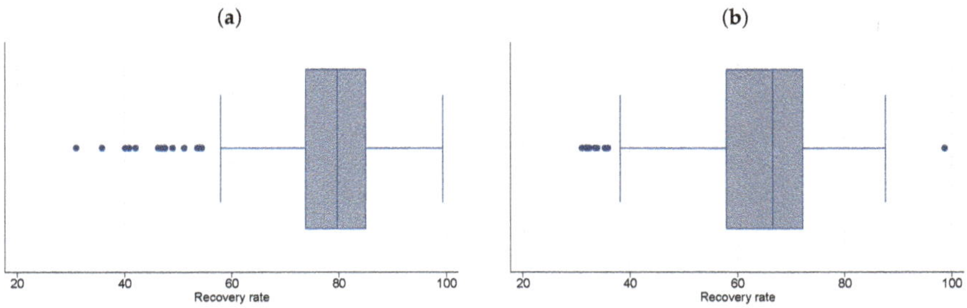

Figure 4. Considering the variable Seniority (field AS26 in the ECB template) we divide secured from unsecured loans. Panel (**a**) reports the box plot for the secured loans included in the total sample (taking into account all the pool cut-off dates), Panel (**b**) shows the box plot for unsecured loans. It is clear that banks expect to recover more from secured loans compared to unsecured ones.

As can be seen in Figure 4, the *originator* estimates a lower recovery rate for unsecured exposures than for secured loans. The average RR for secured exposures is 80.3%, while for unsecured exposures on average the bank expects to recover 66.8% of the amount granted. Figure 5 and Table 9 show the recovery rate calculated by the bank by rating level, it can be seen that the average recovery rate calculated by the bank tends to decrease as the counterparty's rating deteriorates, even if not monotonously.

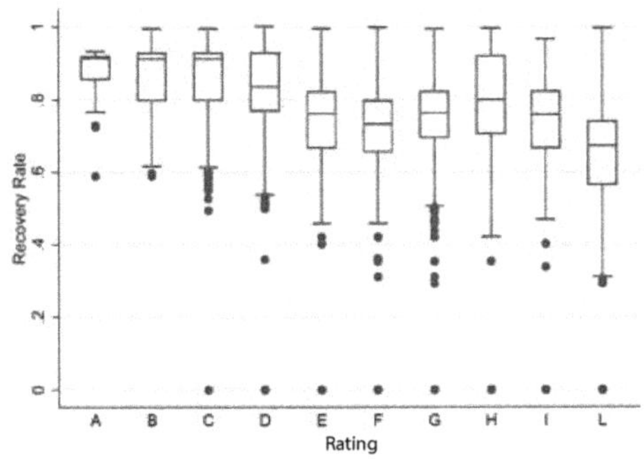

Figure 5. The Figure shows the box plot of the recovery rates computed by the banks divided into the rating classes. We note that the RR decreases from A to L, even though not monotonously.

Table 9. The table shows the average recovery rate derived from the field AS37 of the ECB template. We can see that the RR are decreasing from A-rated to L-rated companies, even though not monotonously.

Rating	Average Recovery Rate (%)
A	87.5
B	86.6
C	86.7
D	83.8
E	75.6
F	72.5
G	75.7
H	77.4
I	70.3
L	62.5

To investigate portfolio loss distribution we implement *CREDITRISK*$^{+TM}$ model on a representative sample of approximately 20,000 counterparties, of which 10,000 refer to loans terminated (repaid or defaulted) before the first pool cut-off date while the remaining 10,000 are active at the latest pool cut-off dates and are used to provide a forecast of the future loss profile of the portfolio.

CREDITRISK^{+TM} can be applied to different types of credit exposure including corporate and retail loans, derivatives and traded bonds. In our analysis we implement it on a portfolio of SMEs credit exposures. It is based on a portfolio approach to modelling credit risk that makes no assumption about the causes of default, this approach is similar to the one used in market risk, where no assumptions are made about causes of market price movements. *CREDITRISK*$^{+TM}$ considers default rates as continuous random variables and incorporates the volatility of default rates to capture default rates level uncertainty. The data used in the model are: (i) credit exposures; (ii) borrower default rates; (iii) borrower default rate volatilities and (iv) recovery rates. In order to reduce the computational difficulties, the exposures are adjusted by anticipated recovery rates in order to calculate the loss in case of default event. We consider recovery rates provided by ED and include them in the database. The exposures, net of recovery rates, are divided into bands with similar exposures. The model assumes that each exposure has a definite known default probability over a specific time horizon. Thus

$$p_A = Annual\ probability\ of\ default\ for\ obligor\ A \tag{14}$$

We introduce the probability generating function (PGF) defined in terms of an auxiliary variable z

$$F(z) = \sum_{n=0}^{\infty} p(n\ defaults) z^n. \tag{15}$$

An individual borrower either defaults or does not default, therefore the probability generating function for a single borrower is[6]:

$$F_A(z) = 1 - p_A + p_A z = 1 + p_A(z-1) \tag{16}$$

CREDITRISK^{+TM} assumes that default events are independent, hence, the probability generating function for the whole portfolio is the product of the individual PGF, as shown in Equation (17)

$$F(z) = \prod_A F_A(z) = \prod_A (1 + p_A(z-1)) \tag{17}$$

and could be written as:

$$logF(z) = \sum_A log(1 + p_A(z-1)). \tag{18}$$

The Credit Risk Plus model CSFB (1997) assumes that a borrower's default probabilities are uniformly small, therefore powers of those probabilities can be ignored and the logarithm can be replaced using the expression[7]

$$log(1 + p_A(z-1)) = p_A(z-1) \tag{19}$$

and, in the limit, Equation (18) becomes

$$F(z) = e^{\sum_A p_A(z-1)} = e^{\mu(z-1)} \tag{20}$$

where

$$\mu = \sum_A p_A \tag{21}$$

represents the expected number of default events in one year from the whole portfolio. $F(z)$ is expanded in its Taylor series in order to identify the distribution corresponding to this PGF:

$$F(z) = e^{\mu(z-1)} = e^{-\mu} e^{\mu z} = \sum_{n=0}^{\infty} \frac{e^{-\mu}\mu^n}{n!} z^n \tag{22}$$

thus considering small individual default probabilities from Equation (22) the probability of realising n default events in the portfolio in one year is given by:

$$\text{Probability (n defaults)} = \frac{e^{-\mu}\mu^n}{n!} \tag{23}$$

where we obtain the Poisson distribution for the distribution of the number of defaults. The distribution has only one parameter, the expected number of defaults μ. The distribution does not depend on the number of exposures in the portfolio or the individual probabilities of default provided that they are uniformly small. Real portfolio loss differs from the Poisson distribution, historical evidence shows in fact that the standard deviation of default event frequencies is much larger than $\sqrt{\mu}$, the standard

6 The Credit Risk Plus model assumes independence between default events. Therefore, the probability generating function for the whole portfolio corresponds to the product of the individual probability generating functions.

7 The approximation ignores terms of degree 2 and higher in the default probabilities. The expression derived from this approximation is exact in the limit as the PD tends to zero, and five good approximations in practice.

deviation of the Poisson distribution with mean μ. We can espress the expected loss in terms of the probability of default events

$$\varepsilon_j = v_j \times \mu_j; \; hence \; \mu_j = \frac{\varepsilon_j}{v_j} = \sum_{A:v_A=v_j} \frac{\varepsilon_A}{v_A} \tag{24}$$

where

$$\mu = \sum_{j=1}^{m} \mu_j = \sum_{j=1}^{m} \frac{\varepsilon_j}{v_j} \tag{25}$$

v_j is the common exposure in the exposure band, ε_j is the expected loss in the exposure band and μ_j is the expected number of defaults in the exposure band. We can derive the distribution of default losses as with $G(z)$ as the PGF for losses expressed in multiples of an unit of exposure L

$$G(z) = \sum_{n=0}^{\infty} p(\text{aggregate losses} = nxL)\; z^n. \tag{26}$$

The inputs that we include are therefore the average of the estimate of the probability of default calculated through the logistic regression and the relative volatility calculated through the pool cut-off dates. The exposure included in the model was calculated net of the recovery rates estimated by the bank. As stated previously, since the data to obtain the recovery rate are not available, we test the model with bank own recovery rates estimates. The mean and volatility values of the default probabilities are shown in Table 10. For the sake of completeness, we have also reported the mean and standard deviation of the default frequencies.

The model's estimate on the historical data of the loans terminated in the first available pool cut-off date provides an indication of the expected loss of 2,661,592 Euro against a total exposure of 48.92 million Euro with a standard deviation of 670,422 Euro (Table 11).

The real loss of the analysed portfolio calculated on all terminated loans is 2.10 million euro, lower than the expected loss computed by the model but within the $EL - \sigma$ threshold. The estimated expected loss by the model is 5.44% of the capital exposed to risk which represents the outstanding amount net of recovery rates.

Table 10. The table reports rating (column 1), mean and standard deviation of the estimated PD from the logistic regression (column 2 and 3), mean and st.dev. of the default frequencies in the sample (column 4 and 5). We use the estimated PD derived from the logistic regression and the Recovery Rates to calculate the loss distribution of the portfolio with the *CREDITRISK*$^{+\text{TM}}$ model.

	Estimate		Frequency	
Rating	**Mean (%)**	**st.dev (%)**	**Mean (%)**	**st.dev (%)**
A	0.27	0.26	0.19	0.38
B	0.43	0.41	0.94	0.77
C	0.74	0.64	1.54	0.45
D	1.15	0.92	1.85	0.79
E	2.06	1.51	1.83	0.55
F	3.15	1.94	2.25	0.55
G	5.43	2.52	3.02	0.98
H	8.70	3.15	2.51	1.42
I	17.45	4.41	26.57	21.84
L	33.93	4.02	68.96	8.61

Table 11. The table illustrated the capital exposed to risk and the thresholds for loss of the portfolio with unactive loans (either repaid or defaulted) at the pool cut-off date of 2014H1. The capital exposed to risk is calculated as the sum of all the portfolio exposures net of recovery rates computed by banks and reported by ED. The total net capital is therefore 48 million euro, with an expected loss (EL) of 2.66 million. The table reports the expected loss threshold (EL $\pm\sigma$), 95th and 99th percentile loss.

Threshold	Amount (€)	Percentage (%)
Capital exposed to risk	48,922,828	100.00
EL $-\sigma$	1,991,170	4.07
EL	2,661,592	5.44
EL + σ	3,332,014	6.81
95th percentile	3,894,574	7.96
99th percentile	4,630,839	9.46

The analysis shows that the portfolio before the first pool cut-off date lost a total of 4.29% of its value against an estimated loss of 5.44%. Even though the model with the input data used overestimates the expected loss, it is in the $EL - \sigma$ range. Due to the small number of counterparts and the lack of homogeneity of the data, an estimation error is possible. With a view to analyzing future performance, only loans active in the last pool cut-off date are kept in the portfolio and estimates of PD and volatility have been used as an approximation of the probability of future default. In a sample of 10,000 current counterparties in last pool cut-off date the capital exposed to the total risk of loss is 247 million with an expected loss of 5.7 million corresponding to 2.31% of the total (Table 12). This means that after the last available report the portfolio would have lost an additional 2.3% of the capital exposed to risk before the withdrawal.

The average loss in the sample is 2.14% while the estimate of the future loss in the pool cut-off dates is a further 2.31%. Figure 6a shows the loss distribution for terminated loans and Figure 6b illustrates the loss distribution for active exposures.

In accordance with the studies conducted by CRIF[8], Italian company specialized in credit bureau and business information, the default rates of Italian SMEs are around 6%, above those calculated in the analyzed sample. Assuming that recovery rates are similar to those of companies not included in the portfolio of securitized exposures, we can assume that the loss profiles for securitized portfolios are less severe than for exposures retained in the bank's balance sheet and not securitized.

8 Available at https://www.crifratings.com/media/1264/short_default-rates-report-for-publishing_07012016_ita.pdf.

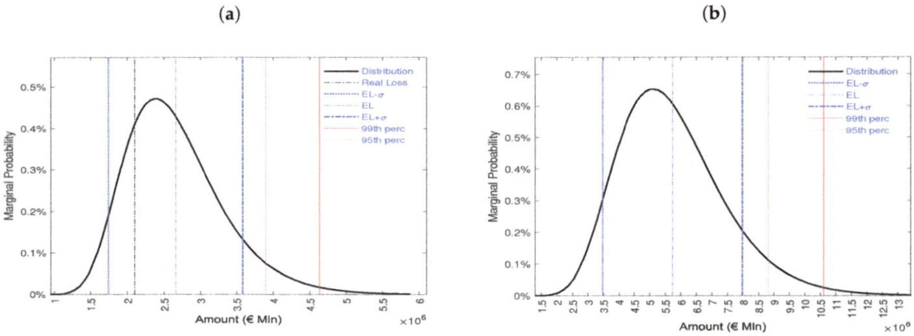

Figure 6. The figure illustrates the loss distribution for unactive loans at the pool cut-off date 2014H1 (Panel (**a**)) and for active loans at the report date 2016H1 (Panel (**b**)). We indicate in the figure loss distribution (black solid line), real loss portfolio loss (black dash-dot line), EL $-\ \sigma$ (blue dotted line), EL (blue dash-dot line), EL + σ (thick blue dash-dot line), 99th percentile (red solid line) and 95th percentile (red dotted line). It is possible to calculate the real portfolio loss only on inactive loans, therefore this threshold is present only in Panel (**a**).

Table 12. The table reports the capital exposed to risk and the thresholds for loss of the portfolio with active loans at the pool cut-off date of 2016H1. The capital exposed to risk is calculated as the sum of all the portfolio exposures net of recovery rates. The total net capital is 447 million Euro, with an expected loss (EL) of 5.72 million. The table reports the expected loss threshold (EL $\pm\ \sigma$), 95th and 99th percentile loss.

Threshold	Amount (€)	Percentage (%)
Capital exposed to risk	247,841,024	100.00
EL $-\ \sigma$	4,026,790	1.62
EL	5,729,076	2.31
EL + σ	7,431,362	2.99
95th percentile	8,828,005	3.56
99th percentile	10,608,768	4.28

4. Conclusions

Small and medium enterprises play a main role in the European Union in terms of jobs and added value in the real economy. These enterprises are largely reliant on bank-related lending channels and do not have easy access to alternative channels such as the securitisation mechanism.

In this paper, we investigated the default probability, recovery rates and loss distribution of a portfolio of securitised loans granted to Italian small and medium enterprises. SMEs have a share in Italy that is larger than the average of the European Union and thus represent an interesting market to be investigated. We make use of loan level data information provided by the European DataWarehouse and employ a logistic regression to estimate their default probability.

The aim of our analysis focused on the comparison of the riskiness of securitised loans with the average of bank lending in the SME market. We collected the SME's exposures from the European DataWarehouse and exploited the informational content of the variables to compute a credit score to estimate the probability of default at a firm level.

Our results indicate that the default rates for securitised loans are lower than the average bank lending for the Italian SMEs' exposures as shown in Caprara et al. (2015). The investigation should be extended to the European level in order to compare the different SME markets using the same timeframe as in the proposed Italian analysis. We leave these aspects for future research.

Author Contributions: The authors have contributed jointly to all of the sections of the paper.

Funding: This research received no external funding.

Acknowledgments: We thank three anonymous Reviewers and Editors for their insightful comments and suggestions.

Conflicts of Interest: The authors declare no conflict of interest.

Appendix A

Equation (A1) reports the regression output for all the analyzed pool cut-off dates. Figure A1 illustrates the relationship between Score and default probability, Figure A2 shows the masterscale and Figure A3 shows masterscale and borrower distribution. Table A1 reports portfolio composition per rating class, Table A2 shows default frequencies in the sample and Table A3 compares default probabilities estimated by regression model and default frequencies in the sample.

$$\begin{aligned}
default2014H1 &= \beta_0 + \beta_1 WeightedAverageLife + \beta_2 Payment_Ratio \\
&\quad + \beta_3 Seniority + \beta_4 Code_Nace \\
&\quad + \beta_5 Geographic_Region + \beta_6 CurrentInterestRateIndex + e \\
default2014H2 &= \beta_0 + \beta_1 Seniority + \beta_2 Payment_Ratio \\
&\quad + \beta_3 Code_Nace + \beta_4 WeightedAverageLife \\
&\quad + \beta_5 Geographic_Region + e \\
default2015H1 &= \beta_0 + \beta_1 Seniority + \beta_2 Payment_Ratio \\
&\quad + \beta_3 Code_Nace + \beta_4 WeightedAverageLife \\
&\quad + \beta_5 Geographic_Region + e \\
default2015H2 &= \beta_0 + \beta_1 Seniority + \beta_2 Payment_Ratio \\
&\quad + \beta_3 Code_Nace + \beta_4 WeightedAverageLife + e \\
default2016H1 &= \beta_0 + \beta_1 Seniority + \beta_2 Payment_Ratio \\
&\quad + \beta_4 Code_Nace + \beta_5 WeightedAverageLife \\
&\quad + \beta_6 Geographic_Region + e
\end{aligned} \tag{A1}$$

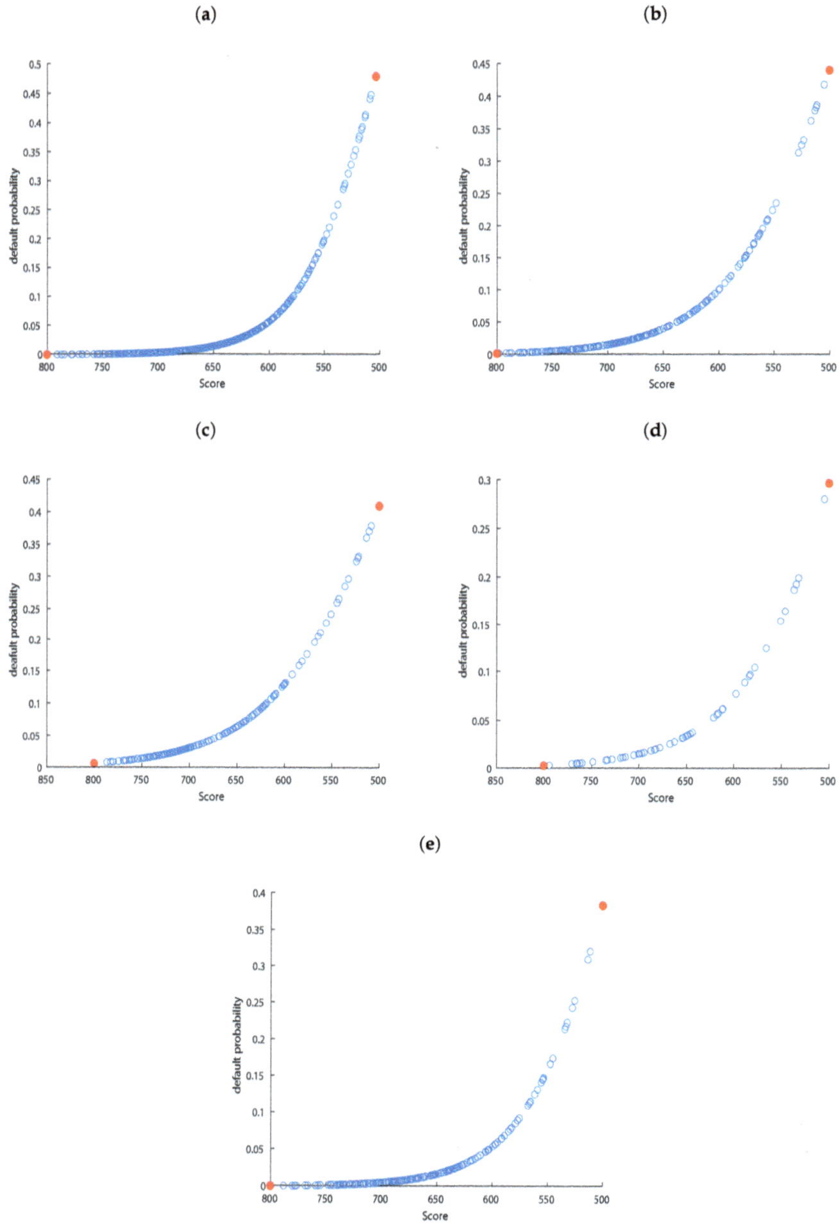

Figure A1. The figure illustrates the relationship between Score (x-axis) and default probability (y-axis) for 2014H1 (Panel (**a**)), 2014H2 (Panel (**b**)), 2015H1 (Panel (**c**)), 2015H2 (Panel (**d**)), 2016H1 (Panel (**e**)).

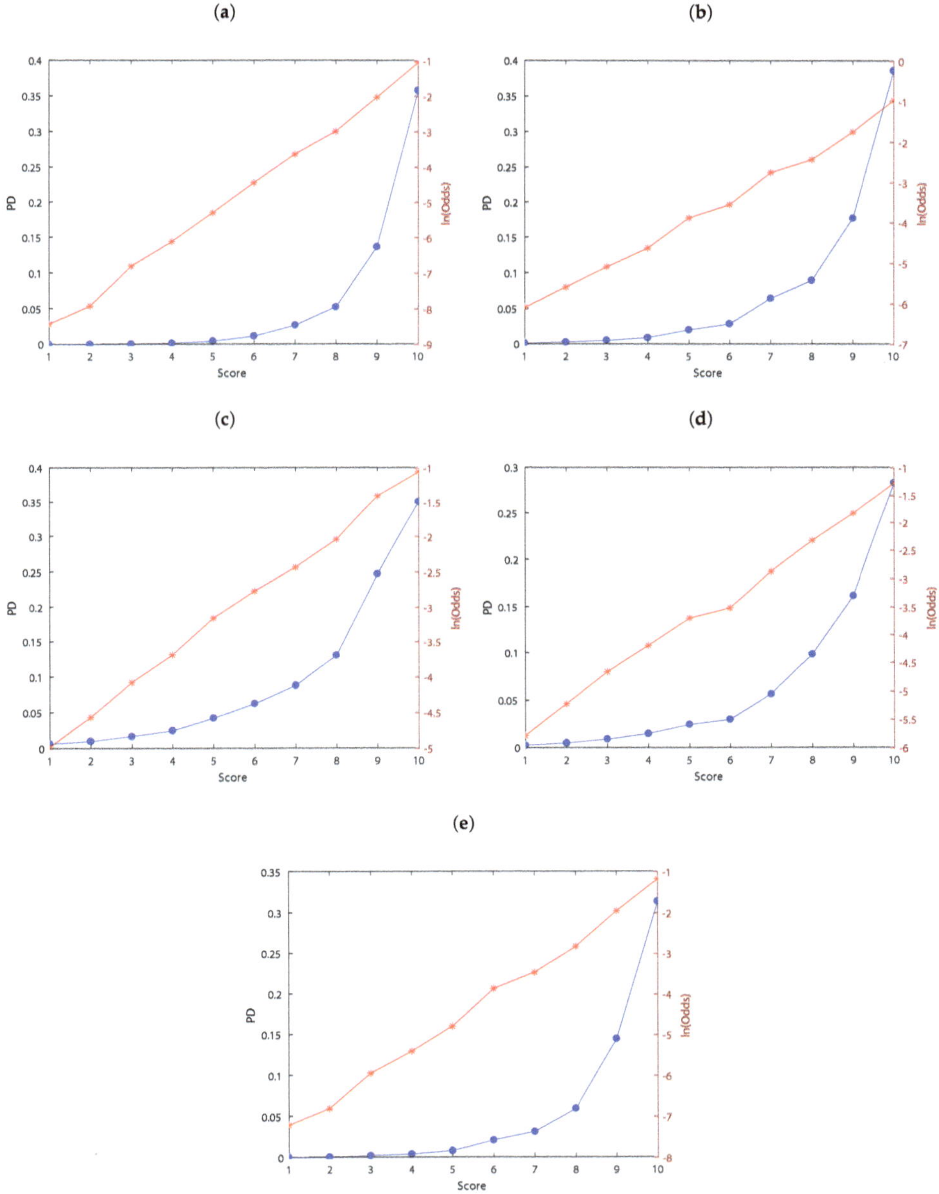

Figure A2. Master scale for the sample. We illustrate 2014H1 (Panel (**a**)), 2014H2 (Panel (**b**)), 2015H1 (Panel (**c**)), 2015H2 (Panel (**d**)), 2016H1 (Panel (**e**)).

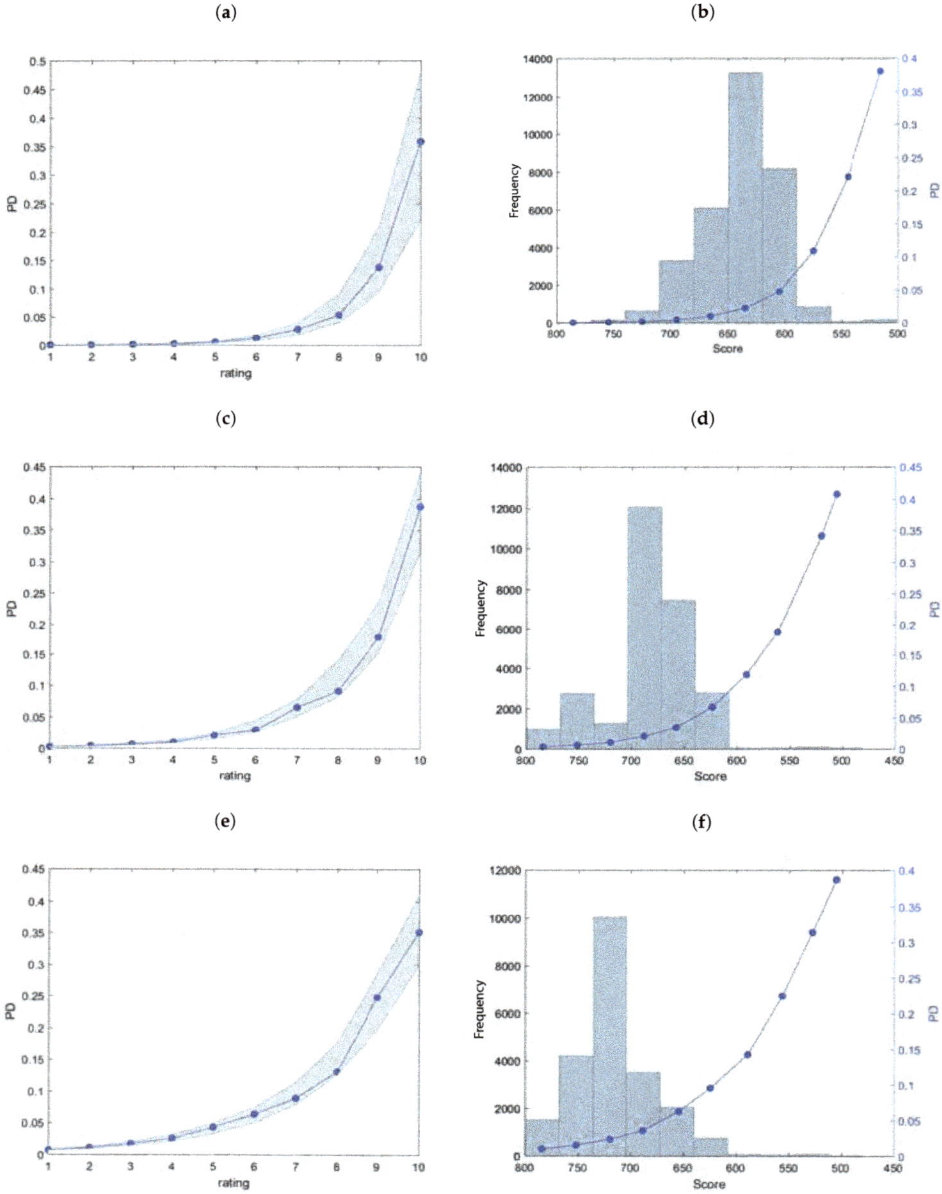

Figure A3. *Cont.*

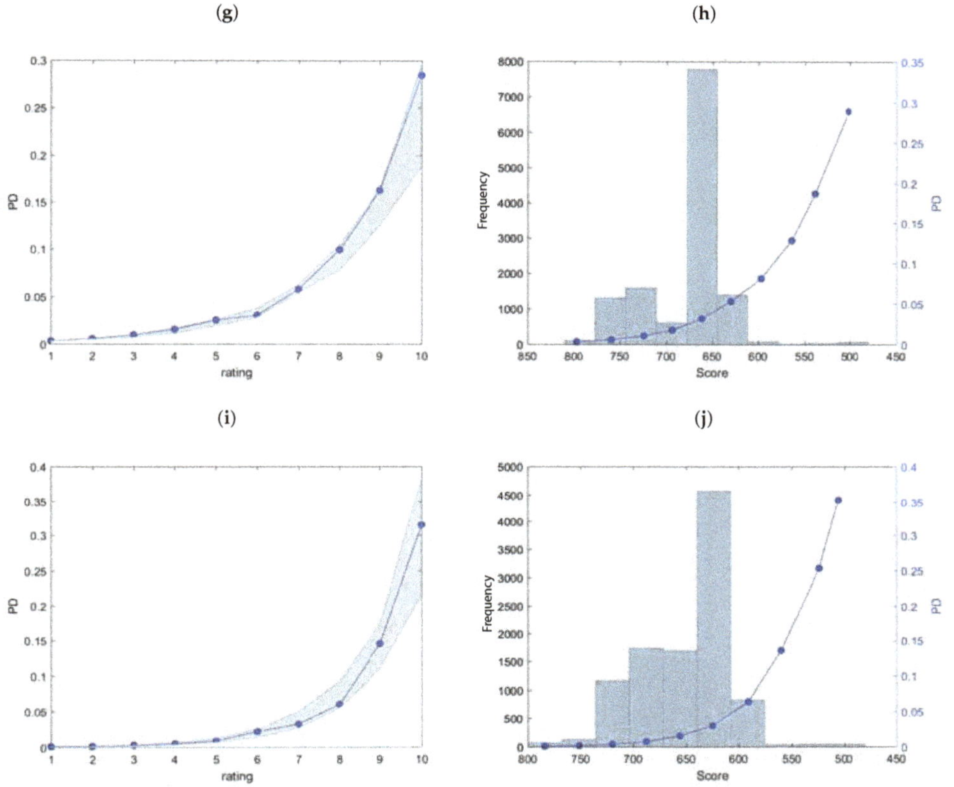

Figure A3. Master scale and borrower distribution for 2014H1(Panel (**a**,**b**)), 2014H2 (Panel (**c**,**d**)), 2015H1 (Panel (**e**,**f**)), 2015H2 (Panel (**g**,**h**)), 2016H1 (Panel (**i**,**j**)).

Table A1. The table shows the portfolio composition per rating across the pool cut-off dates. The distribution of counterparties is mainly concentrated in the intermediate rating classes.

2014H1				2014H2				2015H1				2015H2				2016H1			
Rating	Freq.	Perc.	Cum.	Rating	Freq.	Perc.	Cum.	Rating	Freq.	Perc.	Cum.	Rating	Freq.	Perc.	Cum.	Rating	Freq.	Perc.	Cum.
A	4	0.01	0.01	A	31	0.11	0.11	A	57	0.25	0.25	A	106	0.81	0.81	A	42	0.41	0.41
B	30	0.09	0.10	B	1250	4.52	4.63	B	1919	8.57	8.82	B	1306	10.03	10.84	B	95	0.92	1.33
C	301	0.92	1.02	C	2519	9.11	13.74	C	8002	35.72	44.54	C	1506	11.56	22.41	C	523	5.06	6.39
D	716	2.18	3.20	D	1288	4.66	18.39	D	7610	33.97	78.51	D	502	3.85	26.26	D	1562	15.12	21.50
E	3498	10.65	13.85	E	7355	26.59	44.98	E	1775	7.92	86.43	E	1413	10.85	37.11	E	1149	11.12	32.62
F	7272	22.15	36.00	F	12,165	43.97	88.95	F	2060	9.20	95.63	F	6877	52.81	89.92	F	2988	28.92	61.54
G	15,679	47.75	83.75	G	2660	9.62	98.57	G	751	3.35	98.98	G	1163	8.93	98.85	G	3148	30.47	92.01
H	4984	15.18	98.93	H	150	0.54	99.11	H	72	0.32	99.30	H	30	0.23	99.08	H	711	6.88	98.89
I	153	0.47	99.40	I	82	0.30	99.41	I	115	0.51	99.81	I	39	0.30	99.38	I	32	0.31	99.20
L	197	0.60	100.00	L	164	0.59	100.00	L	42	0.19	100.00	L	81	0.62	100.00	L	83	0.80	100.00

Table A2. The table shows rating (column 1), amount of non-defaulted loans (column 2), amount of defaulted (column 3), default frequency (column 4) and total number of loans included in the sample per rating class (column 5). We report the statistics for the different pool cut-off dates.

2014H1	Non-Defaulted	Defaulted	pd_actual (%)	Total	2014H2	Non-Defaulted	Defaulted	pd_actual (%)	Total
A	4	0	0.00	4		31	0	0.00	31
B	30	0	0.00	30		1229	21	1.68	1250
C	298	3	1.00	301		2482	37	1.47	2519
D	707	9	1.26	716		1267	21	1.63	1288
E	3452	46	1.32	3498		7186	169	2.30	7355
F	7169	103	1.42	7272		11,819	346	2.84	12,165
G	15,264	415	2.65	15,679		2587	73	2.74	2660
H	4810	174	3.49	4984		146	4	2.67	150
I	134	19	12.42	153		58	24	29.27	82
L	62	135	68.53	197		46	118	71.95	164
2015H1	**Non-Defaulted**	**Defaulted**	**pd_actual (%)**	**Total**	**2015H2**	**Non-Defaulted**	**Defaulted**	**pd_actual (%)**	**Total**
A	57	0	0.00	57		105	1	0.94	106
B	1890	29	1.51	1919		1286	20	1.53	1306
C	7825	177	2.21	8002		1478	28	1.86	1506
D	7366	244	3.21	7610		491	11	2.19	502
E	1742	33	1.86	1775		1377	36	2.55	1413
F	2015	45	2.18	2060		6681	196	2.85	6877
G	715	36	4.79	751		1142	21	1.81	1163
H	69	3	4.17	72		30	0	0.00	30
I	37	78	67.83	115		36	3	7.69	39
L	8	34	80.95	42		25	56	69.14	81
2016H1	**Non-Defaulted**	**Defaulted**	**pd_actual %**	**Total**					
A	42	0	0.00	42					
B	95	0	0.00	95					
C	517	6	1.15	523					
D	1547	15	0.96	1562					
E	1136	13	1.13	1149					
F	2929	59	1.97	2988					
G	3050	98	3.11	3148					
H	695	16	2.25	711					
I	27	5	15.63	32					
L	38	45	54.22	83					

Table A3. The table compares default probabilities estimated by the regression model (*pd_model*) and default frequencies (*pd_actual*) across the pool cut-off dates. The values of the two statistics are close, especially for the intermediate rating classes.

	2014H1		2014H2		2015H1		2015H2		2016H1	
	pd_model	pd_actual	pd_model	pd_actual	pd_model	pd_actual	pd_model	pd_actual	pd_model	pd_actual
A	0.02	0.00	0.23	0.00	0.69	0.00	0.31	0.94	0.08	0.00
B	0.04	0.00	0.38	1.68	1.05	1.51	0.55	1.53	0.11	0.00
C	0.11	1.00	0.63	1.47	1.72	2.21	0.95	1.86	0.27	1.15
D	0.23	1.26	1.00	1.63	2.54	3.21	1.53	2.19	0.46	0.96
E	0.52	1.32	2.11	2.30	4.31	1.86	2.51	2.55	0.86	1.13
F	1.23	1.42	2.95	2.84	6.37	2.18	3.02	2.85	2.15	1.97
G	2.78	2.65	6.55	2.74	8.90	4.79	5.74	1.81	3.19	3.11
H	5.34	3.49	9.09	2.67	13.12	4.17	9.92	0.00	6.02	2.25
I	13.77	12.42	17.85	29.27	24.81	67.83	16.26	7.69	14.54	15.63
L	35.87	68.53	38.72	71.95	35.17	80.95	28.42	69.14	31.45	54.22

References

Altman, Edward I. 1968. Financial ratios, discriminant analysis and the prediction of corporate bankruptcy. *The Journal of Finance* 23: 589–609. [CrossRef]

Altman, Edward I. 1977. Predicting performance in the savings and loan association industry. *Journal of Monetary Economics* 3: 443–66. [CrossRef]

Anderson, Raymond. 2007. *The Credit Scoring Toolkit: Theory and Practice for Retail Credit Risk Management and Decision Automation*. Oxford: Oxford University Press.

Barnes, Paul. 1982. Methodological implications of non-normally distributed financial ratios. *Journal of Business Finance & Accounting* 9: 51–62.

Beaver, William H. 1968. Alternative accounting measures as predictors of failure. *The Accounting Review* 43: 113–22.

Blum, Marc. 1974. Failing company discriminant analysis. *Journal of Accounting Research* 12: 1–25. [CrossRef]

Bryant, Stephanie M. 1997. A case-based reasoning approach to bankruptcy prediction modeling. *Intelligent Systems in Accounting, Finance & Management* 6: 195–214.

Buta, Paul. 1994. Mining for financial knowledge with cbr. *Ai Expert* 9: 34–41.

Caprara, Cristina, Davide Tommaso, and Roberta Mantovani. 2015. *Corporate Credit Risk Research*. Technical Report. Bologna: CRIF Rating.

Chesser, Delton L. 1974. Predicting loan noncompliance. *The Journal of Commercial Bank Lending* 56: 28–38.

Cortes, Corinna, and Vladimir Vapnik. 1995. Support-vector networks. *Machine Learning* 20: 273–97. [CrossRef]

CSFB. 1997. *Credit Risk+*. Technical Document. New York: Credit Suisse First Boston.

Deakin, Edward B. 1972. A discriminant analysis of predictors of business failure. *Journal of Accounting Research* 10: 167–79. [CrossRef]

Dietsch, Michel, Klaus Düllmann, Henri Fraisse, Philipp Koziol, and Christine Ott. 2016. *Support for the Sme Supporting Factor: Multi-Country Empirical Evidence on Systematic Risk Factor for Sme Loans*. Frankfurt am Main: Deutsche Bundesbank Discussion Paper Series.

Edmister, Robert O. 1972. An empirical test of financial ratio analysis for small business failure prediction. *Journal of Financial and Quantitative Analysis* 7: 1477–93. [CrossRef]

European Parliament, Council of the European Union. 2013. *Regulation (EU) No 575/2013 on Prudential Requirements for Credit Institutions and Investment Firms and Amending Regulation (EU) No 648/2012*. Brussels: Official Journal of the European Union.

Hamer, Michelle M. 1983. Failure prediction: Sensitivity of classification accuracy to alternative statistical methods and variable sets. *Journal of Accounting and Public Policy* 2: 289–307. [CrossRef]

Hand, David J., and William E. Henley. 1997. Statistical classification methods in consumer credit scoring: A review. *Journal of the Royal Statistical Society: Series A (Statistics in Society)* 160: 523–41. [CrossRef]

Hopkin, Richard, Anna Bak, and Sidika Ulker. 2014. *High-Quality Securitization for Europe—The Market at a Crossroads*. London: Association for Financial Markets in Europe.

Jo, Hongkyu, Ingoo Han, and Hoonyoung Lee. 1997. Bankruptcy prediction using case-based reasoning, neural networks, and discriminant analysis. *Expert Systems with Applications* 13: 97–108. [CrossRef]

Karels, Gordon V., and Arun J. Prakash. 1987. Multivariate normality and forecasting of business bankruptcy. *Journal of Business Finance & Accounting* 14: 573–93.

Kim, Hong Sik, and So Young Sohn. 2010. Support vector machines for default prediction of smes based on technology credit. *European Journal of Operational Research* 201: 838–46. [CrossRef]

Martin, Daniel. 1977. Early warning of bank failure: A logit regression approach. *Journal of Banking & Finance* 1: 249–76.

Mays, Elizabeth, and Niall Lynas. 2004. *Credit Scoring for Risk Managers: The Handbook for Lenders*. Mason: Thomson/South-Western Ohio.

Min, Jae H., and Young-Chan Lee. 2005. Bankruptcy prediction using support vector machine with optimal choice of kernel function parameters. *Expert Systems With Applications* 28: 603–14. [CrossRef]

Mironchyk, Pavel, and Viktor Tchistiakov. 2017. *Monotone Optimal Binning Algorithm for Credit Risk Modeling*. Utrecht: Working Paper.

Müller, Marlene, and Bernd Rönz. 2000. Credit scoring using semiparametric methods. In *Measuring Risk in Complex Stochastic Systems*. Berlin and Heidelberg: Springer, pp. 83–97.

Odom, Marcus D., and Ramesh Sharda. 1990. A neural network model for bankruptcy prediction. Paper Presented at 1990 IJCNN International Joint Conference on Neural Networks, San Diego, CA, USA, June 17–21, pp. 163–68.

Ohlson, James A. 1980. Financial ratios and the probabilistic prediction of bankruptcy. *Journal of Accounting Research* 18: 109–31. [CrossRef]

Park, Cheol-Soo, and Ingoo Han. 2002. A case-based reasoning with the feature weights derived by analytic hierarchy process for bankruptcy prediction. *Expert Systems with Applications* 23: 255–64. [CrossRef]

Refaat, Mamdouh. 2011. Credit Risk Scorecard: Development and Implementation Using SAS. Available online: Lulu.com (accessed on 15 October 2018).

Řezáč, Martin, and František Řezáč. 2011. How to measure the quality of credit scoring models. *Finance a úvěr: Czech Journal of Economics and Finance* 61: 486–507.

Satchel, Stephen, and Wei Xia. 2008. Analytic models of the roc curve: Applications to credit rating model validation. In *The Analytics of Risk Model Validation*. Amsterdam: Elsevier, pp. 113–33.

Siddiqi, Naeem. 2017. *Intelligent Credit Scoring: Building and Implementing Better Credit Risk Scorecards*. Hoboken: John Wiley & Sons.

Sinkey, Jr., Joseph F. 1975. A multivariate statistical analysis of the characteristics of problem banks. *The Journal of Finance* 30: 21–36. [CrossRef]

Stuhr, David P., and Robert Van Wicklen. 1974. Rating the financial condition of banks: A statistical approach to aid bank supervision. *Monthly Review* 56: 233–38.

Tam, Kar Yan, and Melody Y. Kiang. 1992. Managerial applications of neural networks: The case of bank failure predictions. *Management Science* 38: 926–47. [CrossRef]

Thomas, Lyn C., Dabid B. Edelman, and Jonathan N. Crook. 2002. *Credit Scoring and Its Applications: Siam Monographs on Mathematical Modeling and Computation*. Philadelphia: University City Science Center, SIAM.

Van Gestel, Tony, Bart Baesens, Johan Suykens, Marcelo Espinoza, Dirk-Emma Baestaens, Jan Vanthienen, and Bart De Moor. 2003. Bankruptcy prediction with least squares support vector machine classifiers. Paper presented at 2003 IEEE International Conference on Computational Intelligence for Financial Engineering, Hong Kong, March 20–23. pp. 1–8.

Wilson, Rick L., and Ramesh Sharda. 1994. Bankruptcy prediction using neural networks. *Decision Support Systems* 11: 545–57. [CrossRef]

Zeng, Guoping. 2013. Metric divergence measures and information value in credit scoring. *Journal of Mathematics* 2013: 848271. [CrossRef]

Zhang, Guoqiang, Michael Y. Hu, B. Eddy Patuwo, and Daniel C. Indro. 1999. Artificial neural networks in bankruptcy prediction: General framework and cross-validation analysis. *European Journal of Operational Research* 116: 16–32. [CrossRef]

Journal of
Risk and Financial Management

MDPI

Article

Value-at-Risk and Models of Dependence in the U.S. Federal Crop Insurance Program

A. Ford Ramsey [1,*] and Barry K. Goodwin [2]

[1] Department of Agricultural and Applied Economics, Virginia Tech, Blacksburg, VA 24061, USA
[2] Department of Economics and Department of Agricultural and Resource Economics, North Carolina State University, Raleigh, NC 27607, USA; bkgoodwi@ncsu.edu
* Correspondence: aframsey@vt.edu; Tel.: +1-540-231-5032

Received: 29 March 2019; Accepted: 15 April 2019; Published: 16 April 2019

Abstract: The federal crop insurance program covered more than 110 billion dollars in total liability in 2018. The program consists of policies across a wide range of crops, plans, and locations. Weather and other latent variables induce dependence among components of the portfolio. Computing value-at-risk (VaR) is important because the Standard Reinsurance Agreement (SRA) allows for a portion of the risk to be transferred to the federal government. Further, the international reinsurance industry is extensively involved in risk sharing arrangements with U.S. crop insurers. VaR is an important measure of the risk of an insurance portfolio. In this context, VaR is typically expressed in terms of probable maximum loss (PML) or as a return period, whereby a loss of certain magnitude is expected to return within a given period of time. Determining bounds on VaR is complicated by the non-homogeneous nature of crop insurance portfolios. We consider several different scenarios for the marginal distributions of losses and provide sharp bounds on VaR using a rearrangement algorithm. Our results are related to alternative measures of portfolio risks based on multivariate distribution functions and alternative copula specifications.

Keywords: crop insurance; value-at-risk; dependence; copulas; rearrangement algorithm

1. Introduction

The United States federal crop insurance program is one of the largest subsidized agricultural insurance programs in the world. Total liability exceeded 110 billion U.S. dollars in 2018 and resulted in roughly 6.5 billion U.S. dollars in indemnity payments (Risk Management Agency 2018). For major row crops, such as corn and soybeans, in excess of 80% of planted acres are insured under some variant of a federal crop insurance policy. A portion of the actuarially fair premium on the policies is subsidized by taxpayers; for policies with catastrophic coverage the subsidy can be 100 percent of premium but is closer to 60% of premium for the bulk of the policies sold through the program. As the most expensive mechanism for agricultural policy in the United States, any actuarial changes to the program can have major impacts on government expenditures, insurance uptake, and production decisions.

Policies are priced by the Risk Management Agency (RMA) of the U.S. Department of Agriculture (USDA) but are serviced by approved private insurers. These insurers are subject to the Standard Reinsurance Agreement (SRA) which controls several aspects of their relationship with the federal government. The SRA allows private insurers to cede the riskiest portions of their portfolios to a government-backed reinsurance fund. Insurers can generate economic rents if they have a method of pricing that is more accurate than that used by the RMA; they can strategically cede or retain policies (Ker and McGowan 2000). They have an advantage in being able to observe prices from the RMA before choosing which policies to cede. Remaining risk is transferred to international reinsurers who engage in substantial business with the approved insurance providers.

Because of significant government involvement in the program, and following demand from reinsurers, quantifying the risk associated with the entire crop insurance portfolio is an important and challenging problem. Unlike other lines of insurance, losses across members of the insurer's portfolio cannot be considered independent. Latent variables induce dependence by affecting crop production across a number of locations. The most obvious of these latent variables is weather. But many other factors that affect crop production, such as pests, disease, and management practices, are spatially correlated. Positive spatial dependence in crop production has been forwarded as an explanation for the lack of development of private crop insurance markets. However, Holly Wang and Zhang (2003) showed that spatial dependence dissipates at a sufficient speed such that private insurance markets should be feasible. Government involvement may actually crowd out private insurance.

We estimate value-at-risk (VaR) for a hypothetical portfolio of crop insurance policies. The marginal distributions determining the aggregate loss are allowed to follow an arbitrary distribution leading to an inhomogeneous portfolio from the insurer's perspective. Dependence relationships between individual losses are unknown. As any joint distribution can be decomposed into marginal distributions and a copula function, one implication is that the form of the copula is also unknown. In spite of the lack of knowledge about the appropriate copula, reliable bounds on VaR can be computed using the rearrangement algorithm of Embrechts et al. (2013). We calculate the VaR using the rerrangement algorithm and a variety of copula specifications.

The problem of reliable estimates for VaR extends beyond private insurers to reinsurers. Reinsurers handle risks from more than one insurer so the portfolio of the international reinsurer consists of risks from a diverse group of entities. Most crop insurers operate in a geographically concentrated area leading to greater dependence in their portfolios. To develop an aggregate loss distribution for their holdings, the reinsurer is then tasked with pooling loss distributions for the underlying insurers. This can be challenging for reinsurers handling crop insurance portfolios because of difficulties in separating systemic and pool-able losses (Odening and Shen 2014).

Although the federal government can handle any reinsurance losses through the program, budgeting decisions with respect to the crop insurance program take into account the probability of worst-case losses (Hayes et al. 2003). The probability of a large portfolio loss is important for predicting variability in future government outlays. Likewise, insurers and reinsurers engage in loss reserving. Loss reserving models produce an estimated total loss reserve as the required loss reserve (the amount needed to meet all indemnifications) is not known until after indemnities are paid out. The issue of calculating adequate reserves is similar for financial institutions dealing with operational risk. Insurers, reinsurers, and financial institutions often base reserving decisions on VaR calculations; in the insurance industry, VaR is typically termed probable maximum loss (PML).

By calculating VaR under several different dependence models and deriving sharp bounds using the rearrangement algorithm, we also provide estimates of model risk in crop insurance applications. As the marginal distributions are the same in any case, the model risk we describe is specifically related to the dependence model. In line with previous findings by Goodwin and Hungerford (2014), there is a substantial amount of model risk induced by the choice of the dependence structure. Therefore, any top-down approach to loss aggregation should take into account the model risk from dependence in reserving decisions. Because the crop insurance program is publicly funded, the amount of overall risk (of which model risk is one part) in the program causes difficulties in accurately projecting public expenditures.

The general approach we take is to assume marginal distributions and merge them into a joint distribution using a copula function. This approach is referred to by Aas and Puccetti (2014) as top-down aggregation. An alternative approach is bottom-up aggregation where drivers of risk types are identified and a model is developed for the risk factors. Simulations can then be used to aggregate risk over a number of different scenarios for the evolution of the risk factors. Bottom-up aggregation is also frequently used by crop insurance modelers. Because the fundamental driver of yield risk is weather, catastrophe modelers often model the evolution of weather, simulate a number of scenarios, and then translate these weather scenarios into yield losses. In either case, using top-down or bottom-up approaches for risk aggregation, the end result is construction of a measure of portfolio risk from marginal risk information.

2. Crop Insurance Policies and Actuarial Methods

The U.S. federal crop insurance program encompasses a wide range of different policy types, crops, and locations. The most widely purchased policies are yield and revenue insurance policies. These may be purchased at the farm or county level. In the latter case, the loss is determined by the average yield or revenue in the county. Farm level policies are priced using production data from an individual farm. Whether at the farm or county level, the actuarial methods underlying pricing are similar. A number of adjustments are made in pricing farm level policies because these policies usually have a much shorter time series of available data.

Revenue is the product of quantity and price. Quantity is usually given by crop yield: the amount of crop production per unit of land. The loss on revenue and yield insurance policies are determined by prices and yields. To generate the probabilities of loss required to price crop insurance policies, we have the option of modeling losses themselves or directly modeling prices and yields. Up to harvest, yields for the coming year can be considered random variables. Randomness results from the stochastic nature of crop production as affected by weather, pests, and other uncertainties. Both yield and revenue insurance are multiple peril and indemnify losses from a number of different sources of risk.

For yield insurance policies, the loss on the policy is given by

$$\text{loss}_{\text{yield}} = \max\left(0, (\lambda\bar{y} - y)p\right), \tag{1}$$

where $\bar{y}$ is the historical mean yield or expected yield, y is the realized yield, $\lambda \in (0, 1)$ is the coverage level, and p is a deterministic price. The only stochastic element in Equation (1) is y. Under a revenue insurance policy,

$$\text{loss}_{\text{revenue}} = \max\left(0, (\lambda\bar{y}p_p - yp_h)\right), \tag{2}$$

where the variables are similarly defined. In this case, p_p is a projected or planting-time price and p_h is the realized or harvest-time price for the crop. Only the yield y and realized price p_h are stochastic. Some revenue insurance policies extend the guaranteed revenue in Equation (2) from $\lambda\bar{y}p_p$ to $\lambda\bar{y}\max(p_p, p_h)$ to provide additional price coverage.

Both Equations (1) and (2) reveal several interesting aspects of these policies. First, they require a model for the evolution of crop yields. Second, revenue insurance policies also require a model of dependence between the stochastic yield and price. The random variables in the loss equations are likely to be correlated across space. Lastly, because policies in the same county are written at different coverage levels, losses on different policies are also correlated within the same county. Given the complexities in pricing a single policy, determining risk in a portfolio of crop insurance policies is a complicated task.

The actuarial process of pricing individual policies in the federal program has received considerable attention because of the close link between actuarial practices and program losses. The RMA also has a legislative mandate to produce premium rates that are actuarially fair. Early work focused on estimation of the marginal distribution of crop yields and if a best distribution could be found. Applications included parametric distributions (Gallagher 1986; Ozaki and Silva 2009; Sherrick et al. 2004), nonparametric distributions (Goodwin and Ker 1998), and semiparametric distributions (Ker and Coble 2003; Tolhurst and Ker 2014). Although no clear winner has emerged, the tendency has been to gravitate toward the use of flexible parametric distributions that can accommodate skewness and excess kurtosis. Non-parametric approaches are used when large samples are available. Current rating methods employed by the RMA use truncated normal distributions.

In most cases, the distributions are not fitted to observed yields but to normalized yields. Since 1940, average corn yields in the United States have increased roughly 8 times. Better management practices and plant breeding have enabled remarkable growth in the mean of the yield distribution. To account for technological change, observed yields are detrended and probability distributions are estimated on deviations from trend. The detrending procedure has varied but researchers have used robust regression, locally weighted scatterplot smoothing, and deterministic models. Several authors have considered joint estimation of the trend and density using time-varying distributions (Tolhurst and Ker 2014; Zhu et al. 2011).

Revenue insurance is now the most popular form of insurance in the crop insurance program and accounts for over 80% of total liability. The increasing prevalence of revenue insurance has prompted research into dependence between prices and yields. Goodwin and Hungerford (2014) and Hungerford and Goodwin (2014) examined yield-price dependence as it affects systemic risk. One problem with pricing revenue insurance policies is that the samples used to identify the copula, or more specifically dependence between prices and yield, are small in practice. The issue was further considered by Ramsey et al. (2019) who found that, although there was little support for the assumption of a Gaussian copula, the economic impact of choice of copula on pricing for individual policies was minor. Rates were affected more by changes in the marginal distributions.

Because yield risks are spatially correlated, several authors have also examined the measurement of dependence between yields across space. This is important not only for measuring systemic risk but also for informing estimates in locations with little available yield information. If the dependence structure is known, then data from a number of locations can be pooled to arrive at more accurate estimates for individual policies. Okhrin et al. (2013a) examined the diversification effects of weather indices that can be used in lieu of yield and revenue insurance. Porth et al. (2016) discussed an approach for improved pooling of systemic weather risk using simulated annealing. Ker et al. (2015) and Park et al. (2018) developed methods to average or smooth yield distributions across locations and achieve more accurate rates.

While dependence in losses across space has attracted significant attention, there are also dependencies among policies sold at the same location. Because of the way area policies are structured, a policy purchased at the 90% coverage level will always pay out when a policy purchased at the 70% coverage level is indemnified. However, the converse is not true. These dependencies do not present a major practical problem because the majority of policies are sold at the farm level and are usually at the highest coverage levels. However, if we wished to directly model a portfolio of policies across counties and coverage levels, intra-county dependence in the portfolio would also need to be taken into account.

Previous work on the modeling of crop yields is germane to measurement of portfolio risk because one can either model the losses directly or derive the losses from a model of yields. As an example, to determine a loss from the mean, one needs a model or procedure for determining the mean of the distribution. The same factors that generate dependence between yields at different locations cause systemic risk for the crop insurance portfolio. In modeling either losses, loss costs, or yields, several assumptions have to be made on the evolution of the random variables and the stability of the distributions generating the random variables. Unfortunately, there is no single objective criteria for determining which approach is best.

3. Dependence and Portfolio Risk

In many applications, the starting point for assessing the aggregate risk inherent in an insurance portfolio is the value-at-risk (VaR). The aggregate loss S for the portfolio is a function of its individual factor losses x_i so that

$$S = \sum_{i=1}^{K} x_i, \quad (3)$$

for a portfolio comprised of K factors. The VaR for the portfolio is

$$VaR_{\alpha}(S) = F^{-1}(S;\alpha) = \inf(S \in R : F(S) > \alpha), \tag{4}$$

with confidence level α where $F(\cdot)$ is the distribution function of the aggregate loss S. VaR is usually intended to capture the risk of extremely large losses and α takes values in the range of 0.9 to 0.99. For a given portfolio and time horizon, the probability of a loss larger than the VaR is at most α.

To calculate the VaR, we require the distribution function of the aggregate loss or a model for the joint distribution of the factors in the portfolio. There are a number of choices for the model of the joint distribution but some models impose strict assumptions on the behavior of the underlying variables. For instance, the assumption of a Gaussian joint distribution implies that the marginal behavior of the variables is Gaussian. An appealing method for constructing the joint distribution is the use of copulas which allows the analyst to split the problem into choice of the marginals and a dependence structure. The dependence structure is modeled by the copula function.

The copula is a function in K dimensions that allows a joint distribution function to be given by

$$F(x_1, \ldots, x_K) = C(F_1(x_1), \ldots, F_K(x_K)), \tag{5}$$

where $F_i(\cdot)$ is the marginal distribution function of random variable x_i. At least for continuous marginal distributions, the copula C is unique and contains all dependence information in the joint distribution. This result, originally discovered by Sklar (1959), is both powerful and practically useful. As indicated in the preceding section, there are a number of situations where the marginal distributions of the variables have been thoroughly investigated or can be motivated by a reasonable appeal to economic or statistical theory. Less is known about the dependence structure between variables and the copula formulation allows the analyst to concentrate on addressing this unknown dependence.

There are two important copulas known as the Fréchet upper and lower bounds. For a given copula $C(u_1, \ldots, u_K)$

$$\max\left(\sum_{i=1}^{K} u_i - K = 1, 0\right) \leq C(u_1, \ldots, u_K) \leq \min(u_1, \ldots, u_K), \tag{6}$$

for all $C(\cdot)$ and $u_1, \ldots, u_K \in [0,1]$. The copula on the left is the Fréchet lower bound and the copula on the right is the Fréchet upper bound. The upper bound is known as the comonotonic copula because it denotes perfect positive dependence between the random variables. The lower bound is countermonotonic and represents perfect negative dependence, but is only a well-defined copula in two dimensions. All copulas capture dependence structures somewhere between perfect positive and perfect negative dependence, and therefore they must be within the Fréchet bounds.

The likelihood function for the copula is

$$L = \sum_{j=1}^{N} \log C(F_1(x_{j1}), \ldots, F_d(x_{jK})) + \sum_{i=1}^{K}\sum_{j=1}^{N} \log f_i(x_{ji}), \tag{7}$$

with two terms that capture the dependence structure's effect on the likelihood and the contribution of the univariate marginal distributions respectively. The most common approach to obtaining the joint distribution is to use a procedure known as Inference from Margins whereby the parameters of the marginal distributions are first obtained and then the copula part of the likelihood is maximized taking the marginal parameters as given. In many cases, the parameter of the copula has a one-to-one relationship with measures of dependence such as Kendall's tau or Spearman's rho. It is not necessary to maximize the pseudo-likelihood. An estimate of the copula parameter can be obtained by first estimating the dependence measure and transforming the empirical measure to the copula parameter via calibration. Unfortunately, for some copulas (such as the t) there is no direct relationship between common dependence measures and some of the copula parameters.

Important features of copulas are their tail dependence properties. These properties can have large impacts on VaR estimates because VaR is usually concerned with the tail of the loss distribution. Two coefficients

$$\lambda_U = \lim_{u \to 1} Pr(U_1 \geq u | U_2 \geq u) = \lim_{u \to 1} \frac{1 - 2u + C(u,u)}{1 - u}, \tag{8}$$

$$\lambda_L = \lim_{u \to 0} Pr(U_1 \leq u | U_2 \leq u) = \lim_{u \to 0} \frac{C(u,u)}{u} \tag{9}$$

define the upper and lower tail dependence coefficients respectively. Tail dependence is realized whenever one of the coefficients is positive. Among the most popular bivariate copulas, the Gaussian copula has no tail dependence, the t copula has tail dependence in both tails, the Clayton copula has tail dependence in the lower tail, and the Gumbel copula has tail dependence in the upper tail. Both the Gumbel and Clayton copulas can capture asymmetries in tail dependence and have been used in many applications where dependence between the elements of a portfolio is expected to be stronger in the case of major portfolio losses.

While the Archimedean copulas (Gumbel and Clayton) can capture dependence asymmetry, their use in multivariate applications is questionable. They usually are controlled by a single parameter even in many dimensions. For instance, whereas a four-dimensional Gaussian copula describes dependence with essentially six parameters, a four-dimensional Gumbel copula has only a single parameter. Because of this limitation on multivariate Archimedean copulas, several authors have proposed pair-copula constructions that "stack" bivariate copulas and result in more complicated dependence relationships while maintaining parsimony. The most popular methods are hierarchical Archimedean copulas and vine copulas (Nikoloulopoulos et al. 2012; Okhrin et al. 2013b).

Copulas have been used to examine dependence relationships in a number of settings. Yang et al. (2015) considered dependence between international stock markets. In an insurance application, Tamakoshi and Hamori (2014) measured dependence between the credit default swap indices of insurers. Patton (2009) provide a number of examples and applications of copulas to financial time series. Some implications and use of copulas in credibility ratemaking for auto insurance are provided in Frees and Wang (2006). A common theme in all of these works is that the copula model used can have a major impact on portfolio losses and risk—whether in a financial or insurance setting. Unfortunately, there are few methods of choosing the ideal form of the copula. The analyst is usually left with selecting a copula model from a set of possible models that may or may not include the true model.

Because of the relationship shown in Equation (5), it is relatively straightforward to compute the VaR if presented with marginal distributions and the copula function. If the marginals and copula are not known, they can be estimated from the data. Perhaps the easiest approach is to simulate uniform random variables with a given dependence structure by drawing from the estimated copula. The uniform draws are then passed through the marginal inverse cumulative distribution functions producing a simulated dataset from the joint distribution of K random variables. For each iteration of the simulation, the total portfolio loss is calculated. The α VaR is the α empirical quantile of the simulated distribution of portfolio losses.

Embrechts et al. (2013) contains a detailed discussion on the use of VaR in operational risk settings and many of the concepts are immediately applicable in insurance settings. Following Embrechts et al. (2013), define the upper and lower bounds for the VaR of the portfolio as

$$\overline{VaR}_\alpha(S) = \sup(VaR_\alpha(S) : F_i \in \gamma(F_1, \ldots, F_K)) \tag{10}$$

$$\underline{VaR}_\alpha(S) = \inf(VaR_\alpha(S) : F_i \in \gamma(F_1, \ldots, F_K)), \tag{11}$$

where $\gamma(F_1, \ldots, F_K)$ is the Fréchet class of all possible joint distributions for the portfolio having the given marginal distributions. These can be restated in terms of the copula as

$$\overline{VaR}_\alpha(S) = \sup(VaR_\alpha(S) : C \in \epsilon_K)) \tag{12}$$

$$\underline{VaR}_\alpha(S) = \inf(VaR_\alpha(S) : C \in \epsilon_K), \tag{13}$$

where ϵ_K is the set of all copulas of dimension K. Embrechts et al. (2013) define $\overline{VaR}_\alpha$ and $\underline{VaR}_\alpha$ as the worst and best case VaR respectively. Moreover, the bounds given in Equations (10) and (11) cannot be improved without additional information on the dependence structure. The difference between the bounds is the difference in risk that arises from the dependence structure (i.e., copula) and is defined by Aas and Puccetti (2014) as the dependence uncertainty spread.

In general, the VaR for the portfolio is not the sum of VaR for the marginal risk factors. One exception is the case of comonotonic dependence. Comonotonic dependence is a relatively conservative assumption as it implies perfect dependence between the factors. The copula for factors with comonotonic dependence must be the upper Fréchet bound. Interestingly, there are cases where independence results in a worse (larger) VaR restimate than under comonotonicity (Mainik and Embrechts 2013). The point stressed by Embrechts et al. (2013) is that the comonotonic copula is not typically the solution for Equation (10). Likewise the countermonotonic copula is not generally a solution to Equation (11).

Because the comonotonic and countermonotonic copulas do not generally produce the best and worst case VaR, Embrechts et al. (2013) develop a reordering algorithm to compute sharp bounds on VaR under best and worst case dependence scenarios. Determining the bounds is also developed in Puccetti and Rüschendorf (2012) and Puccetti (2013). As explained in Aas and Puccetti (2014), the rearrangement algorithm is relatively simple and consists of rearranging each column of a matrix until they are oppositely ordered to the sum of the other columns. The algorithm terminates in a finite number of steps and the termination condition depends on whether one is calculating $\overline{VaR}_\alpha$ or $\underline{VaR}_\alpha$. Several empirical applications have shown the rearrangement algorithm to generate reasonable VaR estimates conditional on the underlying marginal distributions.

The algorithm can be applied to portfolios of high dimension where the estimation and validation of a given dependence structure can be difficult. It is easy to estimate a Gaussian copula using calibration methods. But in high dimensions, multiple parameter copulas such as the t can cause estimation problems. Optimization is required over a large parameter space. Moreover, the best fitting copula is usually selected according to a fit criteria such as the Akaike information criterion (AIC). There is no guarantee that the set of copulas being considered will include any copula with adequate fit. While the copula paradigm provides a useful approach for constructing a joint distribution and measuring associated portfolio risk, it does not necessarily provide adequate information on dependence uncertainty and model risk. The problem is made even more difficult in cases of limited data where estimation of the copula may be impossible.

Aas and Puccetti (2014) present an interesting application of the rearrangement algorithm to capital requirements for Norway's largest bank: DNB. They also discuss some of the challenges in applying the algorithm in a real situation. In their case, some of the risk factors have limited data and the dependence structure used by the bank is formed on the basis of expert opinion. Fitting several types of copulas and using the rearrangement algorithm, Aas and Puccetti (2014) show that dependence uncertainty can be quite large in practical applications and that VaR can vary significantly based on the type of copula used to capture the dependence structure. Adding more information on dependence among groups of the random variables results in considerably tighter bounds on the VaR.

The VaR is a single measure of the risk of the portfolio and subject to several criticisms. In particular, the VaR is almost always estimated from historical information. To estimate probabilities from historical events, it is necessary to make an assumption that the events are independent and identically distributed. This is rarely the case in practice, especially when dealing with crop yields or revenue. Crop insurers are also routinely confronted by small sample sizes that place practical constraints on the set of admissible models. These difficulties feed over into calculations of dependence and portfolio risk as noted by both Hungerford and Goodwin (2014) and Ramsey et al. (2019).

Many of the problems of estimating a measure of portfolio risk in crop insurance are analogous to problems in the operational risk space (Cope et al. 2009). Estimation of the loss distribution can be highly sensitive to large losses occurring with low frequency. Data is scarce enough that appeals to extreme value theory for the distribution of losses cannot be justified. Very little is known about the dependence process except that losses are correlated across space. This makes the modeling of portfolio risk in crop insurance a challenging problem. The empirical applications that follow present two possible approaches for addressing these concerns and arriving at a measure of portfolio risk.

4. Empirical Applications

We considered two empirical applications aimed at measuring risk in a portfolio of crop insurance policies. The first estimated VaR for a portfolio of corn yield insurance policies in Illinois. The loss in this case was the normalized yield deviation from trend. In other words, we directly modeled the crop yield in each county and constructed losses in terms of a normalized yield. VaR was calculated using data on these yield losses. The second application is more general; we modeled the loss cost ratio for corn policies in a single crop reporting district in Iowa. The loss cost modeling is easily generalized to other crops and locations. It also avoids some of the intricacies in direct modeling of yields. However, there was less data to work with and the loss cost distribution was assumed to be stable across the time period.

4.1. VaR for a Portfolio of Yield Policies

We obtained all-practice corn yields in Illinois at the county level for 102 counties from 1955 to 2015. Because yields change over time with advances in production technology and management practices, the marginal distribution of yields must be normalized. Each observed yield was thought of as being drawn from a unique distribution at each location and in each year (Tack and Ubilava 2013). The distribution of interest from the insurer's perspective was the projected yield distribution for the upcoming year. Therefore, this application considers a purely synthetic portfolio of policies that realize a loss anytime the yield is below its mean. Using Equation (1), the coverage level was 100% of the expected average yield.[1] This approach could be used to capture portfolio dependence among a suite of different policies so long as we are willing to model dependence between policies at different coverage levels.

Because the distribution of yields changes over time, we first fit a trend to the yields in each county using locally weighted scatterplot smoothing (Cleveland and Devlin 1988). The smoothing parameter was selected automatically using a corrected version of AIC suggested in Hurvich et al. (1998). The residuals from trend were then recentered about the last year in the series. Figure 1 shows boxplots of yields from all Illinois counties at five year intervals. We can see that there was significant variation in yields across space and time. Mean and median yields have consistently risen and the standard deviation of the distribution also appears to have increased.

Figure 2 shows yields in Adams County, Illinois along with the fitted locally weighted scatterplot smoothing (LOESS) line. In this case, the trend appears nearly linear. Large losses have occurred over the 50 year period; a notable loss was during the drought conditions that characterized crop production throughout the midwest in 2012. There is also visual suggestion of heteroskedasticity, justifying the recentering procedures. Using the normalized yields, we then constructed losses from the projected mean yield in each year. These losses were used to fit the marginal distributions and copula functions.

1 Policies currently offered in the federal crop insurance program do not allow producers to cover 100% of mean yield. However, most crop insurance is purchased at high coverage levels above 80%.

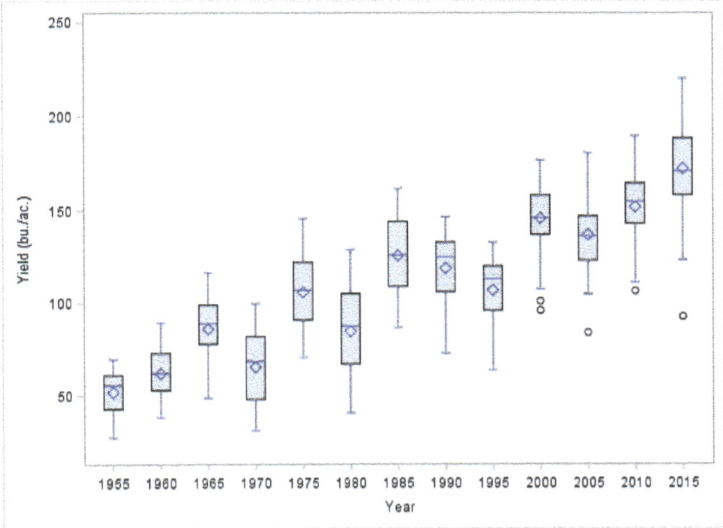

Figure 1. Boxplot of Illinois yields over time.

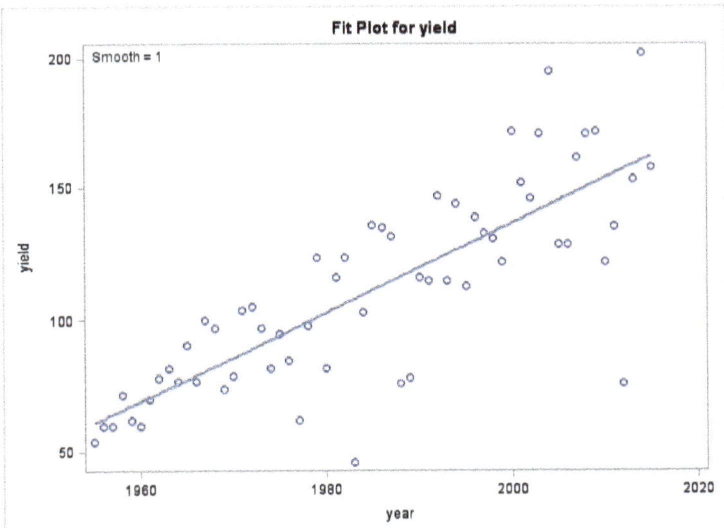

Figure 2. Adams, Illinois corn yields.

Scatterplots of yield losses across five randomly selected Illinois counties are shown in Figure 3. Given the close geographic proximity of the counties, it should be no surprise that there was a high degree of correlation across space. There were a number of years where losses are observed in one county but not another; the important point is that these losses tend to be relatively small. The largest loss in almost all of the counties is observed in a single year: 2012. Pearson correlation coefficients across the same five counties are shown in Table 1. There is high correlation although this should not be considered representative of all counties across the state. It does, however, suggest that dependence across counties could be an important element determining portfolio losses.

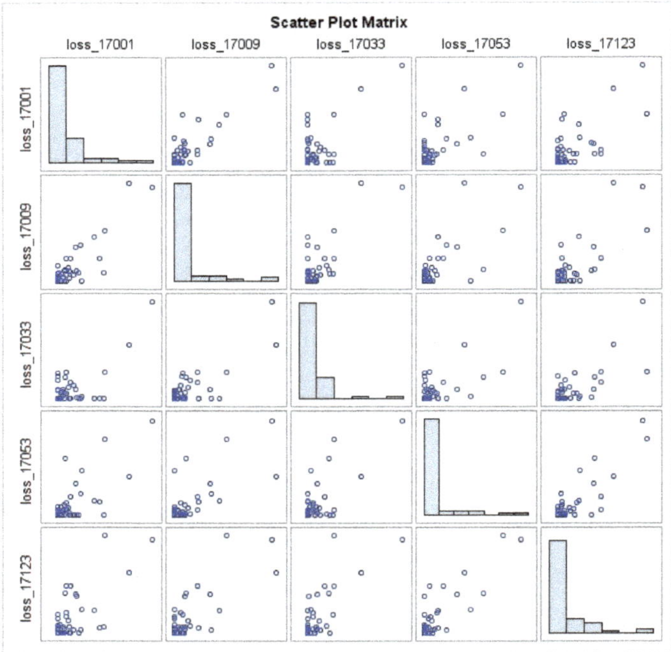

Figure 3. Scatterplot of losses from mean.

Table 1. Pearson correlation of losses across five counties.

County FIPS	Pearson Correlation Coefficients				
	17001	**17009**	**17033**	**17053**	**17123**
17001	1	0.88652	0.70929	0.74421	0.73467
17009	0.88652	1	0.80876	0.74871	0.80017
17033	0.70929	0.80876	1	0.7359	0.77594
17053	0.74421	0.74871	0.7359	1	0.86371
17123	0.73467	0.80017	0.77594	0.86371	1

The aggregate loss for the portfolio of policies is given by

$$S = x_{17001} + \cdots + x_{17203}, \tag{14}$$

and is simply the sum of the losses in the 102 counties of Illinois. The risk factors x_i are indexed by their Federal Information Processing Standards (FIPS) code at the county level. We consider several parametric distributions for the losses including the exponential, gamma, inverse Gaussian, lognormal, and Weibull distributions. These distributions can take a wide range of shapes, offer substantial flexibility, and have non-negative support. Goodness of fit was determined using the Cramer von Mises (CvM) statistic which compares the estimated loss distribution to the empirical cumulative distribution function. The CvM statistic is defined as

$$\text{CvM} = N \int_{-\infty}^{\infty} (F_n(x) - F(x))^2 dF(x), \tag{15}$$

where $F(\cdot)$ is the estimated cumulative distribution function and $F_n(\cdot)$ is the empirical cumulative distribution function. The selected marginal distributions and parameter values for the first ten counties are shown in Table 2. For the majority of counties, the gamma distribution was best fitting (76), followed by the exponential (17), and inverse Gaussian (9). Because the distribution varies across counties, the portfolio is inhomogeneous.

Table 2. Marginal loss distributions and parameter values for 10 counties in Illinois (IL).

County FIPS	Model	Theta	Alpha/Xi
17001	Exponential	8.32	
17003	Exponential	6.63	
17005	Exponential	8.45	
17007	Gamma	158.42	0.04
17009	Inverse Gaussian	14.29	0.12
17011	Gamma	149.04	0.04
17013	Gamma	133.91	0.04
17015	Gamma	185.26	0.04
17017	Inverse Gaussian	13.79	0.08
17019	Gamma	172.67	0.04

Given the selected parametric marginal distributions, we calculated the VaR for the portfolio under different assumptions about the dependence structure. In addition to the rearrangement algorithm of Embrechts et al. (2013), we also compared VaR calculations using a Gaussian copula where the parameters of the copula are estimated from the data. The raw data (normalized yields) were first mapped to the unit interval using the empirical cumulative distribution functions. We estimated the copula using inference from margins where only the copula portion of the joint likelihood was maximized. We then took 100,000 draws from the fitted copulas. These draws were passed through the fitted inverse cumulative distribution functions of the parametric marginals. This produced simulated losses from the joint distribution of the portfolio which can be used to calculate the VaR. The comonotonic VaR was obtained by simply summing the marginal $VaR_{\alpha}(x_i)$ across all of the portfolio constituents.

Table 3 shows the VaR calculated under the assumption of independent marginal risks, a Gaussian copula, and the worst-case VaR calculated using the rearrangement algorithm. The total liability across the portfolio was 16,994 bushels in the last year. The bushel per acre losses in the table could be weighted by the amount of acreage in a county if desired. The table shows that there was a large amount of model risk arising from the chosen dependence structure, and that the amount of risk increased as we considered VaR at higher percentiles. The $\overline{VaR}$ at the 0.975 percentile raised another interesting point.

Table 3. Value-at-risk for synthetic portfolio of crop insurance policies.

α	Independence	Gaussian	$\overline{VaR}$
0.90	1192	1546	6545
0.95	1473	3101	11,446
0.975	1902	5336	18,671

The total liability under the synthetic portfolio was only 16,994 bushels, but the extreme VaR estimates tended to return portfolio losses greater than total liability. The marginal loss distributions were unbounded. Furthermore, there were very few large losses in the data. This result relates to a warning made by Aas and Puccetti (2014) that in considering the worst possible VaR, only the tails matter. Dependence in the other parts of the distribution can be set arbitrarily and will not affect the worst case VaR. They note that there are many situations where a model for the entire distribution might be desired instead of a model for the tails alone.

These results for the VaR of the synthetic portfolio suggest several extensions or improvements. First, the assumptions made about the marginal distributions can be very important. There was also little data to estimate the dependence structure and differences arising from model risk can also be quite large. Nonetheless, insurers should be aware of the impacts that marginal and dependence model assumptions can make in calculation of VaR estimates.

4.2. VaR for a Portfolio Using Loss Costs

Risk in an insurance context is typically expressed using the loss-cost ratio (LCR), which is given by the ratio of indemnities to liabilities, and represents the percentage of liability that is paid out in a given period. Insurers and reinsurers typically use the distribution of the LCR as a metric for determining insurance return periods, probable maximum loss (PML), or the value at risk (VaR) for a portfolio. These concepts are analogous and all represent metrics derived from quantiles of the LCR distribution. An actuarially-sound insurance contract will set the premium rate at the level of the LCR. In cases where catastrophic losses are relevant (i.e., large losses that may occur with a low probability), these metrics play an important role in the determination of loading factors and reserves.

The return period is entirely analogous to the probable maximum loss. Both metrics suggest the worst (or best) outcome expected to occur over a given number of insurance cycles (typically years). A 1 in 10 PML corresponds to the maximum loss that an insurer may be expected to realize over a ten year period. In terms of a probability distribution of losses, this corresponds to the 90th percentile of the distribution. In VaR terms, this corresponds to the maximum amount one may be expected to lose with a 90% level of confidence. Other quantiles of the distribution directly correspond to other PMLs and VaRs.

Corn is the largest US crop and currently accounts for about $40 billion in liability on 70 million acres each year in the US federal crop insurance program. Iowa is a major corn growing state in the US, making an ideal case study for considering alternative metrics of risk. We utilized the annual loss-cost ratios collected over the 1981–2017 period for the Central Crop Reporting District (CRD) in Iowa. The LCRs were summed at the county level and represent coverage of corn across all plans and coverage levels. This district is comprised of 12 counties: Boone, Dallas, Grundy, Hamilton, Hardin, Jasper, Marshall, Polk, Poweshiek, Story, Tama, and Webster. The relevant Iowa counties are illustrated in Figure 4. One would anticipate LCRs across these individual counties to be highly correlated (dependent). We would also anticipate a distribution that is heavily right-skewed, reflecting infrequent but very large loss events. Such events would typically correspond to poor weather such as drought or flood conditions, which is highly systemic in nature.

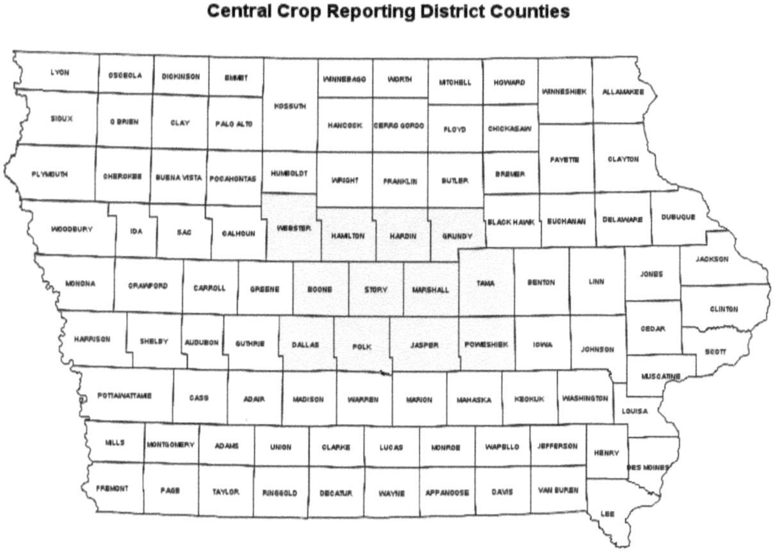

Figure 4. Iowa counties included in the analysis.

Figure 5 illustrates LCR values for each county. The values are suggestive of a high degree of positive skewness in the densities. The first step in our analysis involves fitting a parametric marginal density to each of the county-level LCR histories. We used the Akaike information criterion (AIC) to select the optimal density from among the following candidates—the Burr Type XII, the exponential, the gamma, the log-normal and the Weibull. We then considered chi-square and Kolmogorov–Smirnov (KS) goodness-of-fit tests to evaluate the optimal density. Table 4 presents a summary of the analysis of parametric densities. In every case except for one (Polk County), the optimal parametric density is a log-normal. In the case of Polk County, the Weibull distribution had the minimal AIC value. The goodness of fit tests support the selected distributions in every case.

Figure 6 presents the estimated cumulative and empirical distribution functions for each county's LCR. Figure 7 presents the estimated density functions. The right (positive) skewness associated with the LCR distributions is apparent and extreme, suggesting the potential for substantial VaR values. We evaluated VaR values for each county individually as well as for portfolios constructed from t and Gaussian copula estimates. Table 5 presents estimates of the t and Gaussian copulas. Especially notable in the copula estimates is the relatively small degrees of freedom parameter estimate of 9.33, which suggests considerable tail dependence in the individual densities. This also suggests superior fit for the *t* copula in that it nests a Gaussian model, which is implied for large values of the degree of freedom parameter. This tail dependence is apparent in the copula dependence matrix estimates in Table 5. The dependence is much stronger in the case of the *t* copula. To capture asymmetric dependence we also estimated Clayton and Gumbel copulas. As noted, one would not typically expect multivariate Archimedean copulas to provide a flexible model of dependence as they have a single parameter. The dependence parameters for the Clayton and Gumbel copulas were, respectively, 0.9021 (with a standard error of 0.0360) and 5.1684 (with a standard error of 0.1894).

We used the copula and marginal density estimates to consider two alternative portfolios comprised of LCR values from the 12 counties. The first (portfolio 1) weights each county by 1/12 and the second (portfolio 2) considers a weighted average of experience, using the 2017 liability weights for each county. The estimates were quite similar, reflecting the fact that the liability of the portfolio was somewhat evenly distributed across the 12 counties.

VaR/return-period estimates are presented for each county individually and for each portfolio in Table 6. Again, a 1 in 100 year return period represents the 99th percentile or VaR. The estimates are quite similar and reflect the high degree of spatial dependence inherent in the insurance experience. Insurers would expect to exceed LCR values of about 0.43–0.46 once every one-hundred years. The VaR values are slightly higher for the *t*-copula, reflecting the higher degree of tail dependence. In the loss ratio modeling, the worst case loss ratios were actually in the upper tail of the distribution. Thus we find that the Clayton copula, which can capture tail dependence only in the lower tail, results in much lower VaR estimates at almost all return periods except the one in five case. The results from the Gumbel copula are similar to those of the *t* and Gaussian copulas. The results from modeling of the loss cost ratios again indicate that the choice of the dependence structure can have an important effect on the total risk for the portfolio.

In sum, these empirical applications demonstrate several salient points related to modeling of extreme losses in crop insurance. Both the marginal model and dependence model matter. The loss history is characterized by several extreme losses that can dominate estimates of risk. But because crop yields are only measured once a year, and available data at the county level is limited, it can be difficult to accurately model the appropriate distributions using historical data. While these examples do not solve these fundamental issues, they do suggest additional research that may lead to better understanding of value-at-risk in crop insurance. However, they also highlight the need for continued investigation into the building blocks of the risk models: marginal distributions and dependence structures.

Table 4. Goodness of fit criteria for alternative loss-cost distributions.

County	Marginal	AIC	BIC	Chi-Square	p-Value	Result	AD	CvM	KS	Result
Boone	Logn	−235.7045	−232.4294	7.6808	0.1040	FTR	0.5154	0.0710	0.1018	FTR
Dallas	Logn	−199.1769	−195.9017	3.4220	0.4898	FTR	0.2307	0.0295	0.0976	FTR
Grundy	Logn	−250.9037	−247.6286	3.9948	0.4067	FTR	−0.2656	0.0666	0.0955	FTR
Hamilton	Logn	−229.7353	−226.4601	5.3251	0.2555	FTR	0.3589	0.0447	0.0916	FTR
Hardin	Logn	−216.4420	−213.1668	2.4182	0.6593	FTR	0.3615	0.0496	0.0927	FTR
Jasper	Logn	−214.9949	−211.7197	3.2070	0.5238	FTR	0.3755	0.0555	0.0886	FTR
Marshall	Logn	−229.5464	−226.2712	2.7523	0.6001	FTR	0.2472	0.0403	0.0929	FTR
Polk	Weibull	−187.4824	−184.2073	5.3221	0.2558	FTR	0.4572	0.0837	0.1548	FTR
Poweshiek	Logn	−210.9589	−207.6837	5.3440	0.2538	FTR	0.4152	0.0656	0.0983	FTR
Story	Logn	−228.5102	−225.2350	5.4218	0.2467	FTR	0.4333	0.0606	0.1031	FTR
Tama	Logn	−187.8575	−184.5823	2.0636	0.7241	FTR	0.2076	0.0289	0.0730	FTR
Webster	Logn	−226.3786	−223.1034	3.0586	0.5481	FTR	0.5438	0.0808	0.1213	FTR

'FTR' indicates that the distribution was not rejected at the $\alpha = 0.05$ or smaller level.

Table 5. t and Gaussian copula estimates.

County LCR	Boone	Dallas	Grundy	Hamilton	Hardin	Jasper	Marshall	Polk	Poweshiek	Story	Tama	Webster
Boone		0.9914	0.9753	0.9871	0.9783	0.9882	0.9874	0.9888	0.9822	0.9915	0.9835	0.9859
Dallas	0.8752		0.9614	0.9787	0.9719	0.9818	0.9796	0.9875	0.9773	0.9810	0.9748	0.9760
Grundy	0.6269	0.4647		0.9696	0.9780	0.9748	0.9768	0.9719	0.9646	0.9761	0.9734	0.9691
Hamilton	0.8359	0.7580	0.5911		0.9835	0.9830	0.9841	0.9789	0.9799	0.9886	0.9811	0.9872
Hardin	0.6871	0.6437	0.6444	0.8000		0.9675	0.9763	0.9714	0.9662	0.9792	0.9739	0.9753
Jasper	0.8106	0.7031	0.6581	0.8000	0.5692		0.9854	0.9909	0.9888	0.9869	0.9881	0.9781
Marshall	0.7695	0.6607	0.6199	0.7638	0.6230	0.7580		0.9809	0.9824	0.9855	0.9859	0.9819
Polk	0.7946	0.8384	0.5838	0.7372	0.6265	0.8730	0.7342		0.9834	0.9870	0.9799	0.9743
Poweshiek	0.7157	0.6539	0.4647	0.7031	0.5052	0.8132	0.7000	0.7919		0.9804	0.9857	0.9720
Story	0.8384	0.7250	0.6409	0.8480	0.6773	0.8480	0.7836	0.8527	0.7551		0.9853	0.9847
Tama	0.7189	0.5874	0.5120	0.7609	0.6472	0.8260	0.7695	0.7250	0.8235	0.7521		0.9721
Webster	0.7492	0.6773	0.5198	0.8310	0.6265	0.6054	0.6160	0.5692	0.5432	0.7095	0.4935	

Upper diagonal elements correspond to t copula parameters and lower (shaded) diagonals correspond to Gaussian copula. The t copula has 9.3286 degrees of freedom, with an associated standard error of 1.7004.

Figure 5. Empirical loss-cost data: 1981–2017.

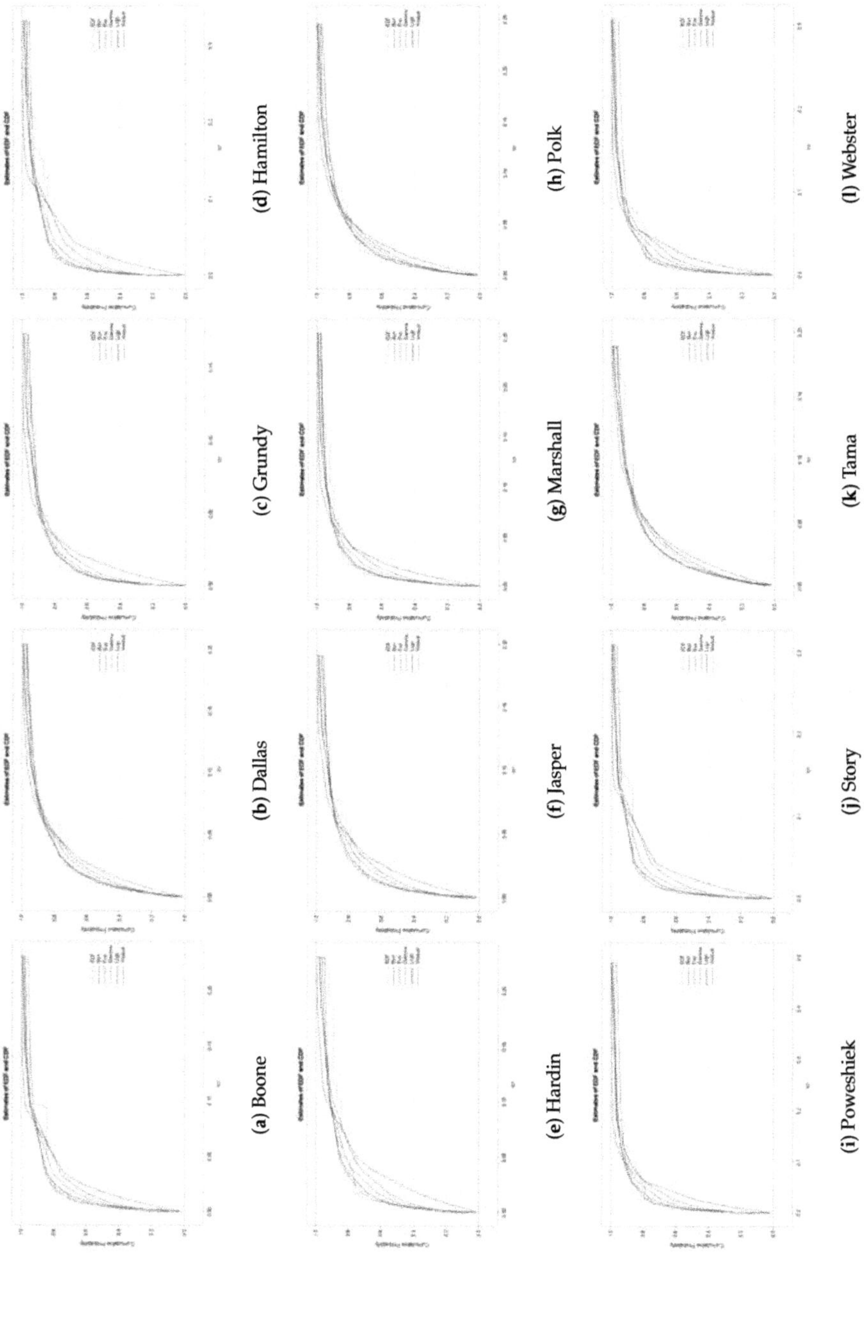

(a) Boone **(b)** Dallas **(c)** Grundy **(d)** Hamilton

(e) Hardin **(f)** Jasper **(g)** Marshall **(h)** Polk

(i) Poweshiek **(j)** Story **(k)** Tama **(l)** Webster

Figure 6. CDF Functions for Iowa County Loss-Cost Ratios.

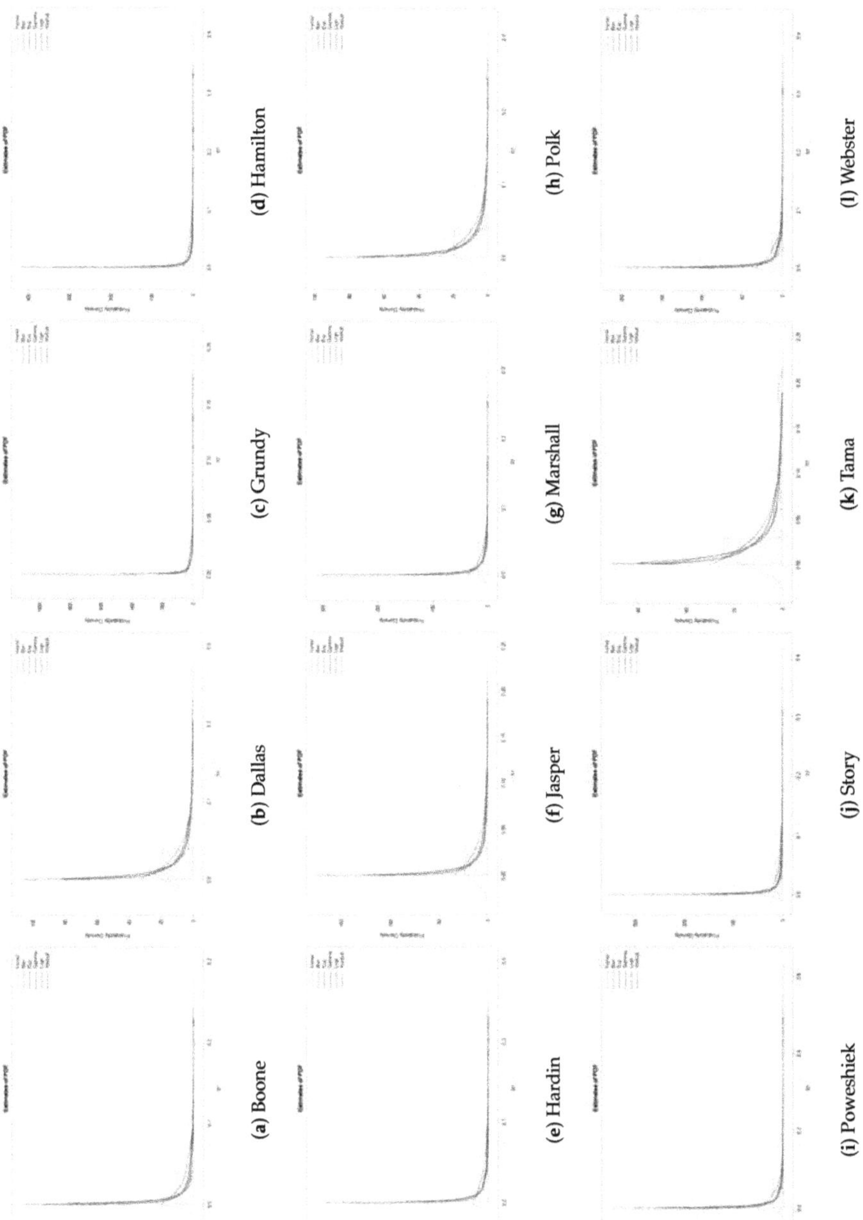

Figure 7. PDF Functions for Iowa County Loss-Cost Ratios.

Table 6. VaR/return period estimates from individual counties and portfolios.

Density	*t* Copula				Gaussian Copula				Clayton Copula				Gumbel Copula			
	1 in 100	1 in 50	1 in 10	1 in 5	1 in 100	1 in 50	1 in 10	1 in 5	1 in 100	1 in 50	1 in 10	1 in 5	1 in 100	1 in 50	1 in 10	1 in 5
Portfolio 1	0.43812	0.27920	0.08003	0.01131	0.43414	0.26790	0.07155	0.00824	0.22934	0.17712	0.08048	0.02090	0.42499	0.27078	0.06748	0.00830
Portfolio 2	0.46545	0.29400	0.08004	0.01074	0.44606	0.27757	0.07132	0.00770	0.24890	0.18486	0.08215	0.02005	0.43985	0.28077	0.06715	0.00779
Boone County, IA	0.37719	0.23366	0.05601	0.00574	0.31351	0.20307	0.05433	0.00593	0.32374	0.20598	0.05612	0.00588	0.31467	0.20361	0.05104	0.00588
Dallas County, IA	0.44318	0.28788	0.08190	0.01028	0.39576	0.25827	0.07993	0.01041	0.42397	0.24646	0.07936	0.01054	0.38156	0.25832	0.07464	0.01044
Grundy County, IA	0.57583	0.34552	0.06021	0.00388	0.54197	0.30180	0.05817	0.00395	0.44884	0.28862	0.05776	0.00392	0.52244	0.29673	0.05566	0.00390
Hamilton County, IA	0.84217	0.47607	0.07856	0.00496	0.71779	0.40096	0.08120	0.00515	0.82710	0.42288	0.08349	0.00513	0.70932	0.41233	0.07425	0.00511
Hardin County, IA	0.71455	0.40185	0.08318	0.00635	0.59942	0.37029	0.08031	0.00684	0.60625	0.36398	0.07669	0.00630	0.58270	0.34088	0.07709	0.00695
Jasper County, IA	0.42586	0.28374	0.07298	0.00796	0.40228	0.25647	0.06924	0.00785	0.45837	0.26377	0.06821	0.00778	0.38974	0.25304	0.06643	0.00797
Marshall County, IA	0.38769	0.26039	0.06036	0.00609	0.36363	0.21975	0.06003	0.00633	0.35996	0.24039	0.06057	0.00636	0.34208	0.21965	0.05539	0.00628
Polk County, IA	0.22775	0.18718	0.08725	0.01524	0.22851	0.17871	0.08526	0.01541	0.23674	0.18255	0.08589	0.01574	0.22151	0.17727	0.08187	0.01538
Poweshiek County, IA	0.62651	0.36814	0.08281	0.00743	0.54077	0.32652	0.08090	0.00780	0.51553	0.34094	0.08276	0.00797	0.49878	0.33102	0.07633	0.00758
Story County, IA	0.49854	0.28090	0.06481	0.00589	0.43580	0.26435	0.06522	0.00614	0.46184	0.27269	0.06719	0.00612	0.39927	0.26672	0.06006	0.00606
Tama County, IA	0.43648	0.28598	0.08735	0.01263	0.38722	0.25609	0.08625	0.01319	0.38582	0.25762	0.08349	0.01289	0.37834	0.25503	0.08220	0.01319
Webster County, IA	0.42491	0.24181	0.06379	0.00661	0.35799	0.23497	0.06233	0.00665	0.38993	0.24340	0.06269	0.00668	0.34738	0.23179	0.05799	0.00664

5. Conclusions

Accurate estimation of loss distributions is difficult when data is limited and theory provides little direction in the model space. Nonetheless, policymakers are often called upon to make decisions in this limited setting. Recent changes to farm legislation have prompted the RMA to make crop insurance available to a wider range of producers than ever before. Expansion of the program entails new actuarial developments for individual policies as well as construction of risk measures for the crop insurance portfolio. One such measure is value-at-risk; VaR gives the loss at high quantiles of the loss distribution. VaR is analogous to the return period or probable maximum loss as more commonly termed in insurance settings.

We examine VaR and PML under a number of alternative dependence scenarios. After modeling the marginal distributions of losses and loss-costs, we use independent, Gaussian, and t copulas to capture dependence among the factors in the portfolio. The algorithm of Embrechts et al. (2013) is used to estimate bounds on the VaR in what can be considered worst-case dependence scenarios. We find that there is a large degree of model risk arising from the dependence structure. Differences in the dependence models should be taken into account when making reserving decisions or forecasting future outlays for the crop insurance program.

These results also serve to highlight the intricacies involved in determining the degree of systemic risk inherent in crop insurance portfolios. Both the marginal distributions and dependence structure can exhibit non-stationary behavior; much attention has been paid to normalizing observed data so that loss distributions can be obtained. Unfortunately, researchers and actuaries must provide loss estimates in situations where the model space is large, but available data is small. New techniques for borrowing information across space have brought increased accuracy in ratemaking. A useful comparison to the top-down approach to VaR would be to compare with bottom-up modeling of the yield risk factors and see if the two methods arrive at roughly the same estimates of portfolio risk.

Several extensions could be made to the methods presented here. Accurate modeling of the marginal distributions is important in calculation of VaR. We have assumed that the distributions of losses and loss costs are stable over time. Moreover, we have not dealt with bounding of the loss distributions. A useful improvement would be to consider marginals that take into account bounds on losses, the possibility of zero inflation (zero loss can be common in crop insurance portfolios, especially at low coverage levels), and changes over time. Although not considered directly in this paper, it seems reasonable that a large portion of the model risk could arise from the marginal models.

Crop insurance is not only a major mechanism for agricultural risk management in the United States, but has become a worldwide phenomenon. Mahul and Stutley (2010) note an increasing reliance on government supported agricultural insurance in developing countries. Agricultural insurance programs, whether completely public, private, or a combination of the two, have a variety of reinsurance schemes. These can vary from full public reinsurance to private reinsurance to coinsurance pools and other arrangements. Policymakers considering public agricultural insurance as a policy tool need accurate estimates of the risk from such programs in making decisions. Value-at-risk is one risk measure for informing policy debates and the design of fiscally sustainable agricultural insurance programs.

Author Contributions: The authors contributed equally to this research.

Funding: This research did not receive any outside funding.

Conflicts of Interest: The authors declare no conflict of interest.

Abbreviations

The following abbreviations are used in this manuscript:

VaR	Value-at-Risk
SRA	Standard Reinsurance Agreement
PML	Probable Maximum Loss
RMA	Risk Management Agency
USDA	U.S. Department of Agriculture

References

Aas, Kjersti, and Giovanni Puccetti. 2014. Bounds on total economic capital: The DNB case study. *Extremes* 17: 693–715. [CrossRef]

Cleveland, William S., and Susan J. Devlin. 1988. Locally weighted regression: An approach to regression analysis by local fitting. *Journal of the American Statistical Association* 83: 596–610. [CrossRef]

Cope, E.W., G. Mignola, G. Antonini, and R. Ugoccioni. 2009. Challenges in measuring operational risk from loss data. *Journal of Operational Risk* 4: 3–27. [CrossRef]

Elaine Hungerford, Ashley, and Barry Goodwin. 2014. Big assumptions for small samples in crop insurance. *Agricultural Finance Review* 74: 477–91. [CrossRef]

Embrechts, Paul, Giovanni Puccetti, and Ludger Rüschendorf. 2013. Model uncertainty and VaR aggregation. *Journal of Banking & Finance* 37: 2750–64.

Frees, Edward W., and Ping Wang. 2006. Copula credibility for aggregate loss models. *Insurance: Mathematics and Economics* 38: 360–73. [CrossRef]

Gallagher, Paul. 1986. US corn yield capacity and probability: Estimation and forecasting with nonsymmetric disturbances. *North Central Journal of Agricultural Economics* 8: 109–22. [CrossRef]

Goodwin, Barry K., and Ashley Hungerford. 2014. Copula-based models of systemic risk in US agriculture: Implications for crop insurance and reinsurance contracts. *American Journal of Agricultural Economics* 97: 879–96. [CrossRef]

Goodwin, Barry K., and Alan P. Ker. 1998. Nonparametric estimation of crop yield distributions: Implications for rating group-risk crop insurance contracts. *American Journal of Agricultural Economics* 80: 139–53. [CrossRef]

Hayes, Dermot J., Sergio H. Lence, and Chuck Mason. 2003. Could the government manage its exposure to crop reinsurance risk? *Agricultural Finance Review* 63: 127–42. [CrossRef]

Holly Wang, H., and Hao Zhang. 2003. On the possibility of a private crop insurance market: A spatial statistics approach. *Journal of Risk and Insurance* 70: 111–24. [CrossRef]

Hurvich, Clifford M., Jeffrey S. Simonoff, and Chih-Ling Tsai. 1998. Smoothing parameter selection in nonparametric regression using an improved Akaike information criterion. *Journal of the Royal Statistical Society: Series B (Statistical Methodology)* 60: 271–93. [CrossRef]

Ker, Alan P., and Keith Coble. 2003. Modeling conditional yield densities. *American Journal of Agricultural Economics* 85: 291–304. [CrossRef]

Ker, Alan P., and Pat McGowan. 2000. Weather-based adverse selection and the US crop insurance program: The private insurance company perspective. *Journal of Agricultural and Resource Economics* 25: 386–410.

Ker, Alan P., Tor N. Tolhurst, and Yong Liu. 2015. Bayesian Estimation of Possibly Similar Yield Densities: Implications for Rating Crop Insurance Contracts. *American Journal of Agricultural Economics* 98: 360–82. [CrossRef]

Mahul, Olivier, and Charles J. Stutley. 2010. *Government Support to Agricultural Insurance: Challenges and Options for Developing Countries*. Washington, DC: The World Bank.

Mainik, Georg, and Paul Embrechts. 2013. Diversification in heavy-tailed portfolios: Properties and pitfalls. *Annals of Actuarial Science* 7: 26–45. [CrossRef]

Nikoloulopoulos, Aristidis K., Harry Joe, and Haijun Li. 2012. Vine copulas with asymmetric tail dependence and applications to financial return data. *Computational Statistics & Data Analysis* 56: 3659–73.

Odening, Martin, and Zhiwei Shen. 2014. Challenges of insuring weather risk in agriculture. *Agricultural Finance Review* 74: 188–99. [CrossRef]

Okhrin, Ostap, Martin Odening, and Wei Xu. 2013. Systemic weather risk and crop insurance: The case of China. *Journal of Risk and Insurance* 80: 351–72. [CrossRef]

Okhrin, Ostap, Yarema Okhrin, and Wolfgang Schmid. 2013. On the structure and estimation of hierarchical Archimedean copulas. *Journal of Econometrics* 173: 189–204. [CrossRef]

Ozaki, Vitor A., and Ralph S. Silva. 2009. Bayesian ratemaking procedure of crop insurance contracts with skewed distribution. *Journal of Applied Statistics* 36: 443–52. [CrossRef]

Park, Eunchun, B. Wade Brorsen, and Ardian Harri. 2018. Using Bayesian Kriging for Spatial Smoothing in Crop Insurance Rating. *American Journal of Agricultural Economics* 101: 330–51. [CrossRef]

Patton, Andrew J. 2009 Copula—Based models for financial time series. In *Handbook of Financial Time Series*. Berlin: Springer, pp. 767–85.

Porth, Lysa, Milton Boyd, and Jeffrey Pai. 2016. Reducing Risk Through Pooling and Selective Reinsurance Using Simulated Annealing: An Example from Crop Insurance. *The Geneva Risk and Insurance Review* 41: 163–91. [CrossRef]

Puccetti, Giovanni, and Ludger Rüschendorf. 2012. Computation of sharp bounds on the distribution of a function of dependent risks. *Journal of Computational and Applied Mathematics* 236: 1833–40. [CrossRef]

Puccetti, Giovanni. 2013. Sharp bounds on the expected shortfall for a sum of dependent random variables. *Statistics & Probability Letters* 83: 1227–32.

Ramsey, A. Ford, Barry K. Goodwin, and Sujit K. Ghosh. 2019. How High the Hedge: Relationships between Prices and Yields in the Federal Crop Insurance Program. *Journal of Agricultural and Resource Economics* 44, forthcoming.

Risk Management Agency. 2018. Summary of Business. Available online: https://prodwebnlb.rma.usda.gov/apps/SummaryOfBusiness (accessed on 3 January 2019).

Sherrick, Bruce J., Fabio C. Zanini, Gary D. Schnitkey, and Scott H. Irwin. 2004. Crop insurance valuation under alternative yield distributions. *American Journal of Agricultural Economics* 86: 406–19. [CrossRef]

Sklar, Abe 1959. Distribution Functions in n Dimensions and Their Margins. *Statistics Publications, University of Paris* 8: 229–31.

Tack, Jesse B., and David Ubilava. 2013. The effect of El Niño Southern Oscillation on US corn production and downside risk. *Climatic Change* 121: 689–700. [CrossRef]

Tamakoshi, Go, and Shigeyuki Hamori. 2014. The conditional dependence structure of insurance sector credit default swap indices. *The North American Journal of Economics and Finance* 30: 122–32. [CrossRef]

Tolhurst, Tor N., and Alan P. Ker. 2014. On technological change in crop yields. *American Journal of Agricultural Economics* 97: 137–58. [CrossRef]

Yang, Lu, Xiao Jing Cai, Mengling Li, and Shigeyuki Hamori. 2015. Modeling dependence structures among international stock markets: Evidence from hierarchical Archimedean copulas. *Economic Modelling* 51: 308–14. [CrossRef]

Zhu, Ying, Barry K. Goodwin, and Sujit K. Ghosh. 2011. Modeling yield risk under technological change: Dynamic yield distributions and the US crop insurance program. *Journal of Agricultural and Resource Economics* 36: 192–210.

Journal of
Risk and Financial Management

MDPI

Article

Herding in Smart-Beta Investment Products

Eduard Krkoska [1] and Klaus Reiner Schenk-Hoppé [1,2,*]

[1] Department of Economics, School of Social Sciences, University of Manchester, Manchester M13 9PL, UK; eduard.krkoska@student.manchester.ac.uk

[2] Department of Finance, NHH–Norwegian School of Economics, 5045 Bergen, Norway

* Correspondence: klaus.schenk-hoppe@manchester.ac.uk

Received: 26 February 2019; Accepted: 18 March 2019; Published: 21 March 2019

Abstract: We highlight herding of investors as one major risk factor that is typically ignored in statistical approaches to portfolio modelling and risk management. Our survey focuses on smart-beta investing where such methods and investor herding seem particularly relevant but its negative effects have not yet come to the fore. We point out promising and novel approaches of modelling herding risk which merit empirical analysis. This financial economists' perspective supplements the vast statistical exploration of implementing factor strategies.

Keywords: herding; factor investing; risk

JEL Classification: G12; G14; G40

---

1. Introduction

Factor-investing is the latest craze among asset managers. As most elegantly put by Bender et al. (2013, p. 2), a factor is "any characteristic relating a group of securities that is important in explaining their return and risk."

Investing according to factors, or "smart-beta" investing, began with Fama and French's (1992, 1993) Nobel-prize winning observation that a substantial proportion of equity returns can be explained by just three factors. As these and other factors yielding excess returns were discovered and gained significant academic attention, their use became adopted by financial managers, who promoted products such as the now popular smart-beta Exchange Traded Funds (ETFs). Practitioners claim that proper use of smart-beta tilts can provide around double the Sharpe ratio of a standard market-value weighted portfolio (Amenc et al. 2014). Famous hedge funds such as AQR Capital Management and Dimensional Fund Advisors are leading proponents of factor investing. The factor-investment industry has seen dramatic annual growth rates of 30% in the assets under management (AUM) in the past five years and at present manages more than $1 trn according to the Economist (2017, 2018). A Financial Times Stock Exchange (FTSE) report (Russell 2018, p. 6) finds that the percentage of investors explicitly using smart-beta strategies nearly doubled between 2015 and 2017. There is also a proliferation of factors used in such strategies. Wiggins (2018) reports there are now more than 300 different factors with about 40 factors being introduced annually. Cochrane (2011) famously referred to this as a "factor zoo".

As fund managers continuously attempt to outperform other funds, their factor strategies become more complex as well as controversial. This occurred firstly with the implementation of multi-factor strategies, which become more complex as there are meaningful correlations between variables. For example, Asness et al. (2013) mention the significant effects of this to Sharpe ratios (Sharpe 1964, 1994). More recently, the debate is with regards to dynamic multi-factor strategies, where the factor weights are continually adjusted. Sundstrom (2018) defends its use by praising its ability to adjust throughout the business cycle, however the selectivity of the asset allocations hints that the investment style lean further towards active and away from passive.

The current paper aims to draw the attention of researchers and practitioners concerned with portfolio modelling and risk management to the potential risks emanating from investors herding into factor-strategies. We stress that this is a financial economists' perspective which contrasts with the vast statistical exploration of implementing factor strategies. For example, Allen and McAleer (2018) provided a comprehensive overview of the "Choosing factors" paper by Fama and French (2018). Despite the detailed statistical insights, the paper, along with many others which concern factors, does not mention risks of herding in popular strategies.

In this paper, we highlight a number of formal frameworks in which herding risk can be modelled as the risk emanating from changes in investor expectations, sluggish price movements or large and sudden cash flows. All of these are mostly unexplored, face difficulties in estimation, and are put forward as open problems for empiricists.

Financial history is littered with fashion turned to bust. (In)famous examples are the 1978 crash following herding in portfolio insurance, the dot-com bubble in 2000 and the more recent 2008 sub-prime lending crisis, all examples of crashes preceded by investors crowding in the financial markets (Chincarini 2012, pp. 2–3). In our view, factors are at present a fashion (with innovation and creation of factors for the sake of generating business) and the lack of reflection that herding in innovative products is often followed by a downfall.

2. Herding in Financial Markets

Bikhchandani and Sharma's (2000, p. 4) review defines herd behaviour as: "an obvious intent by investors to copy the behaviour of other investors". It can be viewed as a rational (Devenow and Welch 1996) or irrational (Welch 2000) bias that investors unwittingly succumb to. Herd behaviour is well documented in financial economics; for example, Wermers (1999) found herding behaviour from mutual funds, especially in certain categories of equity such as smaller firms and growth firms; Graham (1999) and De Bondt and Forbes (1999) found empirical evidence that financial analysts herd, with excessive agreement in their forecasting; and Roider and Voskort (2016) found evidence of investor herding in a laboratory experiment where reputational incentives arise.

2.1. Risks of Herding

In a seminal model of rational herding (Banerjee 1992), a decision maker considers the behaviour of previous decision makers who may have important information; this theoretical framework finds that the behaviour of optimising agents is, in fact, to herd. This implies that if, for example, specialised institutions know that factors yield significant premia, then retail investors may follow their choices and herd in smart-beta products.

Using game theoretic principles, Caginalp et al. (2001) asserted that for the trading price to reflect fundamental value agents rely not only on their own optimisation, but on that of others. Once an overvaluation is observed, agents will have less certainty about the optimisation processes of other agents and may build on the trend, conditional on having enough cash. Once the excess cash and the upwards trend dissipates, the bubble can collapse in an abrupt and unpredictable manner.

Computational models have also been applied to determine the outcomes of herding behaviour. Duffy (2006) surveyed these types of models, which can involve *reinforcement* where higher yielding assets are purchased in larger quantity, whereas the reverse applies for poorly performing assets. Alternatively, *belief-based* learning models allow agents to form expectations about the strategies of other players in the market and then form their own strategy. The models can range from very unsophisticated expectation formation to perfect rationality.

Applying a model of agents with near zero intelligence, Duffy and Ünver (2006) found that this can stimulate asset price bubbles and crashes. Their results also match some features of experimental data from laboratory experiments, reinforcing the model's relevance to reality.

Experimental evidence from Smith et al. (1988) finds that assets whose previous dividend payoffs were known would, on significant occasion, have their price inflated above fundamental value and then crash. This result held when the test subjects were experienced traders, although with a lower frequency. When the subjects participated repeatedly in the test, their deviations from intrinsic value became less pronounced as they learnt from the feedback. The test demonstrates that significant bubbles may emerge, even with experienced traders, if it is difficult to learn from feedback as is the case with new and evolving strategies.

In another experiment, Sgroi (2003) allowed for individuals' decisions to be endogenous, allowing them to take actions when they choose to, rather than forcing sequential decisions. This provides a more realistic experimental framework. Nevertheless, the choices of the first players alone were enough to convince others to herd, despite the option to wait and gather further information.

The literature clearly describes the risks that arise from herding in assets, whether it be return reduction or, more remarkably, asset price bubbles and resulting crashes. These kinds of situations are famous in financial history as the herding was not realised until it was too late.

2.2. History of Herding

In the 1987 financial bubble, which escalated far enough to crash suddenly, Norris (2012) reported that the Dow Jones index "lost 23% of its value". Portfolio insurance is often blamed, with the claim that it gave investors confidence that, if prices were exorbitant, they could exercise their insurance with minimal consequences. If stock prices fell, the institutions' computers would automatically sell futures of the market index, hence offsetting the loss of market decline. This dynamic hedging process was discussed in detail by Ho et al. (2013). Knowing that the insurance was available to them, large institutions watched market prices soar without considering the potential consequences of a large price drop.

What was seemingly not accounted for was that not all investors could simultaneously benefit from trading around a common market risk (Leland 1980, p. 581). To exercise the insurance and sell the futures, another investor must take the other side of the trade. Once stock prices began falling, a significant number of institutions began selling the futures. To sell such a large quantity of futures, their prices had to be driven down. Those buying futures also sold the underlying index to hedge their position, driving down prices further and causing further sales of the future contracts; this eventually resulted in the crash.

Whilst portfolio insurance should theoretically provide investors with further methods of optimising their trading strategy, rather than causing a crisis, Shiller (1988, p. 291) discussed "portfolio insurance as a fad". As this technological advancement itself should not have been sufficient to cause the stock market crash, Shiller discussed overconfident institutional investors, hinting at the acknowledgement of an overpriced market, contributed to by herding in portfolio insurance. A different model was proposed by Jacklin et al. (1992), where the market underestimates the amount of dynamic hedging being utilised, where in fact it is a fad, allowing asset prices to rise. It is only once the market realises the amount of herding in portfolio insurance that it reevaluates its asset pricing relative to fundamentals.

Another event of relevance to present-day smart-beta investing is the 2007 "quant meltdown", as discussed by Rennison and Wigglesworth (2017), whereby the renowned quantitative investment strategies failed, resulting in a financial crash. Whilst the use of these systematic strategies provides several benefits and opportunities, such as return enhancement and risk management, the applications of quant investing by large institutions was highly backed with leverage. There are debates on the exact root of the quant crisis, however there is some consensus that the combination of extreme leverage and crowding in the same trades led to it.

Whilst smart-beta funds are a quantitatively based method of generating returns, the methods are now much more diverse than a decade ago, with a plethora of alternative risk premia spanning asset classes and financial tools such as leverage, short-selling and derivatives and based around both, or either, return enhancement and risk management. This should reduce the risk of herding in the same strategies. However, in terms of implementation, it is likely for several large funds to be based around the same traditional factors, using less complex financial tools. In this case, there is a distinct possibility that these trades are, or will become, overly crowded.

This prospect was mentioned by Brightman (2011, p. 1) who argued that the quant meltdown "deserves more attention by today's investors", than the 2008 financial crisis, as it uncovers the risks that quantitative strategies entail. Relevant to today's fashion in smart-beta products, Brightman (2011, p. 2) claimed that "early success and clever marketing attracts large flows into the funds, which, in turn, drives the prices of securities held by these funds to unsustainable extremes".

Despite the striking similarities of herding in financial history with present-day smart-beta investing, the topic is often bypassed by those analysing the statistical properties of the investment style. The purpose of this paper is to highlight herding as a risk factor which ought to be considered and further investigated by financial economists and mathematicians.

3. Smart-Beta Strategies

Asset allocations based on factor strategies, most notably smart-beta Exchange Traded Funds (ETFs), are marketed as a combination of both active and passive management. Fund managers advertise their products as having the benefits of active strategies with the lower costs of passive index buying. ETFs have traditionally been a popular vehicle for passive investment, tracking an index and traded on a stock-exchange, with significantly lower management costs and more liquidity than active management (Foucher and Gray 2014).

Active fund managers attempt to outperform the market for which they charge a higher fee. French (2008) concluded that the typical investor, under some assumptions, would be better off by switching to a passive portfolio. Furthermore, examining rising fees charged for active management, Malkiel (2013, p. 108) concluded that, "it is hard to think of any other service that is priced at such a high proportion of value".

3.1. Foundations of Factor Investing

The Capital Asset Pricing Model (CAPM) theory of linear market returns has significant documentation of anomalies. Early evidence can go back to Basu (1977), who found that portfolios with low P/E ratios earned higher returns than those with higher ratios, on both a risk-adjusted and absolute basis. The now famous size effect, where risk-adjusted returns on small stocks were higher than those on large stocks, was first reported by Banz (1981). Reinganum (1981) showed that the outperformance related to both the P/E ratio and size was not only short-term, but persisting over six months. The book-to-market, or "value", factor has also been well established (Rosenberg et al. 1985), whereby the investor buys stocks with a high book-value to market-value ratio and sells stocks with a low ratio. The momentum strategy, buying stocks with recent high returns and selling those with low returns, was found to yield significant excess returns by Jegadeesh and Titman (1993). DeBondt and Thaler (1985) found a similar effect in timeseries: portfolios of prior "losers" tend to outperform prior "winners". The phenomenon is not short-term, as it is after thirty-six months that losing stocks earn significantly more than winners. These findings led to the first influential extension of the three-factor model by Carhart (1997), who added the short-term momentum effect as a fourth variable.

Seasonal anomalies are also examined. Thaler (1987b) found that stocks earned significantly higher returns in January than in other months. Thaler (1987a) found "Weekend, Holiday, Turn of the Month, and Intraday Effects". Thaler put forward several behavioural explanations for seasonality, such as the timings of both good and bad news being announced. He also wrote that most proposed explanations have been tested and rejected.

The seminal work of Fama and French (1993) identified five common risk factors that explain returns on both stocks and bonds. Making up the famous three-factor model, the stock factors are market risk, size and book-to-market value, whereas factors related to bond returns are default risk and a factor related to maturity. Doskov et al. (2016) found evidence, however, that aggregate risks in the macroeconomy, such as growth and volatility, not only have significant explanatory power but also dominate the size and value factors.

3.2. The Factor Zoo

As multifactor explanations of asset returns were further investigated in academia, Cochrane (2011) famously proclaimed that we now "have a zoo of new factors". One of the newly discovered factors was investment. Titman et al. (2004) found that firms which engaged in significant capital investment expenditures would experience lower stock returns for the next five years. Novy-Marx (2013) found that profitability, the ratio of gross profits to assets, was as good at explaining cross-sectional stock returns as the value factor. This strategy essentially buys productive stocks and sells unproductive stocks.

One of the latest asset pricing models is the Fama and French (2015) five-factor model, an extension of the three-factor model (Fama and French 1996). The extended model now includes an operating profitability factor; stocks with robust profitability minus those with weak profitability. The final factor is investment; stocks with conservative investment minus aggressive investment stocks. An important result of Fama and French (2015, p. 10) is that the "five-factor model outperforms the Fama and French three-factor model on all metrics and it generally outperforms other models". It was estimated to explain 71–94% of cross-sectional expected returns variation for the portfolios examined. Despite this, the authors observed that the value factor was made redundant in this new model, with its explanatory power being captured by the other variables.

Factor investing has become so widespread that Johnson et al. (2016, p. 3) reported that, "as of 31 December 2015, there were 950 such products that seek to either improve return or alter risk relative to more-traditional market benchmarks". The number of smart-beta products today is even higher.

3.3. Implementation

While we are concerned with conscious smart-beta strategies, it is important to point out that unconscious factor investing is possible. An early example of exposure to systematic factors is illustrated by examining one of the largest institutional investors globally, Norway's government pension fund Norges Bank Investment Management (NBIM) with about $1 trillion under management in 2019. An analysis of the fund's returns by Ang et al. (2009, p. 16) found that a significant part of the active return was "linked to a number of well-recognized systematic factors". In fact, when looking at the factor exposure of active returns, for both fixed-income assets and equity, about 70% of those returns were explained by 10 commonly known factors. Following these reports, NBIM took a more conscientious approach to factors in their investments (NBIM 2009).

Robeco (2018), an international asset management firm with EUR 165 billion AUM, EUR 55 billion based on Quant models, provides a "Guide to factor investing in equity markets", describing a spectrum of smart-beta strategies, from low managerial discretion to high. A low discretion investment could be a single factor ETF, whereas a high discretion investment could be bespoke to the investors preferences. Objectives can include both return enhancement and risk reduction. The different objectives factor investing can take is reflected in the array of smart-beta ETFs available for purchase. For example, they vary in asset class, with some utilising fixed income and others currencies. There is also geographic variation, using emerging markets for example.

Many details of implementation are fiercely debated amongst practitioners, such as factor timing (see, for example, Robeco (2017), Asness (2016), and Arnott et al. (2016)). Another implementation challenge is multifactor allocations, for which Asness et al. (2015, p. 45) found evidence that, with value, momentum, carry and defensive strategies, "combining all four style premia into one portfolio effectively doubles the maximum Sharpe ratio obtainable from any single-style strategy".

4. Risk in Smart-Beta Portfolios

There is a plethora of work detailing statistical insights on smart-beta strategies (for example, Allen and McAleer (2018)). This section describes the implications of herding, promising models of herding risk and data snooping in smart-beta.

4.1. Evidence of Smart-Beta Herding

An explanation of why herd behaviour might be prevalent in smart-beta funds is the (ir)rationality of managers to follow other managers' decisions. Scharfstein and Stein (1990) discussed how reputational concern could incentivise ignoring private information; if they are wrong it is easily justifiable, as the others were wrong also. Scharfstein and Stein (1990, p. 466) called this the "sharing the blame effect". Similarly, Zwiebel (1995) found there are disincentives to use innovations which dominate the industry norm. In fact, it may now be the case that not utilising factor tilts situate managers outside of the norm. There is importance in the reputations of innovators (Katz and Shapiro 1985). Weaker reputation firms favour product compatibility with the high reputation ones. Market leaders being followed in their innovations can be related to big funds' use of factor strategies (such as NBIM discussed above) with smaller funds jumping on the bandwagon. This is especially likely as the early literature on smart-beta was overwhelmingly positive.

Taking a less rational approach to herding, early experimental tests about group thinking (Asch 1955) found that test subjects were highly suggestible to the answer of the majority. Lone managers may not want to disagree with the larger group, potentially on the belief that the group must be correct or that they do not want to be viewed as managers who are failing to utilise the best practice. Asness (2015) mentioned that one risk of smart-beta investing when strategies are well known, as is the case for many traditional factors, is that they may be especially "painful" to the investor in bad times. In bad times, for example, all investors can move cash to reduce this factor bet. The shifting of such a large volume of cash is strikingly similar to our previous example of the Quant crisis. When investors move cash flows synonymously the high volume of trade can in itself be thought of as a risk factor; the risk that in bad times there is a crash on a factor strategy. Asness (2015, p. 2), in fact, compared the "pain" in bad times to be something as bad as career ending.

We provide a formal framework which includes the flow risk of herding in smart-beta, however what this paper highlights is the lack of empirical work in measuring this herding risk. We suggest further empirical research in estimating this.

4.2. Promising Modelling Approaches

Herding as extreme capital movements. Herding in the overall market, investment strategies or specific products can be interpreted as extreme flows of capital. Asness (2015) put forward this view in his narrative of how alpha (excess returns due to investor skill) turns into beta (a risk premium that everyone can reap). The increased volatility due to the possibility of extreme flows of capital, in particular the drawdown, should be a risk factor and thus priced in an efficient market.

Empirical analysis could start from Carhart's (1997) four-factor model

$$R_i - R_f = \alpha_i + \beta(R_M - R_f) + b_s SMB + b_v HML + b_m UMD + \epsilon_i \quad (1)$$

and add a risk factor related to capital flows. Such a factor would have to measure the correlation of a specific strategy i's capital flows and variations in the total market capitalisation.

Several issues in estimating this risk seem to be relevant. First, one should expect an asymmetry between the pattern of outflows and inflows of capital. Just as for the overall stock market, downturns tend to be more rapid than upturns (for example, see Terrones et al. (2011) and Graham (2006, p. 69)), which are particularly pronounced for specialised firms (Opler and Titman 1994). When focusing on a particular investment strategy, one has to disentangle its capital flow and the overall flow in or out of the market. More poetically, one has to account for the old adage "the tide raises all boats". Second, extreme flows are rare events. It is unlikely that flows on most days are distinguishable from noise and thus constitute diversifiable risk, which is not rewarded with a risk premium. Perhaps lessons from catastrophe insurance (see Michel-Kerjan (2010)) can be useful to define a suitable factor for the model in Equation (1). Third, the relation between capital flows and the existing risk factors needs to be assessed. For instance, a momentum strategy reaping the UMD premium should suffer from larger inflows as it bids up prices on the long leg and depresses those on the short leg, and the reverse for outflows. However, outflows are highly dependent on past performance (reference here), which creates another estimation problem in properly disentangling dependent and independent variables.

Herding as toxicity. Research on the toxicity of order flows by Easley et al. (1996) might hold useful lessons for empirical research on risk premium due to herding. Their research considers the pricing behaviour of market makers in response to imbalances in the flow of buy and sell market orders and to changes in the frequency of order arrival.

In this type of model, traders may have information on future stock prices (news) but market makers, who set bid and ask prices and offer liquidity, have not. In an efficient market, the price of a stock at time t is given by

$$E[S_i \mid t] = P_{no\ news}(t)S_i^* + P_{bad\ news}(t)\underline{S}_i + P_{good\ news}(t)\overline{S}_i$$

where bad news means the next period's stock price will be lower than today ($\underline{S}_i$) and good news the opposite ($\overline{S}_i$). The value $S_i^* = \delta\underline{S}_i + (1-\delta)\overline{S}_i$ is the value of the stock before any trading. The market maker also has ex ante beliefs $P_.$ on the probability of future outcomes. These beliefs will change in response to the observed order flow. If market-making is perfectly competitive, then bid and ask prices are set such that market makers' profits are zero:

$$\text{Bid}(t) = E[S_i \mid t] - \frac{\mu P_{bad\ news}(t)}{\epsilon + \mu P_{bad\ news}(t)}\left(E[S_i \mid t] - \underline{S}_i\right)$$

$$\text{Ask}(t) = E[S_i \mid t] + \frac{\mu P_{good\ news}(t)}{\epsilon + \mu P_{good\ news}(t)}\left(\overline{S}_i - E[S_i \mid t]\right)$$

where μ is probability that an informed trader arrives and ϵ is probability that an uninformed order arrives. Often in the literature the latter are called noise traders or liquidity traders, i.e., their trade does not contain information but occurs for exogenous reasons. Calibrating these models is a tricky exercise. However, the main underlying idea is simple. If the orders execute much more often on one side of the market than the other (compared to the marker makers' expectations), then bid and ask can move dramatically. The order flow is toxic.

These models can be interpreted as looking at herding on a micro-scale. It could therefore be possible to carry out related analyses on a macro-scale. Most recently the model (which does not capture today's limit order book markets for stocks) has been modified for a world with high-frequency trading (Easley et al. 2012) and also been applied to the 2010 flash crash (Easley et al. 2011). On the most extreme end of toxicity, one might place rare events (Nassim Taleb's famous black swan). Methods from extreme value theory, such as those highlighted by Singh et al. (2013) in connection with modelling the market events around the 2008 financial crisis, remain unexplored for their potential in modelling sudden shifts in capital allocations. Using these types of models to combine herding and risk premia on capital flows might be a challenging but interesting and fruitful future research problem.

Herding in agent-based models. Agent-based modelling forms a class of approaches that explicitly aim to study herding and market overreaction. There is a wide variety of theoretical approaches (Hens and Schenk-Hoppé 2009) as well as computational methods (Tesfatsion and Judd 2006) for these models. The models that seem to have the greatest potential for combining herding and risk premia are those dealing explicitly with expectations dynamics (for their potential to generate booms and busts) and those using sluggish adjustment of prices (for their potential to generate fat tails and volatility clustering).

Hommes (2013) and Hommes and Wagener (2009) presented many agent-based models in which the price of a risky asset is driven by expectations. In a model with one risky and one risk-free asset, economic agents with mean-variance utility and heterogeneous expectations about future price movements interact. The market price is determined in each period by finding a price that gives zero aggregate excess demand. The price of the risky asset is given by

$$p_t = \frac{1}{1+r}\left[\sum_{h=1}^{H} n_{ht}E_{ht}\left(p_{t+1}+d_{t+1}\right) - a\sigma^2 z^s\right]$$

where r is the risk-free rate, there are H different types economic agents, each type has individual expectations $E_{ht}\left(p_{t+1}+d_{t+1}\right)$ over the next period price p_{t+1} and the expected dividend d_{t+1}. The parameter a is a common risk aversion against variance, σ^2 is the volatility of the risky asset and z^s is the exogenous total supply (shares issued).

Herding in the model coincides with sudden shifts in expectations. It is a demanding task to make this type of model work empirically. First, one has to devise a more parsimonious specification of expectations. Second, if herding were partly predictable, one could use futures and option prices to extract expectations. In general, it is unclear at present which data would be useful in deriving these expectations.

There has been progress along these lines in simpler models (e.g., by Lux (2009) and Chiarella et al. (2009)). These models are based on sluggish adjustment of prices. Consider for instance the simple dynamics of gradual price adjustment and expectations in (Lux 2009, Equations (3.10)–(3.13)). In this continuous-time model (simplified here), the price of an asset adjusts as

$$p_t' = \lambda(P_f - p_t + \pi)$$

where λ measures the speed at which the price reacts to changes in demand, P_f is the price expected by fundamental investors, and π are the expectations of trend-following investors. The expectations of the latter evolve as:

$$\pi_t' = c(p_t' - \pi)$$

where c measures the aggressiveness of trend-followers. Alfarano et al. (2005) calibrated such a type of model to stock market and commodity indexes. They could fit fat tails of the return distribution and volatility clustering using a herding mechanism similar to Kirman (1993). To the best of our knowledge, there has not been any work done in the direction of combining that framework with the analysis of risk premia.

Financial market models with explicit capital flows. Another class of heterogeneous agent models that seems to have potential for calibration and the extraction of a herding risk factor was given by Hens and Schenk-Hoppé (2018). The view put forward there is to model financial markets explicitly in terms of the investment strategies present in the market and their wealth under management as well as a flow of capital between these strategies.

The basic model proceeds in two steps: (1) dynamics consisting of portfolio choice, random payoffs, determination of market prices and realised gains and losses; and (2) a flow of capital based on difference in realised returns or other characteristics. There are K different dividend-bearing assets, a risk-free bond (labelled asset number 0, with net interest rate r), and I different investment strategies with initial capital w_0^i. The strategies are written in terms of proportions

$$\lambda_t^i = (\lambda_{t,0}^i, ..., \lambda_{t,K}^i)$$

Asset prices are endogenous, determined by demand and supply:

$$p_{t,k} = (1-c)\sum_{i=1}^{I}\lambda_{t,k}^i w_t^i \tag{2}$$

where c can be interpreted as a consumption rate. The portfolio at time t is therefore given by

$$\theta^i_{t,k} = (1-c)\lambda^i_{t,k} w^i_t / p_{t,k}$$

and the bond investment is $\theta^i_{t,0} = (1-c)\lambda^i_{t,0} w^i_t$. The random dynamics of wealth is obtained as

$$w^i_{t+1} = \sum_{k=1}^{K} [p_{t+1,k} + D_{t+1,k}]\theta^i_{t,k} + (1+r)\theta^i_{t,0}. \tag{3}$$

with $D_{t+1,k}$ the dividend paid to shareholders. w^i_{t+1} comprises the wealth under management of strategy i after asset payoffs (dividends and interest) are received and capital gains or losses occurred.

Now, reallocation of capital happens. The amounts are subject to a process of withdrawal and redistribution (typically depended on difference in realised performance). Denoting by π^i_t the proportion of capital withdrawn from strategy i and by q^i_t the proportion of the total capital available for reallocation to flow to strategy j, the new distribution of wealth across the strategies is given by:

$$W^i_{t+1} = (1-\pi^i_t) w^i_{t+1} + q^i_t \sum_{i=1}^{I} \pi^i_t w^i_{t+1} \tag{4}$$

All of these equations can be combined in one stochastic non-linear dynamic model as:

$$\begin{aligned} W_{t+1} = & \Big[\mathrm{Id} - (1-c)\Theta_t \Lambda_{t+1}\Big(\mathrm{diag}(\pi_t) + q_t(\mathbf{1}-\pi_t)^T\Big)\Big]^{-1} \times \\ & \Big[\Theta_t D_{t+1} + (1+r)(1-c)\mathrm{diag}(\lambda_{t,0})\left[\pi_t \circ W_t + q_{t-1}(\mathbf{1}-\pi_t)^T W_t\right]\Big] \end{aligned} \tag{5}$$

where Θ_t is the matrix of portfolios at time t with individual entries $\theta^i_{t,k}$.

The empirical challenge is to define investment strategies (a "market ecology") that captures a major part of the capital in the market. Further, one needs to devise and estimate the functions governing the flow of capital between different strategies. Strategies could be passive or active, e.g., based on Fama–French factors, or use information on the holdings of large institutional investors and hedge funds. Modelling this risk factor as a flow is novel and the severity of consequences from the risk is why we provide a framework from which empiricists can make estimates.

4.3. Consequences of Smart-Beta Herding

Potential consequences of herding in smart-beta products are closely related to several other instances of herding in financial markets. Discussing the practical implications of herding, Olsen (1996) suggested that it increases the mean of forecast earnings and reduces the variance of its distribution. As "more optimistic forecasts are usually better for the investment business than less optimistic forecasts" (Olsen 1996, p. 38), the reduced variance can be explained by forecasts being shifted towards other managers' forecasts. If earnings forecasts are consistently above realised earnings, there will be a reduction in returns when asset prices inevitably adjust downwards.

Factor strategies being reported as a financial innovation may be a case of Shiller's (2010) "irrational exuberance", a concept especially important from the financial economist's point of view. Money flowing into the sector could, incorrectly yet intuitively, be viewed as a signal that it is economically sound, initiating herd behaviour. The generally positive economic picture of recent years has likely also fuelled confidence in the strategies, which have been performing well, but under good circumstances. Theoretical work (Hens and Schenk-Hoppé (2018)) also finds evidence that, if value investors are patient, a likely scenario, then not only does the market incur significant price volatility but also both short- and long-term mispricings can occur. Brightman (2011) stressed that the 2007 quant meltdown is all but forgotten in light of the 2008 financial crisis. However, that is at investors' peril as the quant meltdown uncovered the risks that quantitative strategies entail and the role of success and marketing to attract large inflows of capital which eventually carry the seed to destruction. Smart-beta products are fashionable as never before and investors do not take into account potential herding into the same strategies, which may become overvalued and near capacity. Moreover, estimations of capacity are varied and by no means exact.

We can consider two cases: (1) investors all realise that there is an overvaluation and that capacity is nearing, resulting in a sharp decline in value of these strategies; and (2) capacity is reached, perhaps at a lower-bound estimate and a crash follows. Asness (2015, p. 5) frankly acknowledges that "on the risk side it seems clear, and pretending otherwise would hurt not help, that crises or runs on these strategies are more possible now that they're well known".

4.4. Data Snooping

Novy-Marx (2014, p. 137) quipped that "the party of the US president, the weather in Manhattan, global warming, the El Niño phenomenon, sunspots, and the conjunctions of the planets all have significant power predicting the performance of popular anomalies". The lesson here is that, if the methods used to discover factor relationships are believed, then these, seemingly spurious, relationships should also be believed. Overfitting was also discussed by Novy-Marx (2015, p. 2), who simultaneously employed multiple stock-level characteristics to produce high in-sample returns. His results indicate that, "the sorting variables (i.e., the random signals) have no real power, but strategies based on combinations of the 'signals' perform strongly". Hence, the performance of some factor models in backtesting does not indicate any future explanatory power of the models.

Considering data-snooping, Harvey et al. (2015) tested for the significance of 316 factors. Their analysis suggests that the majority of published factor relationships are significant only by chance and that, "there are only a handful of true systematic risk factors" (Harvey et al. 2015, p. 33). Historically validated factors, such as market, value, low volatility, liquidity and momentum, are significant, whilst newer factors tend not to be. This yields the critical question of whether the relationships published are indeed true or exist by chance. Early concern of p-hacking was discussed in a famous medical article, "Why Most Published Research Findings Are False" by Ioannidis (2005). The severity of the issue is further documented by fact that the American Statistical Association issued a statement on p-values (Wasserstein and Lazar 2016).

Li and West (2017) found that the performance of backtests is far superior to a smart-beta index once it becomes live. They blamed, at least partially, data snooping as backtests which are insignificant are far less likely to be published. Another claim is that the lower performance of live indices is due to backtests ignoring significant transaction costs, both explicit and implicit.

5. Conclusions

Smart-beta investments have enjoyed very positive press and academic backing. For example, Amenc et al. (2014) wrote that proper use of smart-beta tilts can provide around double the Sharpe ratio of a standard market-value weighted portfolio. Whilst factor rewards certainly have theoretical underpinning and statistical evidence to back them up, we write this as a warning to look further ahead in these investments. We have provided historical examples of herding in financial markets as well as reasoning why there may be herding into smart-beta products. This paper also highlights the rapidly expanding factor zoo, where many documented anomalies have little theoretical underpinning and may be the result of data snooping.

Several modelling approaches, all of them in their infancy with regards to empirical application, are emphasised. Modelling herding risk is accompanied with many empirical challenges, but is worth pursuing by those who have so far ignored this risk factor. Due to the severity of its consequences, this paper argues that the risk of herding into an investment style is one which ought to be considered by all practitioners in their risk analysis and portfolio modelling.

Author Contributions: The authors have contributed jointly to all sections of the paper.

Funding: This research was funded by The University of Manchester SEI programme.

Acknowledgments: We would like to thank the three anonymous referees for their helpful comments and suggestions. The authors are responsible for any remaining errors or shortcomings.

Conflicts of Interest: The authors declare no conflict of interest.

References

Alfarano, Simone, Thomas Lux, and Friedrich Wagner. 2005. Estimation of agent-based models: The case of an asymmetric herding model. *Computational Economics* 26: 19–49. [CrossRef]

Allen, David E., and Michael McAleer. 2018. 'Choosing Factors' by Fama and French (2018): A Comment. Available online: https://ssrn.com/abstract=3272608 (accessed on 1 February 2019).

Amenc, Noël, Felix Goltz, Ashish Lodh, and Lionel Martellini. 2014. Towards smart equity factor indices: Harvesting risk premia without taking unrewarded risks. *The Journal of Portfolio Management* 40: 106–22. [CrossRef]

Ang, Andrew, William N. Goetzmann, and Stephen Schaefer. 2009. Evaluation of Active Management of the Norwegian Government Pension Fund-Global. Available online: https://www0.gsb.columbia.edu/faculty/aang/papers/report%20Norway.pdf (accessed on 1 October 2018).

Arnott, Robert, Noah Beck, and Vitali Kalesnik. 2016. Timing 'Smart Beta' Strategies? Of Course! Buy Low, Sell High! Available online: https://ssrn.com/abstract=3040956 (accessed on 1 October 2018).

Asch, Solomon E. 1955. Opinions and social pressure. *Scientific American* 193: 31–35. [CrossRef]

Asness, Clifford S. 2015. *How Can a Strategy Still Work If Everyone Knows About It?* Greenwich: AQR Capital Management.

Asness, Clifford S. 2016. The siren song of factor timing. *The Journal of Portfolio Management* 42: 1–6. [CrossRef]

Asness, Clifford, Antti Ilmanen, Ronen Israel, and Tobias Moskowitz. 2015. Investing with style. *Journal of Investment Management* 13: 27–63.

Asness, Clifford S., Tobias J. Moskowitz, and Lasse Heje Pedersen. 2013. Value and momentum everywhere. *The Journal of Finance* 68: 929–85. [CrossRef]

Banerjee, Abhijit. 1992. A simple model of herd behavior. *The Quarterly Journal of Economics* 107: 797–817. [CrossRef]

Banz, Rolf W. 1981. The relationship between return and market value of common stocks. *Journal of Financial Economics* 9: 3–18. [CrossRef]

Basu, Sanjoy. 1977. Investment performance of common stocks in relation to their price-earnings ratios: A test of the efficient market hypothesis. *The Journal of Finance* 32: 663–82. [CrossRef]

Bender, Jennifer, Remy Briand, Dimitris Melas, and Raman Subramanian. 2013. Foundations of Factor Investing. Available online: https://ssrn.com/abstract=2543990 (accessed on 1 October 2018).

Bikhchandani, Sushil, and Sushil Sharma. 2000. *Herd Behavior in Financial Markets: A Review*. Washington, DC: International Monetary Fund.

Brightman, Chris. 2011. The Trouble with Quants. *Research Affiliates Newsletter*, August 4.

Caginalp, Gunduz, David Porter, and Vernon Smith. 2001. Financial bubbles: Excess cash, momentum, and incomplete information. *Journal of Psychology and Financial Markets* 2: 80–99. [CrossRef]

Carhart, Mark, and Sheridan Titman. 1997. On persistence in mutual fund performance. *The Journal of Finance* 52: 57–82. [CrossRef]

Chiarella, Carl, Roberto Dieci, and Xue-Zhong He. 2009. Heterogeneity, market mechanisms, and asset price dynamics. In *Handbook of Financial Markets: Dynamics and Evolution*. Amsterdam: North Holland, Chp. 5, pp. 277–344.

Chincarini, Ludwig B. 2012. *The Crisis of Crowding*. Hoboken: John Wiley & Sons.

Claessens, Stijn, M. Ayhan Kose, and Marco E. Terrones. 2011. Financial cycles: What? how? when? *NBER International Seminar on Macroeconomics* 7: 303–44. [CrossRef]

Cochrane, John H. 2011. Presidential address: Discount rates. *The Journal of Finance* 66: 1047–108. [CrossRef]

De Bondt, Werner, and William P. Forbes. 1999. Herding in analyst earnings forecasts: Evidence from the United Kingdom. *European Financial Management* 5: 143–63. [CrossRef]

De Bondt, Werner, and Richard Thaler. 1985. Does the stock market overreact? *The Journal of Finance* 40: 793–805. [CrossRef]

Devenow, Andrea, and Ivo Welch. 1996. Rational herding in financial economics. *European Economic Review* 40: 603–15. [CrossRef]

Doskov, Nikolay, Tapio Pekkala, and Ruy Ribeiro. 2016. Tradable Aggregate Risk Factors and the Cross-Section of Stock Returns. Available online: https://ssrn.com/abstract=2200889 (accessed on 1 October 2018).

Duffy, John. 2006. Agent-based models and human subject experiments. In *Handbook of Computational Economics, Volume 2, Agent-Based Computational Economics*. Amsterdam: North Holland, chp. 4.

Duffy, John, and M. Utku Ünver. 2006. Asset price bubbles and crashes with near-zero-intelligence traders. *Economic Theory* 27: 537–63. [CrossRef]

Easley, David, Nicholas M. Kiefer, Maureen O'Hara, and Joseph B. Paperman. 1996. Liquidity, information, and infrequently traded stocks. *The Journal of Finance* 51: 1405–36. [CrossRef]

Easley, David, Marcos M. López de Prado, and Maureen O'Hara. 2011. The microstructure of the flash crash: Flow toxicity, liquidity crashes, and the probability of informed trading. *Journal of Portfolio Management* 37: 118–28. [CrossRef]

Easley, David, Marcos M. López de Prado, and Maureen O'Hara. 2012. Flow toxicity and liquidity in a high-frequency world. *The Review of Financial Studies* 25: 1457–93. [CrossRef]

Economist. 2017. Building a beta mousetrap. Buttonwood. *The Economist* 422: 9032.

Economist. 2018. "Factor investing" gains popularity. *The Economist* 414: 9074.

Fama, Eugene F., and Kenneth R. French. 1992. The cross-section of expected stock returns. *The Journal of Finance* 47: 427–65. [CrossRef]

Fama, Eugene F., and Kenneth R. French. 1993. Common risk factors in the returns on stocks and bonds. *Journal of Financial Economics* 33: 3–56. [CrossRef]

Fama, Eugene F., and Kenneth R. French. 1996. Multifactor explanations of asset pricing anomalies. *The Journal of Finance* 51: 55–84. [CrossRef]

Fama, Eugene F., and Kenneth R. French. 2015. A five-factor asset pricing model. *Journal of Financial Economics* 116: 1–22. [CrossRef]

Fama, Eugene F., and Kenneth R. French. 2018. Choosing factors. *Journal of Financial Economics* 128: 234–52. [CrossRef]

Foucher, Ian, and Kyle Gray. 2014. Exchange-Traded Funds: Evolution of Benefits, Vulnerabilities and Risks. *Bank of Canada* 4: 34–46.

French, Kenneth R. 2008. Presidential address: The cost of active investing. *The Journal of Finance* 63: 1537–73. [CrossRef]

Graham, Benjamin. 2006. *The Intelligent Investor*. New York: HarperCollins.

Graham, John R. 1999. Herding among investment newsletters: Theory and evidence. *The Journal of Finance* 54: 237–68. [CrossRef]

Harvey, Campbell R., Yan Liu, and Heqing Zhu. 2015. ... and the cross-section of expected returns. *The Review of Financial Studies* 29: 5–68. [CrossRef]

Hens, Thorsten, and Klaus R. Schenk-Hoppé, eds. 2009. *Handbook of Financial Markets: Dynamics and Evolution*. Amsterdam: North-Holland.

Hens, Thorsten, and Klaus R. Schenk-Hoppé. 2018. Patience is a virtue—In value investing. *International Review of Finance*. Available online: https://onlinelibrary.wiley.com/doi/10.1111/irfi.12251 (accessed on 1 March 2019).

Ho, Lan-chih, John Cadle, and Michael Theobald. 2013. Portfolio insurance strategies. In *Encyclopedia of Finance*, 2nd ed. Boston: Springer.

Hommes, Cars. 2013. *Behavioral Rationality and Heterogeneous Expectations in Complex Economic Systems*. Cambridge: Cambridge University Press.

Hommes, Cars, and Florian Wagener. 2009. Complex evolutionary systems in behavioral finance. In *Handbook of Financial Markets: Dynamics and Evolution*. Amsterdam: North Holland, Chp. 4, pp. 217–76.

Ioannidis, John. 2005. Why most published research findings are false. *PLoS Medicine* 8: e124. [CrossRef]

Jacklin, Charles J., Allan W. Kleidon, and Paul Pfeiderer. 1992. Underestimation of portfolio insurance and the crash of October 1987. *The Review of Financial Studies* 5: 35–63. [CrossRef]

Jegadeesh, Narasimhan, and Sheridan Titman. 1993. Returns to buying winners and selling losers: Implications for stock market efficiency. *The Journal of Finance* 48: 65–91. [CrossRef]

Johnson, Ben, Hortense Bioy, and Dimitar Boyadzhiev. 2016. Assessing the true cost of strategic-beta ETFs. *The Journal of Index Investing* 7: 35–48. [CrossRef]

Katz, Michael L., and Carl Shapiro. 1985. Network externalities, competition, and compatibility. *The American Economic Review* 75: 424–40.

Kirman, Alan. 1993. Ants, rationality, and recruitment. *The Quarterly Journal of Economics* 108: 137–56. [CrossRef]

Leland, Hayne E. 1980. Who should buy portfolio insurance? *The Journal of Finance* 35: 581–94. [CrossRef]

Li, Feifei, and John West. 2017. Live from Newport Beach. It's Smart Beta! *Research Affiliates*, August 24.

Lux, Thomas. 2009. Stochastic behavioral asset-pricing models and the stylized facts. In *Handbook of Financial Markets: Dynamics and Evolution*. Amsterdam: North Holland, Chp. 3, pp. 161–215.

Malkiel, Burton G. 2013. Asset management fees and the growth of finance. *Journal of Economic Perspectives* 27: 97–108. [CrossRef]

Michel-Kerjan, Erwann O. 2010. Catastrophe economics: The national flood insurance program. *Journal of Economic Perspectives* 24: 165–86. [CrossRef]

NBIM. 2009. *Systematic Risk in the Equity Portfolio. Annual Report 2008*. Oslo: Norges Bank Investment Management.

Norris, Floyd. 2012. A Computer Lesson Still Unlearned. *The New York Times*, October 19.

Novy-Marx, Robert. 2013. The other side of value: The gross profitability premium. *Journal of Financial Economics* 108: 1–28. [CrossRef]

Novy-Marx, Robert. 2014. Predicting anomaly performance with politics, the weather, global warming, sunspots, and the stars. *Journal of Financial Economics* 112: 137–46. [CrossRef]

Novy-Marx, Robert. 2015. *Backtesting Strategies Based on Multiple Signals*. Cambridge: National Bureau of Economic Research.

Olsen, Robert A. 1996. Implications of herding behavior for earnings estimation, risk assessment, and stock returns. *Financial Analysts Journal* 52: 37–41. [CrossRef]

Opler, Tim C., and Sheridan Titman. 1994. Financial distress and corporate performance. *The Journal of Finance* 49: 1015–40. [CrossRef]

Reinganum, Marc R. 1981. Misspecification of capital asset pricing. *Journal of Financial Economics* 9: 19–46. [CrossRef]

Rennison, Joe, and Robin Wigglesworth. 2017. No End in Sight for Passive Boom, Says Investing Pioneer. *Financial Times*, November 14.

Robeco. 2017. Factor Investing Challenges: Factor Timing. *Factor Investing Challenges*, August 29.

Robeco. 2018. Guide to Factor Investing in Equity Markets. *Insight*, June 1.

Roider, Andreas, and Andrea Voskort. 2016. Reputational herding in financial markets: A laboratory experiment. *Journal of Behavioral Finance* 17: 244–66. [CrossRef]

Rosenberg, Barr, Kenneth Reid, and Ronald Lanstein. 1985. Persuasive evidence of market inefficiency. *The Journal of Portfolio Management* 11: 9–16. [CrossRef]

Russell. 2018. *Smart Beta: 2018 Global Survey Findings from Asset Owners*. London: FTSE Russell.

Scharfstein, David S., and Jeremy C. Stein. 1990. Herd behavior and investment. *The American Economic Review* 80: 465–79.

Sgroi, Daniel. 2003. The right choice at the right time: A herding experiment in endogenous time. *Experimental Economics* 6: 159–80. [CrossRef]

Sharpe, William F. 1964. Capital asset prices a theory of market equilibrium under conditions of risk. *The Journal of Finance* 19: 425–42.

Sharpe, William F. 1994. The Sharpe ratio. *The Journal of Portfolio Management* 21: 49–58. [CrossRef]

Shiller, Robert J. 1988. Portfolio insurance and other investor fashions as factors in the 1987 stock market crash. *NBER Macroeconomics Annual* 3: 287–97. [CrossRef]

Shiller, Robert J. 2010. *Irrational Exuberance*. Princeton: Princeton University Press.

Singh, Abhay K., David E. Allen, and Powell J. Robert. 2013. Extreme market risk and extreme value theory. *Mathematics and Computers in Simulation* 94: 310–28. [CrossRef]

Smith, Vernon L., Gerry L. Suchanek, and Arlington W. Williams. 1988. Bubbles, crashes, and endogenous expectations in experimental spot asset markets. *Econometrica* 56: 1119–51. [CrossRef]

Sundstrom, Geraldine. 2018. GIS Dynamic Multi-Asset Fund: Flexibility Amid Opportunities and Risks. *Strategy Spotlight*, July 7.

Tesfatsion, Leigh, and Kenneth Judd, eds. 2006. *Handbook of Computational Economics, Volume 2, Agent-Based Computational Economics*. Amsterdam: North Holland.

Thaler, Richard. 1987a. Anomalies: Seasonal movements in security prices ii: Weekend, holiday, turn of the month, and intraday effects. *Journal of Economic Perspectives* 1: 169–77. [CrossRef]

Thaler, Richard. 1987b. Anomalies: The January effect. *Journal of Economic Perspectives* 1: 197–201. [CrossRef]

Titman, Sheridan, K. C. John Wei, and Feixue Xie. 2004. Capital investments and stock returns. *Journal of Financial and Quantitative Analysis* 39: 677–700. [CrossRef]

Wasserstein, Ronald L., and Nicole A. Lazar. 2016. The ASA's statement on p-values: Context, process, and purpose. *The American Statistician* 70: 129–33. [CrossRef]

Welch, Ivo. 2000. Herding among security analysts. *Journal of Financial Economics* 58: 369–96. [CrossRef]

Wermers, Russ. 1999. Mutual fund herding and the impact on stock prices. *The Journal of Finance* 54: 581–622. [CrossRef]

Wiggins, Russ. 2018. Smart Beta Is Making This Strategist Sick. *Institutional Investor*, February 13.

Zwiebel, Jeffrey. 1995. Corporate conservatism and relative compensation. *Journal of Political Economy* 103: 1–25. [CrossRef]

Journal of
Risk and Financial Management

MDPI

Article

The Determinants of Sovereign Risk Premium in African Countries

Jane Mpapalika [1,*] and Christopher Malikane [2]

1 Department of Knowledge Management and Innovation, Economic and Social Research Foundation (ESRF), Ursino Estates P.O. Box 31226, Tanzania
2 Department of Economics, School of Economics and Business Sciences, University of the Witwatersrand, Johannesburg 2000, South Africa; mlk83za@wits.ac.za
* Correspondence: jmpapalika@esrf.or.tz

Received: 4 January 2019; Accepted: 30 January 2019; Published: 9 February 2019

Abstract: This paper investigates the determinants of the sovereign risk premium in African countries. We employ the dynamic fixed effects model to determine the key drivers of sovereign bond spreads. Country-specific effects are fixed and the inclusion of dummy variables using the Bai–Perron multiple structural break test is significant at a 5% level. For robustness, the time-series generalized method of moments (GMM) is used where the null hypothesis of the Sargan Test of over-identifying restrictions (OIR) and the Arellano–Bond Test of no autocorrelation are not rejected. This implies that the instruments used are valid and relevant. In addition, there is no autocorrelation in the error terms. Our results show that the exchange rate, Money supply/GDP (M2/GDP) ratio, and trade are insignificant. Furthermore, our findings indicate that public debt/GDP ratio, GDP growth, inflation rate, foreign exchange reserves, commodity price, and market sentiment are significant at a 5% and 10% level.

Keywords: sovereign risk/debt; risk premium; sovereign defaults; African countries

JEL Classification: H63; G12; N17

1. Introduction

This study investigates the determinants of sovereign risk premium in the selected African countries. As defined by Hilscher and Nosbusch (2010), sovereign risk premium is the difference between the interest rate on the sovereign bond and the interest rate on a risk-free U.S. Treasury bond of comparable maturity. According to Tkalec et al. (2014), the sovereign bond spread is the compensation to investors for default risk in case the realized welfare loss from default exceeds the expected welfare loss. Sovereign spreads are a proxy for the country risk premium which refers to the risk associated with the probability that a country will default on its debts. In general, Olabisi and Stein (2015), note that developing economies are subjected to persistent macroeconomic instabilities, and hence have a higher sovereign risk premium than advanced economies. From the sovereign risk management perspective, it is, therefore, important for policymakers to control the key drivers that influence a country's risk.

Understanding the sovereign risk premium determinants will assist policymakers in formulating sovereign risk management policies oriented towards minimizing sovereign default risks. For instance, Cassard and Folkerts-Landau (1997) argue that the objective of sovereign risk management is to ensure that the government's financing needs are met at the lowest possible cost of debt given a certain level of risk. Therefore, developing sound sovereign risk management policies to determine the key drivers of bond spread is essential to minimize risks and, in turn, achieve macroeconomic stability of the wider economy. In addition, Korinek (2011) point out that the risk premium is an important factor in determining the choice between local currency debt and foreign currency debt, which is also crucial to policymakers. However, the main contribution of the study is to investigate the key drivers of sovereign risk premium in African countries. Our study builds on the works of Martinez et al. (2013), who employ a panel fixed effects model to examine the country risk premium determinants in emerging market economies. For robustness, we employ the Generalized Method of Moments with instrumental variables.

Despite the evidence of sovereign defaults in African economies, limited studies have been done on the determinants of sovereign risk premium in African countries. Studies such as Furceri and Zdzienicka (2012) have shown evidence of sovereign defaults in the selected African countries. However, Siklos (2011), points out that most of the studies focus on the determinants of bond spread in emerging market economies and developed economies. For instance, Kaminsky and Schmukler (1999), find that changes in the foreign interest rate increase the country spread and that the impact is high in countries with low credit ratings. Other studies, such as those by Mendonca and Nunes (2011), find that domestic variables are responsible for determining the risk premium. Hence, the gap that this study seeks to fill is that there are few studies focusing on the determinants of the sovereign risk premium in sub-Saharan Africa.

The rest of the paper is structured as follows: Section 2 reviews the literature; Section 3 presents the model; Section 4 provides the empirical methodology; Section 5 describes data; Section 5.1 summarizes stylized facts; Section 6 analyses empirical findings; and Section 7 concludes with some policy recommendations.

2. Related Literature

The literature on country risk premium determinants in sub-Saharan Africa is relatively scant, despite the empirical evidence of sovereign defaults. Most of the studies, such as that by Martinez et al. (2013), focus on the determinants of sovereign bond spreads in emerging market economies. This study uses quarterly data to estimate a panel fixed effects model on the seven Latin American countries, to investigate the determinants of bond spread. Their study finds inflation, terms of trade, the external debt, and international reserves to GDP ratio/GDP to be key drivers of sovereign bond spreads. Using panel data on emerging market economies, Baldacci and Kumar (2010) investigate the effect of fiscal deficits and public debt on long-term interest rates. They find that higher fiscal deficits lead to a significant increase in long-term interest rates. These self-fulfilling mechanisms suggest that higher fiscal deficits are likely to raise the sovereign risk premium, and hence, sovereign default risks.

According to the theory of fiscal insurance stipulated by Uribe (2006), under certain monetary and fiscal policy regimes, the sovereign risk default is inevitable. In fact, some of the monetary policy rules e.g., interest rate targeting and inflation targeting, are inconsistent with the central bank's objective of price stability. For instance, assume that a country is characterized by chronic fiscal deficits and the central bank's objective is price stability. Then, under this scenario, the probability of a country to default on its sovereign debt is high. More recently, Cuadra et al. (2010) realize that fiscal policy is still procyclical and that defaulting occurs more often in recessions. If the government ran a deficit budget, it has the option of financing this deficit by borrowing from abroad, though at a high interest rate. As observed by Bi (2012), if taxes are more distortionary, it will be more likely that the government will raise its foreign borrowing, and hence, a high likelihood to sovereign default risk.

There has been inconclusive evidence regarding the determinants of sovereign risk premium in developing countries. While some studies, such as those by Baldacci et al. (2011), Iara and Wolff (2014), indicate that domestic fundamentals are responsible for changes in the sovereign risk premium. For instance, Tkalec et al. (2014) demonstrate that an increase in current account deficit raises the level of sovereign risk premium. In addition, De Grauwe and Ji (2012) point out that a high ratio of public debt/GDP increases the debt-servicing burden, which in turn raises debt-servicing costs, along with the likelihood of a sovereign default. Other studies find the market sentiment to be the key driver of sovereign bond spread, in particular, global risk aversion. As noted by Audzeyeva and Schenk-Hoppé (2010), the investor's sentiments significantly affect the bond spread. Similarly, Siklos (2011), highlight that the degree of investor's risk aversion is an important factor in explaining bond spread variations.

The economic literature has identified that most of the variations in the sovereign bond spread are explained by GDP growth. Findings by Sturzenegger (2004), prove that an increase in debt burden is associated with low GDP growth of about 0.6–2.2%. This implies that an improvement in the economic performance of a country contributes to macroeconomic stability. As a result, the probability of sovereign default occurring is minimal. A high level of GDP growth raises the country's ability to service its debt burden, which leads to a reduction in the level of risk premium (Borensztein and Panizza 2009; Maltritz and Molchanov 2013). Other studies, e.g., Galindo et al. (2003) and Gumus (2011), have argued that the contractionary effects of the exchange rate depreciation are associated with currency mismatches and sudden stops, which may lead to financial instability. According to Calvo and Reinhart (2002), this is the main reason many developing countries exhibit the "fear of floating", and therefore, adopt managed floats or soft pegs.

Other studies such as that of Baldacci et al. (2011) find that inflation is significant in influencing the sovereign risks. As described by Martinez et al. (2013), a high inflation rate may be attributed to the monetization of the fiscal deficit and the need for higher interest rates. Hence, Min et al. (2003), illustrate that an increase in inflation rate signaling macroeconomic instability will consequently raise the sovereign risk premium. However, the default risk will be high in an inflation-targeting economy if the government will not raise the short-term interest rate through the central bank to curb inflationary tendencies. The expected sign of inflation on the risk premium is positive.

Foreign exchange reserve/GDP is also an important factor in determining the level of risk premium. The accumulation of foreign exchange reserves should reduce the country's risk. Hence, the hypothesized sign is negative, as shown by (Tkalec et al. 2014). As noted by Bellas et al. (2010) and Martinez et al. (2013), a low ratio of foreign reserves/GDP translates into a high likelihood of sovereign default and liquidity risks. In addition, Ouyang and Rajan (2014), stress that the accumulation of foreign exchange reserves acts as an insurance against sovereign defaults.

Global factors such as global liquidity, risk appetite, and contagion effects are important in determining the country risk. This is in line with findings by Gonzalez-Rozada and Levy-Yeyati (2008) that the level of risk reflects investors' risk aversion. Moreover, Kamin and Kleist (1999), find that bond spreads are mainly explained by the shifts in market sentiments, rather than by variations in fundamentals. Similarly, Maltritz and Molchanov (2013), conclude that market sentiments play an important role in determining the sovereign bond spread over time. However, it is generally argued that developing countries are riskier than advanced economies. The expected sign of market sentiment on the country risk is positive.

3. The Model

Following Ferrucci (2003) and Comelli (2012), a conventional approach to sovereign bond yield is the assumption that the yield spread is a function of the likelihood that a default will occur and the welfare loss following a default. This likelihood of a default occurring depends on a set of macroeconomic fundamentals, e.g., the public debt/GDP ratio, inflation, real exchange rate, and fiscal deficits. Other studies, such as those by Gonzalez-Rozada and Levy-Yeyati (2008), Kamin and Kleist (1999), Maltritz and Molchanov (2013) conclude that market sentiments play an important role in determining the sovereign bond spread over time. In addition, Uribe (2006), makes an important observation regarding the probability of default risks in that, under certain monetary and fiscal policy regimes, the sovereign risk default is inevitable. This is attributed to the inconsistent and conflicting objectives of fiscal and monetary policy regimes.

Therefore, Jankovic and Zivkovic (2014), declare that the bond yield spread is negatively correlated with foreign debt sustainability. As developed by Edwards (1984), the sufficient condition for the optimal share of the investor's funds is given by:

$$\left(1 + r_f\right) = p_w + (1 - p)\left(1 + r^L\right) \tag{1}$$

where r_f is the risk-free interest rate, p is the default probability of the debtor country, p_w is the debtor's payment to the investor in the case a default occurs, and r^L is the rate of return on investment. Then, Bellas et al. (2010), suggest that the probability of default on emerging market sovereign bonds and the risk-free interest rate have the same maturity. In the long-run, however, the probability of sovereign default is constant. Hence, the bond spread over the U.S. Treasury bond, s, is given by:

$$s = r^L - r_f = \frac{p}{1 - p}\left(1 + r_f\right) \tag{2}$$

With respect to Edwards (1984), the probability of default in a logistic form is specified as:

$$p = \frac{\exp\left(\sum_{j=1}^{J} \beta_j x_j\right)}{1 + \exp\left(\sum_{j=1}^{J} \beta_j x_j\right)} \tag{3}$$

By combining Equations (2) and (3), and after taking the logarithm, the sovereign risk premium is provided by:

$$\log s = \log\left(1 + r_f\right) + \sum_{j=1}^{J} \beta_j x_j + \varepsilon_{it} \tag{4}$$

Equation (4) shows that the sovereign bond spread at time t is affected by the country's fundamentals, x_j, and the risk-free interest rate, r_f. Expressing Equation (4) in logs will generate the following log-linear specification with fixed individual effects:

$$\log(embig_{it}) = \alpha_0 + \sum_{j=1}^{n} \alpha_j x_{ijt} + \gamma_j + \lambda_t + \varepsilon_{it} \tag{5}$$

where $embig_{it}$ is the sovereign bond yield spread for country i in time t, x_{ijt} is a vector of independent variables that includes country-specific and global factors, μ_i is the country-specific fixed effects, and ε_{it} are the error terms, which are independently and identically distributed.

4. Empirical Methodology

4.1. Panel Unit Root Tests: LLC and IPS

It is important to carry out the unit root tests in order to determine the order of integration. Moreover, the regression of non-stationary time series data is likely to give spurious results. As noted by Strauss and Yigit (2003), panel unit root tests, address the low power problem in an individual-equation Augmented Dickey–Fuller Test by averaging the t-statistics across the panel and assumes that the disturbance terms are normally distributed. This study will use panel unit root tests developed by Levin et al. (2002) and Im et al. (2003) to determine the order of integration of the underlying variables of interest. The null hypothesis for these unit root tests is that all panels contain a unit root, I(1), except the null hypothesis for the Hadri Unit Root Test that assumes all panels are stationary, I(0).

The Im et al. (2003), based on the Dickey–Fuller procedure specifies each cross-section with individual effects and no time trend as follows:

$$\Delta y_{it} = \alpha_i + \gamma_i y_{i,t-1} + \sum_{j=1}^{p_i} \chi_{ij} \Delta y_{i,t-j} + \varepsilon_{it} \tag{6}$$

where $i = 1, \ldots, N$ and $t = 1, \ldots, T$.

The Im, Pesaran and Shin uses separate unit root tests for the N cross-section units. After estimating the separate Augmented Dickey Fuller regressions, the average of t-statistics for p_1 from the individual ADF regressions, that is:

$$\bar{t}_{NT} = \frac{1}{N} \sum_{i=1}^{N} t_{iT}(p_i \beta i)$$

The t-bar statistic is then standardized and converge to the standard normal distribution as N and T tends to infinity. As shown by Im et al. (2003), the t-bar statistics is robust when N and T are small.

4.2. Residual-Based Panel Cointegration Test

If the null hypothesis of a unit root test is not rejected, then the cointegration test can be performed to determine the long-run relationship in the underlying variables. In a conventional way, cointegration refers to the set of variables that are individually integrated of order one, some linear combination of these variables can be described as stationary, I(0). Earlier works of Pedroni (2004), investigate the properties of residual-based tests for the null of no cointegration for both homogeneous and heterogeneous panels. An interesting observation by McCoskey and Kao (1998) suggests that testing the null hypothesis of cointegration rather than the null hypothesis of no cointegration is interesting, especially in applications, where cointegration is forecasted a priori by economic theory.

However, Pedroni (1999), note that residual-based tests are more robust even in small samples although they cannot determine the number of co-integrated relationships. Our study uses the Pedroni cointegration test suggested by Pedroni (1999). The procedures proposed by Pedroni make use of the estimated residual from the hypothesized long-run regression in its general form, which is given by:

$$y_{it} = \alpha_i + \delta_i t + \beta_i x'_{it} + e_{it} \tag{7}$$

where $i = 1, \ldots, N$ over time periods $t = 1, \ldots, T$. The variables y_{it} and X_{it} are assumed to be integrated of order one, denoted by I(1), and under the null of no cointegration, the residual will also be I(1). The parameters α_i and δ_i allow for the possibility of specific fixed effects and deterministic trends. The slope coefficient β_i is also allowed to vary so that the cointegrating vectors may be heterogeneous across the panel.

Pedroni (1999) suggests the heterogeneous group mean panel test statistics for panel cointegration asymptotic distribution of individual t-statistics is given by:

$$\frac{X_{N,T} \mu \sqrt{N}}{\sqrt{v}} \Rightarrow N(0,1)$$

where $X_{N,T}$ correspond to test statistics, while μ and v are the mean and variance of each test, respectively.

If the variables are cointegrated, then, we proceed to estimate Equation (8) using the panel dynamic fixed effects method. We build our model on the works of Martinez et al. (2013), who investigate the determinants of sovereign risk premium in emerging market economies using panel fixed effects. Panel fixed effect models control for unobservable individual and time-specific effects. According to Csonto and Ivaschenko (2013), a panel model takes into account the individual dimension and the time dimension. As noted by Judson and Owen (1999), the fixed effects model is more robust than the random effects model, because it also controls endogeneity problems. However, the general model of bond spread determinants for country i at time t is given by the following dynamic fixed effects model:

$$y_{it} = \gamma y_{i,t-1} + \sum_{j=1}^{n} \alpha_j x_{ijt} + \gamma_j + \lambda_t + \varepsilon_{it}, \ For \ i = 1 \ldots N \text{ and } t = 1 \ldots T \quad (8)$$

where y_{it} is the sovereign risk premium measured by the interest rate on the sovereign bonds and the 10-year US Treasury bond, which is the benchmark and default-free. Most of the studies use the JP Morgan Emerging Markets Global Bond Index, which is the most comprehensive emerging markets benchmark. Despite the fact that this index incorporates bonds issued in emerging market economies, Asia, Africa, and Europe, it seldom includes all the low-income countries. According to Ebner (2009), some European countries are not included in the JPMBIG index. On the other hand, this benchmark index includes African countries, such as Egypt, South Africa, Nigeria, and Morocco.

However, Ferrucci (2003) and Ebner (2009), use the emerging market benchmark. The vector of independent variables that includes country-specific and global factors is represented by χ_{it}. As shown by Comelli (2012) and Martinez et al. (2013), sound country-specific factors are associated with lower bond spreads. An appreciation of the real exchange rate decreases the country risk premium. Therefore, the expected sign for the exchange rate is negative. In addition, some studies, such as those by Baek et al. (2005); Bellas et al. (2010), and Siklos (2011), find that high GDP growth, greater amounts of reserves and an increase in money supply lower the sovereign bond spread. Hence, this study expects a negative impact on sovereign bond spreads. Other studies, such as Gylfason (1991), point out that higher inflation rates contribute to higher sovereign default risks.

The risk premium is high in heavily indebted countries because of the worsening of fiscal deficit and an increase in investor's sentiments. The hypothesized sign is positive. In addition, the increase in the investors' risk aversion raises the risk premium. In this sense, Bernoth et al. (2012) are of the opinion that in times of uncertain economic conditions, rational investors move to less risky assets, which, in turn, raises the bond spread. In order to control for global factors, the market sentiment is proxied by the consumer's sentiment. Some studies, such as those by Aristei and Martelli (2014), have used direct proxies for market sentiment based on consumer confidence. ζ_i represents the individual country-specific effects, γ_t the time effect, and ε_{it} the error term. This study has also considered two dummy variables in order to capture the effects of the debt crisis. The individual country-specific effect is denoted by γ_i and the time-varying unobservable time effect is denoted by λ_t. The error term is represented by ε_{it}. In addition, we investigate the structural breaks by adding dummy variables.

As a means of robustness, this study uses the system generalized method of moments (GMM) established by Arellano and Bover (1995) and Blundell and Bond (1998). It enhances the difference GMM estimator by creating an additional assumption that first differences of instrument variables are uncorrelated with the fixed effects. The two-step estimator is more efficient than the one-step system GMM and performs better than the differenced GMM and within-group estimators. To address endogeneity and simultaneity bias issues, the explanatory variables are lagged to more than two periods which are used as instruments. If the moment conditions are valid, Blundell and Bond (1998) show that, in Monte Carlo simulations, the GMM-system estimators perform better than the GMM-difference estimator.

We test the validity of the moment conditions by using the Sargan test of over-identifying restrictions. Further tests include an Autoregressive (AR) test to check if the differenced error terms are first and second order serially correlated. The principle of this method is to choose instruments, which satisfy a set of orthogonality conditions, whereby the number of instruments ought not to exceed the number of panels. The order condition requires that the number of instruments must be at least equal to the number of endogenous components, such that $r < K$. Roodman (2009), note that using many moment conditions can improve efficiency but makes the GMM inferences inaccurate.

Bound et al. (1995) argue that the use of an instrumental variable in the case of a weak relationship between instruments and the endogenous explanatory variable causes large inconsistencies in the estimated instrumental variables.

5. Data Description

This study employs annual data covering the period 1971 to 2011 for 10 African countries. The countries selected include Burundi, Egypt, The Gambia, Kenya, Mauritania, Nigeria, Sierra Leone, Swaziland, South Africa, and Zambia. Data is sourced from the International Monetary Fund (IMF)'s International Financial Statistics, the World Bank development indicators; the UNCTAD statistics, the Federal Reserve Bank of St. Louis, and each country's central bank. The country risk premium is measured by the difference between the interest rate on the sovereign bond denominated in US Dollars and the interest rate on the 10-year US Treasury bond, which is the benchmark and default-free. Data on the interest rate of sovereign bond in African countries are obtained from the country's central bank and the Federal Reserve Bank of St. Louis. The 10-year US T-bond is sourced from the Federal Reserve Bank of St. Louis. In addition to the JPEMBIG index, Comelli (2012), point out that this index includes Egypt and South Africa whereas, Bunda et al. (2009), show that the index includes Morocco as well.

The selection of the countries is based on the fact that these countries have a domestic debt market where information on sovereign bonds is available. As noted by Christensen (2005), who investigated the domestic debt markets in sub-Saharan Africa, their choice of countries was limited to non-CFA Franc countries, since CFA Franc countries, until very recently, did not have any domestic debt markets. Among the non-CFA countries, Angola, Botswana, the Democratic Republic of the Congo, Mozambique, and São Tomé and Príncipe did not have domestic government debt markets at the time of collection, that is, in 2005. In cases where these were insufficient, central bank reports or IMF country desk economists helped to fill their gaps.

Inflation is measured by the consumer price index. The exchange rate is defined as the value of domestic currency per unit of foreign currency. GDP growth rate is the real GDP at 2005 prices. Total reserves/GDP is the ratio of reserves to GDP. M2/GDP is the ratio of money supply to GDP where M2 includes M1 with all savings and time-related deposits. The fiscal deficit is measured by the public debt/GDP ratio. Current account/GDP is the sum of the balance of trade, net factor income from abroad, and net cash transfers to GDP growth rate. In order to control for global factors, the proxy for market sentiment is given by the consumer's sentiment. Studies such as Aristei and Martelli (2014) have used direct proxies for market sentiment based on consumer confidence.

5.1. Stylized Facts

Table 1 reports the correlations between the sovereign risk premium and its determinants in African countries. The correlation results show that most of the series are highly correlated with each other. For instance, the correlation between M2/GDP and exchange rate is 0.89; M2/GDP and current account/GDP is 0.85; real GDP and public debt/GDP is 0.70; and the exchange rate and current account/GDP is 0.84. In this case, some insignificant variables will be dropped to avoid the problem of multicollinearity. Most of the studies, e.g., those by Comelli (2012), find a negative correlation between the bond spread and its determinants. This implies that improvement in country-specific fundamentals, such as GDP growth, is associated with low sovereign risk premium. Our results show that there is a negative correlation between the GDP growth rate and the bond spread. The increase in economic growth raises the tax revenue used for servicing debt and, therefore, there is a decline in default risks. This is in line with studies by Siklos (2011) and Maltritz and Molchanov (2013), who show that the bond spread reduces in response to an improvement in the GDP growth rate.

Table 1. Correlation analysis.

Variables	Risk Premium	Reserves/GDP	M2/GDP	Inflation Rate	Real GDP	Exchange Rate	Public Debt/GDP	Consumer Sentiment	Current Account/GDP Ratio
Risk Premium	1								
Reserves/GDP	−0.176 **	1							
M2/GDP	0.648 **	−0.416 **	1						
Inflation rate	0.165 **	−0.032 ***	0.186 **	1					
Real GDP	−0.216 **	0.149 **	0.163 **	−0.152 **	1				
Real exchange rate	−0.723 **	−0.518 **	0.893 **	0.146 **	0.02 ***	1			
Public debt/GDP	0.006 ***	−0.637 **	0.088 **	0.09 **	0.702 **	0.18 **	1		
Consumer sentiment	0.203 **	−0.229 **	−0.355 **	−0.267 **	−0.17 **	−0.30 **	0.400 **	1	
Current account/GDP	−0.431 **	−0.44 **	0.85 **	0.009 ***	0.057 ***	0.842 **	0.134 **	−0.223 **	1

** and *** denotes statistical significance at 5% and 10% level.

There is a negative correlation between foreign exchange reserves/GDP and bond spread. If the level of reserve accumulation declines, then the likelihood of a sovereign default is high. These results are consistent with Tkalec et al. (2014), who show that the accumulation of foreign exchange reserves raises a country's liquidity level, thereby lowering the sovereign bond spread. In practice, foreign exchange reserves are accumulated to raise a country's ability to meet its external debt obligations. More recently, Maltritz and Molchanov (2013), find that foreign reserves/GDP growth is negatively correlated with the sovereign risk premium. In addition, Bellas et al. (2010) and Martinez et al. (2013) argue that a country's foreign exchange reserves can be used to service foreign debt and fix the exchange rate. Hence, the hypothesized sign is negative.

There is a positive correlation between the inflation rate and the sovereign bond spread. A high inflation rate reflects macroeconomic instability and consequently, a rise in the country risk premium. As noted by Calvo et al. (1996), an effective inflation-targeting policy will reduce macroeconomic instabilities by managing inflationary tendencies, which may lead to capital outflows. On the other hand, Baldacci et al. (2011), observe that a rise in the inflation rate, which is attributed to the adoption of an expansionary monetary policy, contributes to a high likelihood of sovereign risks. Other studies, such as those by Martinez et al. (2013), find that the inflation rate is significant at 1% and exhibits the expected positive sign. This means that the bond spread will increase in response to inflationary pressure. More recently, Tkalec et al. (2014) show that sovereign risk premium increases in response to higher inflation in the long run.

The public debt/GDP ratio is positively correlated to the bond spread. It clearly suggests that an increase in public debt/GDP ratio contributes to a rise in the level of the sovereign risk premium. This is consistent with Bernoth et al. (2012), who observe a positive relationship between bond yield spreads and fiscal variables. Similarly, Tkalec et al. (2014), find that the country risk premium increase in response to a higher total debt to GDP ratio, which is attributed to the high cost of debt servicing. In addition, De Grauwe and Ji (2012), affirm that the debt to GDP ratio has a priori expected positive sign towards the bond spread. As noted further by Bi (2012), when the level of public debt is beyond the fiscal limit, sovereign default is likely to occur. On the other hand, the current account balance/GDP ratio is negatively correlated to the sovereign risk premium. According to Özatay et al. (2009) and Martinez et al. (2013), this means that the increase in current account balance/GDP that is current account surplus reduces the probability of sovereign defaults.

Furthermore, market sentiments and bond spreads are positively correlated, which implies that the increase in the investor's risk aversion raises the sovereign risk premium. This is in contrast with Gonzalez-Rozada and Levy-Yeyati (2008), who observe that the emerging market bond spread is negatively correlated with the international risk appetite. Other studies, e.g., Dailami et al. (2008), reveal that an increase in global risk aversion increases the sovereign bond spreads through the contagion effect. An increase in market sentiments is reflected by the improvement in the sovereign credit rating. As shown by Ebner (2009) and Zinna (2013), emerging market sovereign risk is driven by the degree of investors' risk aversion.

6. Empirical Results

6.1. IPS and LLC Unit Root Tests

Table 2 presents the panel unit root tests using studies by Levin et al. (2002) and Im et al. (2003). The optimal lag length selection is chosen based on the Schwarz Information Criterion (SIC) and the optimal bandwidths of LLC; IPS unit root tests are determined based on the Newey–West criterion. Unit root test procedures are designed to investigate the stationarity of each individual series in the panel. Most of the variables, e.g., the exchange rate, M2/GDP ratio, public debt, foreign exchange reserve, and trade accept the null hypothesis of a unit root. However, after first differencing these series, they become stationary at the 5% significance level, with individual linear trends. This is consistent with the findings of Martinez et al. (2013). Other series such as the GDP growth rates, inflation rates, market sentiment, sovereign risk premium, and commodity prices are stationary. We then carry out the Pedroni residual-based cointegration after stationarity of the series.

Table 2. Panel unit root test.

Variables	Level (Without Trend)		Difference (With Trend)	
	Levin, Lin, and Chu	Im, Pesaran, and Shin	Levin, Lin, and Chu	Im, Pesaran, and Shin
GDP	−22.38 **	−21.06 **	−19.66 **	−19.63 **
Exchange rate	1.86 ***	5.51 ***	−9.03 **	−5.03 **
Inflation rate	−17.57 **	−14.24 **	−16.85 **	−12.71 **
M2/GDP	0.01 ***	2.05 ***	−25.03 **	−29.26 **
Public debt/GDP			−23.00 **	−24.34 **
Foreign exchange reserves			−10.27 **	−13.41 **
Risk premium	−2.29 **	−2.79 **		
Market sentiment	−6 **	−7.8 **		
Trade/GDP			−11.03 **	−18.77 **
Commodity price	−3.09 **	−7.29 **		

(i) The null hypothesis of no unit root is rejected if p-value < 0.05. (ii) ** and *** denotes 5% and 10% *** significance level.

6.2. Panel Residual-Based Cointegration Test

Table 3 reports the residual-based panel co-integration results. According to Pedroni (1999) and Kao (1999), the advantage of a residual-based test over the maximum-likelihood based co-integration test is that they are robust, even in small samples. However, Banerjee (1999), points out that they are unable to determine the number of co-integrated relationships. Our test shows that the null hypothesis of no co-integration is strongly rejected in the series under investigation. Since there are co-integrating relationships between the bond spread and its determinants, we proceed to estimate the key drivers of sovereign bond spread in African countries using the Dynamic Fixed Effects model and the Generalized Method of Moments for robustness.

Table 3. Pedroni residual-based cointegration test.

Variable	Without Deterministic Trend	With Deterministic Trend
Sovereign risk premium	−2.66 **	−2.38 **

(i) ** and *** denotes 5% and 10% significant levels. (ii) Null hypothesis is rejected if p-value < 0.05.

6.3. Dynamic Fixed Effects Estimation

Table 4 reports the estimation results for dynamic fixed effects on the sovereign risk premium determinants. The specification allows country-fixed effects to account for cross-country heterogeneity that affects all countries. As pointed out by Bordo et al. (2010), a dynamic fixed effects estimator is robust to heteroscedasticity and serial correlation in the individual dimension. In Table 4, column (1) is the baseline specification, which includes all the variables of interest, where the exchange rate and M2/GDP are insignificant. Column (2) shows the insignificant variables. Column (3) incorporates the dummy variables. It turns out that the inclusion of time dummies affects the significance of trade/GDP ratio, where it becomes insignificant. Our results are consistent with Martinez et al. (2013), who confirm that the exchange rate is insignificant in emerging market economies. In contrast, Ebner (2009), find that the exchange rate is highly significant in African countries.

Table 4. Dynamic Fixed Effects estimation results.

Variables	(1)	(2)	(3)
$Risk_{t-1}$	0.65(0.04) **	0.72(0.03) **	0.63(0.04) **
GDP	0.07(0.01) **	0.04(0.01) **	0.07(0.01) **
Exchange rate	−0.06(0.09)		
Inflation rate	0.04(0.01) **	0.03(0.01) **	0.04(0.01) **
M2/GDP	0.06(0.06)		
Public debt/GDP	0.03(0.007) **	0.01(0.007) **	0.03(0.007) **
Foreign exchange reserves	−0.06(0.01) **	−0.06(0.01) **	−0.06(0.017) **
Market sentiment	0.19(0.09) **	0.21(0.10) **	0.17(0.09) ***
Trade/GDP	−0.07(0.05) **	−0.11(0.05) **	
Commodity price	−0.11(0.03) **	−0.15(0.03) **	−0.12(0.03) **
D1979			0.16(0.04) **
D1980			0.16(0.04) **
D2001			0.17(0.04) **
D2007			0.20(0.04) **
D2008			0.13(0.04) **
R^2	0.64	0.61	0.67
Durbin–Watson statistics	1.79	1.65	1.83
Observations	344	344	344
Prob(F-statistics)	0.0000	0.0000	0.0000

Notes: (i) ** and *** indicates statistical significant at 5% and 10%, respectively. (ii) Standard errors in parentheses.

The results of this study show that a 1% increase in GDP growth, contributes to a decline in the sovereign risk premium by 0.65%. The coefficient on the GDP growth is statistically significant at 5% and displays the expected negative sign. In contrast, Martinez et al. (2013) find that the GDP growth and the public debt/GDP ratio are statistically insignificant, although they present the correct sign. However, our findings are in line with those of Baek et al. (2005), Siklos (2011), Maltritz and Molchanov (2013), who note that high growth rates reduce the sovereign default risk. This means that the increase in the general economic performance of a country raises the macroeconomic stability in the fiscal variables hence, lowering the probability of a sovereign default. For instance, Guillaumont et al. (1999), indicate that macroeconomic fluctuations lower economic growth in African countries. Intuitively, the coefficient on real GDP growth shows that low-growth countries are penalized when issuing bonds as they tend to do so at higher spreads.

The coefficient on the inflation rate is significant and has a positive sign. This implies that a 1% increase in the inflation rate leads to an increase in the sovereign risk premium by 4%. This is in contrast with the findings of Mendonca and Nunes (2011) and Maltritz (2012), where inflation is statistically insignificant in influencing the level of risk premium. However, our findings are consistent with Baldacci et al. (2011), who find that a rise in sovereign bond spread leads to a high inflation rate. In practice, there is a strong link between inflationary tendencies and sovereign defaults. For instance, Reinhart and Rogoff (2011) singled out Zimbabwe, which has weak fiscal and monetary institutions and is significantly exposed to high inflation and the risk of a sovereign default. Using an inflation threshold of 20%, their study finds that Zimbabwe's annual inflation rate exceeds 500%. On the other hand, Eichengreen et al. (2002), cites that inflation-forecast targeting countries like South Africa and Chile, which have strong monetary, fiscal, and financial institutions, normally experience a lower sovereign risk premium.

However, further analysis indicates that Egypt, Ghana, and South Africa are effectively implementing inflation targeting as a monetary policy rule, so as to keep inflation in check. Some studies, such as those by Aron and Aron and Muellbauer (2005), find that since the Reserve Bank of South Africa implemented inflation targeting to manage its inflation in the 2000s, monetary policy credibility increased, and the GDP growth improved, as a result, it lowers the sovereign risks. Similarly, Kyereboah-Coleman (2012), confirms that inflation targeting is successful in managing inflation, lowering the exchange rate pass-through, and improving the credibility of the monetary policy in Ghana. On the contrary, Malikane and Mokoka (2012) find that since the implementation of inflation targeting, monetary policy is not credible when managing inflation. Countries with high inflation rates do not need to issue large amounts of debt, as the inflation tax is a major source of government revenue. For instance, Claessens et al. (2007), show that high inflation is associated with macroeconomic instability, and occasionally, with general government defaults.

A 1% increase in the public debt/GDP ratio raises the sovereign risk premium by 0.03% and the coefficient on the public debt/GDP is highly significant. This suggests that as the public debt/GDP ratio increases, the debt-servicing burden also rises. In turn, indebtedness affects the sovereign's creditworthiness, which leads to a high level of country risks. This observation is in contrast with the findings by Bernoth et al. (2012) and Bernoth and Erdogan (2012), where the coefficients on the debt variable are insignificant. Importantly, it is advisable that a low public debt/GDP ratio is desirable so as to maintain macroeconomic stability in the fiscal variables. The study findings further confirm the existence of the "debt-overhang hypothesis" in Sub-Saharan Africa. The fact that most African economies with the exception of South Africa have high shares of foreign currency liabilities reflects the presence of poor sovereign debt risk management policies and weak institutions.

A 1% reduction in foreign exchange reserves leads to an increase in the sovereign risk premium by 0.06% and is significant at 5% level. The accumulation of foreign exchange reserves is associated with the increase in liquidity, which, in turn, reduces the bond spread. The results of this study contrast with those of Heinemann et al. (2014), who find that the foreign exchange reserve is insignificant in all specifications. However, our findings are consistent with those of Tkalec et al. (2014) and Maltritz and Molchanov (2013) who demonstrated the decline in the sovereign bond spread following an increase in reserve accumulation. However, Gelos et al. (2011) and Olabisi and Stein (2015) reserve accumulation as a monetary policy instrument for providing liquidity acts as an insurance against sovereign defaults. Monetary authorities usually use foreign exchange reserves when there is high exchange rate volatility, in order to fix the exchange rate. Another motive identified by Jeanne and Ranciere (2011) is that countries hold reserves covering three months' worth of imports.

The coefficient on the market sentiment has the expected positive sign and is statistically significant at 5%. This indicates that the bond spread increases by 0.19% (19 basis points) in response to a 1% reduction in the investor's risk aversion. These results are in line with Bernoth et al. (2012) who note that the increase in the bond spread is caused by the rise in the investors' risk aversion. More recently, Tkalec et al. (2014) confirm that the sovereign risk premium rises in response to high market sentiments. In addition, Cuadra et al. (2010) observe that when investors perceive the likelihood of sovereign defaults, country risks will start rising. In this case, a rise in investor's sentiments could be interpreted as a lack of sound risk management strategies to maintain macroeconomic stability. However, our findings also show that African countries are significantly exposed to commodity price shocks. As investigated by Claessens and Qian (1992), African economies depend heavily on the undiversified primary export commodities, which are highly volatile.

Diagnostic checks, such as the Durbin–Watson Test statistics, show no autocorrelation, and the R-squared shows that the model fits our data well. The R-squared increases due to additional explanatory variables. Similarly, Hilscher and Nosbusch (2010) find that adding country-specific variables leads to a substantial increase in the adjusted R-squared. The inclusion of dummy variables is significant in all the specifications.

6.4. Robustness Check: GMM

Table 5 reports the time-series analysis based on the GMM model to determine the key drivers of sovereign risk premium in sub-Saharan Africa. Our results show that the exchange rate, M2/GDP, and trade are insignificant in influencing the sovereign risk premium. This is consistent with the findings of Martinez et al. (2013). We perform the Hansen J-Test of over-identifying restrictions for OIR proposed by Sargan (1958), which tests for the overall validity and relevance of the instruments used. In addition, we carry out the Arellano–Bond Test of no autocorrelation in the error terms. The null hypothesis for the Hansen J-Test is that the instruments are valid and relevant. While, the null hypothesis of the

Arellano and Bond autocorrelation tests of first and second order AR (1) and AR (2), is that there is no autocorrelation. Our results do not reject the null hypothesis of these tests. To address endogeneity issues, Blundell and Bond (1998) suggest the use of instrumental variables by lagging the explanatory variables to two or more lags.

Table 5. Generalized Method of Moment estimation results.

Variables	Inflation Rate	GDP	Public Debt/GDP	Reserves	Sentiment	Trade/GDP	Commodity Price
Burundi	0.14(0.04) **		0.02(0.01) ***				−0.5(0.18) **
Egypt	0.12(0.07) **				3.44(0.57) **		
Gambia	−0.31(0.13) **						
Kenya		0.97(0.5) ***			4.18(2.24) ***		
Mauritania				−0.31(0.15) **	0.99(0.34) **		
Nigeria		−0.26(0.09) **		0.86(0.21) **			
Sierra Leone	0.47(0.10) **			0.97(0.18) **	1.64(0.87) ***		
Swaziland				−0.19(0.05) **			−0.32(0.09) **
South Africa							
Zambia	0.73(0.11) **	0.29(0.10) **					

(i) ** and *** indicates statistical significant at 5% and 10%, respectively. (ii) Standard errors in parentheses. (iii) Instrumental variables include lagged risk premium, lagged exchange rate, lagged M2/GDP, lagged GDP growth, lagged trade/GDP, lagged inflation rate, lagged public debt/GDP, lagged market sentiment, and lagged commodity price (instrumented to one lag).

An important rule of thumb when choosing the number of instruments is that the number of instruments should be at least or equal to the number of regressors, in order not to violate the order condition and limit the number of lags of endogenous variables to $t-1$ and $t-2$. However, for instruments to be valid, they should be strictly exogenous. According to Stock et al. (2002), weak instruments arise when the instruments are weakly correlated with the endogenous variables. The model uses lagged values of the endogenous variable and differences of independent variables as valid instruments. In addition, the exchange rate and M2/GDP ratio are used as instruments. The instrumental variables used are correlated with the endogenous variable such that there is reverse causality. For instance, Devereux and Lane (2003), demonstrate that there is potential endogeneity between risk premium and the exchange rate, as well as the M2/GDP ratio. However, the seven fundamental variables and five time dummies are taken as strictly exogenous. According to Kennedy (1998), the instrumental variable technique provides consistent estimates.

The coefficient estimate on the inflation rate is significant at 5% level in Burundi, Egypt, Gambia, Sierra Leone, and Zambia. This is in line with the findings by Ferrucci (2003), who respectively suggest that macroeconomic variables such as domestic inflation rates are significant determinants of sovereign risk spreads. However, several studies, e.g., Fischer (1993) and Barro (1999), show a negative correlation between inflation and growth, because countries that experience poor growth performance normally have high inflation rates. Again, they respond to growth slumps by printing more money. Bua et al. (2014) explain that printing money might fuel inflationary tendencies in a country. In theory, the seignorage government revenue obtained from printing money can become an important means of deficit financing in the short-run. As noted by Guerrero (2006), the average rate of inflation in Zambia is 82.79%, in Sierra Leone is 27.55%, in Burundi, is 10.36%, in The Gambia is 8.72%, and in Egypt is 7.68%.

An observation by Nkurunziza (2005), is that economic instability in Burundi in the 1990s led to a decline in government revenue, which induced the government to rely more on inflation tax. Burundi, which has an unstable government, may prefer high inflation. In turn, Nkurunziza (2001), emphasize that high inflation may signal poor policies and institutions, which cannot implement inflation-reducing policies, such as inflation-forecast targeting policy rules. A study by Boyd et al. (2001) summarizes the causes of high inflation in Burundi that were attributed to an increase in food prices. As a result, inflation rose from an average of 5% annually in the 1970s and 1980s to 16% in the 1990s. Another study by Cukierman et al. (1992), shows that the increase in the price of imported goods prompted the government to devalue its official exchange rate at the time.

In this case, the drawing down of foreign exchange reserves increased the sovereign risk premium. On the other hand, Deme and Fayissa (1995) point out that in the early 1980s in Egypt, inflation steadily rose, reaching an annual growth rate of 14.6%.

According to a monetarist approach, a rise in the growth of the money supply positively influences the domestic inflation for Egypt. This suggests that monetary policy can be applied to control inflation in Egypt. However, Bruno and Easterly (1998), emphasize that a country is considered to be in an inflation crisis if it is above the 40% threshold level of inflation. At this point, growth turns sharply negative, until the end of the inflation crisis period. Countries that had hyperinflation like Zimbabwe experienced negative economic growth. As suggested by Hegerty (2016), sub-Saharan Africa should improve its macroeconomic performance by adopting inflation targeting. In practice, however, most African economies are still using monetary aggregate targeting, and only a few countries like Ghana and South Africa have shifted to rule-based inflation-forecast targeting.

Another study by Kallon (1994), found high inflationary tendencies in Sierra Leone. In particular, the average inflation rate rose from 15.33% in the 1970s to 63% in the 1980s. Despite the fact that the Sierra Leonean economy is an open economy, and relatively small in size, Sierra Leone is still exposed to significant external risks. On the other hand, Odhiambo (2012) investigates the effects of inflation on financial development in Zambia during the period between 1980 and 2011. Since the 1990s, Baldini et al. (2012) points out that Zambian monetary policy focuses on achieving macroeconomic stability through price stability and exchange rate stability. By way of contrast, the country's inflation rate has been noticeably high. This is attributed to deteriorating terms of trade, due to a decline in copper prices during the period 2008 and 2009, exchange rate volatility, high public debt, and supply shocks.

The coefficient on the public debt to GDP ratio is significant at 10% level in Burundi and has a positive sign. This is similar to Teles and Mussolini (2014), who observe that the increase in public debt/GDP ratio can negatively affect economic growth and hence, pushes up the sovereign risk premium. Moreover, Hatchondo et al. (2012) point out that in countries with an undiversified export base such as Burundi, a high public debt/GDP ratio may be interpreted as the outcome of implementing stricter fiscal rules, in order to restore their credibility. Meanwhile, we obtain a significant coefficient on the commodity price in Burundi and the hypothesized negative sign. A rise in commodity prices increases export earnings used to service debt burden, hence, low sovereign risks. This is in line with the findings by Collier (2007). On the other hand, Bruckner and Ciccone (2010) find that a decline in the commodity price worsens the economic conditions in African economies and that as a result, sovereign risks increase. Moreover, Muhanji and Ojah (2011) note that African countries rely on few primary export commodities, which are highly volatile. Further analysis by Senhadji (1997), argues that favorable commodity prices prompt developing countries to over-borrow with the perception that these favorable commodity prices will last a long time. However, commodity prices are usually uncertain, if taking into account circumstances like the oil price shocks of the 1970s. In turn, commodity price booms are short-lived, and as a result, low commodity export earnings lead to high debt accumulation.

The coefficient on GDP growth is significant at 5% and 10% level in Kenya, Nigeria, Zambia, and South Africa and has mixed signs. As explained by Siklos (2011), this implies that an improvement in economic performance may either increase or decrease the sovereign risk premium. Our results show that the improvement in economic growth reduces sovereign risks in Nigeria and South Africa, whereas it doesn't reduce sovereign risks in Zambia and Kenya. Our findings are in line with those of Baek et al. (2005) and Maltritz and Molchanov (2013), who note that a high growth rate reduces the sovereign default risk. Generally, our results confirm that the "resource curse hypothesis" exists in African economies. This means that African economies have a high sovereign risk premium, due to low economic growth, despite the fact that they are richly endowed with the kind of resources that could boost their export earnings. In particular, Auty (2007), defines the "natural resource curse" as the situation where countries endowed with natural resources experience low economic growth. Some studies, such as those by Sachs and Warner (1999), confirm the negative effects on economic growth. On the contrary, Alexeev and Conrad (2009), disagree.

The coefficient on the foreign exchange reserve is significant in Mauritania, Nigeria, Sierra Leone, and Swaziland. As pointed out by Dreher and Vaubel (2009), the accumulation of the foreign exchange reserve is expected to increase with the economic size and the volume of a country's foreign transactions. Countries with a diversified export base and open economies with high growth rates are expected to hold more reserves. In addition, Bordo et al. (2010) suggest that since foreign currency debt is associated with currency risks, which in turn, push up the sovereign bond spread, holding more reserves might minimize the negative effects of exchange rate risks. Hence, holding an adequate amount of reserves is associated with exchange rate management policies.

The coefficient on the market sentiment is significant at 5% and 10% in Kenya, Mauritania, and Sierra Leone. This is in line with Gonzalez-Rozada and Levy-Yeyati (2008), as well as Bernoth et al. (2012), who find that the increase in the sovereign bond spread is attributed to fluctuations in the investor's risk aversion. High investor's sentiments are interpreted as an increase in the macroeconomic instability, which causes investors to demand a higher risk premium. More recently, Teles and Leme (2010), argue that ratings are used as a guide to investors, where a low sovereign credit rating implies the country carries considerable risk, scaring away potential investors. However, countries with a history of recent defaults have been rated as less risky than countries that have never defaulted. According to Julius et al. (2010), investor's confidence is important when determining the riskiness of a country. Ensuring investors' confidence enhances investors' participation in the market and encourages capital accumulation. On the other hand, Adjasi and Biekpe (2006) find a positive correlation between stock market development and investor confidence in Kenya.

7. Conclusions

This study investigates the key drivers of the sovereign risk premium in African countries. The country risk premium is an important factor in determining the choice between foreign currency borrowing and local currency borrowing. As noted by Olabisi and Stein (2015), a high-risk premium in African countries prompts sovereign borrowers to opt for foreign currency borrowing, which exposes them to exchange rate risks and currency mismatches. In particular, Korinek (2011) demonstrates that developing countries are exposed to high sovereign risks due to macroeconomic volatility, which may increase the probability of a sovereign debt crisis. According to the theory of fiscal insurance forwarded by Uribe (2006), under certain monetary and fiscal policy regimes, sovereign risk default is inevitable. From the sovereign risk management perspective, Baldacci and Kumar (2010), indicate that it is, therefore, important for policymakers to control the key drivers that influence a country's risk. However, our study uses a panel-dynamic fixed effects model to identify the key drivers of a country's risk premium.

Our findings indicate that public debt/GDP, GDP growth, inflation rate, foreign exchange reserve, market sentiment, and commodity price are highly significant in influencing the sovereign risk premium. This is consistent with Gonzalez-Rozada and Levy-Yeyati (2008), Ferrucci (2003), Csonto and Ivaschenko (2013), who note that both the fundamental factors and market sentiment influence the sovereign risk premium. In contrast, Martinez et al. (2013) find that the GDP growth and the public debt/GDP ratio are statistically insignificant, although they present the correct sign. Further analysis reveals that the exchange rate, M2/GDP ratio, and trade/GDP ratio are insignificant. On the contrary, Claessens and Qian (1992) and Ebner (2009) find that the exchange rate is highly significant in African countries. Generally, countries with sound sovereign risk management policies and strong fiscal institutions experience lower sovereign risks.

There are a number of important policy implications for African countries. Policymakers should design appropriate sovereign risk management policies oriented towards achieving institutional reforms that will ensure macroeconomic stability is sustainable. For instance, Claessens et al. (2007), claim that the institutional and macroeconomic framework including the monetary, financial, and fiscal aspects may reflect the level of sovereign risks. In addition, Morgan (2001) suggests that policymakers should set up institutional mechanisms that will manage commodity price uncertainty by issuing commodity-linked bonds and diversifying their export base.

Author Contributions: J.M. and C.M. conceived of the presented idea. J.M. developed the theory and derived the model. C.M. supervised all the work. Both authors discussed the results and contributed to the final manuscript.

Funding: This research received no external funding.

Conflicts of Interest: The authors, Jane Mpapalika and Christopher Malikane declare no conflict of interest.

References

Adjasi, Charles, and Nicholas Biekpe. 2006. Stock market development and economic growth: The case of selected African countries. *African Development Bank* 18: 144–61. [CrossRef]

Alexeev, Michael, and Robert Conrad. 2009. The elusive curse of oil. *Review of Economics and Statistics* 91: 586–98. [CrossRef]

Arellano, Manuel, and Olympia Bover. 1995. Another look at the instrumental variable estimation of error-components models. *Journal of Econometrics* 68: 29–51. [CrossRef]

Aristei, David, and Duccio Martelli. 2014. Sovereign bond yield spreads and market sentiment and expectations: Empirical evidence from Euro area countries. *Journal of Economics and Business* 76: 55–84. [CrossRef]

Aron, Janine, and John Muellbauer. 2005. Monetary policy, macro-stability and growth: South Africa's recent experience and lessons. *World Economics* 6: 123–47.

Audzeyeva, Alena, and Klaus Reiner Schenk-Hoppé. 2010. The role of country, regional and global market risks in the dynamics of Latin American yield spreads. *Journal of International Financial Markets, Institutions and Money* 20: 404–22. [CrossRef]

Auty, Richard M. 2007. Natural resources, capital accumulation and the resource curse. *Ecological Economics* 61: 627–34. [CrossRef]

Baek, In-Mee, Arindam Bandopadhyaya, and Chan Du. 2005. Determinants of market-assessed sovereign risk: Economic fundamentals or market risk appetite? *Journal of International Money and Finance* 24: 533–48. [CrossRef]

Baldacci, Emanuele, and Manmohan Kumar. 2010. *Fiscal Deficits, Public Debt and Sovereign Bond Yields*. IMF Working Paper WP/10/184. Washington, DC: International Monetary Fund, pp. 1–29.

Baldacci, Emanuele, Sanjeev Gupta, and Amine Mati. 2011. Political and fiscal risk determinants of sovereign spreads in Emerging markets. *Review of Development Economics* 15: 251–63. [CrossRef]

Baldini, Alfredo, Jaromir Benes, Andrew Berg, Mai Dao, and Rafael Portillo. 2012. *Monetary Policy In Low Income Countries in the Face of the Global Crisis: The Case of Zambia*. IMF Working paper, WP/12/94. Washington, DC: International Monetary Fund, pp. 1–47.

Banerjee, Anindya. 1999. Panel data unit roots and cointegration: An overview. *Oxford Bulletin of Economics and Statisics* 61: 607–29. [CrossRef]

Barro, Robert. 1999. Notes on optimal debt management. *Journal of Applied Economics* 2: 281–89. [CrossRef]

Bellas, Dimtri, Michael Papaioannou, and Iva Petrova. 2010. *Determinants of Emerging market Sovereign Bond Spreads: Fundamentals vs. Financial Stress*. IMF Working paper, WP/10/281. Washington, DC: International Monetary Fund, pp. 1–24.

Bernoth, Kerstin, and Burcu Erdogan. 2012. Sovereign bond yield spreads: A time-varying coefficient approach. *Journal of International Money and Finance* 31: 639–56. [CrossRef]

Bernoth, Kerstin, Jürgen Von Hagen, and Ludger Schuknecht. 2012. Sovereign risk premiums in the European government bond market. *Journal of International Money and Finance* 31: 975–95. [CrossRef]

Bi, Huixin. 2012. Sovereign default risk premia, fiscal limits, and fiscal policy. *European Economic Review* 56: 389–410. [CrossRef]

Blundell, Richard, and Stephen Bond. 1998. Initial conditions and moment restrictions in dynamic panel data models. *Journal of Econometrics* 87: 115–43. [CrossRef]

Bordo, Michael D., Christopher M. Meissner, and David Stuckler. 2010. Foreign currency debt, financial crises and economic growth: A long-run view. *Journal of International Money and Finance* 29: 642–65. [CrossRef]

Borensztein, Eduardo, and Ugo Panizza. 2009. The costs of sovereign default. *IMF Economic Review* 56: 683–741.

Bound, John, David A. Jaeger, and Regina M. Baker. 1995. Problems with instrumental variables estimation when the correlation between the instruments and the endogenous explanatory variable is weak. *Journal of the American Statistical Association* 90: 1–443. [CrossRef]

Boyd, John H., Ross Levine, and Bruce D. Smith. 2001. The impact of inflation on financial sector performance. *Journal of Monetary Economics* 47: 221–48. [CrossRef]

Bruckner, Markus, and Antonio Ciccone. 2010. International commodity prices, growth and the outbreak of civil war in Sub-Saharan Africa. *The Economic Journal* 120: 519–34. [CrossRef]

Bruno, Michael, and William Easterly. 1998. Inflation crises and long-run growth. *Journal of Monetary Economics* 41: 3–26. [CrossRef]

Bua, Giovanna, Juan Pradelli, and Andrea F. Presbitero. 2014. Domestic public debt in Low-Income Countries: Trends and structure. *Review of Development Finance* 4: 1–19. [CrossRef]

Bunda, Irina, A. Javier Hamann, and Subir Lall. 2009. Correlations in emerging market bonds: The role of local and global factors. *Emerging Markets Review* 10: 67–96. [CrossRef]

Calvo, Guillermo, and Carmen Reinhart. 2002. Fear of floating. *Quarterly Journal of Economics* 116: 379–408. [CrossRef]

Calvo, Guillermo, Leornado Leiderman, and Carmen Reinhart. 1996. Inflows of capital to Developing countries in the 1990s. *Journal of Economic Perspectives* 10: 123–39. [CrossRef]

Cassard, Marcel, and David Folkerts-Landau. 1997. *Risk Management of Sovereign Assets and Liabilities*. IMF Working Paper, WP/97/166. Washington, DC: International Monetary Fund, pp. 1–53.

Christensen, Jakob. 2005. Domestic debt markets in sub-Saharan Africa. *IMF Staff Papers* 52: 518–38. [CrossRef]

Claessens, Stijn, and Ying Qian. 1992. *Risk Management in Sub-Saharan Africa*. IMF Working Paper, WPS 593. Washington DC: International Monetary Fund, pp. 1–58.

Claessens, Stijn, Daniela Klingebiel, and Sergio L. Schmukler. 2007. Government bonds in domestic and foreign currency: The Role of institutional and macroeconomic factors. *Review of International Economics* 15: 370–413. [CrossRef]

Collier, Paul. 2007. Managing commodity booms: Lessons of international experience. In *Centre for the Study of African Economics*. Oxford: Oxford University, pp. 1–16.

Comelli, Fabio. 2012. Emerging market sovereign bond spreads: Estimation and back-testing. *Emerging Markets Review* 13: 598–625. [CrossRef]

Csonto, Balazs, and Iryna Ivaschenko. 2013. *Determinants of Sovereign Bond Spreads in Emerging Markets: Local Fundamentals and Global Factors vs. Ever-Changing Misalignments*. IMF Working Paper, WP/13/164. Washington, DC: International Monetary Fund, pp. 1–42.

Cuadra, Gabriel, Juan M. Sanchez, and Horacio Sapriza. 2010. Fiscal policy and default risk in emerging markets. *Review of Economic Dynamics* 13: 452–69. [CrossRef]

Cukierman, Alex, Miguel Kiguel, and Nissan Liviatan. 1992. How much to commit to an exchange rate rule? Balancing credibility and flexibility. *Economic Analysis Review* 7: 73–90.

Dailami, Mansoor, Paul Masson, and Jean Jose Padou. 2008. Global monetary conditions versus country-specific factors. *Journal of International Money and Finance* 27: 1325–36. [CrossRef]

Deme, Mamit, and Bichaka Fayissa. 1995. Inflation, money, interest rate, exchange rate, and casuality: The case of Egypt, Morocco, and Tunisia. *Applied Economics* 27: 1219–24. [CrossRef]

Devereux, Michael B., and Philip R Lane. 2003. Understanding Bilateral Exchange Rate Volatility. *Journal of International Economics* 60: 109–32. [CrossRef]

Dreher, Axel, and Roland Vaubel. 2009. Foreign exchange intervention and the political business cycle: A panel data analysis. *Journal of International Money and Finance* 28: 755–75. [CrossRef]

Ebner, André. 2009. An empirical analysis on the determinants of CEE government bond spreads. *Emerging Markets Review* 10: 97–121. [CrossRef]

Edwards, Sebastian. 1984. LDC foreign borrowing and default risk: An empirical investigation. *American Economic Review* 74: 726–34.

Eichengreen, B., R. Hausmann, and H. Panizza. 2002. *Original Sin: The Pain, the Mystery, and the Road To Redemption.Currency and Maturity Matchmaking: Redeeming Debt from Original Sin*. Washington, DC: Inter-American Development Bank, pp. 1–56.

Ferrucci, Gianluigi. 2003. *Empirical Determinants of Emerging Market Economies' Sovereign Bond Spreads*. IMF Working Paper (205). Washington DC: International Monetary Fund, pp. 1–38.

Fischer, Stanley. 1993. The role of macroeconomic factors in growth. *Journal of Monetary Economics* 32: 485–511. [CrossRef]

Furceri, David, and Aleksandra Zdzienicka. 2012. How costly are debt crises? *Journal of International Money and Finance* 31: 726–42. [CrossRef]

Galindo, Arturo, Ugo Panizza, and Fabio Schiantarelli. 2003. Debt composition and balance sheet effects of currency depreciation: A summary of the micro evidence. *Emerging Markets Review* 4: 330–39. [CrossRef]

Gelos, R. Gaston, Ratna Sahay, and Guido Sandleris. 2011. Sovereign borrowing by developing countries: What determines market access? *Journal of International Economics* 83: 243–54. [CrossRef]

Gonzalez-Rozada, Martin, and Eduardo Levy-Yeyati. 2008. Global factors and emerging market spreads. *The Economic Journal* 118: 1917–36. [CrossRef]

De Grauwe, Paul, and Yuemei Ji. 2012. Mispricing of sovereign risk and macroeconomic stability in the Eurozone. *Journal of Common Market Studies* 50: 866–80. [CrossRef]

Guerrero, Federico. 2006. Does inflation cause poor long-term growth performance? *Japan and the World Economy* 18: 72–89. [CrossRef]

Guillaumont, Patrick, Sylviane Guillaumont Jeanneney, and Jean-Francois Brun. 1999. How instability lowers African growth. *Journal of African Economies* 8: 87–107. [CrossRef]

Gumus, Inci. 2011. Exchange rate policy and sovereign spreads in emerging market economies. *Review of International Economics* 19: 649–63. [CrossRef]

Gylfason, Thorvaldur. 1991. Inflation, growth, and external debt: A View of the landscape. *The World Economy* 14: 279–97. [CrossRef]

Hatchondo, Juan Carlos, Francisco Roch, and Leonardo Martinez. 2012. *Fiscal Rules and the Sovereign Default Premium*. IMF Working Paper WP/12/30. Washington, DC: International Monetary Fund, pp. 1–38.

Hegerty, W. Scott. 2016. Commodity-price volatility and macroeconomic spillovers: Evidence from nine emerging markets. *North American Journal of Economics and Finance* 35: 23–37. [CrossRef]

Heinemann, Friedrich, Steffen Osterloh, and Alexander Kalb. 2014. Sovereign risk premia: The link between fiscal rules and stability culture. *Journal of International Money and Finance* 41: 110–27. [CrossRef]

Hilscher, Jens, and Yves Nosbusch. 2010. Determinants of sovereign risk: Macroeconomic fundamentals and the pricing of sovereign debt. *Review of Finance* 14: 235–62. [CrossRef]

Iara, Anna, and Guntram Wolff. 2014. Rules and risk in the Euro area. *European Journal of Political Economy* 34: 222–36. [CrossRef]

Im, Kyung So, Hashem Pesaran, and Yongcheol Shin. 2003. Testing for unit roots in heterogeneous panels. *Journal of Econometrics* 115: 53–74. [CrossRef]

Jankovic, Irena, and Bosko Zivkovic. 2014. An analysis of the effect of currency mismatch on a country's default risk. *Economic Annals* 59: 85–121. [CrossRef]

Jeanne, Olivier, and Romain Ranciere. 2011. The optimal level of international reserves for emerging market countries: A new formula and some applications. *The Economic Journal* 121: 905–30. [CrossRef]

Judson, Ruth, and Ann Owen. 1999. Estimating dynamic panel data models: A guide for macroeconomists. *Economics Letters* 65: 9–15. [CrossRef]

Julius, Bitok, Kiplangat Andrew, Tenai Joel, and Rono Lucy. 2010. Determinants of investor confidence for firms listed at the Nairobi stock exchange, Kenya. *International Journal of Finance and Management* 1: 160–73.

Kallon, Kelfala. 1994. An econometric analysis of inflation in Sierra Leone. *Journal of African Economies* 3: 201–30. [CrossRef]

Kamin, Steven, and Karsten von Kleist. 1999. *The Evolution and Determinants of Emerging Market Credit Spreads in the 1990s*. BIS Working Paper No. 68. Washington, DC: Federal Reserve System, pp. 1–40.

Kaminsky, Graciela, and Sergio Schmukler. 1999. What triggers market jitters? A chronicle of the Asian crisis. *Journal of International Money and Finance* 18: 537–60. [CrossRef]

Kao, Chihwa. 1999. Spurious regression and residual based tests for cointegration in panel data. *Journal of Econometrics* 90: 1–44. [CrossRef]

Kennedy, Peter. 1998. *A guide to Econometrics*. Cambridge: MIT Press.

Korinek, Anton. 2011. Foreign currency debt, risk premia and macroeconomic volatility. *European Economic Review* 55: 371–85. [CrossRef]

Kyereboah-Coleman, Anthony. 2012. Inflation targeting and inflation management in Ghana. *Financial Economic Policy* 4: 25–40. [CrossRef]

Levin, Andrew, Chien-Fu Lin, and Chia-Shang James Chu. 2002. Unit root tests in panel data: Asymptotic and finite sample properties. *Journal of Econometrics* 108: 1–24. [CrossRef]

Malikane, Christopher, and Tshepo Mokoka. 2012. Monetary policy credibility: A Phillips curve view. *The Quarterly Review of Economics and Finance* 52: 266–71. [CrossRef]

Maltritz, Dominik. 2012. Determinants of sovereign yield spreads in the Eurozone: A Bayesian approach. *Journal of International Money and Finance* 31: 657–72. [CrossRef]

Maltritz, Dominik, and Alexander Molchanov. 2013. Analyzing determinants of bond yield spreads with Bayesian model averaging. *Journal of Banking and Finance* 37: 5275–84. [CrossRef]

Martinez, Lisana, Antonio Terceno, and Mercedes Terruel. 2013. Sovereign bond spreads determinants in Latin American countries: Before and during the XXI financial crisis. *Emerging Markets Review* 17: 60–75. [CrossRef]

McCoskey, Suzanne, and Chihwa Kao. 1998. A residual-based test for the null of cointegration in panel data. *Econometric Reviews* 17: 57–84. [CrossRef]

Mendonca, Helder Ferreira de, and Marcio Nunes. 2011. Public debt and risk premium: An analysis from an emerging economy. *Journal of Economic Studies* 38: 203–17. [CrossRef]

Min, Hong-Ghi, Duk-Hee Lee, Changi Nam, Myeong Cheol Park, and Sang-Ho Nam. 2003. Determinants of emerging-market bond spreads: Cross-country evidence. *Global Finance Journal* 14: 271–86. [CrossRef]

Morgan, Wallet. 2001. Commodity futures markets in LDCs: A review and prospects. *Progress in Development Studies* 1: 139–50. [CrossRef]

Muhanji, Stella, and Kalu Ojah. 2011. External shocks and persistence of external debt in open vulnerable economies: The case of Africa. *Economic Modelling* 28: 1615–28. [CrossRef]

Nkurunziza, Janvier. 2001. Exchange rate policy and the parallel market for foreign currency in Burundi. *African Journal of Economic Policy* 8: 69–121.

Nkurunziza, Janvier. 2005. Political instability, inflation tax and asset substitution in Burundi. *Journal of African Development* 7: 42–72.

Odhiambo, Nicholas. 2012. The impact of inflation on financial sector development: Experience from Zambia. *The Journal of Applied Business Research* 28: 1497–508. [CrossRef]

Olabisi, Michael, and Howard Stein. 2015. Sovereign bond issues: Do African countries pay more to borrow? *Journal of African Trade* 2: 87–109. [CrossRef]

Ouyang, Alice, and Ramkishen Rajan. 2014. What determines external debt tipping points? *Journal of Macroeconomics* 39: 215–25. [CrossRef]

Özatay, Fatih, Erdal Özmen, and Gulbin Şahinbeyoğlu. 2009. Emerging market sovereign spreads, global financial conditions and U.S. macroeconomic news. *Economic Modelling* 26: 526–31. [CrossRef]

Pedroni, Peter. 1999. Critical values for cointegration tests in heterogeneous panels with multiple regressors. *Oxford Bulletin of Economics and Statistics* 61: 653–70. [CrossRef]

Pedroni, Peter. 2004. Panel Cointegration; Asymptotic and Finite Sample Properties of Pooled Time Series Tests, with an Application to the PPP Hypothesis. *Econometric Theory* 20: 597–625. [CrossRef]

Reinhart, Carmen, and Kenneth Rogoff. 2011. From financial crisis to debt crisis. *American Economic Review* 101: 1676–706. [CrossRef]

Roodman, David. 2009. A note on the theme of too many instruments. *Oxford Bulletin of Economics and Statistics* 71: 135–58. [CrossRef]

Sachs, Jeffrey, and Andrew Warner. 1999. The Big push, natural resource booms and growth. *Journal of Development Economics* 59: 43–76. [CrossRef]

Sargan, John Denis. 1958. The estimation of economic relationships using instrumental variables. *Econometrica* 26: 393–415. [CrossRef]

Senhadji, Abdelhak. 1997. *Sources of Debt Accumulation in a Small Open Economy*. Washington, DC: International Monetary Fund, IMF Working Paper, WP/97/146. pp. 1–26.

Siklos, Pierre. 2011. Emerging market yield spreads: Domestic, external determinants, and volatility spillovers. *Global Finance Journal* 22: 83–100. [CrossRef]

Stock, James, Jonathan Wright, and Motohiro Yogo. 2002. A survey of weak instruments and weak identification in Generalized Method of Moments. *Journal of Business and Economic Statistics* 20: 518–29. [CrossRef]

Strauss, Jack, and Taner Yigit. 2003. Shortfalls of panel unit root testing. *Economics Letters* 81: 309–13. [CrossRef]

Sturzenegger, Federico. 2004. Tools for the analysis of debt problems. *Journal of Restructuring Finance* 1: 201–23. [CrossRef]

Teles, Vladimir Kuhl, and Maria Carolina Leme. 2010. Fundamentals or market sentiment: What causes country risk? *Applied Economics* 42: 2577–85. [CrossRef]

Teles, Vladimir Kuhl, and Caio Cesar Mussolini. 2014. Public debt and the limits of fiscal policy to increase economic growth. *European Economic Review* 66: 1–15. [CrossRef]

Tkalec, Marina, Maruska Vizek, and Miroslav Verbic. 2014. Balance sheet effects and original sinners' risk premiums. *Economic Systems* 38: 597–613. [CrossRef]

Uribe, Martin. 2006. A fiscal theory of sovereign risk. *Journal of Monetary Economics* 53: 1857–75. [CrossRef]

Zinna, Gabriele. 2013. Sovereign default risk premia: Evidence from the default swap market. *Journal of Empirical Finance* 21: 15–35. [CrossRef]

Journal of
Risk and Financial Management

MDPI

Article

Time–Scale Relationship between Securitized Real Estate and Local Stock Markets: Some Wavelet Evidence

Kim Hiang Liow [1,*], Xiaoxia Zhou [2], Qiang Li [1] and Yuting Huang [1]

[1] Department of Real Estate, National University of Singapore, 4 Architecture Drive, Singapore 117566, Singapore; rstlq@nus.edu.sg (Q.L.); huangyuting@u.nus.edu (Y.H.)

[2] School of Finance, Shanghai University of Finance and Economics, 100 Wudong Road, Shanghai 200433, China; zhou.xiaoxia@shufe.edu.cn

* Correspondence: rstlkh@nus.edu.sg

Received: 10 December 2018; Accepted: 15 January 2019; Published: 20 January 2019

Abstract: This study revisits the relationship between securitized real estate and local stock markets by focusing on their time-scale co-movement and contagion dynamics across five developed countries. Since securitized real estate market is an important capital component of the domestic stock market in the respective economies, it is linked to the stock market. Earlier research does not have satisfactory results, because traditional methods average different relationships over various time and frequency domains between securitized real estate and local stock markets. According to our novel wavelet analysis, the relationship between the two asset markets is time–frequency varying. The average long run real estate–stock correlation fails to outweigh the average short run correlation, indicating the real estate markets examined may have become increasingly less sensitive to the domestic stock markets in the long-run in recent years. Moreover, securitized real estate markets appear to lead stock markets in the short run, whereas stock markets tend to lead securitized real estate markets in the long run, and to a lesser degree medium-term. Finally, we find incomplete real estate and local stock market integration among the five developed economies, given only weaker long-run integration beyond crisis periods.

Keywords: wavelet coherence and phase difference; rolling wavelet correlation; multiresolution analysis; contagion; securitized real estate and local stock markets

---

1. Introduction

Securitized real estate (real estate stocks and real estate investment trusts) is a major capital asset component of the domestic stock market in many economies. Due to its dual nature, the value of securitized real estate is a function of the market value of its property holdings and stock market valuation (Morawski et al. 2008). According to Markowitz's (1952) portfolio theory, if the two asset markets are closely linked, then the differential risk premium will eventually disappear to the extent to which there will not be any potential for cross-asset and cross-border diversification for global investors and country funds. Moreover, higher interdependences between securitized real estate and stock markets may imply more or faster transmission of a crisis, indicating that there is less opportunity for spreading risk, at least across the major developed securitized real estate and stock markets, than it was the case in the previous decades (Liow and Schindler 2011). Consequently, the question of how closely securitized real estate is linked to stock is thus of great concern to portfolio investors and financial institutions who invest in both asset markets.

Although traditional research has generally reported a reasonably close link between the two asset markets, one major shortcoming is that such knowledge ignores the possibility that the direction and strength of the real estate–stock link may vary over different frequencies. Recognizing financial markets have many time scales (Loh 2013), the relationships between real estate and stock markets are probably time-scale dependent to the extent that heterogeneity in investment horizon will affect the cross real estate and stock links differently in the short-run, medium-term, and long-run (Zhou 2010). This can happen due to the presence of different types of behaviorally motivated market players such as short-term speculative traders and long-term strategic portfolio investors operating in various real estate and stock markets. Moreover, the existing literature employs one or more of traditional time series methods (such as correlation coefficient, co-integration analysis, and GARCH-related models) to measure the level of dynamic real estate-stock return correlations. Thus, there is room for an alternative approach to provide novel and informative evidence or give fresh insights on the complex interactions between securitized real estate and local stock markets.

Despite much academic effort regarding the time–frequency relationships across stock markets using continuous wavelet transform (CWT) (e.g., Aguiar-Conraria et al. 2008; Loh 2013; Dima et al. 2015; and Tiwari et al. 2016) and maximal overlap discrete wavelet transform (MODWT) (e.g., Ranta 2013; Deora and Nguyen 2013; and Dewandaru et al. 2016) since the last decade, previous time-scale studies on real estate markets, as well as between real estate and stock markets, are lacking, with the exceptions of Zhou (2010, 2012), Li et al. (2015), and Liow et al. (2018a, 2018b). This knowledge gap will be filled by the present study. Our study can be clearly distinguished from the previous studies in focusing on the twin aspects of market "interdependence", and "contagion", and offering a comprehensive exploration of the time-scale real estate-stock connection in an international environment.

Assembling a sample of five major developed securitized real estate markets and their corresponding domestic stock markets, this paper revisits the relationship between the two asset markets by focusing on the time–scale co-movement and contagion dynamics across the five countries. The study provides novel and informative contribution by appealing to wavelet analysis to decompose time series into various time–frequency domains. Wavelets are mathematical functions that divide data into different frequency components and then study each component with a resolution appropriate for its overall scale (Ramsey 2002). Wavelet methodology is a refinement of Fourier analysis (spectral analysis). Subsequently, it was followed by the development of multiresolution analysis by Mallat (1989) and the introduction of orthogonal wavelet bases by Daubechies (1992). In addition to revisiting the average relationship between the two asset markets, we examine the nature and pattern of co-movement of five Western developed countries' real estate-local stock markets at different time scales/investment horizons. We also compare the differences in the time-scale co-movement between the US and European markets during the global financial crisis (GFC) and European debt crisis (EDC). In so doing, this paper adds itself to an understanding of the varying time–frequency relationship between securitized real estate and stock markets, an issue which has been insufficiently addressed in previous empirical studies.

On the first issue examining real estate-stock co-movement, one key message delivered to investors from the previous studies is that increased co-movement between real estate and stock markets may diminish the advantage of internationally diversified asset portfolios. Some of these time-series real estate studies include Liu et al. (1990); Ambrose et al. (1992); Eichholtz (1996); Okunev and Wilson (1997); Ling and Naranjo (1999); Quan and Titman (1999); Okunev et al. (2000); Ling and Naranjo (2002); Bond et al. (2003); Michayluk et al. (2006); Schindler (2011); Liow (2012); Yunus et al. (2012); and Hoesli and Oikarinen (2012).

On the second issue relating to financial contagion, since any increase in the real estate and stock co-movement from the pre-crisis period to the crisis period may take the form of interdependence or contagion, there is the suspicion that the observed co-movement between securitized real estate and local stock markets is caused by contagion in the context of globalization. Whilst some researchers such as Rua and Nunes (2009) and Ranta (2013) presume that contagion is a temporary increase of short time-scale co-movement (or "pure" contagion, Dornbusch et al. (2000)), we also consider whether the detected real estate-stock co-movement is also affected by "fundamentals-based" contagion (Kaminsky and Reinhart 2000). "Pure" contagion describes a situation where an excessive transmission of shocks due to a crisis is beyond any idiosyncratic disturbances and fundamental linkages, and is relatively fast and disappears in a short period. Using wavelets, if short time-scale co-movement increases while long time-scale co-movement remains relatively stable, then such real estate-stock link is a function of "pure" contagion. In contrast, "fundamentals-based" contagion refers to a situation which involves a transmission of shocks, due to financial market and real linkages in crisis and non-crisis periods, and reflects market interdependence across countries. Given this basic contagion framework, we examine if the real estate-stock co-movement increases after the GFC and EDC crisis episodes over the three investment horizons specified. Prior time-series real estate studies include Hui and Chan (2013); Hoesli and Reka (2015) and Hui and Chan (2016).

The plan of this paper is as follows. Section 2 briefly discuss the various methods used in this study. An explanation of the data requirement is in Section 3. With Section 4, reports and discusses the relevant empirical results, Section 5 concludes the paper.

2. Research Methods

We adopt a holistic perspective by taking on a three-step empirical strategies. To save space, we only provided below an intuitive sketch of the wavelet approach and the three methods applied.[1]

2.1. The Essence of Wavelet Analysis

Wavelet analysis transforms time series into different frequency components with a resolution matched to its scale. There are two ways of wavelet decomposition, one is known as the CWT which is designed to work with time series over the entire axis (Grinsted et al. 2004); another one is the DWT which deals with time series with finite range. Additionally, the MODWT is a subsampling of the CWT at dyadic scales, but the number of coefficients can be the same length with the original time series. Both the DWT and MODWT draw on multiresolution analysis (MRA) to decompose a time series into lower and lower levels of resolution. This level of multiresolution decomposition is referred as scales in wavelet studies. Following literature, the interpretation of lower/higher resolution in this study using daily frequency returns is: scale d1 (2–4 days), scale d2 (4–8 days), scale d3 (8–16 days), scale d4 (16–32 days), scale d5 (32–64 days), scale sd6 (64–128 days) and scale d7 (128–256 days), using the Daubechies' (1992) least asymmetric wavelet filter, LA (8).

2.2. Wavelet-Based Modelling

One major contribution of this study lies in combining wavelet analysis and the coherence/phase difference analysis, static and rolling percentage of total volume analysis (PTV), rolling wavelet correlation contagion analysis, and multi-resolution asymmetric dynamic conditional correlation analysis (ADCC-GARCH). They are briefly presented below:

(a) Wavelet Coherence and Phase Difference Analysis

Wavelet coherency allows for a three-dimensional analysis, which simultaneously considers the time and frequency elements, as well as the strength of correlation between the time series (Loh 2013). The coherence captures the correlation coefficients around each moment in time and for each frequency. Using the wavelet coherence plot, the x-axis and y-axis represent time and frequency respectively. From there, we observe how the real estate-stock correlations vary over frequencies and time intervals. Additionally, phases are indicated by arrows, which indicate the nature of lead–lag linkages. All computations will be done using MATLAB.

The wavelet coherence is defined by Torrence and Webster (1999) as the squared absolute value of the smoothed cross-wavelet spectra divided by the product of the smoothed individual wavelet power

[1] Interested readers, please consult various source references for the mathematical functions.

spectra of the two selected time series. This wavelet coherence coefficient is in the range between 0 and 1. As a measure of studying market co-movement, values that are close to zero indicate low correlations; in contrast, values that are close to one indicate the presence of strong correlations. This concept is very useful for determining the regions in the time–frequency domain where the time series share significant co-movements. Finally, we employ the static and rolling percentage of total volume (PTV) of the wavelet coherence to complement the graphic observations derived from the coherence plots.

(b) Rolling Wavelet Correlations

Inspecting the rolling correlations between real estate-stock market returns can observe whether there is a rising trend of correlation across the scales. In this study, we will implement a wavelet based real estate-stock rolling correlation analysis on a scale-by-scale basis, using windows of 125 days (half a year of trading), rolled forward one day at a time, resulting in a time series of wavelet correlation, and are decomposed by the MODWT with a Haar filter.[2]

Moreover, a t-test was performed to compare the level of rolling correlation before and after the GFC and EDC. Following Ranta (2013), we conclude there is evidence of 'pure" contagion if short time-scale co-movements increase, while the long time-scale co-movements remain about the same. In addition, we address whether the real estate-stock co-movement is affected by the "fundamentals-based" contagion after the crisis episodes following the theoretical contagion framework outlined above.

By applying the transformation, the adjusted correlation coefficient (z) is:

$$z = 0.5 * \ln(\frac{1+r}{1-r})$$

The t-test statistic is:

$$t = \frac{z_1 - z_2}{\sqrt{\frac{1}{n_1-3} + \frac{1}{n_2-3}}}$$

Thus, with the time windows used before and after the two crises that have 250, 125, and 500 days respectively, we can compare the equality of coefficients, and test whether the contagion is statistically significant across the real estate and stock markets. Since any "pure" contagion is usually confined to shorter time scales and investment horizons, we use the first four scales (d1, d2, d3, and d4). We also assess the "fundamentals-based contagion" using another three longer time scales (d5, d6, and d7).

(c) Further Analysis: Multi-Resolution Analysis (MRA)-Conditional Correlation Analysis

We combine MRA with a bivariate AR (1)-ADCC-GARCH model of Engle (2002) and Cappiello et al. (2006). Evidence from this analysis will provide support on the varying time scale real estate-stock correlation behavior, and whether the average conditional real estate-stock correlation will increase or decrease when the level of decomposition increases. We expect that since different groups of investors can operate on their time horizons, the real estate-local stock market correlation in an international setting may differ across time scales.

The conditional ADCC-GARCH model is adopted because it keeps the simple interpretation of the univariate GARCH models, as well as providing a consistent estimate of the dynamic correlation matrix. Moreover, the model considers the leverage effects of return volatility. Its estimation comprises

---

2 After experimenting with Daubechies LA (8) and Haar filters, the latter was chosen in the MODWT. It is the simplest of all wavelet filters and avoids the boundary problem of filtering. Moreover, the choice of the length of the window is not straightforward, since a longer window implies the loss of time information, and a shorter window implies the loss of frequency information. Ranta (2013) find that calculations using different DWT filters produce very similar results. In this study, we use the 250-day window (one year trading) as the base case, with the 125 days and 500 days used to test the robustness of the results.

three steps, as detailed in the literature.[3] Using the model, we will evaluate and validate the strength of the real estate-stock market co-movement in the short-run (scales d1 + d2: 2–eight days, one week approx.), medium-term (scales d3 + d4: 8–32 days, one-month approx.) and long-run (scales d5 + d6 + d7, 32–256 days, one year approx.).

Related empirical studies are very limited. Deora and Nguyen (2013) finds from their wavelet-based DCC-GARCH model that the conditional correlations between the Indian and world equity markets vary considerably across time scales. Some other studies such as Lee (2004); Huang (2011) and Khalfaoui et al. (2015) focus on the time-scale mean and volatility spillovers rather than conditional correlations.

3. Sample and Data

A sample of five major developed securitized real estate markets, and their corresponding domestic stock markets are included in this study. Of them, the four major European markets are the UK, France, Germany, and Netherlands, as well as the US (from North America). These five securitized real estate markets represent over 70% of global real estate market capitalization, and they have a combination of listed REITs and real estate stocks in their respective stock markets, with the percentage of REITs in the index being 100% (France), 100% (Netherlands), 99% (US), 84% (UK), and 5% (Germany). Among them, the US has the world's largest real estate market, which is also the most transparent securitized real estate market, and it is largely dominated by REITs. The listed real estate companies have a long history in Europe, with the UK being the largest European securitized real estate market. While Germany has a long history of indirect real estate vehicles such as open-ended funds, closed-ended funds, and listed real estate companies, Netherlands has an established and relatively large securitized real estate market that accounts for above 10% of the European developed securitized real estate market.[4]

The daily FTSE/EPRA public real estate price indexes and the FTSE stock market price indexes of the five countries, both in local dollars, are sourced from the Datastream, and the sample period runs from 3 January 2000 until 29 April 2016. Daily returns are calculated as the difference in the natural logarithm of the price indexes. After excluding public holidays and adjusting for trading hour synchronization, we had 4204 daily compounded returns. Table 1 provides the usual descriptive statistics for the daily returns of the five countries (10 series) over the full study period. One main observation is that all return series are rejected for normality, as indicated by the respective significant Jarque–Bara tests at least at the five percent level.

3 Interested readers, please consult Cappiello et al. (2006) for the relevant mathematical details. Empirically, the model can be estimated using RATS or Ox metrics software packages.

4 The analysis of real estate and stock market returns may need to control for the fact that the real estate securities are embedded in the country specific stock indexes. Whilst this may be probably needed for some Asian markets, such as Japan, Hong Kong, and Singapore, where real estate firms represent a sizeable portion of the overall market valuation, this is probably not that much of a concern for the US and four other European markets in our sample where securitized real estate is a relatively small part of the overall market index. Thus, examining the connection between public real estate and the overall stock market has the flavor of regressing a dependent variable on itself.

Table 1. Descriptive statistics of daily public real estate and stock returns (local dollars).

	REFR	REGE	RENE	REUK	REUS
Real Estate Returns (RE)					
Mean	0.00036	0.00001	0.00011	0.00018	0.00045
Median	0.00084	0.00026	0.00060	0.00099	0.00165
Maximum	0.09329	0.14111	0.09014	0.15391	0.32583
Minimum	−0.10357	−0.14563	−0.08610	−0.16445	−0.32277
Std. Dev.	0.01555	0.01805	0.01506	0.02286	0.02511
Skewness	−0.12634	−0.03566	−0.22948	−0.44756	−0.31375
Kurtosis	7.04311	10.25292	7.21583	9.34468	30.22439
Jarque-Bera	2874.59	9215.50	3150.17	7191.67	129,896.80
Probability	0	0	0	0	0
Stock Retruns (ST)					
	STFR	**STGE**	**STNE**	**STUK**	**STUS**
Mean	0.00002	0.00005	−0.00003	−0.00010	0.00014
Median	0.00045	0.00058	0.00031	0.00057	0.00086
Maximum	0.11890	0.11654	0.10577	0.14800	0.12332
Minimum	−0.11684	−0.09723	−0.11362	−0.14699	−0.13310
Std. Dev.	0.01605	0.01649	0.01591	0.01950	0.01689
Skewness	−0.01915	−0.06913	−0.10200	−0.28101	−0.39447
Kurtosis	8.87680	7.38654	8.61356	9.42605	8.69940
Jarque-Bera	6049.95	3373.86	5527.15	7288.69	5799.00
Probability	0	0	0	0	0

Notes: The sample period is from 3 January 2000 to 29 April 2016. FR, GE, NE, UK, US stand for France, Germany, Netherlands, United Kingdom, and United States, respectively. The returns are continuously compounded returns. (Source: FTSE/EPRA and Datastream).

4. Empirical Results

4.1. Time-Scale Decomposed Returns

Although the maximum wavelet decomposition level is $\log_2 T$, (T is number of data), we choose seven scales, only because the feasible wavelet coefficients become smaller with higher levels of decomposition. Table 2 provides the mean and standard deviation of the time scale decomposed returns using the MODWT method with the LA (8) filter. One key observation is that the estimated wavelet standard deviation for all return series decreases when the scale increases.

A wavelet variance decomposition analysis (Table 3) illustrates that most of the volatility in the return series is captured by lower levels of MODWT wavelet coefficients. The MODWT coefficients at scale 1 (the highest frequency) represent the highest level of energy. The level 1 MODWT wavelet coefficients, indicating short-term fluctuations occurring due to shock occurring up to four days, capture between 20.74% and 50.74% (stock), as well as between 18.31% and 47.49% (real estate) of the total energy of the market returns. Additionally, the first four scales (up to the monthly horizon) represent between 90.02% and 93.99% (real estate), as well as between 91.89% and 95.68% (stock) of the variances of the decomposed returns.

Table 2. Mean and standard deviation (SD) of decomposed returns at different scales.

Real Estate	Time Scales	I	II	III	IV	V	VI	VII	VIII
Panel A: Public Real Estate Markets									
FR	Mean	-1.53×10^{-19}	-6.02×10^{-20}	-4.55×10^{-20}	1.47×10^{-19}	-1.65×10^{-20}	1.02×10^{-20}	-1.37×10^{-21}	5.23×10^{-20}
	SD	0.0102	0.0068	0.0050	0.0031	0.0021	0.0017	0.0011	0.0012
GE	Mean	5.05×10^{-19}	3.70×10^{-20}	7.81×10^{-20}	1.32×10^{-19}	4.79×10^{-20}	6.25×10^{-20}	-3.16×10^{-20}	-9.52×10^{-20}
	SD	0.0117	0.0079	0.0058	0.0038	0.0026	0.0024	0.0012	0.0013
NE	Mean	1.37×10^{-19}	-2.03×10^{-20}	7.49×10^{-20}	3.40×10^{-20}	-2.34×10^{-20}	7.86×10^{-20}	1.19×10^{-20}	1.22×10^{-19}
	SD	0.0098	0.0065	0.0051	0.0032	0.0021	0.0017	0.0011	0.0011
UK	Mean	-1.52×10^{-19}	1.31×10^{-19}	2.40×10^{-19}	2.90×10^{-19}	-1.73×10^{-19}	2.07×10^{-19}	2.62×10^{-20}	1.08×10^{-19}
	SD	0.0085	0.0110	0.0099	0.0071	0.0041	0.0036	0.0018	0.0026
US	Mean	1.61×10^{-19}	-4.78×10^{-19}	-8.68×10^{-20}	1.16×10^{-19}	-1.49×10^{-19}	1.58×10^{-19}	1.16×10^{-19}	3.73×10^{-20}
	SD	0.0121	0.0122	0.0099	0.0056	0.0041	0.0037	0.0016	0.0018
Panel B: Stock Markets									
FR	Mean	6.92×10^{-20}	3.40×10^{-19}	2.80×10^{-20}	-5.09×10^{-20}	-1.03×10^{-19}	3.04×10^{-20}	3.89×10^{-20}	-9.28×10^{-20}
	SD	0.0108	0.0071	0.0048	0.0031	0.0020	0.0017	0.0009	0.0009
GE	Mean	2.34×10^{-19}	-1.65×10^{-19}	3.60×10^{-20}	-8.66×10^{-21}	5.74×10^{-20}	1.44×10^{-19}	3.72×10^{-20}	7.30×10^{-21}
	SD	0.0111	0.0071	0.0051	0.0034	0.0022	0.0018	0.0010	0.0010
NE	Mean	8.82×10^{-20}	9.18×10^{-20}	-4.56×10^{-20}	-8.71×10^{-21}	-3.00×10^{-20}	-4.12×10^{-21}	8.68×10^{-20}	7.56×10^{-20}
	SD	0.0106	0.0070	0.0048	0.0030	0.0021	0.0018	0.0009	0.0010
UK	Mean	-6.62×10^{-20}	-6.97×10^{-20}	1.24×10^{-19}	2.52×10^{-20}	-1.90×10^{-19}	-6.55×10^{-20}	3.85×10^{-20}	-7.10×10^{-21}
	SD	0.0076	0.0102	0.0079	0.0054	0.0034	0.0026	0.0013	0.0016
US	Mean	-6.39×10^{-20}	-2.00×10^{-19}	4.22×10^{-19}	5.98×10^{-21}	-7.83×10^{-20}	-1.07×10^{-20}	1.09×10^{-19}	9.81×10^{-20}
	SD	0.0071	0.0085	0.0070	0.0045	0.0031	0.0024	0.0012	0.0012

Notes: The public real estate and stock returns at different time scales are generated using maximal overlap discrete wavelet transform (MODWT) with a Daubechies LA (8) filter. The countries are: France (FR), GE (Germany), Netherlands (UK), the UK, and the US.

Table 3. Wavelet variance decomposition by time scales.

Panel A: Public Real Estate Markets					
VAR	**FR**	**GE**	**NE**	**UK**	**US**
d1	47.49%	46.54%	46.74%	18.31%	29.00%
d2	26.48%	26.34%	25.44%	31.73%	33.83%
d3	14.31%	14.23%	15.36%	26.06%	21.70%
d4	6.00%	6.35%	6.45%	14.17%	7.48%
d5	2.88%	3.16%	3.01%	4.86%	4.01%
d6	1.91%	2.72%	2.09%	3.57%	3.17%
d7	0.94%	0.65%	0.91%	1.32%	0.81%
Panel B: Stock Markets					
VAR	**FR**	**GE**	**NE**	**UK**	**US**
d1	50.74%	50.19%	49.99%	20.74%	23.58%
d2	27.10%	26.07%	26.87%	37.73%	34.94%
d3	12.64%	12.91%	12.80%	22.95%	23.59%
d4	5.20%	5.79%	5.21%	10.84%	9.79%
d5	2.32%	2.70%	2.71%	4.55%	4.92%
d6	1.48%	1.70%	1.88%	2.38%	2.46%
d7	0.52%	0.64%	0.54%	0.81%	0.73%

Notes: this table presents the percentage of the wavelet variance at seven different scales for each stock market returns generated using MODWT with a Daubechies LA (8) filter; d1–d7 (scale 1 to scale 7).

4.2. CWT: Wavelet Power Spectrum, Cross Wavelet Power Spectrum, and Wavelet Coherency

Figure 1 displays the continuous wavelet power spectrum for the five real estate market indexes.[5] In these plots, the dark black contour line in regions with energy indicates the 5% significant level estimated from Monte Carlo simulations. The areas outside the cone of influence (the thin black line) are heavily affected by the edge effects. One key observation is that the volatilities of the real estate markets decline as the wavelet scale rises. Moreover, all of the real estate market volatilities are relatively high and are statistically significant regardless of the time scales. During 2006–2010, much stronger volatility effects are evident at the medium-term and long-run investment horizons, implying that capital markets todays face higher longer run shocks.

The wavelet coherency is displayed through five contour graphs (Figure 2). In the context of wavelets, the coherence captures the correlation coefficients around each moment in time, and for each frequency. Through this graph we can detect the regions in a time–frequency space where the real estate and stock markets co-vary and capture both time and frequency-varying features. In each plot shown in Figure 2, the horizontal axis represents the time-period during the sample years 2000–2016, whereas the vertical axis refers to the time scales. The thick dark curved line indicates the 5% significance level, such that the region outside the boundary is considered statistically insignificant at the 95% confidence level. The color code for power ranges from blue (low coherency, near zero) to yellow (high coherency, near one). Finally, the arrows pointing to the right mean that the returns are in phase (positively correlated). Moreover, the first series is "lagging" when the arrow are pointing up; whereas the first series is leading when the arrows are pointing down. On the other hand, the two series are out of phase if the arrows are moving to the left. Also to the left and up means that the two series are negatively correlated and the first series is lagging; the first series is leading when the arrow is pointing down.

[5] The stock market plots are not shown to conserve space.

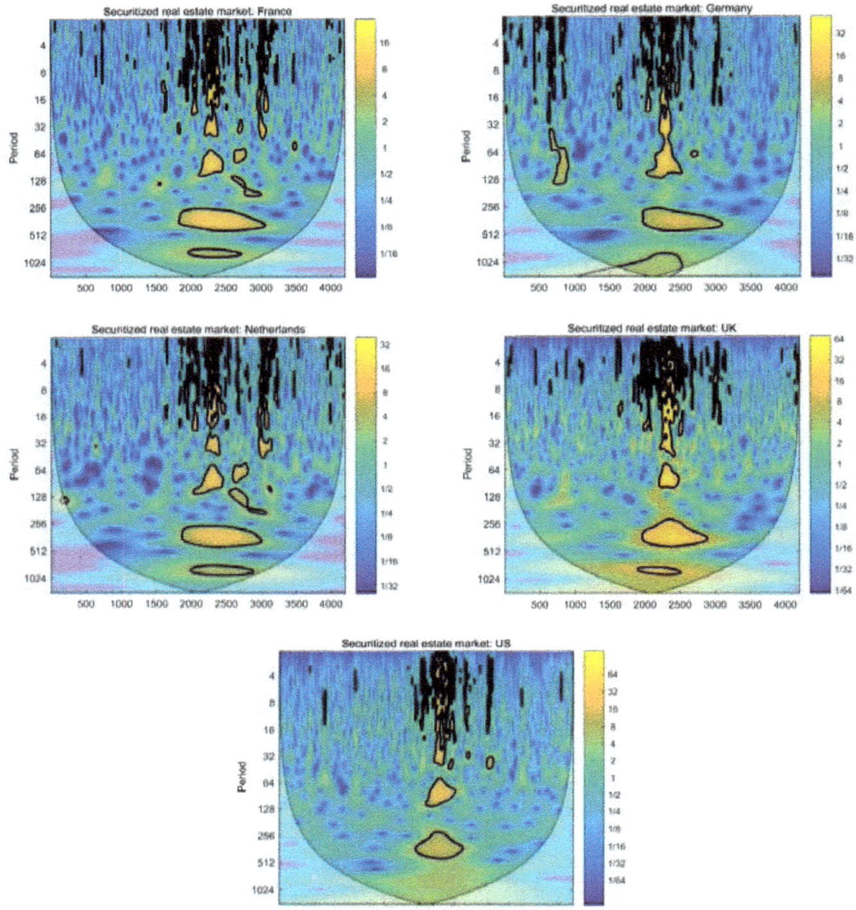

Figure 1. Wavelet power spectrum for securitized real estate market indexes. Notes: Contours are for the wavelet spectrum. The color bar on the right-hand-side of each graph ranges from low power spectrum (dark blue color) to high coherency (yellow color). The thick dark lines indicate the 5% significant level for wavelet coherencies.

Together with the cross-wavelet power plots (Figure 3) that show the movement of real estate-stock covariance and capture regions in time–frequency space where the two series display high common power, we make some important observations. Overall, the results show that the cross real estate-stock movement is varying, and that the patterns of the relationship are not consistent across time scales/investment horizons.

A relatively high degree of real estate-stock market co-movement appears to present in the short-run for all five countries. Moreover, the co-movement becomes more frequent at the shortest time scales (two to eight days) in the crisis years 2007–2010, which can be linked to the US subprime crisis and followed by the EDC. This observation is similar with previous stock market findings that there was an increase in co-movement at shorter-time scales during the financial crisis.

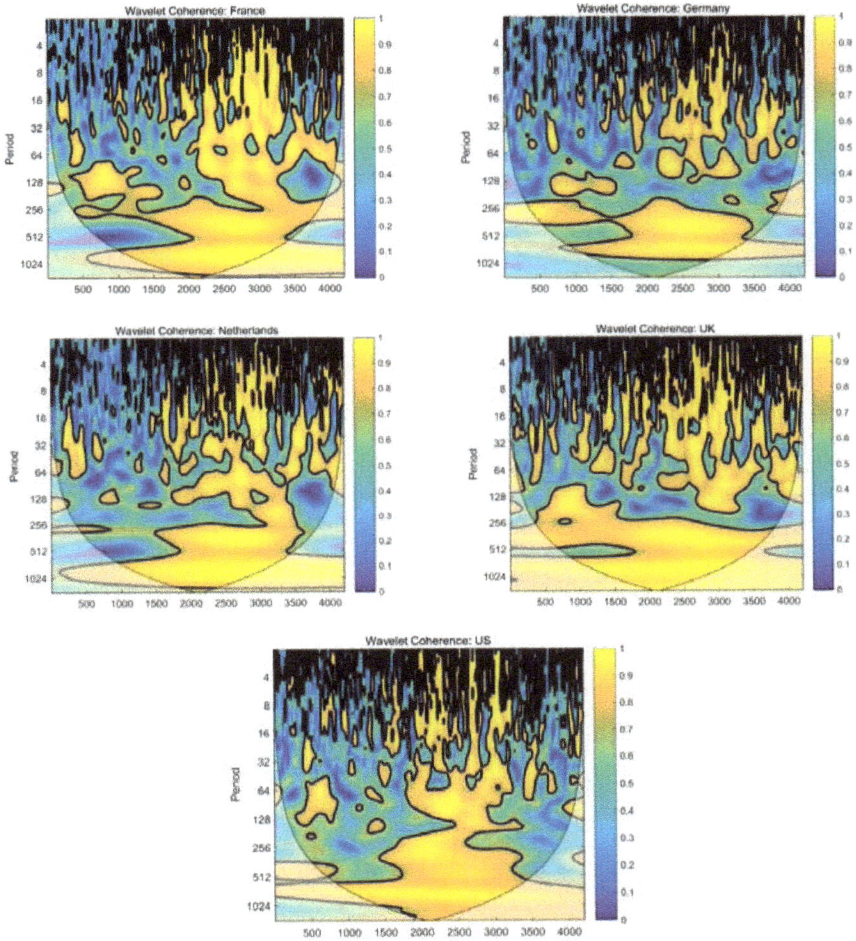

Figure 2. Wavelet coherence between securitized real estate and local stock markets. Notes: Contours are for wavelet coherence. The color bar on the right-hand side of each graph range from low coherency (dark blue color) to high coherency (yellow color). The thick dark lines indicate the 5% significant level for wavelet coherence. The arrows indicate the phase difference, which can determine the lead–lag relationship between the series.

For the medium-term investment horizon between eight and 32 trading days, there is a significant increase in the coherence area for the four European countries. Most of their cross-asset market movement concentrates at these time scales, implying that the gain from domestic real estate-stock portfolio diversification for the European countries is relatively lower and less significant in the medium term. Moreover, some small areas of high coherence are observed at the end of 2000 for the four European countries, due to the bursting of dotcom bubble in 2000, and the terrorist attack in the US in September 2001. The cross-wavelet power plots also indicate shocks to volatilities between the real estate-stock market co-movement during these periods. Additionally, some periods of strong real estate-stock co-movement are observed around mid-2006 for the four European countries, with a very large area of high coherence detected in the four plots during the GFC and EDC periods, indicating much stronger real estate-stock return correlations due to these two crises. This is supported by the cross-wavelet power plots, which highlight that these crisis periods were associated with high volatility regimes in their financial markets, and caused structural break in the real estate-stock market relationship after 2007. In contrast, the US economy shows milder levels of real estate-stock correlations at these intermediate frequencies until the GFC, where they are more visible and stronger, and they are associated with common high volatility regimes in the two asset markets during this crisis period. Overall, these observations are consistent with stock market literature, which finds an increase in the correlations between markets during financial crisis.

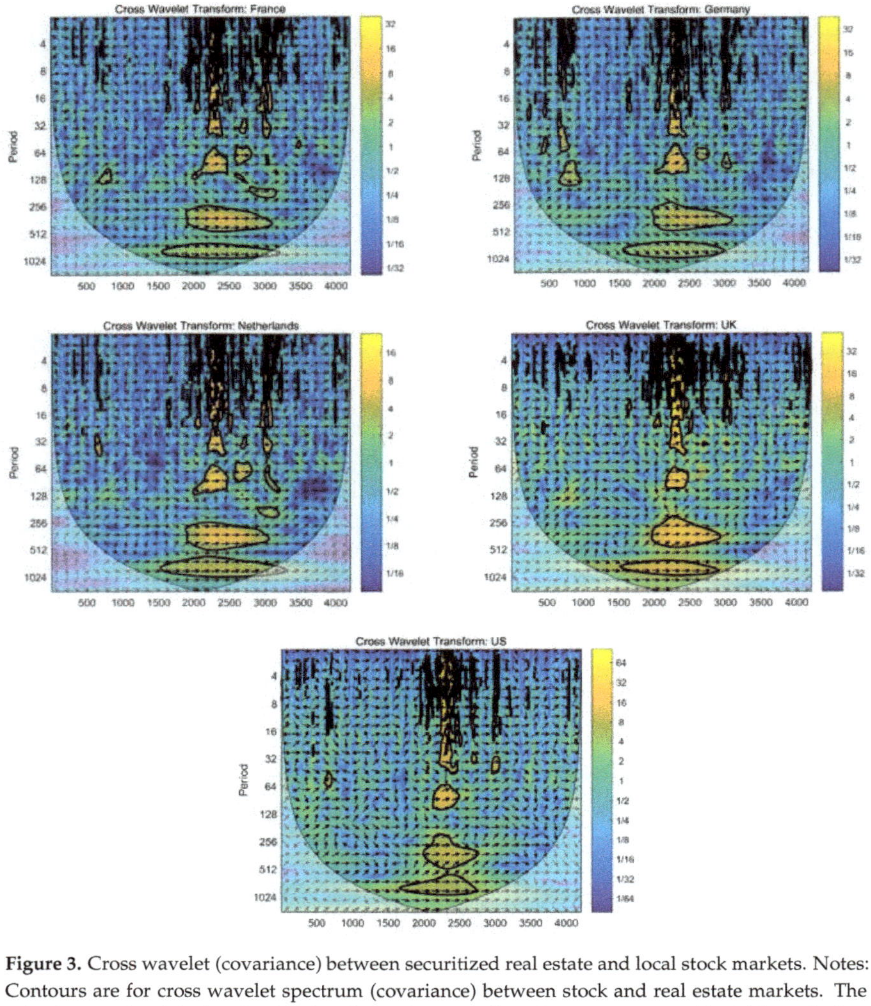

Figure 3. Cross wavelet (covariance) between securitized real estate and local stock markets. Notes: Contours are for cross wavelet spectrum (covariance) between stock and real estate markets. The color bar on the right-hand-side of each graph ranges from low co-spectrum (dark blue color) to high co-spectrum (yellow color). The thick dark lines indicate the 5% significant level for cross wavelet spectrum.

Turning our attention to the cross-asset market movement in the long run, although the cross-wavelet plots indicates the absence of a common high-volatility regime at these higher scales, we observe some relatively high real estate-stock correlations at 32–64 days for the four European countries between 2000 and the beginning 2007, as well as for the UK at 128–256 days from end of 2001 to beginning of 2002, possibly in response to the US 911 terrorist attack. Between mid-2007 and end-2012, strong real estate-stock correlations are clearly visible for all four European countries, with the cross-wavelet power plots displaying common high volatility regimes for these four European countries in two specific periods: October 2007–September 2009 (GFC) and November 2009–December 2011 (EDC). Similarly, the US real estate-stock market co-movement becomes more frequent and stronger, and concentrates at these longer-run scales (32–256 days) during the subprime GFC/EDC, over 2007–2012. Overall, the crises (especially the GFC) have generated relatively more high-power volatility areas at these low-frequency bands. Consequently, in recent years, markets will present a higher volatility, regardless of whether they are stable or volatile.

The phase arrows all points to right, indicating that the identified real estate-stock linkages are in the phase or positively correlated. During crises, the directions of the phase arrows are both up and downs, indicating bi-directional cross-asset causality relationship. Additionally, the lead–lag relationships vary as scale changes. In general, securitized real estate markets lead stock markets in the short run. In contrast, stock markets tend to lead public real estate markets in the long run and to a lesser degree during the medium-term. This lead–lag relationship between stock and public real estate market is consistent with findings by Zhou (2010), in which the US REIT market leads its stock market in the short run, while stock market is the leader in the medium- and long-run.

4.3. CWT: PTV and Rolling PTV Analysis

The PTV of the wavelet coherence summarizes in a single number the degree of coherence between the real estate-stock co-movement examined, and is the average of the estimated wavelet correlations (rescaled from 0 to 100). This wavelet tool complements the graphic observations derived from the coherence plots. Table 4 reports the results. For the four European nations, there is an increase in the cross-asset correlation from the GFC to EDC at the three investment horizons, with the cross-asset movement being more pronounced at the medium-term investment horizon (8–32 days) during the EDC. In contrast, the cross-asset relationship in the US is relatively stronger during the GFC, and manifests itself in all three investment horizons. The difference in these co-movement dynamics could be due to the result of the different nature of the two crises, or a change in volatility regime in the respective real estate or stock markets. Another important observation is with the exception for France, the average lowest correlation level between both asset markets is detected at the long investment horizon of 32–256 days in the other four countries. Moreover, the correlations between the two asset markets in the long run are mostly weaker than in the medium-term during the pre-crisis, GFC and EDC and post-crisis periods.

Figure 4 displays five rolling window estimations of PTV plots of the wavelet coherence, with a window of fixed size one-year being used. Overall, the plots indicate that all five countries experience both time variation and scale variation in their cross-asset co-movement. The cross-asset movements are relatively less stable across all three investment horizons during the GFC and EDC high volatility periods. Moreover, all five economies appear to show a declining trend of the real estate–stock correlation, especially in the long run in recent years. One possible explanation is that the long-term impact factors (both fundamental and idiosyncratic) for the real estate and local stock markets are more distinctive than the short-run impact factors or shocks of the two asset markets. Our additional knowledge also indicates that these developed securitized real estate markets appear to be more correlated with the world stock market, in their efforts to promote greater real estate asset securitization by attracting more international capital to their respective REIT markets. The declining long run real estate–local stock correlation evidence is broadly in agreement with Ling and Naranjo's (2002) observation that securitized real estate has become increasingly less sensitive to local stock market's long-run influence in some developed countries in recent years. In the long-run, securitized real estate is thus less similar with stock in these developed countries. It follows that international investors should be less dependent on the long-run stock market performance to predict the corresponding securitized real estate performance.

Table 4. Percentage of total volume (PTV) of wavelet coherence between real estate and stock markets for each country.

Country	Scale	Full Period (%)	Pre-Crisis (%)	GFC (%)	EDC (%)	Post-Crisis (%)
FR	All	65.19	53.68	74.84	84.19	66.53
	2–8 days	57.54	43.79	68.61	80.17	64.66
	8–32 days	61.38	49.84	74.33	85.16	63.07
	32–256 days	60.43	53.64	71.01	84.14	55.16
GE	All	59.14	50.89	66.28	72.19	61.85
	2–8 days	53.79	41.57	62.6	70.35	62.39
	8–32 days	57.74	46.87	65.57	78.82	62.33
	32–256 days	50.18	45.54	59.88	63.88	46.42
NE	All	63.45	52.35	72.27	79.22	66.43
	2–8 days	57.33	43.84	65.33	75.52	67.79
	8–32 days	59.14	47.89	70.66	80.04	62.49
	32–256 days	53.14	44.81	63.25	75.47	51.57
UK	All	68.91	63.96	68.82	81.46	68.18
	2–8 days	63.38	53.31	69.96	79.16	69.82
	8–32 days	67.53	60.71	73.64	82.98	68.71
	32–256 days	57.41	56.49	53.63	75.79	52.19
US	All	64.3	57.93	79.51	77.72	55.9
	2–8 days	61.72	55.48	76.56	76.82	57.33
	8–32 days	57.7	49.87	77.93	71.26	56.43
	32–256 days	55.92	50.12	78.06	77.93	43.48

Notes: this table presents the values of the PTV of wavelet coherence between real estate-stock market returns inside the cone of influence for the full sample period as well as for the pre-crisis period (4 January 2000–1 August 2007), Global financial crisis (2 August 2007–31 March 2009), European debt crisis (5 November 2009–1 December 2011), and post-crisis period (2 December 2011–29 April 2016) for each country.

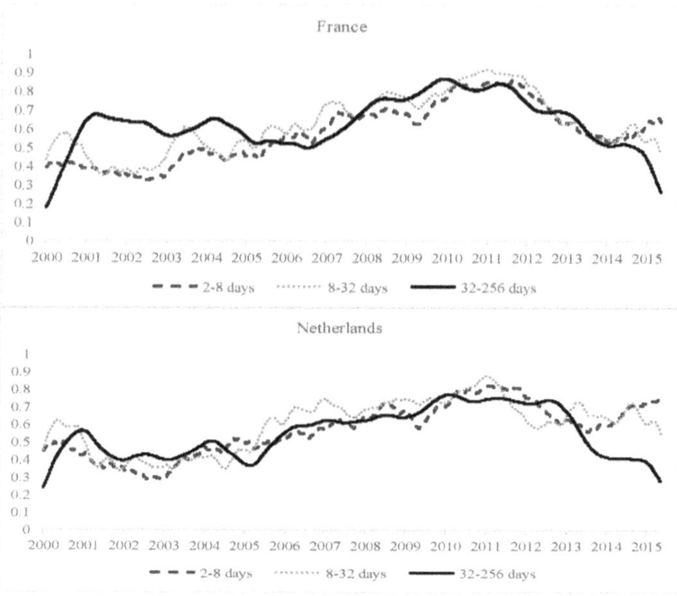

Figure 4. *Cont.*

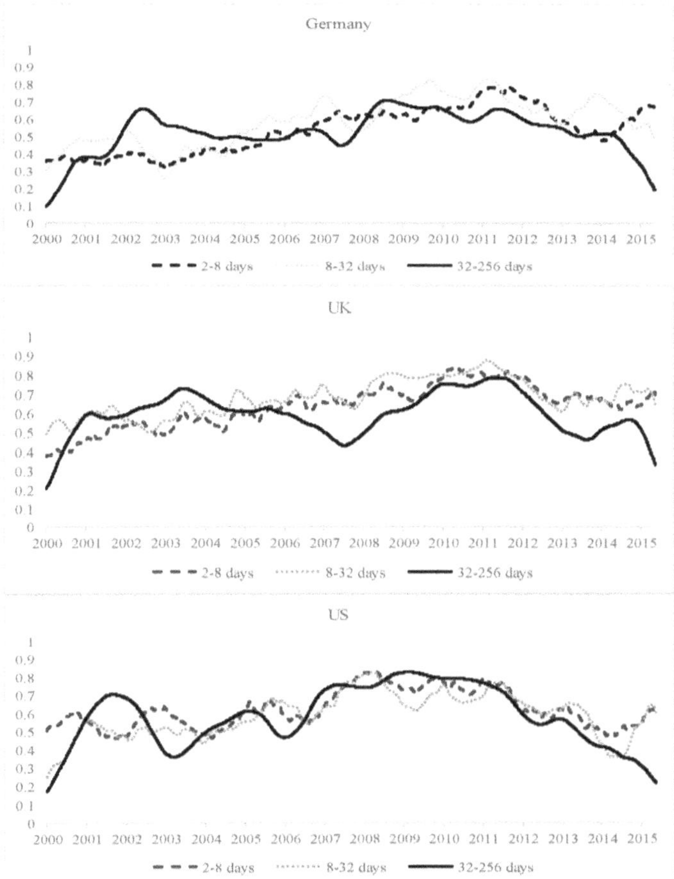

Figure 4. Rolling estimation of the PTV of wavelet coherence between the securitized real estate and stock markets over the three investment horizons. Notes: This figure displays the rolling estimates of the PTV of wavelet coherence between pubic real estate and the stock markets for the five economies inside the cone of influence with a rolling window of 250 trading days (around one year). Dotted lines represent the rolling estimates corresponding to the frequency band from two to eight trading days (short run). Dashed lines show the rolling estimates from eight to 32 trading days (medium-term) and the solid lines refer to the frequency band from 32–256 days (long-run).

4.4. Contagion Across Real Estates and Local Stock Markets

Turning now our attention to contagion, Figure 5 presents the rolling wavelet correlation series for the three investment horizons for the five economies. We observe that the wavelet correlation level fluctuates from one time-scale to another, and oscillate considerably in the long-run. More importantly, the plots show some strong signs of "pure" contagion around the GFC and EDC for some European countries. Strong "fundamentals-based" contagion also extends to the long run in the plots. Although there are some periods of stronger long-run real estate-stock co-movement after the GFC, the long run real estate-stock co-movement becomes weaker relative to the shorter investment horizons after the

EDC, implying that the two asset markets are subject to less common market influences in more recent years. In almost all cases, we observe a decrease in the correlation level after the EDC.[6]

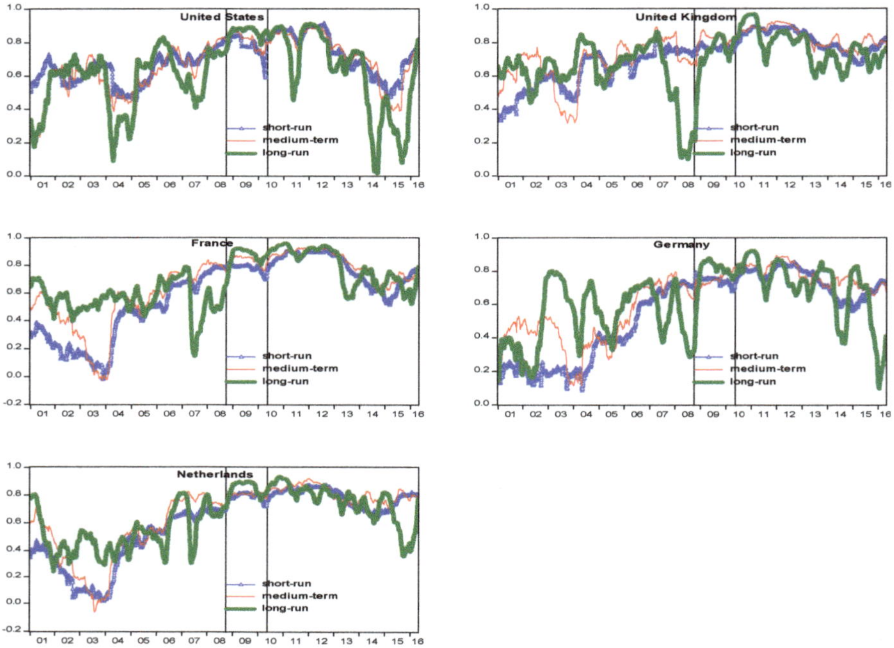

Figure 5. Rolling wavelet correlations between securitized real estate and local stock markets in the short-run, medium-term and long-run. Notes: The investment horizons are defined as: short-run (2–8 days), medium-term (8–32 days) a long-run (32–256 days). The window size is 250 days with a Haar filter. The two vertical lines in each plot indicates two crisis events: Lehman Brothers collapse (left line, 15 September 2008) and European sovereign debt crisis (right line, 2 May 2010).

To confirm the presence of contagion (or otherwise), a paired-sample t-test evaluates if there is a significant increase in the wavelet correlation coefficient after the two crises.[7] Overall, the results (Table 5) agree with those of wavelet coherence analysis, i.e., real estate–stock co-movement is visible at all levels of decomposition. After the crises, the contagion level increases, which indicates higher correlation and stronger co-movement from d1 to d4 (short-run and medium-term), while the real estate-stock interdependence level also increases, implying higher correlation from d5 to d7 (long-run).

6 We inspect another two rolling wavelet correlation series using windows of 125 days and 500 days respectively (the plots are not displayed to conserve space). Although the rising correlation trends of 125-days are quite similar with those using the 250-day windows, the co-movement patterns are more volatile for the 500-day windows. However, the chosen filter (the Haar filter) and the window sizes do not appear to have any significant effect on the results.

7 Ranta (2013) used the same methodology in investigating contagion across major stock markets.

Table 5. Average rolling wavelet real estate–stock correlations (250 days window) and t-tests before and after the crises.

Panel A: Lehman Brothers Collapse (15 September 2008)												
	d1 (2–4 days)				d2 (4–8 days)				d3 (8–16 days)			
Events	Corr. Before	Corr After	Diff.	*t*-stat	Corr. Before	Corr After	Diff.	*t*-stat	Corr. Before	Corr After	Diff.	*t*-stat
FR	0.7489	0.7823	0.0334	15.93 *	0.7835	0.8096	0.0261	20.07 *	0.7998	0.8271	0.0273	13.38 *
GE	0.7165	0.7552	0.0386	45.70 *	0.7205	0.7468	0.0263	13.49 *	0.7311	0.6989	−0.0322	−22.92 *
NE	0.6722	0.7791	0.1069	38.86 *	0.7142	0.8043	0.0902	50.71 *	0.7384	0.7970	0.0586	15.40 *
UK	0.7503	0.7619	0.0116	10.31 *	0.7519	0.7764	0.0245	12.99 *	0.7840	0.8114	0.0275	5.70 *
US	0.7671	0.8054	0.0383	11.87 *	0.7717	0.8168	0.0451	14.51 *	0.8128	0.8489	0.0360	16.18 *
	d4 (16–32 days)				d5 (32–64 days)				d6 (64–128 days)			
	Corr. Before	Corr After	Diff.	*t*-stat	Corr. Before	Corr After	Diff.	*t*-stat	Corr. Before	Corr After	Diff.	*t*-stat
FR	0.8122	0.8663	0.0541	25.93 *	0.6754	0.8668	0.1914	34.93 *	0.5354	0.8540	0.3186	14.0 *
GE	0.7125	0.7360	0.0235	2.64 *	0.6045	0.7628	0.1583	9.43 *	0.5066	0.7549	0.2483	10.32 *
NE	0.7808	0.7903	0.0096	2.51 *	0.6871	0.8264	0.1393	18.66 *	0.7069	0.8414	0.1345	20.4 *
UK	0.6965	0.8053	0.1087	10.48 *	0.4949	0.7325	0.2375	13.57 *	0.3227	0.7062	0.3835	26.66 *
US	0.7578	0.8359	0.0781	22.65 *	0.7246	0.8057	0.0811	16.39 *	0.7675	0.8817	0.1143	41.19 *
	d7 (128–256 days)											
	Corr. Before	Corr After	Diff.	*t*-stat								
FR	0.3366	0.8842	0.5476	53.78 *								
GE	0.4032	0.7641	0.3609	33.76 *								
NE	0.7017	0.8974	0.1957	−36.19 *								
UK	0.0338	0.5236	0.4898	−16.99 *								
US	0.5618	0.8958	0.3340	−22.77 *								
Panel B: European Debt Crisis (2 May 2010)												
	d1 (2–4 days)				d2 (4–8 days)				d3 (8–16 days)			
Events	Corr. Before	Corr After	Diff.	*t*-stat	Corr. Before	Corr After	Diff.	*t*-stat	Corr. Before	Corr After	Diff.	*t*-stat
FR	0.7799	0.8466	0.0668	26.46 *	0.7712	0.8527	0.0815	13.06 *	0.8077	0.8907	0.0830	28.07 *
GE	0.7440	0.7813	0.0374	14.40	0.7249	0.8044	0.0794	27.06	0.7224	0.8456	0.1232	64.42
NE	0.7967	0.8189	0.0223	9.70 *	0.7927	0.8243	0.0316	6.76 *	0.8043	0.8476	0.0433	15.85 *
UK	0.7536	0.8500	0.0964	39.21 *	0.7814	0.8591	0.0777	35.30 *	0.8014	0.8598	0.0584	28.85 *
US	0.7480	0.8612	0.1132	32.59 *	0.7567	0.8637	0.1070	27.25 *	0.8024	0.8528	0.0504	12.57 *

Table 5. *Cont.*

Panel B: European Debt Crisis (2 May 2010)												
	d4 (16–32 days)				d5 (32–64 days)				d6 (64–128 days)			
	Corr. Before	Corr After	Diff.	*t*-stat	Corr. Before	Corr After	Diff.	*t*-stat	Corr. Before	Corr After	Diff.	*t*-stat
FR	0.8438	0.8664	0.0226	6.00 *	0.8447	0.9226	0.0778	15.08 *	0.8783	0.9188	0.0405	8.54 *
GE	0.8160	0.8286	0.0127	5.58 *	0.8275	0.8675	0.0400	13.85 *	0.8114	0.8462	0.0348	3.28 *
NE	0.7999	0.8420	0.0421	29.72 *	0.8376	0.8698	0.0322	8.81 *	0.8367	0.9009	0.0642	9.32 *
UK	0.8386	0.8795	0.0409	18.81 *	0.7911	0.9115	0.1204	27.13 *	0.7851	0.9179	0.1327	24.96 *
US	0.7747	0.8322	0.0576	16.83 *	0.7676	0.8418	0.0742	16.73 *	0.9212	0.8692	−0.0521	−16.98 *
	d7 (128–256 days)											
	Corr. Before	Corr After	Diff.	*t*-stat								
FR	0.8991	0.9506	0.0515	12.98 *								
GE	0.7943	0.8821	0.0878	15.16 *								
NE	0.8780	0.9100	0.0319	6.05 *								
UK	0.7893	0.9295	0.1402	18.21 *								
US	0.8991	0.8280	−0.0710	−11.3 *								

Note: The null hypothesis for the *t*-test is the rolling wavelet correlations between real estate–stock markets before and after the two financial turbulences is equal. The shaded results refer to cases where the before-correlation is greater than the after-correlation. * indicates the rejection of the null hypothesis at 5% critical value.

The first crisis event is represented by the collapse of Lehman Brothers on 15 September 2008 (Panel A of Table 5). Real estate-stock co-movement in the US increases after the crisis at the d1, d2, and d3 levels of decomposition. Then from d4 through d7 levels, the increase in correlation is much higher as the scale increases. With a minor exception for Germany that the correlation is lower after the crisis at the d3 decomposition level, we also notice a similarly rising trend for France, UK, and Netherlands. Thus, we may conclude the correlations increase after the crisis in the short-run and medium-term ("pure" contagion), while in the long-run, the correlations are stronger after the crisis ("fundamentals-based" contagion) for the five countries.

Moving on to the second crisis event (EDC—2 May 2010, Panel B of Table 5), we encounter a different situation. We note that the correlations after the crisis from the d1 to d4 levels of decomposition are all significantly higher than the before-crisis correlation, indicating that the respective real estate-stock co-movements are affected by "pure" contagion. In the long run, whilst the US real estate-stock correlation is higher after the crisis for d5; its correlation at the d6 and d7 levels of decomposition are lower, indicating no evidence of long-run contagion across its real estate and stock markets. In contrast, for the four European countries, their real estate-stock co-movements are significantly higher after the crisis in the long-run (from d5 to d7), an outcome which is reasonably expected, as they are affected by a common and regional financial crisis.

Finally, we repeat another two sets of contagion analyzes with 125-day and 500-day windows. We find the results are largely similar with the 250-day window estimations.[8] Thus, we may conclude that contagion is an important factor in affecting the short-run and medium-term real estate-stock link during and after the GFC and EDC periods for the developed countries studied. The structure of real estate–stock relationship along scales changes during periods of turmoil, indicating the presence of both "pure" and "fundamentals-based" contagion channels across the two asset markets. Previous studies found that the correlations between public real estate and the stock market increased significantly during the global financial crisis period, whether using local, regional or global stock market as references (Liow 2012), especially for US market. Their results can be seen as average results of our multi-resolution analysis. As such, investors and policymakers can learn something fresh and informative along the time–scale contagion relationship reported here.

4.5. Wavelet-Based Multi-Resolution Asymmetric Dynamic Conditional Correlation (ADCC)-GARCH Model

Table 6 indicates that all of the estimated ARCH and GARCH parameters (a, b), as well as the asymmetric coefficient (g) for the five countries' raw ADCC models are highly significant. The estimated average dynamic conditional correlation between the real estate and stock markets is 0.5594 (Germany), 0.6011 (France), 0.6029 (Netherlands), 0.6717 (US) and 0.6879 (UK). However, these average results are not helpful for heterogeneous groups of investors, as the results suggest that not much diversification benefits are expected from investing in the two asset markets. This motivates the investigation of the time-scale cross-asset conditional correlations at the three investment horizons.

The decomposed investment horizon results (Table 6) indicates that the asymmetric correlation coefficient (g) is statistically significant in the two short run investment horizons, as well as being the largest in almost every case of medium-term investment horizon. In contrast, g is only statistically significant in the long-run for the UK-securitized real estate market. We may thus conclude that the asymmetric real estate–stock correlation concentrates at shorter to medium time-scales for our sample of the developed real estate markets.

---

[8] The corresponding correlation and t-test results are not presented to conserve space.

Table 6. Estimation results of the Asymmetric Dynamic Conditional Correlation (ADCC-GARCH) model for the full period and three levels of decomposition: securitized real estate and local stock market return.

		a	*b*	*g*	*Mean*	*SD*	*Maximum*	*Minimum*
France	**Short**	0.0736 ***	0.9147 ***	0.0043	0.5751	0.2613	0.9415	−0.2965
	Medium	0.6193 ***	0.3102 ***	0.2158 ***	0.5610	0.5230	0.9921	−0.8290
	Long	0.795 ***	0.1667 ***	0.0713 ***	0.5262	0.7447	0.9978	−0.9275
	Raw data	0.0258 ***	0.9696 ***	0.0054	0.6011	0.2177	0.9144	−0.0007
Germany	**Short**	0.0677 ***	0.9199 ***	0.0011	0.5272	0.2522	0.8938	−0.3286
	Medium	0.6315 ***	0.3025 ***	0.0591 *	0.5277	0.5408	0.9896	−0.8912
	Long	0.7841 ***	0.1731 ***	0.0577 ***	0.4541	0.7715	0.9963	−0.9199
	Raw data	0.0158 ***	0.9818 ***	0.0034	0.5574	0.2074	0.8712	0.0565
Netherlands	**Short**	0.0716 ***	0.9080 ***	0.0277 **	0.5945	0.2350	0.9277	−0.2543
	Medium	0.6157 ***	0.3177 ***	0.1073 ***	0.5397	0.5286	0.9911	−0.8616
	Long	0.7758 ***	0.1870 ***	0.0956 ***	0.5315	0.7371	0.9974	−0.9077
	Raw data	0.0185 ***	0.9781 ***	0.0033	0.6029	0.2069	0.8842	0.0073
UK	**Short**	0.1583 ***	0.7785 ***	0.0172	0.6029	0.2082	0.9668	−0.3337
	Medium	0.6282 ***	0.2836 ***	0.2656 ***	0.6029	0.4570	0.9931	−0.7660
	Long	0.7861 ***	0.1741 ***	0.0907 ***	0.6029	0.7548	0.9972	−0.9085
	Raw data	0.0510 ***	0.9319 ***	0.0060	0.6029	0.1422	0.9084	0.1061
US	**Short**	0.1693 ***	0.7302 ***	0.0581 **	0.6029	0.1863	0.9577	−0.1926
	Medium	0.6369 ***	0.281 ***	0.1536 ***	0.6029	0.4915	0.9909	−0.8335
	Long	0.7514 ***	0.2156 ***	0.0279 ***	0.6029	0.8185	0.9952	−0.9545
	Raw data	0.0611 ***	0.8758 ***	0.0734 ***	0.6029	0.1304	0.9100	0.0672

Notes: a is the estimated ARCH coefficient, and b is the estimated GARCH coefficient, g is the estimates of asymmetric coefficient in the AR (1) ADCC-GARCH model, mean refers to the average values of conditional correlations estimated by the model. The decomposed returns are estimated by MODWT with a Daubechies LA (8) filter. * Significant at the 10% confidence level, ** significant at 5% confidence level, *** significant at 1% confidence level. Short-run corresponds to the frequency band from two to eight trading days; medium-term is from 16 to 32 trading days, and long-run refers to the frequency band from 64–256 days (long run).

As the level of the investment horizon increases, the average correlation decreases, thus suggesting a decline in the cross-asset relationship, and an improvement of the potential diversification benefits for longer horizon investors and financial institutions that hold these two investment asset types. As an example, the average US real estate–stock correlation in the short-run is 0.6634. This value then becomes weaker in the medium-term (the correlation is 0.5842) and continues to decline to a lower level of 0.3662 in the long run (Table 6), suggesting that these two asset markets are moving away from each other in the long-run. One significant implication from this finding is that the cross real estate-stock diversification over longer investment horizons may be still attractive because of the weakest real estate–stock correlation detected. These findings complement Liow et al.'s (2018a) study on three Greater China (China, Hong Kong, and Taiwan) securitized real estate markets. Accordingly, securitized real estate is an essential asset class providing institutional and private investors with the corresponding diversification benefits for both time- and scale-motivation in mixed real estate–stock portfolios in the long run. Our finding may also imply that securitized real estate behaves more like stock over the shorter investment horizons. This appears to support Lizieri and Satchell's (1997) view that property stocks are stocks in the short-run, as well as Ling and Naranjo's (2002) evidence that the securitized real estate may have become increasingly less sensitive to common stocks in some developed countries in recent years, especially in the long run.

5. Conclusions

The relationship between the real estate and local stock market is very important, and there is a lot of research about it. Because financial markets have many time scales (Loh 2013), the main thrust of this paper is an empirical revisit of the time-scale real estate and stock relationship on a select group of five developed countries from the US and Europe. A novel feature of our empirical work is the use of the wavelet-based modelling approaches in the form of wavelet coherency and the phase difference graphical analysis, the static and rolling percentage of the total volume analysis, rolling wavelet correlation contagion analysis, and multi-resolution ADCC-GARCH analysis, making the study more comprehensive and useful for investors, because traditional methods cannot decompose the variables into different time-scale components.

Specifically, understanding the dynamic behavior of the real estate and the local stock market relationship from the interdependence and contagion perspective is important, because it has practical implications in implementing investment and risk analysis, risk modelling, and risk management. Wavelet approaches enhance the understanding of this dynamic behavior at different time scales or investment horizons. Because participants in the real estate and stock markets have different time horizons in their investment strategies, the wavelet approaches are just the appropriate tool for this purpose. From the wavelet analysis, they can extract the time-scale that most interests them, and make decisions according to this time-scale.

According to our novel wavelet analysis, the relationship between the securitized real estate and local stock markets is time-scale-dependent. Moreover, the average long-run real estate–stock correlation fails to outweigh the average short-run correlation, indicating that the real estate markets may have become increasingly less sensitive to the domestic stock markets in the long-run in recent years. Securitized real estate markets appear to lead stock markets in the short run. In contrast, stock markets tend to lead securitized real estate markets in the long run, and to a lesser degree, the medium-term. Additionally, we find incomplete real estate and local stock market integration among the five developed economies, given only weaker long-run integration beyond the crisis periods.

Although the asset markets are different, our results expands previous works with similar stock market results of Lee (2004); Huang (2011) and Deora and Nguyen (2013). Additionally, there are some papers that have explored this wavelet style GARCH approach with commodity markets (Jammazi 2012; Khalfaoui et al. 2015; and Liu et al. 2017). There are at least three important implications arising from our financial markets (securitized real estate and local stock markets) study. First, our results are intuitive enough to remind investors that the failure to consider the existence of time-scale dimension of the cross real estate–stock connection will probably result in inaccurate assessment of portfolio performance and diversification benefits. Our finding that "as the investment horizon increases, the correlation between securitized real estate and stock is lower" can be very valuable for investors, policymakers, and financial institutions holding investment portfolios in the two asset markets. It implies that securitized real estate can be a competitive investment tool for long-term investors in developed countries. Since investors may be better off by holding risky assets over a long-run investment horizon (time diversification), our results of weaker long-run real estate-stock co-movement may indicate that an international investor would be able to simultaneously achieve the benefits of portfolio diversification and time diversification.

The second implication of distinguishing between excessive and normal co-movement (or between interdependence and contagion) is an important issue from the perspective of portfolio diversification, especially during periods of high volatility. Since contagion is an influential time-scale factor in affecting the short-run, medium-term and long-run real estate-stock market co-movement dynamics differently, policymakers may refer to our results to intervene in the crisis periods where the contagion level between the two asset markets grows stronger, and the markets are dominated by speculators. Additionally, the regional differences regarding the crisis influence on the real estate–stock co-movement at different investment horizons may be valuable for portfolio investors, financial institutions, and policymakers in managing their real estate–stock portfolios in different regions.

The final and general implication is that although our paper reads like an applied econometric paper, it contributes to a real estate audience by increasing an awareness of the wavelet approach to understand the time-scale risk analysis and modelling, in relation to the co-movement and financial contagion in international stock and securitized real estate markets.

Author Contributions: Conceptualization: K.H.L.; methodology: K.H.L. and X.Z.; software, data collection and gathering: Y.H.; formal analysis and investigation: K.H.L. and X.Z.; original draft preparation: Q.L.; wring, review and editing: K.H.L.; funding acquisition: K.H.L.

Funding: This research was supported by Humanity and Social Science Fund, National University of Singapore, grant number R-297-000-132-646.

Acknowledgments: Kim Hiang LIOW wishes to acknowledge the financial support provided by NUS on the research project R-297-000-132-646 which this paper is derived from.

Conflicts of Interest: The authors declare no conflict of interest.

References

Aguiar-Conraria, Luís, Nuno Azevedo, and Maria Joana Soares. 2008. Using wavelets to decompose the time–frequency effects of monetary policy. *Physica A: Statistical mechanics and its Applications* 387: 2863–78. [CrossRef]

Ambrose, Brent W., Esther Ancel, and Mark D. Griffiths. 1992. The fractal structure of real estate investment trust returns: The search for evidence of market segmentation and nonlinear dependency. *Real Estate Economics* 20: 25–54. [CrossRef]

Bond, Shaun A., G. Andrew Karolyi, and Anthony B. Sanders. 2003. International real estate returns: A multifactor, multi-country approach. *Real Estate Economics* 31: 481–500. [CrossRef]

Cappiello, Lorenzo, Robert F. Engle, and Kevin Sheppard. 2006. Asymmetric dynamics in the correlations of global equity and bond returns. *Journal of Financial Econometrics* 4: 537–72. [CrossRef]

Daubechies, Ingrid. 1992. *Ten Lectures on Wavelets*. Philadelphia: Society for Industrial and Applied Mathematics, pp. 198–202.

Deora, Rahul, and Duc Khuong Nguyen. 2013. Time-scale co-movement between the Indian and world stock markets. *Journal of Applied Business Research* 29: 765–76. [CrossRef]

Dewandaru, Ginanjar, Rumi Masih, and A. Mansur M. Masih. 2016. Contagion and interdependence across Asia-Pacific equity markets: An analysis based on multi-horizon discrete and continuous wavelet transformations. *International Review of Economics & Finance* 43: 363–77.

Dima, B., Ş. M. Dima, and Flavia Barna. 2015. A wavelet analysis of capital markets' integration in Latin America. *Applied Economics* 47: 1019–36. [CrossRef]

Dornbusch, Rudiger, Yung Chul Park, and Stijn Claessens. 2000. Contagion: Understanding how it spreads. *The World Bank Research Observer* 15: 177–97. [CrossRef]

Eichholtz, Piet M. A. 1996. Does international diversification work better for real estate than for stocks and bonds. *Financial Analysts Journal* 52: 56–62. [CrossRef]

Engle, Robert. 2002. Dynamic conditional correlation: A simple class of multivariate generalized autoregressive conditional heteroskedasticity models. *Journal of Business & Economic Statistics* 20: 339–50.

Grinsted, Aslak, John C. Moore, and Svetlana Jevrejeva. 2004. Application of the cross-wavelet transform and wavelet coherence to geophysical time series. *Nonlinear Processes in Geophysics* 11: 561–66. [CrossRef]

Hoesli, Martin, and Elias Oikarinen. 2012. Are REITs real estate? Evidence from international sector level data. *Journal of International Money and Finance* 31: 1823–50. [CrossRef]

Hoesli, Martin, and Kustrim Reka. 2015. Contagion channels between real estate and financial markets. *Real Estate Economics* 43: 101–38. [CrossRef]

Huang, Shian-Chang. 2011. Wavelet-based multi-resolution GARCH model for financial spillover effects. *Mathematics and Computers in Simulation* 81: 2529–39. [CrossRef]

Hui, Eddie C. M., and Ka Kwan Kevin Chan. 2013. The European sovereign debt crisis: Contagion across European real estate markets. *Journal of Property Research* 30: 87–102. [CrossRef]

Hui, Eddie C. M., and Ka Kwan Kevin Chan. 2016. Is there any contagion among major equity and securitized real estate markets? Analysis from a new perspective. *Journal of Real Estate Finance and Economics* 56: 1–20. [CrossRef]

Jammazi, Rania. 2012. Oil shock transmission to stock market returns: Wavelet-multivariate Markov switching GARCH approach. *Energy* 37: 430–54. [CrossRef]

Kaminsky, Graciela L., and Carmen M. Reinhart. 2000. On crises, contagion, and confusion. *Journal of international Economics* 51: 145–68. [CrossRef]

Khalfaoui, Rabeh, M. Boutahar, and H. Boubaker. 2015. Analyzing volatility spillovers and hedging between oil and stock markets: Evidence from wavelet analysis. *Energy Economics* 49: 540–49. [CrossRef]

Lee, Hahn Shik. 2004. Price and volatility spillovers in stock markets: A wavelet analysis. *Applied Economics Letters* 11: 197–201.

Li, Xiao-Lin, Tsangyao Chang, Stephen M. Miller, Mehmet Balcilar, and Rangan Gupta. 2015. The co-movement and causality between the US housing and stock markets in the time and frequency domains. *International Review of Economics & Finance* 38: 220–33.

Ling, David C., and Andy Naranjo. 1999. The integration of commercial real estate markets and stock markets. *Real Estate Economics* 27: 483–515. [CrossRef]

Ling, David C., and Andy Naranjo. 2002. Commercial real estate return performance: A cross-country analysis. *Journal of Real Estate Finance and Economics* 24: 119–42. [CrossRef]

Liow, Hiang Kim. 2012. Co-movements and correlations across Asian securitized real estate and stock markets. *Real Estate Economics* 40: 97–129. [CrossRef]

Liow, Kim Hiang, and Felix Schindler. 2011. *An Assessment of the Relationship between Public Real Estate Markets and Stock Markets at the Local, Regional, and Global Levels.* ZEW-Centre for European Economic Research Discussion Paper, No. 11-056. Berlin: ZEW-Centre for European Economic Research.

Liow, KimHiang, Xiaoxia Zhou, Qiang Li, and Yuting Huang. 2018a. Co-movement of Greater China real estate markets: Some time-scale evidence. *Journal of Real Estate Research.* forthcoming.

Liow, KimHiang, Xiaoxia Zhou, Qiang Li, and Yuting Huang. 2018b. Dynamic interdependence between the US and the securitized real estate markets of the Asian-Pacific economies. *Journal of Property Investment and Finance.* forthcoming. [CrossRef]

Liu, Crocker H., David J. Hartzell, Wylie Greig, and Terry V. Grissom. 1990. The integration of the real estate market and the stock market: Some preliminary evidence. *Journal of Real Estate Finance and Economics* 3: 26. [CrossRef]

Liu, Xueyong, Haizhong An, Shupei Huang, and Shaobo Wen. 2017. The evolution of spillover effects between oil and stock markets across multi-scales using a wavelet based GARCH-BEKK model. *Physica A* 465: 374–83. [CrossRef]

Lizieri, Colin, and Stephen Satchell. 1997. Interactions between property and equity markets: An investigation of linkages in the United Kingdom 1972–1992. *Journal of Real Estate Finance and Economics* 15: 11–26. [CrossRef]

Loh, Lixia. 2013. Co-movement of Asia-Pacific with European and US stock market returns: A cross-time-frequency analysis. *Research in International Business and Finance* 29: 1–13. [CrossRef]

Mallat, Stephane G. 1989. A theory for multiresolution signal decomposition: The wavelet representation. *IEEE Transactions on Pattern Analysis and Machine Intelligence* 11: 674–93. [CrossRef]

Markowitz, Harry. 1952. Portfolio selection. *The Journal of Finance* 7: 77–91.

Michayluk, David, Patrick J. Wilson, and Ralf Zurbruegg. 2006. Asymmetric volatility, correlation and returns dynamics between the US and UK securitized real estate markets. *Real Estate Economics* 34: 109–31. [CrossRef]

Morawski, Jaroslaw, Heinz Rehkugler, and Roland Füss. 2008. The nature of listed real estate companies: Property or equity market? *Financial Markets and Portfolio Management* 22: 101–26. [CrossRef]

Okunev, John, and Patrick J. Wilson. 1997. Using nonlinear tests to examine integration between real estate and stock markets. *Real Estate Economics* 25: 487–503. [CrossRef]

Okunev, John, Patrick Wilson, and Ralf Zurbruegg. 2000. The causal relationship between real estate and stock markets. *Journal of Real Estate Finance and Economics* 21: 251–61. [CrossRef]

Quan, Daniel C., and Sheridan Titman. 1999. Do real estate prices and stock prices move together? An international analysis. *Real Estate Economics* 27: 183–207. [CrossRef]

Ramsey, James B. 2002. Wavelets in economics and finance: Past and future. *Studies in Nonlinear Dynamics & Econometrics* 6: 1–27.

Ranta, Mikko. 2013. Contagion among major world markets: A wavelet approach. *International Journal of Managerial Finance* 9: 133–49. [CrossRef]

Rua, António, and Luís C. Nunes. 2009. International co-movement of stock market returns: A wavelet analysis. *Journal of Empirical Finance* 16: 632–39. [CrossRef]

Schindler, Felix. 2011. Long-term benefits from investing in international securitized real estate. *International Real Estate Review* 14: 27–60.

Tiwari, Aviral Kumar, Mihai Ioan Mutascu, and Claudiu Tiberiu Albulescu. 2016. Continuous wavelet transform and rolling correlation of European stock markets. *International Review of Economics & Finance* 42: 237–56.

Torrence, Christopher, and Peter J. Webster. 1999. Interdecadal changes in the ENSO-monsoon system. *Journal of Climate* 12: 2679–90. [CrossRef]

Yunus, Nafeesa, J. Andrew Hansz, and Paul J. Kennedy. 2012. Dynamic interactions between private and public real estate markets: Some international evidence. *Journal of Real Estate Finance and Economics* 45: 1021–40. [CrossRef]

Zhou, Jian. 2010. Co-movement of international real estate securities returns: A wavelet analysis. *Journal of Property Research* 27: 357–73. [CrossRef]

Zhou, Jian. 2012. Multiscale analysis of international linkages of REIT returns and volatilities. *Journal of Real Estate Finance and Economics* 45: 1062–87. [CrossRef]

Journal of
Risk and Financial Management

MDPI

Article

A Communication Theoretic Interpretation of Modern Portfolio Theory Including Short Sales, Leverage and Transaction Costs

Giorgio Arici [1], Marco Dalai [1,*], Riccardo Leonardi [1] and Arnaldo Spalvieri [2]

[1] Department of Information Engineering, University of Brescia, Via Branze 38, 25123 Brescia, Italy; g.arici005@unibs.it (G.C.); riccardo.leonardi@unibs.it (R.L.)

[2] Department of Electronics, Information and BioEngineering, Politecnico di Milano, Via Ponzio 34/5, 20133 Milan, Italy; arnaldo.spalvieri@polimi.it

* Correspondence: marco.dalai@unibs.it; Tel.: +39-030-3715915

Received: 16 November 2018; Accepted: 25 December 2018; Published: 29 December 2018

Abstract: Modern Portfolio Theory is the ground upon which most works in portfolio optimization context find their foundations. Many studies attempt to extend the Modern Portfolio Theory to include short sale, leverage and transaction costs, features not considered in Markowitz's seminal work from 1952. The drawback of such theories is that they complicate considerably the simplicity of the original technique. Here, we propose a simple and unified method, which takes inspiration from, and shows connections with the matched filter theory in communications, to evaluate the best portfolio allocation with the possibility of including a leverage factor and short sales. Finally, we extend the presented method to also consider the transaction costs.

Keywords: modern portfolio theory; portfolio optimization; matched filter

1. Introduction

Let $(\gamma_{1,k}, \gamma_{2,k}, \cdots \gamma_{N,k})$ be the prices of N goods at discrete time instant k. The evolution of the price can be modelled for $n = 1, 2, \cdots, N$ and $k = 0, 1, \cdots$ as

$$\gamma_{n,k+1} = \gamma_{n,k}(1 + x_{n,k}), \tag{1}$$

where $\gamma_{n,0} > 0$ is the initial price of good n and $x_{n,k}$ is the relative price change of the nth good between time k and time $k+1$. Thus, if the price of good n raises by 3% between time k and time $k+1$, then $x_{n,k} = 0.03$. The returns $x_{n,k}$ are random variables whose knowledge is only limited at the level of some statistical properties. Thus, it is common practice to diversify the investor's wealth among the N goods, so that the entire capital is not reserved to a single good and that, in the case of a disastrous event (bankrupt), affect only the portion allocated to the unsuccessful good.

Markowitz's Modern Portfolio Theory Markowitz (1952), sometimes referred as *Mean–Variance Approach*, provides a method to choose an optimal allocation of wealth in view of knowledge of few statistical properties of the return variables. In particular, as the name suggests, this approach is based on the evaluations of the first- and second-order moments of $x_{n,k}$, and the investor can adopt the portfolio that maximizes the expected return given a maximum level of risk accepted. The relevance of this theory is enormous and it has been usually taken as a starting point in a variety of works in the context of portfolio optimization, as shown in Elton and Gruber (1997). Many of these works focus on overcoming some constraints of the original formulation of the Modern Portfolio theory. A point that has been deeply investigated in the past is how to deal with the estimation error that, due to the limited sample size, affects the mean and the variance (see DeMiguel et al. (2009), Kritzman et al. (2010)).

In addition, the mean–variance approach has been compared to competitor approaches in the presence of unavoidable estimation errors (e.g., DeMiguel et al. (2007), Adler and Kritzman (2007)). A criticism that has been moved to the mean–variance approach is about the possibility of describing the distribution of the returns in terms of two parameters only, the mean and the variance (basically, an assumption of Gaussianity). Papers that explore portfolio construction when distribution asymmetries and higher order moments are considered include those by Cremers et al. (2004), Low (2017), and Low et al. (2013, 2016).

Two assumptions impose severe limitations on modern portfolio theory. First, much of the literature assumes that mean and variance are knowable and known. Second, scholars often assume these two parameters alone describe the entire distribution. In addition, modern portfolio theory, as originally laid out, often presumptively forbids the use of short sales and leveraged positions. In other words, conventional works on portfolio design exclude borrowing, either for the purpose of profiting from declines in stock prices (short sales) or for the purpose of increasing the total volume of the investment and correspondingly the resulting profit or loss (leverage). Most studies concerned with these aspects (see Jacobs and Levy (2013a, 2013b) and Pogue (1970)) are based on complex methods and cannot be considered as simple extensions of the original theory.

In this paper, we move back to the original mean–variance approach assuming that mean and variance are known and present a simple extension of Markowitz's theory, inspired by a well known principle in communication theory, that handles simultaneously short-sales and leverage. Finally, we also show that even transaction costs can be taken into account in a straightforward manner. The scope of the paper is thus two-fold: showing a connection between portfolio optimization and matched filter theory in communications, and providing a simple unified presentation of the mentioned important extensions to Markowitz's original theory.

2. Trader Portfolio

We consider here the financial activity commonly called *trading*. The distinction that we make between investing and trading, and that we exploit in the present paper, is that in the latter short trading and leveraged trading are allowed. Basically, this means that in trading money is used not merely to buy assets, but to guarantee risky positions that can remain open until the occurrence of a stop loss condition. When the stop loss condition occurs, the position is closed and money used to guarantee it is lost.

The time evolution of a *leveraged* position on good n is

$$\zeta_{n,k+1} = \zeta_{n,k}(1 + s_{n,k}\lambda_{n,k}x_{n,k}), \tag{2}$$

where $\zeta_{n,k} \geq 0$ is the money invested on good n at time k, $\lambda_{n,k} \geq 0$ is the leverage factor (we return on the meaning of $\lambda_{n,k} \leq 1$ later on), and $s_{n,k} \in \{\pm 1\}$ is the long/short indicator. Hence, $s_{n,k} = 1$ when the position on good n at time k is long, while $s_{n,k} = -1$ when the position is short. In the following, we assume that

$$\zeta_{n,k+1} = 0 \text{ if } s_{n,k}\lambda_{n,k}x_{n,k} \leq -1, \tag{3}$$

meaning that position on good n has been closed at time $k + 1$ because all money used to guarantee it has been lost. Basically, Equation (2) describes the evolution of a financial product that invests with directionality indicated by $s_{n,k}$ and leverage $\lambda_{n,k}$ on good n, and that consolidates its value at each iteration.

The portfolio is the sum of leveraged positions, that is

$$\pi_k = \sum_{n=1}^{N} \zeta_{n,k}. \tag{4}$$

The evolution of the portfolio for $k = 0, 1, \cdots,$ is

$$\pi_{k+1} = \pi_k + \sum_{n=1}^{N} s_{n,k}\lambda_{n,k}\zeta_{n,k}x_{n,k}. \tag{5}$$

The iteration terminates at time instant K such that

$$\pi_K \leq 0. \tag{6}$$

The relative return of the positions taken at time k, which is the focus of the following analysis, is

$$r_k = \frac{\pi_{k+1}}{\pi_k} - 1 = \frac{\sum_{n=1}^{N} s_{n,k}\lambda_{n,k}\zeta_{n,k}x_{n,k}}{\sum_{n=1}^{N} \zeta_{n,k}}. \tag{7}$$

In the following, we consider one step of the iteration and withdraw the time index, thus writing

$$r = \frac{\sum_{n=1}^{N} s_n\lambda_n\zeta_n x_n}{\sum_{n=1}^{N} \zeta_n}. \tag{8}$$

It is convenient to write the relative return of the portfolio as

$$r = \sum_{n=1}^{N} v_n r_n, \tag{9}$$

where

$$r_n = s_n \lambda x_n \tag{10}$$

is the relative return of position n with

$$\lambda = \frac{\sum_{n=1}^{N} \lambda_n\zeta_n}{\sum_{n=1}^{N} \zeta_n}, \tag{11}$$

and

$$v_n = \frac{\lambda_n\zeta_n}{\lambda \sum_{i=1}^{N} \zeta_i}. \tag{12}$$

Note that

$$v_n \geq 0, \;\; n = 1, 2, \cdots, N, \tag{13}$$

$$\sum_{n=1}^{N} v_n = 1, \tag{14}$$

hence v_n is the relative money invested on good n and λ is a leverage factor that can be set equal for all goods without affecting the relative return of the portfolio. Although the leverage factor of stocks is often an integer, the trader may obtain any real value of the leverage by mixing positions on the same good with different leverages. Note that leverages between 0 and 1 can also be obtained simply by investing with leverage 1 a fraction λ of the available money while letting a fraction $1 - \lambda$ be cash. In the end, the real limit on λ is determined by the maximum leverage available on the financial market, which is in practice so high that we can ignore the limits that it poses.

3. Portfolio Optimization

Let boldface lowercase characters denote column vectors and boldface uppercase characters denote matrices, and let

$$\mathbf{x} = (x_1, x_2, \cdots, x_N)^T, \tag{15}$$

where the superscript ^{T} denotes transposition, be a multivariate random process representing the market behavior with mean vector

$$\boldsymbol{\mu}_{\mathbf{x}} = (E\{x_1\}, E\{x_2\}, \cdots, E\{x_N\})^T, \tag{16}$$

and covariance matrix

$$\boldsymbol{\Psi}_{\mathbf{x},\mathbf{x}} = E\{(\mathbf{x} - \boldsymbol{\mu}_{\mathbf{x}})(\mathbf{x} - \boldsymbol{\mu}_{\mathbf{x}})^T\} \tag{17}$$

where $E\{\cdot\}$ denotes expectation. In the following, we assume that the above mean vector and covariance matrix are known.

For any $\lambda \geq 0$, portfolio optimization requires of finding the relative money allocation vector

$$(s_1 v_1, s_2 v_2, \cdots, s_N v_N)^T \tag{18}$$

that maximizes the mean value of the relative return (Equation (9)) with a fixed variance of the relative return. Note that the optimal portfolio will include only positions with

$$E\{r_n\} = s_n \lambda E\{x_n\} \geq 0, \tag{19}$$

that is with

$$s_n = \frac{E\{x_n\}}{|E\{x_n\}|},$$

because positions with negative expected return will be outperformed by cash. For this reason, without losing generality, we consider in the following only

$$s_n = 1, \;\; E\{x_n\} \geq 0, \tag{20}$$

being understood that, when $E\{x_n\} \leq 0$, one takes $s_n = -1$ and then puts

$$-x_n \leftarrow x_n, \quad s_n = 1. \tag{21}$$

With these assumptions, for any $\lambda \geq 0$, portfolio optimization requires of determining the vector

$$\mathbf{v} = (v_1, v_2, \cdots, v_N)^T,$$

that maximizes the expected relative return with a fixed variance of the relative return and with the constraints in Equations (13) and (14). This is a classical constrained optimization problem that can be worked out by maximizing the Lagrangian

$$\mathcal{L}(\mathbf{v}) = 2\alpha E\{r\} - E\{(r - E\{r\})^2\}, \tag{22}$$

where $\alpha \geq 0$ is the Lagrange multiplier and the constraints are Equations (13) and (14). Writing the relative return as

$$r = \mathbf{r}^T \mathbf{v} = \lambda \mathbf{x}^T \mathbf{v}, \tag{23}$$

one promptly finds that the mean value and the variance of the relative return are

$$E\{r\} = \lambda \boldsymbol{\mu}_{\mathbf{x}}^T \mathbf{v} \tag{24}$$

and

$$E\{(r - E\{r\})^2\} = \lambda^2 \mathbf{v}^T \boldsymbol{\Psi}_{\mathbf{x},\mathbf{x}} \mathbf{v}, \tag{25}$$

respectively. Hence, the Lagrangian is

$$\mathcal{L}(\mathbf{v}) = 2\alpha\lambda\boldsymbol{\mu}_{\mathbf{x}}^T\mathbf{v} - \lambda^2\mathbf{v}^T\boldsymbol{\Psi}_{\mathbf{x},\mathbf{x}}\mathbf{v}. \tag{26}$$

Assuming that $\boldsymbol{\Psi}_{\mathbf{x},\mathbf{x}}$ is definite positive, hence invertible, it is easy to see that the unique maximum of Equation (26) is achieved with

$$\mathbf{v} = \frac{\alpha}{\lambda}\cdot\boldsymbol{\omega}, \tag{27}$$

where

$$\boldsymbol{\omega} = \boldsymbol{\Psi}_{\mathbf{x},\mathbf{x}}^{-1}\boldsymbol{\mu}_{\mathbf{x}}. \tag{28}$$

Imposing Equation (14), one finds

$$\alpha = \frac{\lambda}{\sum_{n=1}^{N}\omega_n}, \tag{29}$$

which, substituted in Equation (27), leads to

$$\mathbf{v} = \frac{\boldsymbol{\omega}}{\sum_{n=1}^{N}\omega_n}. \tag{30}$$

Note that, since $\boldsymbol{\Psi}_{\mathbf{x},\mathbf{x}}$ is definite positive, its inverse is also definite positive and, since all the entries of $\boldsymbol{\mu}_{\mathbf{x}}$ are non-negative, all the entries of $\boldsymbol{\omega}$ are non-negative, and hence the constraint in Equation (13) is always satisfied. Equations (28) and (30) say that the relative weights of positions in the optimal portfolio are fixed and independent of the risk that the trader wants to take, while the balance between expected return and risk can be tuned by tuning the leverage according to Equations (24) and (25).

The performance of the optimal portfolio is characterized by the following expected relative return and variance of the relative return

$$\mu_r = \alpha\boldsymbol{\mu}_{\mathbf{x}}^T\boldsymbol{\omega}, \tag{31}$$

$$\sigma_r^2 = \alpha^2\boldsymbol{\mu}_{\mathbf{x}}^T\boldsymbol{\omega}. \tag{32}$$

The *unconstrained efficient frontier* is a straight line in the first quadrant of the plane (σ_r, μ_r) that departs from $(\sigma_r = 0, \mu_r = 0)$ and that has slope

$$\frac{\mu_r}{\sigma_r} = \sqrt{\boldsymbol{\mu}_{\mathbf{x}}^T\boldsymbol{\omega}}, \tag{33}$$

that is the Sharpe ratio (see Sharpe (1966)), a figure that has been object of many studies after the original paper by Sharpe (see, e.g., Bailey and Lopez de Prado (2012) for estimates of the Sharpe ratio when $\boldsymbol{\mu}_{\mathbf{x}}$ and $\boldsymbol{\Psi}_{\mathbf{x},\mathbf{x}}$ cannot be assumed to be known). The entire efficient frontier can be visited by sweeping α from 0 (zero expected return) to ∞ (infinite expected return). Note that including explicitly a risk free position in the portfolio would lead to a covariance matrix that is not invertible, while, with our approach, the risk free position is automatically brought into the portfolio when $\lambda < 1$, because a fraction $1 - \lambda$ of the portfolio is cash.[1]

1 Including the risk free position in the classical portfolio theory is possible, provided that a work around is made to circumvent problems encountered in matrix inversion (see Merton (1972)). Insights on portfolios with and without can be traced back to Tobin (1958).

As shown in North (1963) and Turin (1960), Equations (28) and (33) are very well known in the context of narrowband discrete-time Single Input Multiple Output (SIMO) transmission systems affected by correlated additive noise, e.g. interference. In that context, the transmission channel is characterized by applying an impulse to the input and by collecting the N channel outputs into vector $\boldsymbol{\mu}_{\mathbf{x}}$. In addition, channel's output is affected by zero-mean additive noise with covariance matrix $\boldsymbol{\Psi}_{\mathbf{x},\mathbf{x}}$. Vector ω is the *matched filter* (MF), that is the vector of weights that, applied to the multiple outputs, that is to the goods held in the portfolio, produces through Equation (9) the least noisy version of the input impulse in the mean-square error sense, while μ_r^2/σ_r^2 is the *Signal-to-Noise Ratio* (SNR) after the matched filter. The application of the matched filter in portfolio optimization is not new, as illustrated by Pillai (2009), where however it is shown only how the said communication theory technique can be exploited in investing contexts, without any extension to trading. To put more light on the link between communication theory and the subject treated in this paper, we point out that, in the context of communication theory, the random vector $\mathbf{x}$ introduced in Equation (15) can be regarded as the vector signal at the output of a SIMO channel excited by an input impulse of unit amplitude:

$$\mathbf{x} = \boldsymbol{\mu}_{\mathbf{x}} + \mathbf{n}, \tag{34}$$

where $\boldsymbol{\mu}_{\mathbf{x}}$ is a vector that, in the communication context, is the impulse response of the SIMO channel, and $\mathbf{n}$ is a random noise vector having zero mean values and covariance matrix $\boldsymbol{\Psi}_{\mathbf{xx}}$ (also the covariance matrix of the noise vector is assumed here to be known). As pointed out by an anonymous referee, the suggestion of regarding the variability in financial returns as the effect of noise (the Brownian motion of gas) dates back to Bachelier's thesis Bachelier (1900). At the receiver side, the received vector is passed through the matched filter (Equation (30)), getting

$$r = \lambda \mathbf{x}^T \mathbf{v}, \tag{35}$$

where, in the context of communication, the scaling factor λ is set to

$$\lambda = (\boldsymbol{\mu}_{\mathbf{x}}^T \mathbf{v})^{-1}, \tag{36}$$

so that

$$E\{r\} = 1, \tag{37}$$

meaning that r recovers the unit amplitude of the input impulse keeping minimum the mean squared error $E\{(r - E\{r\})^2\}$, hence achieving the maximum of Equation (33). Besides this, the matched filter has another interesting property that is well known in the context of communication and information theory. Let a be a random scalar parameter that, in the context of communication, is the information-carrying amplitude, e.g., $a \in \{0, 1\}$. When an impulse of amplitude a is applied at channel input, the channel output is

$$\mathbf{s} = a\boldsymbol{\mu}_{\mathbf{x}} + \mathbf{n}\,. \tag{38}$$

With Gaussian noise, the matched filter output

$$r = \lambda \mathbf{s}^T \mathbf{v} \tag{39}$$

is a *sufficient statistic* for the hidden a. This means that r can be seen as a synthetic representation of $\mathbf{s}$ that fully preserves the possibility of making inference, for instance, maximum likelihood detection, about the hidden a based on r alone. In a more technical language, this concept is expressed by saying that the information processing inequality

$$I(a, \mathbf{s}) \geq I(a, T(\mathbf{s})), \tag{40}$$

where $I(x, y)$ is Shannon information between x and y, is met with equality when the transformation $T(\mathbf{x})$ is the right hand side of Equation (38). The interested reader is referred to Chapter 2 of Cover and Thomas (2006) for the basics about Shannon information, for the concept of sufficient statistic and for the meaning of the information processing inequality.

An example illustrates similarities and differences between the leveraged portfolio and classical Markowitz's portfolios. Consider three goods with

$$\boldsymbol{\mu}_{\mathbf{x}} = 10^{-2} \times (1, 2^2, 2^3)^T, \tag{41}$$

$$\boldsymbol{\Psi}_{\mathbf{xx}} = 10^{-4} \times \begin{pmatrix} 1 & 0 & 0 \\ 0 & 2 & 0 \\ 0 & 0 & 2^6 \end{pmatrix}. \tag{42}$$

For the leveraged portfolio, the optimal money allocation vector is proportional to

$$\omega = 10^2 \times (1, 2, 2^{-3})^T,$$

and the slope of the efficient frontier is

$$\frac{\mu_r}{\sigma_r} = \sqrt{10}.$$

Figure 1 reports μ versus σ for the individual goods and the efficient frontiers for the leveraged portfolio and for the Markowitz's portfolios with and without the possibility of holding cash.

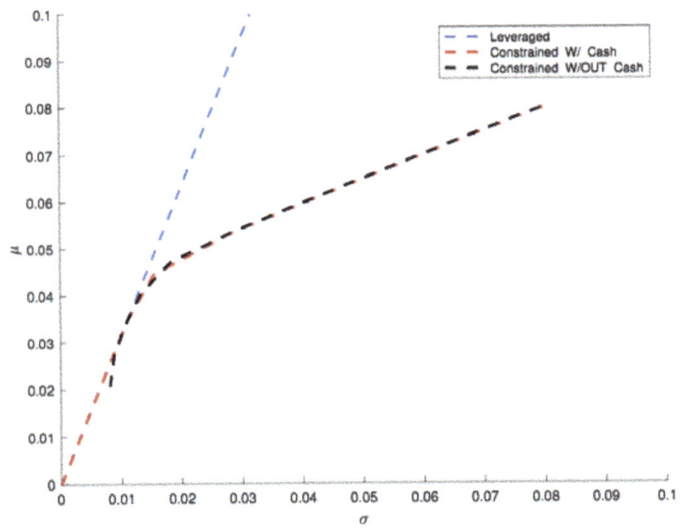

Figure 1. Comparison between leveraged portfolio with the classical Markowitz's portfolio with the statistical hypotheses of Equations (41) and (42).

What happens is that the efficient frontier of the Markowitz's portfolio without cash is equal to the efficient frontier of the leveraged portfolio until

$$\lambda \leq 1, \tag{43}$$

because the fraction $(1 - \lambda)$ of cash of the leveraged portfolio is invested in the non-leveraged portfolio on the low risk stocks, thus leaving the performance of Markowitz's portfolio only slightly worse than the performance of the leveraged portfolio. In the limit, including the possibility of holding cash in Markowitz's portfolio would close the gap between leveraged and non-leveraged portfolios until the inequality in Equation (43) is satisfied. Differences between the two portfolios become bigger and bigger as $\lambda \to \infty$ because, while the leveraged portfolio continues taking profit from diversification by maintaining the optimal mix between goods thanks to the big leverage, the absence of leverage forces the Markowitz's portfolios to renounce to diversification, leading in the limit to a portfolio composed by only one good, the one that offers the greater expected return, even if, as it happens in the example, this portfolio could be easily outperformed also by a portfolio made by only one good with better μ/σ, simply by leveraging it.

4. Cost of Transactions

Another relevant feature not considered in Markowitz's original paper is the cost deriving from a transaction on the market. *Transaction costs* may influence portfolio's optimization, and, for this reason, transaction costs have been widely considered in the subsequent literature (Lobo et al. (2007), Mansini et al. (2003), Mansini and Speranza (1999, 2005)). Type and structure of transaction costs depend on the financial operator (e.g., broker or bank) and on the type of stocks that the trader uses for her/his operation (e.g., Exchange Trade Commodities, Exchange Traded Funds, or Contract for Difference). Let us consider a general case where the relative cost is of the type

$$\lambda\delta_n(\lambda), \quad \delta_n(\lambda) \geq 0, \quad n = 1, 2, \cdots, N, \tag{44}$$

where, here again, without losing generality, we assume that the leverage factor is common to all the goods and consider a transaction cost that can depend on the specific good and on the leverage factor. The relative return of the nth position is

$$r_n = \lambda(s_n x_n - \delta_n(\lambda)). \tag{45}$$

By following the steps of Equations (19)–(21), we consider only the case in Equation (20), with the more demanding condition

$$E\{r_n\} = \lambda(E\{x_n\} - \delta_n(\lambda)) \geq 0. \tag{46}$$

The above inequality means that a position that does not meet the above inequality cannot be in the portfolio, because it is outperformed by cash. A brief comment about the dependence of δ_n on λ is in order. Consider the investment in bonds with one-year life emitted by a very trusted central bank. If the time step is one year and the return of the bond is higher than the cost of transaction, then one could borrow money to buy bonds. Actually, this is allowed in our model, because borrowing money simply means increasing λ. However, in a case like the one of this example, borrowing money is a cost that increases the cost of transaction, so that, in the end, the cost of transaction becomes higher than the return of the bond. When this happens it is the dependence of δ_n on λ that, through Equation (46), rules out this position from the leveraged portfolio. Actually, a realistic cost model for such a case is

$$\lambda\delta_n(\lambda) = \begin{cases} \beta_1\lambda & \lambda \leq 1 \\ \beta_1\lambda + \beta_2(\lambda - 1) & \lambda > 1 \end{cases} \tag{47}$$

where β_1 takes into account costs such as bank commissions that apply when investor's money is employed, that is for $\lambda \leq 1$, while β_2 takes into account the cost of borrowing money, which applies to a fraction $(\lambda - 1)$ of the investment. If, for $\lambda > 1$,

$$\lambda(\beta_1 + \beta_2) - \beta_2 > \lambda E\{x_n\},$$

then the condition in Equation (46) is violated and the position on good n with leverage λ cannot be included in the portfolio.

The constrained optimization is again Equation (22) with the usual constraints, but now

$$E\{r\} = \lambda(\boldsymbol{\mu}_{\mathbf{x}} - \delta(\lambda))^T \mathbf{v}, \tag{48}$$

$$E\{(r - E\{r\})^2\} = \lambda^2 \mathbf{v}^T \boldsymbol{\Psi}_{\mathbf{x},\mathbf{x}} \mathbf{v}. \tag{49}$$

The optimal portfolio and the efficient frontier are found by the same means as in the previous section, simply putting $(\boldsymbol{\mu}_{\mathbf{x}} - \delta(\lambda))$ in place of $\boldsymbol{\mu}_{\mathbf{x}}$. The only difference is that, when the cost of transactions depends on λ, the optimal portfolio will depend on λ and the efficient frontier will no longer be a straight line.

As an example, we consider again the example of Section 3 where the statistical properties are described by Equations (41) and (42) with the addition of the following transaction costs

$$\lambda\delta(\lambda) = \begin{cases} 5 \times 10^{-3}\lambda & \lambda \leq 1 \\ 5 \times 10^{-3}\lambda + 10^{-2}(\lambda - 1) & \lambda > 1 \end{cases} \tag{50}$$

equal for the three goods. Figure 2 displays a new comparison between Markowitz's portfolios and leveraged portfolio with the inclusion of transaction costs (Equation (50)). The first region corresponds to $\lambda \leq 1$, where the efficient frontier of the leveraged portfolio is a straight line since we are in the first case of Equation (50), where $\delta(\lambda)$ is actually a constant since there is no dependance of λ. The breakpoint between the straight line and the second region is at $\lambda = 1$, where the transaction cost changes and is no longer independent of λ as in the second case of Equation (50). The separation between the second and the third region is at $\lambda = 2$, where $\delta(\lambda) = E\{x_n\} = 10^{-2}$ and good 1 is ruled out by Equation (46). Finally, as $\lambda \to \infty$, the efficient frontier approaches a straight line, because $\delta(\lambda)$ approaches the constant 1.5×10^{-2}. These features are not easily noticed in Figure 2. Thus, in Figure 3, the efficient frontier of the leveraged portfolio is illustrated from a different perspective, where the division in three different regions highlighted by green dots is more visible.

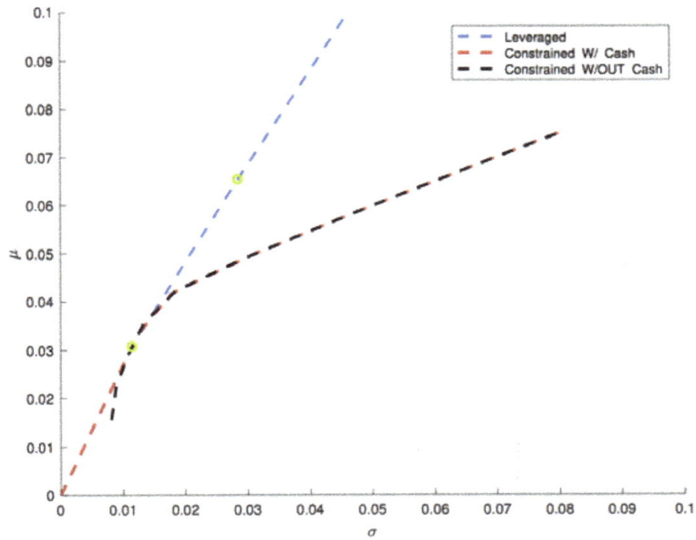

Figure 2. Comparison between leveraged portfolio with the classical Markowitz's portfolios with the statistical hypotheses of Equations (41), (42) and (50).

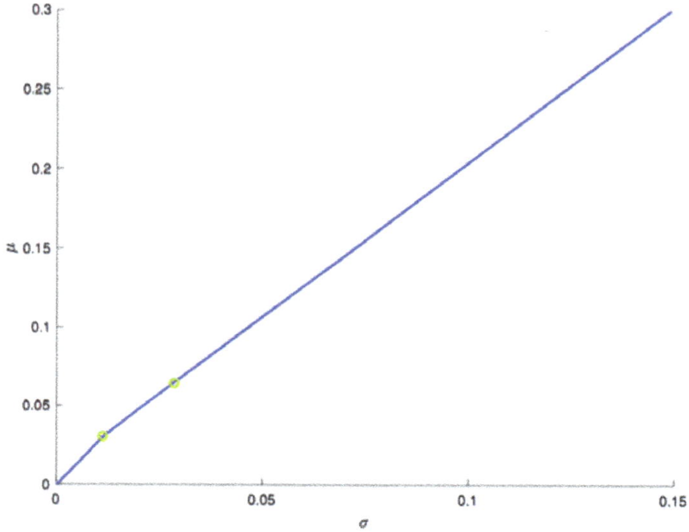

Figure 3. Comparison between leveraged portfolio with the classical Markowitz's portfolios with the statistical hypotheses of Equations (41), (42) and (50).

5. Conclusions

In this work, we propose a method that takes inspiration from matched filter, a known concept in communication theory, and that extends Markowitz's Modern Portfolio Theory to account for short-sales, leverage and transaction costs. The illustrated method differs from the other known techniques in its simplicity and for the universality that allows the trader to simultaneously consider all the extensions to the original theory or just a part of them.

Author Contributions: Conceptualization, investigation and writing original draft: G.A. and A.S.; formal analysis: G.A., M.D., R.L. and A.S.; software: G.A.; resources: R.L. and A.S.; supervision, validation reviewing and editing: M.D., R.L. and A.S.

Funding: This research received no external funding.

Conflicts of Interest: The authors declare no conflict of interest.

References

Adler, Timothy, and Mark Kritzman. 2007. Mean–variance versus full-scale optimisation: In and out of sample. *Journal of Asset Management* 7: 302–11. [CrossRef]

Bachelier, Louis. 1900. Théorie de la spéculation. *Annales Scientifiques de l'École Normale Supérieure 3e Série* 17: 21–86. [CrossRef]

Bailey, David H., and Marcos Lopez de Prado. 2012. The sharpe ratio efficient frontier. *Journal of Risk* 15: 3–44. [CrossRef]

Cover, Thomas M., and Joy A. Thomas. 2006. *Elements of Information Theory (Wiley Series in Telecommunications and Signal Processing)*. New York: Wiley-Interscience.

Cremers, Jan-Hein, Mark Kritzman, and Sebastien Page. 2004. Optimal hedge fund allocations: Do higher moments matter? *Revere Street Working Paper* 272-13. [CrossRef]

DeMiguel, Victor, Lorenzo Garlappi, Francisco J. Nogales, and Raman Uppal. 2009. A generalized approach to portfolio optimization: Improving performance by co nstraining portfolio norms. *Management Science* 55: 798–812. [CrossRef]

DeMiguel, Victor, Lorenzo Garlappi, and Raman Uppal. 2007. Optimal versus naive diversification: How inefficient is the 1/n portfolio strategy? *The Review of Financial Studies* 22: 1915–53. [CrossRef]

Elton, Edwin J., and Martin J. Gruber. 1997. Modern portfolio theory, 1950 to date. *Journal of Banking & Finance* 21: 1743–59.

Jacobs, Bruce I., and Kenneth N. Levy. 2013a. Leverage aversion, efficient frontiers, and the efficient region. *The Journal of Portfolio Management* 39: 54–64. [CrossRef]

Jacobs, Bruce I., and Kenneth N. Levy. 2013b. A comparison of the mean-variance-leverage optimization model and the markowitz general mean-variance portfolio selection model. *The Journal of Portfolio Management* 40: Fall 2013.

Kritzman, Mark, Sébastien Page, and David Turkington. 2010. In defense of optimization: The fallacy of 1/n. *Financial Analysts Journal* 66: 31–39. [CrossRef]

Lobo, Miguel Sousa, Maryam Fazel, and Stephen Boyd. 2007. Portfolio optimization with linear and fixed transaction costs. *Annals of Operations Research* 152: 341–65. [CrossRef]

Low, Rand Kwong Yew. 2017. Vine copulas: Modeling systemic risk and enhancing higher-moment portfolio optimization. *Accounting & Finance* 58: 423–63.

Low, Rand Kwong Yew, Jamie Alcock, Timothy Brailsford, and Robert W. Faff. 2013. Canonical vine copulas in the context of modern portfolio management: Are they worth it? *Journal of Banking & Finance* 37: 3085–99.

Low, Rand Kwong Yew, Robert W. Faff, and Kjersti Aas. 2016. Enhancing mean-variance portfolio selection by modeling distributional asymmetries. *Journal of Economics and Business* 85: 49–72. [CrossRef]

Mansini, Renata, Włodzimierz Ogryczak, and M. Grazia Speranza. 2003. On lp solvable models for portfolio selection. *Informatica* 14: 37–62.

Mansini, Renata, and Maria Grazia Speranza. 1999. Heuristic algorithms for the portfolio selection problem with minimum transaction lots. *European Journal of Operational Research* 114: 219–33. [CrossRef]

Mansini, Renata, and M. Grazia Speranza. 2005. An exact approach for portfolio selection with transaction costs and rounds. *IIE Transactions* 37: 919–29. [CrossRef]

Markowitz, Harry. 1952. Portfolio selection. *The Journal of Finance* 7: 77–91. [CrossRef]

Merton, Robert C. 1972. An analytic derivation of the efficient portfolio frontier. *The Journal of Financial and Quantitative Analysis* 7: 1851–72. [CrossRef]

North, D. Oo. 1963. An analysis of the factors which determine signal/noise discrimination in pulsed-carrier systems. *Proceedings of the IEEE* 51: 1016–27. [CrossRef]

Pillai, Unnikrishna Sreedharan. 2009. Matched Filter Approach to Portfolio Optimization. US Patent 7,502,756, March 10.

Pogue, Gerald A. 1970. An extension of the markowitz portfolio selection model to include variable transactions' costs, short sales, leverage policies and taxes. *Journal of Finance* 25: 1005–27. [CrossRef]

Sharpe, William F. 1966. Mutual fund performance. *The Journal of Business* 39: 119–38. [CrossRef]

Tobin, James. 1958. Liquidity preference as behavior towards risk. *The Review of Economic Studies* 25: 65–86. [CrossRef]

Turin, George. 1960. An introduction to matched filters. *IRE Transactions on Information Theory* 6: 311–29. [CrossRef]

Journal of
Risk and Financial Management

MDPI

Article

Risk Assessment of Housing Market Segments: The Lender's Perspective

Mats Wilhelmsson [1,*] and Jianyu Zhao [2]

1. Royal Institute of Technology (KTH), Department of Real Estate and Construction Management, S-100 44 Stockholm, Sweden
2. Department of Civil of Engineering, Aalto University, 02130 Espoo, Finland; jianyu.zhao@aalto.fi

* Correspondence: mats.wilhelmsson@abe.kth.se

Received: 30 August 2018; Accepted: 14 October 2018; Published: 26 October 2018

Abstract: It is well known that risk factors influence how investment portfolios perform from a lender's perspective; therefore, a thorough risk assessment of the housing market is vital. The aim of this paper was to analyze the risks from housing apartments in different housing market segments by using the Stockholm, Sweden, owner-occupied apartment market as a case study. By applying quantitative and systems engineering methods, we (1) established the relationship between the overall housing market and several housing market segments, (2) analyzed the results from the quantitative model, and (3) finally provided a feasible portfolio regarding risk control based on the given data. The goal was to determine how different housing segment factors could reveal risk towards the overall market and offer better outlooks for risk management when it comes to housing apartments. The results indicated that the risk could be reduced at the same time as the return increased. From a lender's perspective, this could reduce the overall risk.

Keywords: mortgage portfolio; housing segments; risk assessment; hedonic modeling; analytic hierarchy process

---

1. Introduction

Over the past 20 years, housing prices in Sweden have risen rapidly. Sweden's present housing price boom started in the mid-1990s, after the recovery from a financial crisis caused by a previous housing boom. According to public data, during the period of 1996 to 2007, caused by increasing average disposable income, the house prices in Stockholm increased by more than 200 percent, at the same time as the reduction in the cost of capital due to the low-interest rate environment in Sweden and elsewhere worldwide. It is worth noting that Sweden did not experience any plunge in house prices during the global financial crises. After the crises, between 2008 and 2017, house prices have risen by almost 75%.

Higher house prices, however, have increased the interest rate sensitivity as the household debt (higher leverage) has increased substantially over this period. For example, in a recent article by Cerutti et al. (2017), the results indicated that the risk in the economy increased if both a financial boom and a house price boom were observed. Hence, risks exist because the housing market is sensitive due to changes in economic-social characteristics such as income, interest rates, and household formation as well as irrational and speculative behavior from buyers and sellers (Shiller 2014). Since the value of real estate properties is usually high relative to income, it requires financial leverage. Hence, it could lead to major impacts on the economy if the economic situation changes and when the interest rate starts to rise. For example, Agnello and Schuknecht (2011) showed that the probability for booms and busts in housing markets were determined by, for example, domestic credit liquidity and interest rates. As Crowe et al. (2013) concluded, neglecting house price booms can have substantial effects on the economy.

Specific risks in the housing market can include refinancing risks, government policy risks, interest rate risks, and vacancy risks, as well as location risks and specific risks of different housing segments. Our focus here was on specific housing segment risks, that is, the risk that is attributed to the object. Analyzes of housing market segments have previously been investigated in several studies such as Goodman and Thibodeau (2003), Bourassa et al. (1999), and Wilhelmsson (2004). However, there have not been any analyses regarding housing market segment risk.

This risk can be analyzed from different perspectives. For example, the housing segment risk can be analyzed from the lender's perspective, the house owner perspective, the investor perspective, or the public perspective. Here, we analyzed the housing segment risk from the lenders' perspective. From the lenders' perspective, the risk can be divided into credit risk and market risk. In some sense, they are each other's counterparts. Analyzing the object risk will impact the lender through two different channels: (1) the credit risk channel through the value of the collateral, and (2) the market risk channel through the equity price risk, which can both be mitigated through diversification. That is, how can housing segment risks be accurately identified to come up with a portfolio mix of mortgages that could reduce the risk measured as volatility and risk measured as a higher expected return? The answer to this question is not easy. Here, we illustrated the risk characteristics from a lender's perspective in the owner-occupied apartment market of Stockholm, Sweden. With the help of the application of quantitative and systems engineering methods, the results could be added to create a risk-reduced investment portfolio.

Previously, Corgel and Gay (1987) investigated the benefits of diversification across several metropolitan areas in the U.S. in a non-housing real estate mortgage portfolio context. They used a mean-variance portfolio analysis and found that geographical mortgage diversification outperformed alternative portfolio strategies. Moreover, Ogden et al. (1989) found that geographical diversification reduced the mortgage portfolio foreclosure risk and Clauretie (1988) found comparable results in his analysis. However, recently, Cotter et al. (2015) investigated whether housing risk could be geographically diversified and their results showed that increased market integration reduced the geographical diversification potential. Likewise, Pu et al. (2016) showed that an increasing correlation between property segments could lead to increased losses. Hence, geographical diversification of the mortgage portfolio might have worked before housing market integration. Contrary to earlier studies, we investigated diversification not only by interregional geographical diversification. Instead, we analyzed the housing market diversification in dimensions other than geography, such as the size and age of the housing as well as intraregional segments.

The aim of this paper was to (1) diversify the systematic housing segment risk, (2) analyze how stable the relationship between different segments of the housing market were, (3) develop a simple method to assess the internal risk on the housing market, and (4) evaluate the proposed method.

Our contribution was that we used a novel method to assess different housing market segment risks that involved a combination of the hedonic method, beta analysis, and analytic hierarchy process (AHP), which, together with the mean-variance portfolio analysis, has not been previously used in this context. The hedonic and beta analyses were implemented to avoid the "interviews" in the preliminary phase of a classical implementation of the AHP, and allowed us to obtain the weights for each segment risk from the revealed (and not the declared) market preferences. The research results indicated how housing prices in Stockholm have changed over the years and how sensible different impact factors in housing contributed to these changes. Our innovative model was also validated to propose a risk-reduced portfolio by comparing market internal risks to housing segment risks using systems engineering methods. The proposed method is not limited for use only in the construction of portfolios, but can also, for example, be used to evaluate specific housing segment risk between different housing markets or sub-markets to be used in housing market analysis.

The rest of this paper is organized as follows: Section 2 discusses risk assessment and risk management; Section 3 presents the methods applied; and Section 4 presents the econometric and portfolio analysis results. Finally, Section 5 summarizes and concludes our analysis.

2. Risk Assessment and Risk Management

Risk assessment and risk management has been a topic in both the academic and popular press since the 2008 financial crisis when thousands of families lost their homes as society underestimated the risk in both the financial and housing markets. The high and increasing risk level came from, among other things, a lack of knowledge on how real asset prices are determined and irrational decision-making patterns. How the financial market identifies the risk factors, analyzes them, and manages them are key elements to maximize profitability and determine the overall risk level.

From the lenders' perspective, two different types of risks can be identified: credit risk and market risk. Credit risk comes from the risk that the household defaults on debt, that is, the borrower fails to make payments on the mortgage and it is the risk that the collateral will not cover the claim. Households borrow capital from the bank to buy houses and use the house as collateral. The loan-to-value ratio becomes important for the lender to analyze. Everything else being equal, credit risk is lower if the value of the collateral increases. Credit risk management is about mitigating financial losses that can be diversified away. On the other hand, market risk affects the whole market. Here, we are especially interested in an equity price risk that can be both systematic and unsystematic. Increased housing price volatility increases the market risk, but some of it can be diversified away. That is, the object risk will impact the lender through two different channels—credit risk and market risk—where both can be mitigated to some extent by diversification.

In the capital market literature, it is known that the rate of return is equal to the risk-free interest rate plus the risk premium. In an efficient market, the unique unsystematic risks are disturbed away, so it is important to determine the systematical risks to analyze the overall risks in the financial market. Systematic risk captures the aspect of investment risk that cannot be eliminated by diversification. Higher volatility for a certain asset when compared to the overall volatility indicates that the systematic risk is higher. Hence, from a lenders' perspective, it is important to understand the sensitivity of systematic risk. Using references from CAPM (Capital Asset Pricing Model) from Sharpe (1964) and Lintner (1975), the beta-value can reveal the risk from a certain asset when compared to the market portfolio of investments.

Since the beta-value can provide information about the overall performance of an investment portfolio as a reference to obtain an expected rate of return, it is often regarded as a useful tool to weigh the potential risks and produce a reference for the value of the investment (Rosenberg and Guy 1995). Beta is also assumed to be the only feature in an investment portfolio that would make an impact on the rate of return requested from a rational investor in an efficient market (Campbell and Vuolteenaho 2004).

In general, banks are more willing to give loans to investments that are more correlated to systematic risks in a capital market where the risks can be tracked and analyzed more easily. This would lead to a situation where many banks try to carefully analyze the beta-value of investment portfolios before they invest in the market, which, in turn, indicates that a good portfolio would consist of investments that can well undertake and share the integral market risks and are also less sensitive with lower volatility.

There exist theories regarding risk assessment from the lenders' perspective (Huang et al. 2012). However, risk itself is a very vague concept that is hard to quantify, so when it comes to analyzing the risk, it is difficult to know what exactly is needed to identify or calculate it. Applying quantitative and systems engineering methods to set up the modeling type on risk assessment can be a very interesting interdisciplinary field to explore potential risks, especially in the property market.

Real estate including the housing market, in contrast to the financial market, has its own characteristics of risks which include fixed physical attributions, specific locations, long-lived and illiquid assets, as well as large indivisible investments (Ibbotson and Siegel 1984; Firstenberg et al. 1988). Huffman (2003) analyzed the risk associated with corporate real estate and divided them into three categories: financial, physical, and regulatory risks.

Diversification is one possible risk management strategy. Therefore, real estate companies, together with their financial lenders, are exposed to both geographical and business cycle risks in their core business, which can affect both their balance sheets and income statements. Since property value is sensitive to changes in both macro- and microeconomic conditions, monetary and fiscal policy together with demand and supply factors can influence the total risk levels in the real estate market (Afonso and Sousa 2011).

Additionally, properties in an owner-occupied housing market have a high need of being purchased since residents require places to live (Domian et al. 2015). It suggests a relatively higher demand than other markets, so practitioners and some academic research have implied that residential real estate has high returns with low risk (Beracha and Skiba 2011). However, this view has been debated in recent years as the actual potential risks in the housing market could be bigger than what has been often thought (Favilukis et al. 2017). One reason could be due to its special characteristics as a kind of tradable commodity property (Domian et al. 2015), which contains a high value, a bigger uncertainty of pricing prediction, and business cycle effects. This means that economic features and risks can vary a lot during the long-time duration of investments on real estate since they may be influenced by a lag in construction, myopic expectation, and elasticity from supply and demand. In all, it brings up a unique and interesting topic of analyzing risk factors in the housing market in terms of its own financial characteristics and arguments.

It is also worth mentioning that there is usually a default and foreclosure risk involved when buyers cannot continue to pay off their loans from the banks and lose their ownership of the properties (Chatterjee and Eyigungor 2015). These risks, which symbolize the uniqueness in the housing market, can lead to an important consideration where the limitation of households with wealth or fund liquidity is more likely to take place (Brown 2016).

3. Methodology

We utilized four distinct and very different methodologies to analyze the housing market segment risk and develop a method to assess the internal risk on the housing market. The first model relates apartment prices with its attributes on a number of different segments in the housing market. The segments consist of both geographical segments as well as apartment type segments. By estimating the hedonic price equations, it is possible to derive property price indices for those segments, which can be used to estimate the risk of each segment. By doing this, we are able to measure whether the segments behave like the overall markets or if they have more or less risk. These risk factors are then used in a third modeling approach: the analytic hierarchy process (AHP). The objective here was to objectively derive the portfolio with the lowest risk. Finally, we needed to evaluate the results. Here, we used measures such as return and standard deviation, skewness and kurtosis as well as Value-at-Risk (VaR).

3.1. Hedonic Modeling

In real estate economics, hedonic modeling is often used to estimate the value or demand (e.g., Wilhelmsson 2002; Ayan and Erkin 2014). It decomposes the integral pricing factor into several constituent characteristics and examines the value of each characteristic by putting them into a regression analysis. More specifically, hedonic pricing methods have been developed based on this principle, which were used in this paper. In hedonic pricing methods, it is assumed that the price of one certain product reflects the embodied characteristic's value from its different internal segments, which are also usually coefficients that relate its attributes in the regression model. This implies that independent variables that are chosen for the regression analysis would include "performance-related product and service attributes" (Baltas and Freeman 2001), so the relationship between the pricing factor and market-segment effects would successfully be made for the differences in measurable product performances.

Following this principle, housing transaction activities can also be divided into many different characteristics and those, in turn, make up an integral expected property value like other products sold on the market (Wilhelmsson 2002; Monson 2009). By applying hedonic pricing methods, housing transaction prices are often viewed as a composition of their internal features and the method tries to measure the marginal effects of its own characteristics back on the price (e.g., Donner et al. 2016; Zietz et al. 2008). The fundamental hedonic price function is often referred to in the form of

$$\ln P_t = \alpha_0 + \alpha_i X_{it} + \lambda_t T_t + \varepsilon_{it} \tag{1}$$

where P is the vector of the sale prices; X represents the explanatory variables; T is a time dummy; α is the vector of the regression coefficients; λ is equal to the price index; and ε is the error term. Apartment transaction price P_t is in the natural logarithm as the semi-log form provides more reliable estimates in terms of heteroscedasticity, which is often used in cross-section datasets in real estate research (Malpezzi 2003). Furthermore, it is better for an economic interpretation, as will be illustrated in a later section. X_{it} represents the influential factors in line with the certain time series t. If compared with the first time series, which was January 2005 in this case, λ stands for the changed value in the index number when compared to the default period.

Here, the hedonic pricing model estimated a vector of time dummy coefficients and used them to calculate the house price index as in Song and Wilhelmsson (2010), and more recently in Wu et al. (2014). The basic principle of the hedonic regression model is that the transaction price of apartments in the Stockholm region is related to other factors that could affect the price was used as the independent variable.

In practice, many empirical applications of the hedonic pricing model have introduced the concept of segmentation such as different housing markets (e.g., Wilhelmsson 2004; Brasington and Hite 2005). The idea of market segmentation comes from the notion "a means by which a product is differentiated by buyers or investors in a way which allows them to target the preferences and needs of identifiable sub-groups of demanders" (Jones et al. 2004). This regression analysis of market segmentation is a helpful and meaningful method to carry out the intrinsic value of each attribute, indirectly revealing the preferences of the buyers (Baudry and Maslianskaia-Pautrel 2015), which also helps to predict the transaction prices by analyzing empirical data from the past. Here, we defined the segmentation of the housing market in three different dimensions: geographical segmentation, apartment size segmentation, and house age segmentation. More sophisticated statistical methods to define housing submarkets can be used such as the principal component and cluster analysis methods demonstrated by Bourassa et al. (1999).

3.2. Beta Modeling

Beta modeling, which is also known as a systematic risk in finance, plays a significant role in risk management, capital budgeting applications, and asset pricing in an investment portfolio (Ferreira et al. 2011). The sensitivity of the expected rate of return from an investment to the rate from the overall market portfolio is quantified by beta in the model (Bollen and Gharghori 2015). For example, systematic risks in an investment portfolio often decide the degree of how much funds are raised, while the expected risks (beta) are based on the expected weighted average betas from every single asset in the portfolio (Reeves and Wu 2013). Not surprisingly, estimating this systematic risk or beta is linked to that problem (Scholes and Williams 1977). A similar approach, in a real estate context, was used in Cannon et al. (2006) where they investigated risk and return in the housing market by utilizing an asset-pricing approach.

A beta (β) of an investment stands for the volatility degree compared to the market. It statistically indicates if the investment would be more or less volatile to the market investment based on an assumption that the market portfolio of all investments has a beta of exactly 1 (Sharpe 1964). More specifically, if the beta is larger than 1, it indicates that the investment tends to be more volatile than the market; if the beta is between 0 and 1, it indicates that the investment appears to be less volatile than the market or not highly correlated with the market; if however, the beta is lower than 0, it suggests that the price of the chosen investment probably would move up when the market value moves down. As the reference from the capital asset pricing model, beta risk should be the only factor for which investors would get an expected return that is higher than the interests of risk-free assets (Fama 1976). Thus, beta measures the additional risk degree that has been added to the diversified portfolio of the funds from the same type (Ilmanen 2014).

Beta is important to risk assessment because it highlights the systematic risks in the market that cannot be reduced by diversification. Moreover, beta can provide a slope that represents the connection ratio of the volatility of the rate of return from an investment and the volatility of the rate of return from the market index (Tofallis 2008), which can be calculated from the hedonic index in the housing market. Hence, it can have a guiding effect for banks or other financial institutions to evaluate the risk of an investment/debt portfolio compared to the market and make decisions of how much they could put their financial mortgage upon a certain portfolio. In mathematical function, the beta model is usually given as:

$$r_{i,t} = \beta_0 + \beta_i r_{m,t} + e_{i,t} \tag{2}$$

where $r_{i,t}$ is the excess return of the investment; $r_{m,t}$ is the market rate of return; β_i is the beta value for systematic risks; and $e_{i,t}$ stands for the error term (Ortas et al. 2014). However, nowadays it is more and more recognized that this linear model does not really perform as accurately as expected empirically, so it has led to the more revised version of the function model developed for further improvement (Fouque and Tashman 2012).

As for the modeling in this paper, the linear regression of the indexes from the hedonic model was set up following the basic form above. The improved function is shown below:

$$\ln\left(\frac{\text{index}_i^t}{\text{index}_i^{t-1}}\right) = \beta_0 + \beta_1 \ln\left(\frac{\text{index}_{\text{market}}^t}{\text{index}_{\text{market}}^{t-1}}\right) + e \tag{3}$$

where index_i^t is equal to the house price index based on the housing segment of i at time t; β_1 is equal to the beta value for the housing segment of i; and $\text{index}_{\text{market}}^t$ is the index of the market portfolio at time t. The function is in natural logarithm form to calculate the return. The letter i could mean different housing market segment utilized into the analysis, such as the size of the apartments, the location or/and the age of the apartments.

3.3. AHP Modeling

The mathematical model of AHP stands for the analytic hierarchy process and was developed by Saaty (1980). AHP is a systematical technique for measuring, organizing, and analyzing decisions with complexes, and applied with a series of calculations and psychology patterns (Dey 2010). AHP is built based on a human's intrinsic judgments, followed by their perceptions or knowledge hierarchically (Zhu and Xu 2014), so it can be applied to settings in group decision making (Saaty and Peniwati 2008). Since it also has a standard means of calculation and process, it can be used in a very wide variety of decision situations such as business development, risk management, portfolio management, regional planning, and education (Bender et al. 1997; Zhao et al. 2011, 2013a; Saracoglu 2013). In a real estate context, the method has been used by Bender et al. (1997) and Srinivasan (1994). In Zopounidis (1999), AHP, as an example of a multi-criteria method, was used in solving financial decision problems.

Compared to modern portfolio theory (MPT), which is often used in the risk assessment of investments, AHP provides a whole new image on how to define risk levels in a systematic way from another perspective. MPT provides a mathematical framework to assess the risks of individual assets to market overall risks (Markowitz 1952), but does not yet offer possibilities to access risk levels in different segments of the portfolio. By comparing pre-defined impact factors, AHP can help make better decisions for a risk-reduced portfolio by creating different hierarchy levels based on segments in investments (Zhao et al. 2013b). For example, in this paper, a four-level hierarchy structure system was made for risk assessment in different types of real estate properties thanks to the previous regression results of the index analysis. Then, AHP can be used to summarize how much of the weight sets of each factor should be considered through a series of matrix calculations (Zhao et al. 2011). This is of high significance for a suggested risk-reduced portfolio in a later stage since weight sets here refer to the importance of each individual housing segment in an investment portfolio.

Through AHP, a subjective comparison between different factors can be objectively quantified. Therefore, in a way, the risks can be quantified in an assessment together combined with a qualitative analysis. The major processes of AHP to obtain the weight sets of all housing segments regarding their risks are as follows:

1. **Analyze the relationship among the influential factors in different hierarchical levels**

First, it is important to build an overall model structure with different hierarchy levels according to the logic of the problem to be solved. Next, the impact factors are placed into the levels and are compared one by one between every two factors to create the judgment matrices. The judgment matrices can tell which factors are seen as more important than another (Saaty 2008). In this case, it is the degree of how risky each factor is compared to one and another that is used. Judgment matrices are the key to weight sets for relevant factors.

2. **Carry out the weight sets**

With the help of the judgment matrices from the previous steps, the weight sets in each hierarchy can be calculated. There are several mathematical ways of doing this, though, in this case, the process included: (1) obtaining eigenvector W as well as the maximum eigenvalue λ_{max}, and (2) standardizing the eigenvector W for the final adjusted weight sets among the different factors.

3. **Test consistency for the judgment matrices in each level**

For more than two factors in the same level of the structure, there is a need to ensure that the importance of each factor does not conflict with one another (Hyun et al. 2015). For example, if the C1 factor is more important than C2, and C2 is more important than C3, then naturally C1 is more important than C3, and not the other way around. The method proposed by Saaty (1980) to measure the reliability of the relative weights is the consistency ratio. To perform the consistency ratio test, first, the consistency index (CI) should be obtained, defined as

$$CI = \frac{\lambda_{\max} - n}{n - 1} \tag{4}$$

where $\lambda_{\max}$ is the maximum eigenvalue from step 2. Following that, the consistency ratio (CR) can be calculated, which equals CI divided by the average random consistency index (RI). RI is defined and can be obtained by sampling matrices in the statistics (Saaty 1980). A consistency test is necessary only when the number of factors in the same level is more than 2. If the CR is less than 0.1, it indicates that the consistency test is passed (Bender et al. 1997), and therefore the weight sets can now be used correctly.

Since AHP can be applied for better estimations in risk management (Dey 2010), the judgment matrices in this paper were set according to the beta in different housing segments instead of experts' grading for the establishment of priorities in the hierarchy levels (Zheng and Xu 2010). In this way, the risk assessment methods were better connected with the AHP by beta values.

The process of the whole calculation was illustrated through the application of AHP by creating a risk-reduced portfolio in different housing segments in a later section. Compared with other decision-making theories, it has its own advantages such as (1) the results (weight sets for impact factors) are objectively quantified, so that the potential bias could be avoided to the maximum degree

(Bhushan and Rai 2004); (2) it is followed by a series of standard mathematical calculations that are simple and can be applied in many interdisciplinary areas (Forman and Gass 2001); and (3) by comparing each relevant factor and examining the evaluation for inconsistencies where the results were of high confidence and accuracy.

3.4. Evaluation

The evaluation was carried out by using measures such as return, standard deviation, skewness, kurtosis, and Value-at-Risk. A portfolio with a higher return reduces the risk for the lender as the underlying collateral in their portfolio has appreciated more than the average, and therefore, lowers the loan-to-ratio in the mortgage portfolio. Lower volatility, measured as the standard deviation of the return, in the underlying assets in the mortgage portfolio is preferable, all else is equal. Skewness and kurtosis provide measures if the return deviates from a normal distribution. Skewness to the right is better than skewness to the left, all else is equal. The literature suggests that the mean-variance-skewness is more desirable than the mean-variance measure (Joro and Na 2006).

We also utilized the concept of Value-at-Risk (Duffie and Pan 1997; Saita 2008). The VaR measurement answered the question of what the maximum loss the housing portfolio could experience the few next days with a probability of alpha (Boffelli and Urga 2016). Three different approaches can be used to estimate VaR: the parametric model, the historical simulation, and the Monte Carlo simulation. Here, we utilized the parametric model. We estimated the mean and standard deviation for the underlying housing price index and the AHP weighted housing price index using a generalized method of moments (GMM) method, and after that, a nonlinear combination of the parameter estimates to obtain point estimates of the Value-at-Risk together with the confidence interval. Two different distributions were used in the computation of the confidence interval: normal distribution and t-distribution. The estimating procedure is outlined in Boffelli and Urga (2016).

In a recent article, Bernard et al. (2017) assessed the model uncertainty of credit risk portfolios. Their conclusion was that "VaR assessments of credit portfolios/ ... / remain subject to significant model uncertainty and are not robust". Moreover, one of the drawbacks with VaR is that it does not give a measure of the severity of the loss (Boffelli and Urga 2016). Hence, we used the VaR measurement as one of many alternative measures of the benefit of diversification.

4. Empirical Analysis

4.1. Data

In co-operation with Valueguard AB, we empirically analyzed the data containing information on transactions of apartments in co-operative housings as well as apartment characteristics. Table 1 presents the descriptive statistics concerning the apartment characteristics. In the hedonic modeling, we used around 140,000 observations over a period of 12 years (from January 2005 to June 2017). We only used data from metropolitan Stockholm, Sweden, which can be considered as the housing market with several different segments.

The structure of the housing market in Stockholm can be divided into three distinct sections: the rental apartment market, the owner-occupied co-operative apartment market, and the owner-occupied single-family housing market. We only analyzed the owner-occupied co-operative apartment market. Around 400,000 dwellings in Stockholm can be found in multi-family houses, and around 45,000 in single-family houses. The most common dwelling in multi-family houses is co-operative apartments where around 55% of the apartments are co-operative apartments. The rest are rental apartments in both the private and public housing sector. A co-operative apartment is a type of housing tenure, known as bostadsrätt, where members own a share in the co-operative that entitles them to an apartment within the commonly owned stock. However, most co-operative housing societies have been organized as such from the outset, at the time of building. While not strictly speaking owner-occupied, residents may occupy the apartment for as long as they see fit and they are free to sell. It is also possible to use the apartment as collateral when getting a mortgage. In other respects, however, such as renting it out second hand or making major alterations, actions are subject to the control of the co-operative. Usually, the co-operative is rather restrictive when it comes to subletting, which means that households only own one co-operative apartment. Speculation by owning more than one apartment and subletting them is not common at all. Residents also pay a monthly fee to the society for daily up-keep and long-term maintenance, and the size of the fee, in turn, influences the sale price of the apartments in this segment of the market (and, therefore, needs to be controlled for in any analysis).

Table 1. The descriptive statistics apartment data.

Variable	Unit	Mean	Standard Deviation
Price	SEK	3,088,164	1998.972
Living area	m^2	60.96	25.44
Rooms	Number	2.29	0.98
Age	Year	62.95	36.07
Floor level (apt)	Number	2.74	2.03
Floor level (property)	Number	4.79	1.91
Fee	SEK	3117.74	1266.04
Top floor	Binary	0.19	0.40
Ground floor	Binary	0.17	0.37
Distance CBD	Meter	4354.71	2907.49

The variable used in the hedonic model consisted of eight apartment/property characteristics. The measuring size with the square meters of the living area and number of rooms, the age of the property at the time of the transaction, the height of the property, and the floor level of the apartment as well as the fee to the co-operative for maintenance. We also included two binary variables indicating if the apartment was located on the first (ground) floor or on the top floor. We also used neighborhood characteristics in the form of the distance from the central business district (CBD) and the binary variables for each parish in the municipality of Stockholm.

The average price over the period was around 3 million SEK and variation around its mean was high, almost two million SEK. The average size of the apartment was 60 m^2 with a standard deviation of 25 square meters and the average number of rooms was equal to 2.3. The average apartment was located almost on the third floor in a property of five floors. Besides the living area, the fee was the most important characteristic explaining the apartment prices. The average fee was 3100 SEK with a standard deviation of almost 1300 SEK. Almost 20% of the apartments were located on the top floor and slightly less were located on the ground floor. The expected sign of the apartment/property attributes were positive, except for the ground floor and fee. Of the neighborhood characteristics, only the distance to the CBD was displayed here. The average apartment was located around four kilometers from the city center and the standard deviation was as high as three kilometers. The next step was to estimate the hedonic price equation that related the transaction price to the apartment/property characteristics and neighborhood characteristics.

4.2. Hedonic Modeling

The stochastic hedonic model we used relates the apartment price to several independent variables about the apartment and the house as well as location. Aside from the variables that we described in the data section, the model also included binary variables such as parish and time. The coefficients concerning time were of primary interest. Table 2 shows the results from the hedonic regression model. Here, we only present the model for Stockholm's housing market. The first model was a default model where all transactions were included (OLS—ordinary least square), and the second model was a so-called outlier robust estimation.

Table 2. The hedonic regression model (OLS and outlier model).

	OLS Model		Outlier Model	
	Coefficient	t-Value	Coefficient	t-Value
Living area	0.8561	278.35	0.8418	327.79
Rooms	0.0762	34.36	0.0730	37.08
Age	−0.0117	−18.92	−0.0111	−21.15
Floor level (apt)	0.0477	38.90	0.0427	37.03
Floor level (property)	−0.0209	−10.95	−0.0192	−11.97
Fee	−0.1918	−77.33	−0.1512	−78.45
Top floor	0.0187	12.12	0.0168	13.26
Ground floor	0.0106	6.30	0.0048	3.29
Distance CBD	−0.2553	−97.72	−0.2282	−115.26
Constant	13.7090	133.02	13.2311	183.72
R^2	0.8997		0.9193	
No. of observations	136,892		136,891	
VIF	4.04		-	
Breusch-Pagan	2515.86		-	

Note: Additionally included in the model are 30 binary variables concerning the parish and 154 binary variables concerning month. Coefficients are not shown in the table. The VIF (Variance Inflation Factor) value is the average VIF value concerning the binary variables for time.

The overall goodness-of-fit was as high as 90%. Even though we only included nine explanatory variables in the hedonic price equation, by all standards, the explanation power was high. We could not rule out omitted variable bias even if the probability was low. The Breusch-Pagan test showed that we had problems with heteroscedasticity. Therefore, the t-values were based on White robust variance estimates. The robust outlier model explained the overall variation in price a little more, 92% when compared to 89%. As the estimated parameters were very similar in the two models, we chose the simple OLS model of the hedonic models. The VIF value measures the extent of multicollinearity. This problem exists, but is only a problem for the neighborhood characteristics. The average VIF value for the monthly binary variables was around four, that is, lower than the threshold value of five (Berggren et al. 2017).

For individual coefficients concerning the apartment/property characteristics, both the economic interpretation and the statistical interpretation were in accordance with our expectations. All t-values were extremely high, which were natural when the number of observations was as high as it was. The size of the apartment increased the expected value of the apartment. If the space (m^2) of the living area increased by 1%, the expected price increased by 0.86%. If the fee increased by 1%, the expected price decreased by 0.20%. If the distance from the CBD increased, the expected price will also decline. To summarize, all estimates of the apartment/property characteristics and neighborhood characteristics were of reasonable magnitude and expected sign. Hence, we were confident that our estimates concerning the monthly binary variables were robust and accurate.

Earlier studies showed that spatial dependency was often present in real estate data (see e.g., Wilhelmsson 2002). However, its effect on the price indices seemed to be limited (Song and Wilhelmsson 2010), whose conclusion was "Although there is a presence of spatial dependency in our hedonic models, this seems not to spill over to the price indexes". We, therefore, did not estimate a spatial autoregressive or spatial lag hedonic model.

As discussed earlier, we analyzed the segmentation in three dimensions: (1) geographical; (2) apartment size; and (3) the age of the house. The geographical segmentation divided the market into inner-city and suburbs. Here, we defined inner-city with a distance of 5000 meters from the CBD. The apartment size segmentation divided the market into three submarkets: the market for one-room apartments, 2–3 room apartments, and the market for apartments with four rooms or more (here up to 10 rooms). The age of the house segmentation defined older houses as those older than 15 years after construction. Newer houses were built less than 15 years ago when the apartments were sold.

Figures 1–4 show the estimated price indices for the Stockholm markets and for the different segments of the market.

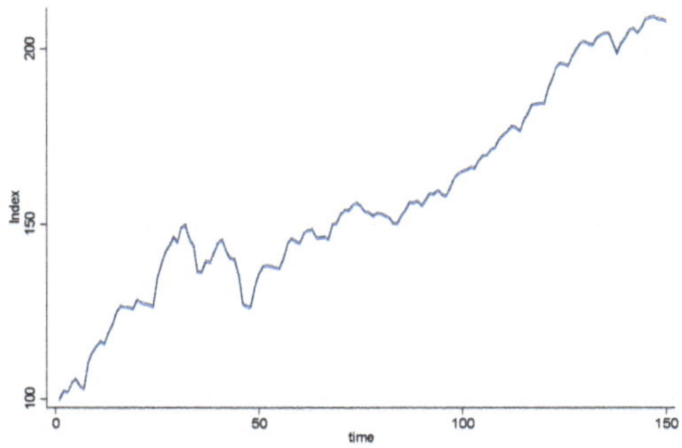

Figure 1. Stockholm housing market. Note: The apartment price index. The Stockholm housing market and segments of the market (the x-axis is the measuring price index and the y-axis is the measuring time).

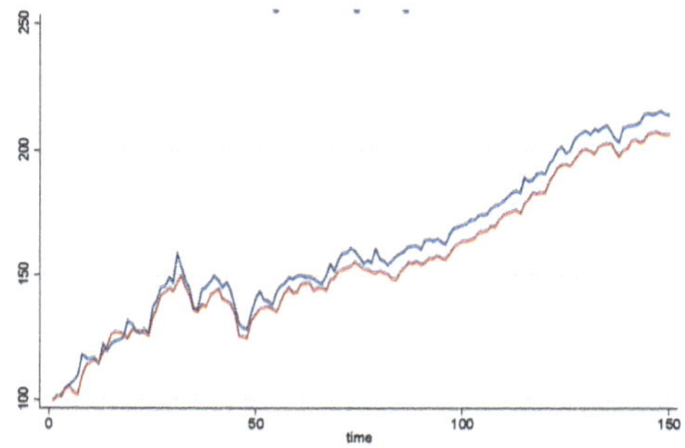

Figure 2. Age segments. Note: The apartment price index. The Stockholm housing market and segments of the market (the x-axis is the measuring price index and the y-axis is the measuring time). The red line is equal newer apartment and the blue is equal older apartments.

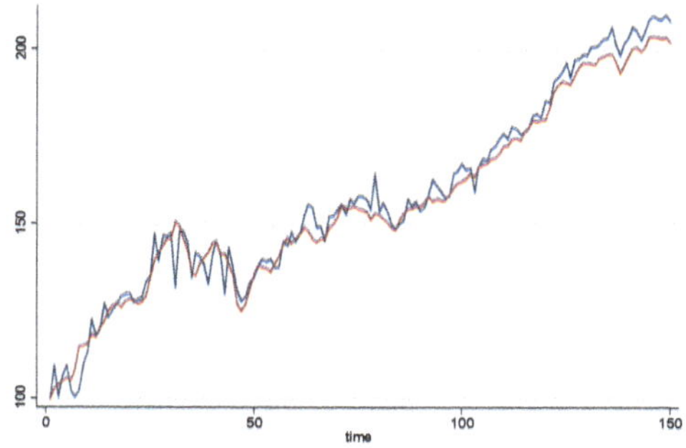

Figure 3. Geography segments. Note: The apartment price index. The Stockholm housing market and segments of the market (the x-axis is the measuring price index and the y-axis is the measuring time). The red line is equal inner city and the blue is equal outer city.

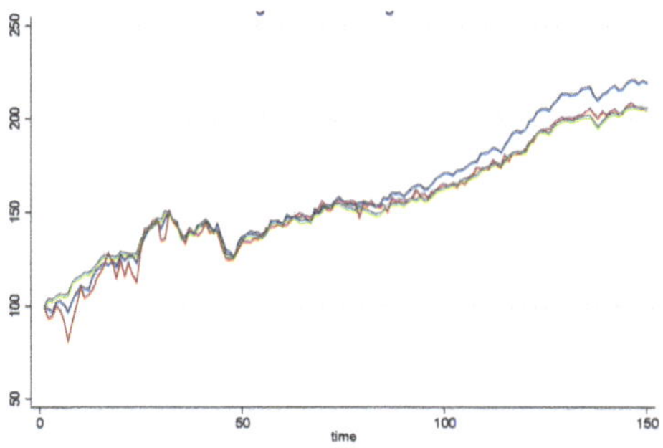

Figure 4. Size segments. Note: The apartment price index. The Stockholm housing market and segments of the market (the x-axis is the measuring price index and the y-axis is the measuring time). The red line is equal one-room apartments, the blue is equal 2–3 room apartments and the green line equal large apartments.

Figure 1 clearly shows that the transaction price in the housing market in the Stockholm area has risen over the past few decades in general, up to an index value of 208 in June 2017 from 100 in January 2005. This means that the price for an apartment in 2017 was more than twice as expensive as it was in 2005. However, the price index also demonstrates that the price did not only rise. After the first peak at the index of 150 in August 2007, the price rapidly dropped and eventually reached 128 in November 2008, which can be attributed to the impact from the financial crisis starting in the USA in early 2008. During the period from the middle of 2006 to the end of 2009, the fluctuation of the transaction price in the Stockholm market showed an unstable market for apartments. That led to an increased risk when compared to the time after the end of 2011 when the prices rose consistently. However, the drop in the Stockholm apartment market is not comparable to some of the metropolitan regions in Europe and elsewhere.

Over the analyzed time period, the one-room apartment price index was generally higher than the total index for the same time frame, which probably means that the demand for one-room apartments can be considered to be higher when compared to the other types. Compared with other room types of apartments in Stockholm, the price index fluctuated for apartments with four or more rooms, which were more volatile most of the time and also faced a dramatic drop starting from early 2015.

Both apartment price indexes in the inner-city and suburbs of Stockholm were in line with the total index roughly from the period of early 2007 to mid-2011. However, the price development in the suburbs showed a lower price development when compared with the overall apartment market before 2007 and higher transaction prices after 2011. This could demonstrate that people may have switched preferences from previously buying apartments near central Stockholm to a tendency of nowadays moving out from central Stockholm. This could be a consequence of the fact that apartment prices in the inner-city are too expensive, so the demand has been pressed out to the suburbs.

The index of apartments that were older than 15 years was highly correlated with the total index during this period, which showed a good stability of transaction in this segment. Newer apartments had a higher volatility in prices as expected, as prices grew higher, especially during the early period, the sale prices were generally lower than the average market according to the index comparison shown above.

To summarize, most of the housing market segments have had more or less the same rapid apartment price development over the studied period. In general, the housing market in Stockholm faced a rather unstable period during the global financial crisis from early 2008 and then started to gradually increase afterward in terms of the transaction price. The most recent number has pointed out that the price is higher than twice its price in 2005. However, the volatility in the series differs.

Some of the housing market segments exhibit more risk in the form of higher volatility and some other segments have had less risk. We will thoroughly analyze the price indices in the next section.

4.3. Beta Modeling

We estimated seven different beta models where we related the return on each segment of the housing market to the overall housing market. First, the descriptive statistics for each return series are presented in Table 3. The return series was derived from the apartment price indices by calculating the log return. The descriptive statistics for each return series were the following measures: average, standard deviation, kurtosis, skewness, and Dickey–Fuller test for non-stationarity together with the Durbin–Watson test for autocorrelation as well as an ARCH-LM test for heteroscedasticity in the return series.

Table 3. The descriptive statistics: prices indices data.

	Mean	Standard Deviation	Skewness	Kurtosis	ARCH-LM	Durbin-Watson	Dickey–Fuller
Stockholm	0.0049	0.0187	0.3399	6.81	0.04	1.78	−10.89
1 room	0.0050	0.0231	0.6629	5.11	0.28	1.99	−12.08
2–3 rooms	0.0049	0.0191	0.0755	5.41	0.03	1.81	−11.70
>3 rooms	0.0047	0.0515	−0.2718	6.72	0.00	2.67	−17.42
Inner-city	0.0047	0.0146	−0.3686	5.53	0.00	1.21	−8.19
Suburbs	0.0053	0.0225	0.2254	4.15	0.00	2.19	−13.28
Newer	0.0048	0.0411	0.0974	4.85	0.00	2.38	−14.86
Older	0.0048	0.0182	0.0988	6.59	0.14	1.84	−11.32

We concluded that the average monthly returns were almost of the same magnitude, however, the variation measured with the standard deviation showed that variation in volatility was high. The volatility was higher in the older apartments segment, in the suburbs, and in larger apartments. None of the series were normally distributed. A close to normal distribution could be found in the newer apartment segment and in the suburbs. The distribution concerning older apartments was highly skewed to the right. All series peaked more than what could be expected when compared to a normal distribution. ARCH-LM tests showed if there was any heteroscedasticity over time in the return series, that is, if the volatility changed over time. The hypothesis about heteroscedasticity was rejected in the overall housing market and in the newer and older apartment segments as well as in the segment for one-room apartments. The Durbin–Watson test tests the hypothesis about the presence of serial correlation (or temporal autocorrelation). A value around two indicates that there is no serial correlation. Almost all series showed the presence of serial correlation. The Dickey–Fuller test is a test of stationarity. All the statistics in the table indicated that all series were stationary.

The model was first estimated using OLS and then tested for serial correlation. In all models, the serial correlation was present. As a remedy to the problem, we utilized the Cochrane–Orcutt regression technique. All t-values were based on White's heteroscedasticity robust estimates (White 1980). Table 4 presents the results from these estimations.

Table 4. The beta-analysis (Cochrane–Orcutt regression).

	Beta	t-Value	95% Conf. Interval		R^2	Durbin-Watson
1 room	0.822	9.68	0.65	0.99	0.459	2.03
2–3 rooms	0.983	32.41	0.92	1.04	0.939	2.20
4+ rooms	1.328	6.34	0.91	1.74	0.329	2.10
Inner-city	0.639	11.09	0.52	0.75	0.618	2.03
Suburbs	1.006	20.41	0.91	1.10	0.798	2.25
Newer	1.337	7.75	1.00	1.68	0.457	2.06
Older	0.935	39.71	0.89	0.98	0.953	2.20

The overall goodness-of-fit showed a substantial variation among the eight different segments of the housing market. The variation in R^2 ranged from 0.33 to 0.95. In the beta-model, the R-squared measures how closely each change in the price of a housing segment correlated to a benchmark, that is, the overall housing market. A low R-square value may indicate that the estimated beta values are less reliable. There is a risk of potential omitted variable bias in our estimates. One way to remedy this problem would be to also include social-economic variables in the model. However, this was not done in the present research. The measurements indicated that the market risk was very high in the new apartment, apartments in the inner-city, and one-room apartment segments. All these sub-markets followed the general trends in the overall market. However, segment specific risk was especially identified in the segments of the suburbs and 2–3 room apartments. All models exhibited serial correlation; therefore, the Cochrane–Orcutt approach was applied. After the transformation, all temporal autocorrelation was reduced to acceptable levels.

The beta model related the log returns for each segment against the return of the overall market. The average integral risk in the housing market of Stockholm was set to one, so any other beta in different types of housing segment could be compared with one. If it was more than 1, it meant that the price in this type of housing segment was more volatile than the overall market, thus bigger risks existed.

The beta also contained economical and quantified implications. For example, in the room size segment, the beta for one room, 2–3 rooms, and four or more rooms were 0.822, 0.983, and 1.328, respectively. It indicated that if the transaction price of the total market went up by 1%, the prices in these three kinds of apartments would be 0.822%, 0.983%, and 1.328%, respectively. This is a very important benchmark for later analysis in AHP methods for the suggestion of a risk-reduced portfolio proposal. The beta results regarding the correlation between the total market and apartment size segment had a relatively good accuracy. All estimates were statistically significantly different from zero. However, a more relevant hypothesis was to test whether the beta values were significantly different from one. Here, we noticed that the estimate concerning four rooms or more was not statistically different from one.

The beta coefficients concerning the geographical segmentation suggested that both markets had less risk than the overall market. However, only the estimate concerning the inner-city was statistically different from one. That is, the inner-city segment exhibited a lower risk than the overall housing market and the suburbs exhibited the same risk as the overall market. Concerning the age segmentation, we can conclude that none of the two estimates were statistically significantly different from one, indicating that both age groups exhibited the same risk.

4.4. Analytic Hierarchy Process Modeling

The first step in analytic hierarchy process modeling is to construct a hierarchy structure. Since three impact factors (geography, apartment size, and age) were chosen, the hierarchy was constructed based on this. Figure 5 depicts the structure of AHP for the different housing market segments.

Each impact factor was different. For example, D1 represents apartments that were older than 15 years, located in the inner-city, and had one room; D5 represents apartments that were older, located in the inner-city but had two or three rooms. So, D1 and D5 were actually different factors. Since there were 21 different impact factors, there were 21 different indexes created for AHP. For example, the index of B1 was the index for apartments that had one room while the index of D1 was the index for apartments that had one room, that were located in the inner-city, and that were older than 15 years. The order from higher level to lower level could be changed, which means, for example, that the B level could present a distance factor or age factor, and the D level could also present the room size factor. This order of the structure is just an example for constructing a risk-reduced portfolio in housing apartments.

Since there were 21 different indexes constructed for the AHP when applying the same beta model, 21 different betas could also be carried out. Together with different hierarchies in the model, the beta matrices were created, which were used for the judgment matrices.

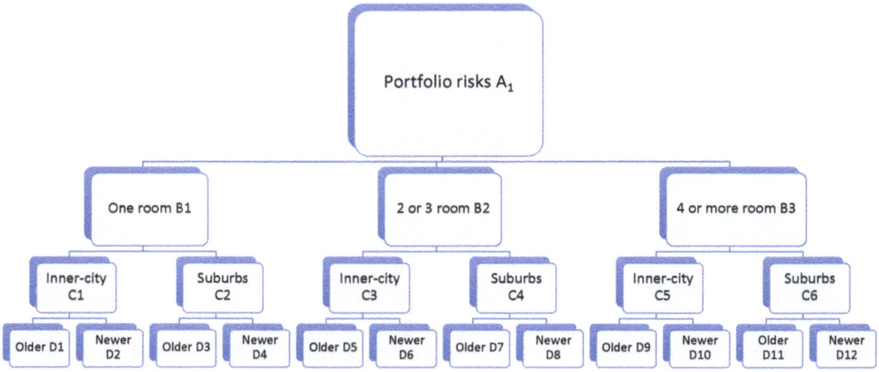

Figure 5. The structure of AHP for different housing segments in Stockholm.

The first step was to determine the risks of the different housing segments in a different hierarchy if the market price increased by 1%. As the beta matrix shows the risk connection between the upper level and lower level in the AHP model, it was easy to estimate how many percentages of the price in each housing segment in a different hierarchy would increase if the market price increased by 1%. Table 5 presents the results of how much the price would appreciate each housing market segment if the overall housing price increased by 1%.

Table 5. How much each segment would increase if the overall market price increased by 1.

Segment	Percent	Segment	Percent
D1	0.81	C1	0.62
D2	0.62	C2	0.88
D3	0.99	C3	0.57
D4	0.82	C4	1.10
D5	0.34	C5	0.53
D6	0.57	C6	1.15
D7	0.72		
D8	1.05		
D9	0.19		
D10	0.55	B1	0.82
D11	0.88	B2	0.98
D12	1.08	B3	1.33

According to the AHP model structure, if the market price increased by 1%, B1 would increase by 0.82%, which equaled its beta; and if B1 increased by 1%, C1 would increase by 0.75%, which equaled its beta. Hence, this means that if the market price increased by 1%, C1 would increase by $0.82 \times 0.75 = 0.62\%$, which was the same number as shown above for C1. Following this principle, the direct risks at different levels to the market price could be carried out as in the table above.

In the next step, we calculated the risk-reduced portfolio weight according to AHP. As the weight sets in each hierarchy and betas from each lower level to higher level are given, the risk-reduced portfolio was created following the suggested weight sets from each factor level. The advantage of this portfolio is that the overall risks can be equally distributed from a higher level down to a lower level, which in turn, lessens the risks of the portfolio. A risk-reduced portfolio allows the market risk to be equally distributed into the lower level and makes the total portfolio less risky.

To obtain the risk-reduced portfolio weight in AHP, we needed to calculate the judgment matrices and weight set in the B, C, and D levels. Since the beta values in each hierarchy are already known, which presents the relationship between every lower impact factor to the upper impact factors, it is easy to reconstruct the relationship between every two factors in the same level. For example, in the beta values of A–B, if the A level increases by 1%, B1, B2, and B3 would increase to 0.82%, 0.98%, and 1.33%, respectively. This also showed a relationship between B1, B2, and B3 themselves when compared with each other. If "less risky" is taken as a higher score, the judgment matrices can be created by having each beta of an impact factor divide one another on the same level.

The judgment matrix in the B level:

A	B1	B2	B3
B1	1	1.20*	1.62*
B2	0.84	1	1.35
B3	0.62	0.74	1

Note: *: 1.20 = 0.98 (beta of B2)/0.82 (beta of B1), this means, in a way, that the B1 factor is 1.2 times more important than the B2 factor based on the principle that the less risky factor (smaller beta) scores are higher than those with the bigger risk. **: Following the same principle, 1.62 = 1.33/0.82; this way covers every number in the matrix and so on.

The judgment matrix in the C level:

B1	C1	C2
C1	1	1.422
C2	0.703	1

B2	C3	C4
C3	1	1.933
C4	0.517	1

B3	C5	C6
C5	1	2.170
C6	0.461	1

The judgment matrix in the D level:

C1	D1	D2
D1	1	0.768
D2	1.303	1

C2	D3	D4
D3	1	0.834
D4	1.198	1

C3	D5	D6
D5	1	1.702
D6	0.587	1

C4	D7	D8
D7	1	1.460
D8	0.685	1

C5	D9	D10
D9	1	2.916
D10	0.343	1

C6	D11	D12
D11	1	1.226
D12	0.815	1

After the judgment matrices, the weight sets stand for how many percentages of the investment are suggested for the allocation between the sub-markets in, for example, the mortgage portfolio, to reduce the overall investing risks. Weight sets can be calculated in the AHP principle and are shown in Table 6.

Table 6. The illustration of the weight set calculation for the B level.

B Level	B1 (1)	B2 (2)	B3 (3)	Weight Sets (4)	Weight Sets Adjusted (5)
B1	1	1.20	1.62	1.245	0.4073
B2	0.84	1	1.35	1.041	0.3406
B3	0.62	0.74	1	0.771	0.2521

Note: (4) = $\sqrt[3]{(1) \times (2) \times (3)}$.(5) = (4)/sum(4) (Standardize weight sets).

Since the consistency test is necessary only when the number of factors in the same level is more than two, this means that only the judgment matrix in the B level needs examining. The result is as follows:

$$AW = \begin{bmatrix} 1 & 1.20 & 1.62 \\ 0.84 & 1 & 1.35 \\ 0.62 & 0.74 & 1 \end{bmatrix} \begin{bmatrix} 0.407 \\ 0.341 \\ 0.252 \end{bmatrix} = \begin{bmatrix} 1.222 \\ 1.022 \\ 0.756 \end{bmatrix} \quad \begin{matrix} \lambda max = 3 \\ CI = 0 \\ RI = 0.571 \\ CR = 0 < 0.1 \end{matrix} \quad \text{(Judgment Matrix)} \tag{5}$$

Since the CR is smaller than 0.1, this result passes the consistency test so the weight sets can be used for a risk-controlled portfolio.

Following the same principle, it is easy to calculate the weight sets for the C and D levels as shown in Tables 7 and 8:

Table 7. The weight set calculation for the C level.

	B1	B2	B3	Weight Set	Description
	0.4073 (1)	0.3441 (3)	0.2521 (5)		
C1	0.5871 (2)	0 (4)	0 (6)	0.2391 (7)	(7) = (1) × (2) + (3) × (4) + (5) × (6)
C2	0.4129	0	0	0.1682	Same principle as (7)
C3	0	0.6590	0	0.2245	Same principle as (7)
C4	0	0.3410	0	0.1161	Same principle as (7)
C5	0	0	0.6846	0.1726	Same principle as (7)
C6	0	0	0.3154	0.0795	Same principle as (7)

Table 8. The weight set calculation for the D level.

	C1	C2	C3	C4	C5	C6	Weight Set
	0.2391	0.1682	0.2245	0.1161	0.1726	0.0795	
D1	0.4343	0	0	0	0	0	0.1038
D2	0.5657	0	0	0	0	0	0.1353
D3	0	0.4549	0	0	0	0	0.0765
D4	0	0.5451	0	0	0	0	0.0917
D5	0	0	0.6300	0	0	0	0.1414
D6	0	0	0.3700	0	0	0	0.0830
D7	0	0	0	0.5934	0	0	0.0689
D8	0	0	0	0.4066	0	0	0.0472
D9	0	0	0	0	0.7446	0	0.1285
D10	0	0	0	0	0.2554	0	0.0441
D11	0	0	0	0	0	0.5508	0.0438
D12	0	0	0	0	0	0.4492	0.0357

Table 9 presents all of the optimal weights and risk weights. The overall market risk was equal to one. The interpretation of the weight set was, for example in the B level, the suggested portfolio that would be invested, containing 41% of one-room apartments, 34% of two or three room apartments, and 25% of four or more room apartments in Stockholm, Sweden.

Table 9. The optimal weight sets for the B, C, and D levels.

	Risks in B Level	Weights %	B Level Portfolio Risk
B1	0.822	40.73	0.3348
B2	0.983	34.06	0.3348
B3	1.328	25.22	0.3348
		Total Risk:	**1.004**
	Risks in C Level	**Weights %**	**C Level Portfolio Risk**
C1	0.6199	23.91	0.1482
C2	0.8813	16.82	0.1482
C3	0.5667	22.45	0.1272
C4	1.0954	11.61	0.1272
C5	0.5311	17.26	0.0916
C6	1.1527	7.95	0.0916
		Total Risk:	**0.7342**

Table 9. *Cont.*

	Risks in D Level	Weights %	D Level Portfolio Risks
D1	0.8059	10.38	0.0836
D2	0.6187	13.53	0.0836
D3	0.9869	7.65	0.0755
D4	0.8235	9.17	0.0755
D5	0.3372	14.14	0.0477
D6	0.5743	8.30	0.0477
D7	0.7172	6.89	0.0494
D8	1.0468	4.72	0.0494
D9	0.1889	12.85	0.0243
D10	0.5507	4.41	0.0243
D11	0.8814	4.38	0.0386
D12	1.810	3.57	0.0386
		Total Risk:	0.6384

To summarize, this means that this is the best percentage of each segment factor in the portfolio that takes equal risk distribution into the next level. The total risk of the portfolio would be around 1.00, 0.73, and 0.64 for the B, C, and D levels, respectively, when compared with the market. Hence, level D minimizes the portfolio risk. It is not enough to diversify by only apartment size and space, the age of the property is also needed in the diversification.

4.5. Evaluation

The evaluation was carried out by comparing the Stockholm house price index with an index using optimal weight. In order to evaluate the proposed method, we used measures such as the average, standard deviation, kurtosis, and skewness on the monthly return series. The value-at-risk (VaR) was also utilized as an alternative measure of diversification benefit. Table 10 presents the descriptive statistics.

Table 10. The evaluation of the results.

	Stockholm	Opt-MPT	Opt-D	Opt-C
Return	0.00486	0.00499	0.00509	0.00499
Standard deviation	0.01864	0.01619	0.02400	0.01642
Skewness	0.2589	−0.0798	0.0583	−0.2419
Kurtosis	6.4182	5.7998	5.1957	5.6726
ARCH-LM	0.0178	0.0012	0.0004	0.0363
Durbin-Watson	1.7874	1.5681	2.1649	1.6766
Dickey–Fuller	−10.921	−9.728	−13.245	−10.259
VaR	−0.0258	−0.0216	−0.0344	−0.0220

The results showed that with the optimal weight, the average return was higher, that is, the appreciation of the houses in the lenders' portfolio increased more over time at the same time that the risk/volatility was lower (lower standard deviation). It is also interesting to note that the skewness of the return series was very different. The optimal weight (AHP-D) return series was skewed to the right, that is, the right tail of the distribution was long relative to the left tail. Both the AHD-C and MPT series were skewed to the left. The VaR at one month for a position on the Stockholm index was −2.6% at the 95% confidence level when compared to AHP-D at −3.4%. However, the difference was not statistically different at a 95% significance level.

5. Conclusions

Apartment size is usually seen as a very important impact factor in apartment sales, therefore, analyzing the data from 2005 to early 2017 in this paper showed a relatively accurate volatility of each size segment in terms of the transaction price. By setting up hedonic and beta modeling, the apartment pricing indexes and the relationship of each segment towards the overall market could be constructed. From the data analysis, a conclusion could be drawn that apartments that had four or more rooms in Stockholm had the most volatility when compared with other size type apartments, which also means that the investments put in this segment contained a higher risk.

Stockholm, Sweden, is often regarded as a city with a shortage of accommodation nowadays in the city center, which the data analysis also indicated. From both the results of the hedonic and beta modeling, it was shown that, interestingly, households had a tendency to purchase apartments in the city center from 2005 to 2007 that shifted to the urban area after 2011. Meanwhile, the two location segments were highly in line with the total market. This implies that nowadays, accommodation in the Stockholm city center is becoming more and more limited, so it has pushed people to think about buying the apartments further from city center, which probably means that today, apartments further away from the city center have more investment value than ones closer to the center.

Without any doubt, the results have shown that the newer apartments (less than 15 years) have a higher pricing volatility than older apartments, which means that they contain more investment risk than the other. However, this phenomenon has cooled down a bit in recent years since apartments in those two age segments are more and more in line with the total market for the last few years in Stockholm.

After examining the correlation between different housing segments and the overall market, it is interesting, going further, to determine what a reduced-risk apartment investment portfolio should be, and how much of each housing segment should be contained in this portfolio. By applying beta modeling and AHP methods from systems engineering, the weight set of each segment can be carried out, which represents how much investment funding from each segment should be put into the portfolio to reduce the risks as much as possible.

In this paper, the housing segments of apartment size, age, and location, in general, are chosen and three hierarchies were created. The calculation results showed that for a given investment portfolio for apartments, it is wise to put the most funds into apartments that have one room, are older, and are located in the inner-city, followed by apartments that have one room, are older, but further from the city center. This portfolio arrangement can reduce the bundled total risk to a level that is lower than the market risk by allowing the risks to be equally distributed into the next hierarchy level.

What are the policy implications for the lender? Typically, the lender analysis will be of both the borrower and the object, the apartment. The focus has been on the borrower. The lender looks at the loan-to-value ratio, income in relation to debt service, and of course, the credit history of the borrower. The main objective has been to reduce the default probability. A lender to a real estate developer typically focuses more on the object, for example, the net operating income, vacancy rates, and break-even levels, than the borrower. What we proposed in this paper was that the mortgage lender could also benefit by more carefully analyzing the object and specifically the housing market segment more carefully. By controlling borrower characteristics, the risk for the lender can be reduced by utilizing a strategy considering the distribution of mortgages in different housing market segments. Even within a metropolitan housing market, as we investigated in this paper, diversifying does entail potential benefits (higher return and less risk). The benefits are probably even higher if inter-regional diversification is considered.

Author Contributions: Conceptualization, M.W. and J.Z.; Methodology, M.W. and J.Z.; Software, M.W.; Validation, M.W. and J.Z.; Formal Analysis, M.W. and J.Z.; Investigation, M.W. and J.Z.; Resources, M.W.; Data Curation, M.W.; Writing—Original Draft Preparation, M.W. and J.Z.; Writing—Review & Editing, M.W. and J.Z.; Visualization, M.W.; Supervision, M.W.

Funding: This research received no external funding.

Conflicts of Interest: The authors declare no conflict of interest.

References

Afonso, António, and Ricardo M. Sousa. 2011. The macroeconomic effects of fiscal policy. *Applied Economics* 44: 4439–54. [CrossRef]

Agnello, Luca, and Ludger Schuknecht. 2011. Booms and busts in housing markets: Determinants and implications. *Journal of Housing Economics* 20: 171–90. [CrossRef]

Ayan, Ebubekir, and H. Cenk Erkin. 2014. Hedonic Modeling for a Growing Housing Market: Valuation of Apartments in Complexes. *International Journal of Economics and Finance* 6: 188. [CrossRef]

Baltas, George, and Jonathan Freeman. 2001. Hedonic Price Methods and the Structure of High-Technology Industrial Markets: An Empirical Analysis. *Industrial Marketing Management* 30: 599–607. [CrossRef]

Baudry, Marc, and Masha Maslianskaia-Pautrel. 2015. Revisiting the hedonic price method in the presence of market segmentation. *Environmental Economics and Policy Studies* 18: 1–29. [CrossRef]

Bender, Andre, Allan Din, Philippe Favarger, Martin Hoesli, and Janne Laakso. 1997. An analysis of Perception Concerning the Environmental Quality of Housing in Geneva. *Urban Studies* 34: 503–13. [CrossRef]

Beracha, Eli, and Hilla Skiba. 2011. Findings from a cross-sectional housing risk-factor model. *Journal of Real Estate Financial Economics* 47: 289–309. [CrossRef]

Berggren, Björn, Andreas Fili, and Mats Håkan Wilhelmsson. 2017. Does the increase in house prices influence the creation nof business startups? The case of Sweden. *Region* 4: 1–16. [CrossRef]

Bernard, Carole, Ludger Rüschendorf, Steven Vanduffel, and Jing Yao. 2017. How robust is the value-at-risk of credit risk portfolios? *The European Journal of Finance* 23: 507–34. [CrossRef]

Bhushan, Navneet, and Kanwal Rai. 2004. *Strategic Decision Making: Applying the Analytic Hierarchy Process*. London: Springer, ISBN 1-85233-756-7.

Zhu, Bin, and Zeshui Xu. 2014. Analytic hierarchy process-hesitant group decision making. *European Journal of Operational Research* 239: 794–801. [CrossRef]

Boffelli, Simona, and Giovanni Urga. 2016. *Financial Econometrics Using STATA*. College Station: Stata Press.

Bollen, Bernard, and Philip Gharghori. 2015. How is β related to asset returns? *Applied Economics* 48: 1925–35. [CrossRef]

Bourassa, Steven C., Foort Hamelink, Martin Hoesli, and Bryan D. MacGregor. 1999. Defining Housing Submarkets. *Journal of Housing Economics* 8: 160–83. [CrossRef]

Brasington, David M., and Diane Hite. 2005. Demand for environmental quality: A spatial hedonic analysis. *Regional Science and Urban Economics* 35: 57–82. [CrossRef]

Brown, Scott R. 2016. The Influence of Homebuyer Education on Default and Foreclosure Risk: A Natural Experiment. *Journal of Policy Analysis and Management* 35: 145–72. [CrossRef]

Campbell, John Y., and Tuomo Vuolteenaho. 2004. Bad beta, good beta. *American Economic Review* 94: 1249–75. [CrossRef]

Cannon, Susanne, Norman G. Miller, and Gurupdesh S. Pandher. 2006. Risk and Return in the U.S. Housing Market: A Cross-Sectional Asset-Pricing Approach. *Real Estate Economics* 34: 519–52. [CrossRef]

Cerutti, Eugenio, Jihad Dagher, and Giovanni Dell'Ariccia. 2017. Housing finance and real-estate booms: A cross-country perspective. *Journal of Housing Economics* 38: 1–13. [CrossRef]

Chatterjee, Satyajit, and Burcu Eyigungor. 2015. A quantitative analysis of the US housing and mortgage markets and the foreclosure crisis. *Review of Economic Dynamics* 18: 165–84. [CrossRef]

Clauretie, Terrence. 1988. Regional Economic Diversification and Residential Mortgage Default Risk. *Journal of Real Estate Research* 3: 87–97.

Corgel, John B., and Gerald D. Gay. 1987. Local Economic Base, Geographic Diversification, and Risk Management of Mortgage Portfolios. *AREUEA Journal* 15: 256–67. [CrossRef]

Cotter, John, Stuart Gabriel, and Richard Roll. 2015. Can Housing Risk be Diverfied? A Cautionary Tale from the Housing Boom and Bust. *The Review of Financial Studies* 28: 913–36. [CrossRef]

Crowe, Christopher, Giovanni Dell'Ariccia, Deniz Igan, and Pau Rabanal. 2013. How to deal with real estate booms: Lessons from country experiences. *Journal of Financial Stability* 9: 300–19. [CrossRef]

Dey, Prasanta Kumar. 2010. Managing project risk using combined analytic hierarchy process and risk map. *Applied Soft Computing* 10: 990–1000. [CrossRef]

Domian, Dale, Rob Wolf, and Hsiao-Fen Yang. 2015. An assessment of the risk and return of residential real estate. *Managerial Finance* 41: 591–99. [CrossRef]

Donner, Herman, Han-Suck Song, and Mats Wilhelmsson. 2016. Forced sales and their impact on real estate prices. *Journal of Housing Economics* 34: 60–68. [CrossRef]

Duffie, Darrell, and Jun Pan. 1997. An overview of Value at Risk. *Journal of Derivatives* 4: 7–49. [CrossRef]

Fama, Eugene F. 1976. *Foundations of Finance: Portfolio Decisions and Securities Prices.* New York: Basic Books.

Favilukis, Jack, Sydney C. Ludvigson, and Stijn Van Nieuwerburgh. 2017. The macroeconomic effects of housing wealth, housing finance, and limited risk sharing in general equilibrium. *Journal of Political Economy* 125: 140–223. [CrossRef]

Ferreira, Eva, Javier Gil-Bazo, and Susan Orbe. 2011. Conditional beta pricing models: A nonparametric approach. *Journal of Banking & Finance* 35: 3362–82.

Firstenberg, Paul M., Stephen A. Ross, and Randall C. Zisler. 1988. Real estate: The whole story. *Journal of Portfolio Management* 14: 22–34. [CrossRef]

Forman, Ernest H., and Saul I. Gass. 2001. The Analytic Hierarchy Process: An Exposition. *Operations Research* 49: 469–86. [CrossRef]

Fouque, Jean-Pierre, and Adam P. Tashman. 2012. Option pricing under a stressed-beta model. *Annals of Finance* 8: 183–203. [CrossRef]

Goodman, Allen C., and Thomas G. Thibodeau. 2003. Housing market segmentation and hedonic prediction accuracy. *Journal of Housing Economics* 12: 181–201. [CrossRef]

Ilmanen, Antti. 2014. Expected Returns: An Investor's Guide to Harvesting Market Rewards. *Quantitative Finance* 14: 581–82.

Huang, Xin, Hao Zhou, and Haibin Zhu. 2012. Assessing the systemic risk of a heterogeneous portfolio of banks during the recent financial crisis. *Journal of Financial Stability* 8: 193–205. [CrossRef]

Huffman, Forrest E. 2003. Corporate real estate risk management and assessment. *Journal of Corporate Real Estate* 5: 31–41. [CrossRef]

Ibbotson, Roger G., and Laurence B. Siegel. 1984. Real estate returns: A comparison with other investments. *Real Estate Economics* 12: 219–42. [CrossRef]

Jones, Colin, Chris Leishman, and Craig Watkins. 2004. Intra-Urban migration and housing submarkets: Theory and evidence. *Housing Studies* 19: 269–83. [CrossRef]

Joro, Tarja, and Paul Na. 2006. Portfolio performance evaluation in a mean-variance-skewness framework. *European Journal of Operational Research* 175: 446–61. [CrossRef]

Hyun, Ki-Chang, Sangyoon Min, Hangseok Choi, Jeongjun Park, and In-Mo Lee. 2015. Risk analysis using fault-tree analysis (FTA) and analytic hierarchy process (AHP) applicable to shield TBM tunnels. *Tunnelling and Underground Space Technology* 49: 121–29. [CrossRef]

Lintner, John. 1975. The Valuation of Risk Assets and the Selection of Risky Investments in Stock Portfolios and Capital Budgets. *Stochastic Optimization Models in Finance* 51: 220–21. [CrossRef]

Malpezzi, Stephen. 2003. Hedonic pricing models: A selective and applied review. In *Housing Economics and Public Policy*. Oxford: Blackwell Publishing.

Markowitz, Harry. 1952. Portfolio selection. *Journal of Finance* 7: 77–91.

Monson, Matt. 2009. Valuation using hedonic pricing models. *Cornell Real Estate Review* 7: 10.

Ogden, William, Nanda Rangan, and Thomas Stanley. 1989. Risk Reduction in S&L Mortgage Loan Portfolios Through Geographic Diversification. *Journal of Financial Service Research* 2: 39–48.

Ortas, Eduardo, Manuel Salvador, and Jose Moneva. 2014. Improved beta modeling and forecasting: An unobserved component approach with conditional heteroscedastic disturbances. *The North American Journal of Economics and Finance* 31: 27–51. [CrossRef]

Pu, Ming, Gang-Zhi Fan, and Chunsheng Ban. 2016. The pricing of mortgage insurance premiums under systematic and idiosyncratic Shocks. *Journal of Risk and Insurance* 83: 447–74. [CrossRef]

Reeves, Jonathan J., and Haifeng Wu. 2013. Constant versus Time-Varying Beta Models: Further Forecast Evaluation. *Journal of Forecasting* 32: 256–66. [CrossRef]

Rosenberg, Barr, and James Guy. 1995. Prediction of Beta from Investment Fundamentals. *Financial Analysts Journal* 51: 101–12. [CrossRef]

Saaty, Thomas L. 1980. *The Analytical Hierarchy Process*. New York: McGraw-Hill.

Saaty, Thomas L. 2008. *Decision Making for Leaders: The Analytic Hierarchy Process for Decisions in a Complex World. Pittsburgh.* Pittsburgh: RWS Publications, ISBN 0-9620317-8-X.

Saaty, Thomas L., and Kirti Peniwati. 2008. *Group Decision Making: Drawing out and Reconciling Differences*. Pittsburgh: RWS Publications, ISBN 978-1-888603-08-8.

Saita, Francesco. 2008. *Value at Risk and Bank Capital Management. Risk Adjustment Performances, Capital Management and Capital Allocation Decision Making. Burlington*. Waltham: Academic Press publications, Elsevier.

Saracoglu, Burak Omer. 2013. Selecting industrial investment locations in master plans of countries. *European Journal. of Industrial Engineering* 7: 416–41. [CrossRef]

Scholes, Myron, and Joseph Williams. 1977. Estimating betas from nonsynchronous data. *Journal of Financial Economics* 5: 309–27. [CrossRef]

Sharpe, William F. 1964. Capital asset prices: A theory of market equilibrium under conditions of risk. *The Journal of Finance* 19: 425–42.

Shiller, Robert J. 2014. Speculative Asset Prices. *The American Economic Review* 104: 1486–517. [CrossRef]

Song, Han-Suck, and Mats Wilhelmsson. 2010. Improved price index for condominiums. *Journal of Property Research* 27: 39–60. [CrossRef]

Srinivasan, Venkat C. 1994. Using the analytical hierarchy process in house selection. *Journal of Real Estate Finance and Economics* 9: 69–85.

Tofallis, Chris. 2008. Investment volatility: A critique of standard beta estimation and a simple way forward. *European Journal of Operational Research* 187: 1358–67. [CrossRef]

White, Halbert. 1980. A Heteroscedasticity-Consistent Covariance Matrix Estimator and a Direct Test for Heteroskedasticity. *Econometrica* 40: 817–38. [CrossRef]

Wilhelmsson, Mats. 2002. Spatial models in real estate economics. *Housing, Theory and Society* 19: 92–101. [CrossRef]

Wilhelmsson, Mats. 2004. A method to derive housing sub-markets and reduce spatial dependency. *Property Management* 22: 276–88. [CrossRef]

Wu, Jing, Yongheng Deng, and Hongyu Liu. 2014. House price index construction in the nascent housing market: The case of China. *The Journal of Real Estate Finance and Economics* 48: 522–45. [CrossRef]

Zhao, Xiaogang, Yi Zhou, and Jianyu Zhao. 2011. Fire safety assessment in oil depot based on Comprehensive Grey Relational Analysis. Paper presented at Reliability, Maintainability and Safety (ICRMS), 2011 9th International Conference on, Guiyang, China, June 12.

Zhao, Xiaogang, Yi Zhou, and Jianyu Zhao. 2013a. Application of Fuzzy Analytic Hierarchy Process in Selection of Electrical Heat Tracing Elements in Oil Pipelines. *Applied Mechanics and Materials* 367: 452–56. [CrossRef]

Zhao, Jian Yu, Yi Zhou, and Xiao Yang Cai. 2013b. Selection of Engineering Management University Internship Projects Based on Fuzzy Analytic Hierarchy Process. *Advanced Materials Research* 787: 1002–5. [CrossRef]

Zheng, Xiao, and Shui Tai Xu. 2010. The Risk Assessment Research on Real Estate Projects in View of Fuzzy-Synthetical Evaluation. *Applied Mechanics and Materials* 29: 2455–61. [CrossRef]

Zietz, Joachim, Emily Norman Zietz, and G. Stacy Sirmans. 2008. Determinants of house prices: A quantile regression approach. *Journal of Real Estate Finance and Economics* 37: 317–33. [CrossRef]

Zopounidis, Constantin. 1999. Multicriteria decision aid in financial management. *European Journal of Operational Research* 119: 404–15. [CrossRef]

Journal of
Risk and Financial Management

MDPI

Article

Credit Ratings and Liquidity Risk for the Optimization of Debt Maturity Structure

Faiza Sajjad * and Muhammad Zakaria

Department of Management Sciences, COMSATS University, Islamabad 44000, Pakistan; mzakaria@comsats.edu.pk
* Correspondence: faiza@ciit.net.pk

Received: 19 March 2018; Accepted: 8 May 2018; Published: 11 May 2018

Abstract: The purpose of this study is to examine the relationship between credit rating scales and debt maturity choices. A liquidity hypothesis is used to formulate the testable proposition and conceptual framework. Generalized linear model (GLM) and pooled ordinary least square (OLS) are utilized by SAS programming to test the proposed hypothesis. Other different estimation techniques are also used for robust evidence. Results suggest that companies with high and low ratings have a shorter debt maturity. Companies with medium ratings have longer debt maturity structure. Liquidity shows a negative association with longer debt maturity structure. It is evident that at high rating scale with high liquidity, and at lower rating scales with lower liquidity firms have a shorter debt maturity. Mid rated firms with a low probability of refinancing risk show longer debt maturity structure. Considering refinancing risk by Asian companies make the nonlinear relationship between credit ratings and debt maturity choices. Results suggest the importance of credit ratings for the optimization of debt maturity structure of Asian firms, which was totally overlooked by the past studies. The findings of this study are consistent with the liquidity hypothesis. The findings also motivating financial managers and investors to consider credit ratings as a measure of financial constraints.

Keywords: credit ratings; debt maturity structure; liquidity risk; Asian firms

---

1. Introduction

There are several studies in the finance discipline that are mostly concentrated on the choice between debt and equity in the Asian markets, but there is another area of interest that is debt maturity structure, which can be of the same importance but is generally not a focus of financial research. There is rather little empirical evidence on the determinants of debt maturity structure of Asian firms.

The failure of non-financial institutions such as Lehman Brothers and the Bear Stearns during the recent financial crisis once again focused attention on the risk arising from short-term debts. It is now consistently recognized that the adjacent cause for the collapse of such institutions was their refinancing risk due to larger dependability on short-term debts, (Chen et al. 2013). The theoretical literature has acknowledged the refinancing risk arising from the short-term debt, (Dang and Phan 2016; Parise 2017). Optimal debt maturity choices play a vital role in the firm's financial structure. It is assumed from previous studies that right proportion of short-term debt and long-term debt can decrease the cost of financing, (Fan et al. 2012; He and Milbradt 2016; Khurana and Wang 2015), agency cost (Flannery 1986), and information asymmetry, (Diamond 1991). (Diamond 1991) shows that in the "presence of credit market frictions, firms may face difficulty in rolling over short-term debt, especially if refinancing coincides with a deterioration in either firm fundamentals or credit market conditions". The contemporary theoretical literature argues that refinancing or liquidity risk may itself be an additional source of credit risk because short-term debt increases the possibility of a run on the firm and worsen the conflict of interest between debt holders and shareholders, (Dimitrov et al. 2015; He et al. 2017; Wang and Zhang 2017).

Others have argued (Antoniou et al. 2006; Valta 2016) that the optimal debt maturity structure also reduces the cost of capital and bankruptcy risk. Some research (Wang and Zhang 2017) argues that even when there is an equal value of short-term debt and long-term debt, there is still a need for the right decision about the maturity of debt financing to avoid liquidity risk.

The selection of debt financing is dependent on the private information in which the management is concerned about the quality of the firm, (Öztekin and Flannery 2012). This fact can be related to the credit ratings that portray the quality of firms and reduces the information asymmetry between investors and borrowers. There is very little research on the importance of credit ratings in debt maturity choices, (Diamond 1991; Guedes and Opler 1996; Naeem 2012). The study of (Flannery 1986), on debt financing choices, is considered as one of the pioneering studies that put the focus on the importance of signaling in the debt maturity structure.

Credit rating agencies also obtain information from the public and private sectors which is crucial for firms so that they know about current and future economic trends. To be precise, to meet issuers' demand for financial information, the credit rating agencies provide a clear and realistic financial picture of firms in terms of codes and symbols that fulfill the demands of the issuer. Moreover, credit rating provides accurate pricing of securities, and visibly reduces the cost of each transaction due to use of shortcodes. Therefore, it is expected that rated firms would gain the assistance of credit rating agencies to grab attention from investors. Credit ratings also provide perks of giving financial flexibility, decreasing the chances of incorrect and asymmetric information in the market (Lok and Richardson 2011).

In addition, credit ratings give encouragement to firms to sustain a good level of ratings in the market. Today, credit ratings are used by banks, plan sponsors, fund managers and trustees of financial firms not only in the US but also across the globe for financial portfolio management (Cantor 2004). The stature, pertinence, and value of credit rating agencies have ascended with the passage of time as it is clearly observed that investors and firms depend on these agencies for their output and performance. The inspiration for this investigation started with the perception that an organization's financial managers, regulatory authorities, investors, and speculators are concerned about credit ratings when making their investment and financing choices. Credit ratings can also helpful for optimal debt maturity choices.

Generally, studies on debt maturity structures are based on the U.S. and European market, among those first papers is that of Morris (1976), which focused on U.S. companies. Moreover, other researchers also cover mainly U.S. firms (CScherr and Hulburt 2001; Mark Hoven Stohs 2002), and there is only a restricted list of studies focused on cross-country comparisons (Antoniou et al. 2006; Fan et al. 2012). In the emerging economies, there are limited studies on the corporate debt maturity structure, even there is no evidence on the relationship between credit ratings and the debt maturity structure of Asian firms. The aforementioned scenario also highlights the need for a considered approach towards financial risk management that would support firms in a changing financial environment. Asian financial markets, like other regions, have also observed a remarkable growth in the development of credit rating agencies. Therefore, a comprehensive study to examine the effect of credit ratings on the debt maturity structure of Asian firms is required. The main objective of this research is to "examine the relationship between credit ratings and the debt maturity structure of Asian firms".

Moreover, this study is the first attempt to empirically examines the Diamond (1991) framework to elaborate the influence of each rating scale on the debt maturity choices and further complements it by assuming the importance of refinancing risk. Although there is a big lapse of academic literature on debt maturity structure for the Asian market, it is understood from the previous discussion that a different and distinct setting is presented by Asian markets providing an opportunity to analyze this issue with more elaboration. Therefore, in this context, the key research question of this study is as below:

Do credit rating scales have any explanatory power for the debt maturity structure of Asian companies? Or is there any relevance of the debt maturity structure of firms for credit ratings?

The paper is structured as follows. After the introduction, a literature review and theoretical framework are presented in Section 2. The Section 3 presents an explanation of research methodology and estimation procedure. Section 4 consists of the empirical results and interpretations. The Section 5 presents the conclusion of the paper.

2. Literature Review

Theoretical debate on debt maturity structure started from the proposition of (Stiglitz 1988), that the debt maturity structure of firms is irrelevant to their value in perfect capital markets; a rationale like the irrelevance proposition for capital structure of firms presented by (Modigliani and Miller 1958). As it is evident to understand that none of the capital markets is perfect, due to taxation, cash inflows, and outflows, information asymmetry, agency cost, and interest rate etc. Therefore, there are numerous empirical as well as theoretical studies that negate and challenge the idea of irrelevance propositions for determination of maturity structure of debt. Four theories have been established for studying the irrelevance proposition for debt maturity structure: (i) the hypothesis of agency costs; (ii) the asset maturity hypothesis; (iii) tax liabilities in debt maturity structures; (iv) signaling theories for debt maturity structure as well as information asymmetry.

Agency cost theory stated that the potential or absolute conflict between bondholders and shareholders can be reduced with the help of debt maturity structure (Jensen and Meckling 1976). The conflict can also originate when the firm's capital structure has a risky debt inclusion to execute positive NPV (net present value) projects. These profits should be shared between bondholders and shareholders (Ataullah et al. 2018; Khurana and Wang 2015). There are some other ways argued by (Myers 1977), that the maturity debt reduction also reduces the underinvestment problems despite having other means of conflict resolution e.g., including restrictive covenants to debt contracts. Asset maturity hypothesis proposed that debt maturity has a risk of being unable to process fixed outflows of cash along with inflows that are generated by business processes. This risk can be mitigated with the matching of cash inflows and outflows (Myers and Majluf 1984). This can be a prevaricating policy for firms so that the maturity of the asset can be compatible with the debt maturity. In such cases, firms should have sufficient funds that are generated from assets.

(Brick and Ravid 1985) argued that a positive relationship is already established between the debt maturity structure and taxation, and the optimal strategy to work on the firms is to increase the long-term debt.

Signaling theory stated that the selection of debt maturity structure is dependent on the private information by which management is concerned about the quality of the firm. (Flannery 1986) are considered as pioneering studies that put the focus on the signaling of debt maturity structure. (Flannery 1986) proposed an argument that debt maturity structure of firms can indicate a firm's quality to outsiders and can impact an investor's decision. The model of Flannery proposes the assumption that the short-term debt is issued frequently for a long term can raise the fixed transaction cost of firms as compared to long-term debt.

There are numerous research studies that present an empirical view, specifying important factors established on theoretical models. The research design of many past studies relies on the firm's level measures such as growth opportunities, size, matching for the maturity of assets, interest ratio, firm's quality, liquidity etc. (Ataullah et al. 2018; Dang and Phan 2016; Katper et al. 2017). Moreover, some studies have been more focused on institutional or industrial classification, (Debortoli et al. 2017; Fan et al. 2012; Jõeveer 2013; Martins et al. 2017; Naeem 2012).

A firm's financing decision is significantly affected by the economic environment of the country, particularly in the case of developing countries. Very few studies incorporate macroeconomic factors in financing decisions (Chen et al. 2013; Debortoli et al. 2017; Deesomsak et al. 2004; He et al. 2017; Wang and Zhang 2017; Faiza Sajjad 2018).

In advanced and third wave literature is an increasing number of studies investigating whether credit ratings issued by external credit rating agencies, such as Moody's or Standard and Poor's, are helpful in explaining firms' financial structure behaviour (Chen et al. 2013; Chong et al. 2015; De Haan 2017; Efing and Hau 2015; Fracassi et al. 2016; Gopalan et al. 2014; Gul and Goodwin 2010; Naeem 2012; Faiza Sajjad 2018).

Since the complexity of financial markets and borrowers' and lenders' diversity is increasing, credit rating has now become a reliable parameter to assess the creditworthiness of firms, regulators, and investors (Kedia et al. 2017). The perceptional changes of market participants are mainly influenced by credit ratings issued by rating agencies. After that, numerous borrowers and different financial institutions have settled certain credit standards in the market and has successfully achieved the attention of regulatory bodies in various countries (Wojewodzki et al. 2017). To be precise, the 2008 financial crisis has made it important to search more into the importance of financial decision-making process for firm's productivity. There are numerous advantages of rated firms i.e., extending the base of investors, accurate security pricing, and reduction of dependence on conventional funding sources e.g., debt markets. It is contended by (Bolton et al. 2012; CFR.org 2015; Chava et al. 2014) that even in the state of financial crises, firms with ratings are not facing any major issue in raising funds.

Two survey-based studies (Graham and Harvey 2000; Mittoo and Zhang 2008), on firms in US and European markets, claim that refinancing risk is another subsequent element which is considered by firms while making debt maturity structure decisions. Liquidity risk is also explored by past studies as an important determinant of debt maturity structure. Firms are likely to get liquidation and more costly financing if they become incapable of rolling over debt to the next period. In these cases, the costs and advantages of selecting a certain level of maturity in the financial structure can be evaluated from the prospect of liquidity risk. (Bancel and Mittoo 2004) show that 70% of a sample consider liquidity risk as the second major factor for debt maturity decisions. The increased liquidity risk of firms is also raised by the intensity of information asymmetry between lenders and borrowers (Bruche and Segura 2015; Chen et al. 2013; Mian and Santos 2017).

Diamond's model suggests that short-term debt is not the priority of all firms. This fact can be related to the credit ratings that portray the quality of firms when the information is updated in a systematic manner for investors so that the issue of information asymmetry between investors and insiders can be resolved. (Diamond 1991) defines the liquidity risk as '... a solvent risk due to which the illiquid borrower becomes unable to attain an interest in refinancing parties' (p. 710). After that, firms prefer to do trade off costs between the benefits of choosing short-term debt and the cost of liquidity risk. (Diamond 1991), stated that a non-monotonic relationship exists between debt maturity structure and liquidity risk as it is assessed by credit ratings. Low risk and high rated firms, and high risk and low rated firms tend to issue high debt for the short-term and intermediate firms having more issuance of long-term debt.

Numerous empirical studies test the non-monotonicity between credit ratings and financial structure based on the U.S. market. However, a mixed relationship is found. For example, (Barclay and Smith 1995) a study on U.S. firms is inconsistent with the non-monotonic relationship and (Naeem 2012; Mark Hoven Stohs 2002) find strong evidence of non-monotonicity between debt maturity structure and credit ratings by assuming liquidity risk.

Several studies in the literature have been conducted to determine the optimal debt maturity structure as well as the importance of credit ratings, but no empirical study has been conducted on the relevance of each credit rating scale for the optimization of debt maturity structure in Asian markets. The aforementioned research gaps leave some room for additional research. Hence, the purpose of this research is to investigate the importance of each rating scale for the optimal debt maturity structure of Asian firms. Country factors, firms' factors, and industry dummies are also used as proxy measures for robust evidence. Therefore, by following the argument made by Diamond (1991), a hypothesis for the present study is suggested as follows:

Hypothesis (H1). *There is a non-linear (inverted U-shaped) relationship between rating scales and debt maturity choices by assuming liquidity risk, with other factors being steady.*

Through a literature review, the following variables are identified for the theoretical framework of the present study. The dependent variable is longer debt maturity (DML), the independent variable is individual credit ratings (ICR) because this paper tests the explanatory power of each rating scale on the maturity structure of debts.

Control variables include a firm's factors such as tangibility (FAR), interest coverage ratio (IR), quality (AR), liquidity (LIR), profitability (PR), size (SIZ). Industry dummies (ID) consist of nine industries classified by DataStream, (Basic material (BMD), consumer goods (CGD), consumer services (CSD), industrial (INDSD), technology (TECD), telecommunication (TELD), utility (UTILD), healthcare (HCD), oil and gas (OGD). Country factors are GDP growth (GD), domestic stock market (SM), real interest rate (RI), inflation rate (INF) (World bank database). Figure 1 shows the conceptual framework of the study.

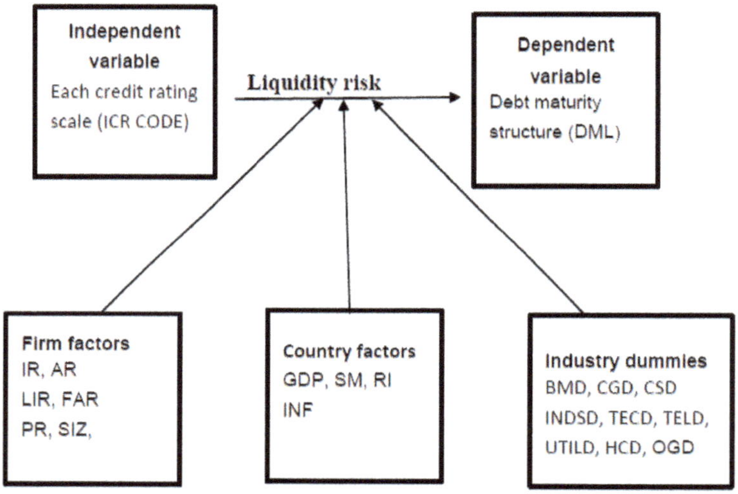

Figure 1. A conceptual framework.

This study is expected to contribute to both the literature on the maturity structure of debts and on credit ratings by presenting empirical evidence to the formulated theoretical framework, that refinancing risk induces a non-linear inverted u-shaped relationship between each rating scale and the maturity structure of debt.

Although the theoretical and empirical literature identifies liquidity risk as an important determinant of debt maturity structure, (He and Xiong 2012; Parise 2017) but credit rating is totally ignored as an important determinant of debt maturity structure by past studies. Therefore, this study is unique in this context and expected to present novel findings of the non-linear relationship between rating scales and the maturity structure of debt for Asian firms by assuming liquidity risk.

3. Research Methodology

3.1. Model Specification and Data Selection

The research sample consists of non-financial listed Asian companies that are rated by Standard and Poor's rating agency. A sample of Asian rated firms by Standard and Poor's are small as compared to non-rated firms and the main objective of the study is to determine the optimal debt maturity structure of rated firms and their behavior according to each rating scale. Therefore, that sample is important to draw an accurate conclusion for a special group of rated firms and their behavior.

Non-financial companies are chosen from eight selected Asian regions (Japan, South Korea, Singapore, China, Hong Kong, Indonesia, Malaysia, India, (JSSCHIMI)). The financial data was extracted from DataStream based on nine industrial classifications. Long-term issuer credit ratings by Standard and Poor's are used. Macroeconomic data are extracted from the World Bank database. Financial firms and firms with missing observations during sample years are excluded. For the empirical evidence the data set employed consists of the balanced panel data of 137 rated firms; for 17 years (2000–2016), resulting in 2329 observations.

The theoretical framework for this study comprised two aspects i.e., First the research studies on credit ratings and debt maturity structure. Second control variables include a firm's factors, country factors, and industry dummies. A coding methodology is used to measure the credit ratings of each company and test the influence of credit assessment on debt maturity structure. According to (Kisgen 2006, 2009), coding schemes are established by the actual credit ratings given by Standard and Poor's rating agency. A numerical code of 1 to 16 is allocated to each rating level or individual rating category (See Table 1).

Table 1. Long-term issuer ratings and assigned numerical coding.

Credit Ratings	Individual Rating Coding
AA+	1
AA	2
AA−	2
A+	4
A	5
A−	6
BBB+	7
BBB	8
BBB−	9
BB+	10
BB	11
BB−	12
B+	13
B	14
B−	15
CCC+	16

The theoretical framework is formulated from the extensive literature review and from Diamond's 1991 liquidity hypothesis. Table 2 shows the selected variables of the current study, such as debt maturity ratio (longer debt maturity) as a dependent variable, credit ratings as an independent variable, control variables, (a firms' factors, country factors, and industry dummies).

Table 2. The theoretical framework.

Dependent Variable	Symbol	Formula
Debt maturity ratio	DML	Long-term debts/total debts
Independent Variable		
Credit rating scales	ICR	Credit ratings issued by Standard and Poor's (long-term issuer) and measured by ordinal numbering or codes
Control Variables		
Firms factors		
Profitability	PR	Return on assets
Interest coverage ratio	IR	EBIT/total interest
Tangibility	FAR	Fixed assets/total assets
Size	SIZ	Log of sales
Liquidity	LIR	Current assets/total assets
Quality	AR	Total assets turnover ratio (activity ratio)
Country factors		
GDP Growth	GDP	World Bank database
Domestic stock market	SM	Percentage of market capitalization to GDP growth
Inflation rate	INF	Inflation deflators (World Bank database)
Real interest rate	RI	World Bank database
Industry dummies	ID	Nine industries from DataStream

3.2. Model for Maturity Structure of Debt and Credit Ratings

To empirically test the relevance of each rating scales and the debt maturity structure, following equation is specified. ICR^2 is used to test the non-monotonic relationship between DML and ICR.

$$\begin{aligned} DML \; &= \overline{\alpha}_0 + \overline{\alpha}_1 ICR_{it} + \overline{\alpha}_2 ICR_{it}^2 + \Phi_3 IR_{it} + \Phi_4 AR_{it} + \Phi_5 FAR_{it} + \Phi_6 LIR_{it} \\ &+ \Phi_7 PR_{it} + \Phi_8 SIZ_{it} + \Phi_9 ID_{it} + \Phi_{10} GDP_{it} + \Phi_{11} SM_{it} \\ &+ \Phi_{12} RI_{it} + \Phi_{13} INF_{it} + \varepsilon_{it} \end{aligned} \tag{1}$$

DML = Debt maturity structure
ICR = each rating scale/ individual credit rating
ICR^2 = Square of individual credit ratings

All other are control variables such as firm factors (IR, AR, FAR, LIR, PR, SIZ), Industry dummies (ID) and Country factors (GDP, SM, RI, INF).

3.3. Estimation Techniques

Generally, past studies on the corporate debt maturity structure were using pooled OLS. The present study is using a new technique that is a generalized linear model (GLM) along with pooled OLS for strong evidence. GLM represent a class of regression models that allow generalizing the linear regression to adjust many types of response variables including binary, count, continuous, positive and proportion distributions, (Fox 2008; Wulff 2007). It is considered a valuable statistical technique due to its flexibility in solving different statistical complication and is widely used. According to (Fox 2008), in the past twenty years, GLM has been referred as the most substantial development in regression analysis. GLM has "the ability to handle a larger class of error distributions and data types and this is the key improvement of GLMs over linear models".

Moreover, for robust evidence and solving the different problems of data, such as endogeneity, autocorrelation and heteroskedasticity, estimation techniques such as fixed effect (FE), heteroskedastic consistent variance (HCV) and generalized method of moment (GMM) are employed to examine the influence of each rating scale on the debt maturity structure.

According to prior studies, dynamic panel models play a significant role in corporate finance research. Currently, GMM is extensively used for estimating dynamic financial structure decision, (Antoniou et al. 2008; Cheng 2014; Lu et al. 2015; Öztekin and Flannery 2012). The two-step GMM is employed in this study. For dynamic panel data, GMM is generally used in situations like heteroskedasticity, autocorrelation, fixed individual effect, endogeneity and if the data sample has small T time period and large individuals N", (Cheng 2014; Faiza Sajjad 2018).

4. Results and Discussion

Descriptive statistics are presented before properly examining the link between the debt maturity structures and credit ratings. Table 3 shows the statistical summary of all variables including the dependent, independent, and control variables.

Table 3. Descriptive statistics.

Var	N	Mean	Std Dev	Minimum	Maximum
DMS	2329	0.499	0.295	0.000	0.99
DML	2329	0.500	0.295	0.000	0.99
ICR	2329	6.87	3.065	1.00	15.00
IR	2329	30.60	177.47	−234.1	7654
AR	2329	0.88	0.797	0.010	12.30
LIR	2329	1.764	1.610	0.048	21.84
PR	2329	3.544	7.323	−94.03	52.25
FAR	2329	2.74	25.47	−0.024	653.42
SIZ	2329	8.315	10.81	1.053	428.35
GD	2329	4.419	3.59	−5.41	17.29
SM	2329	252.11	367.73	14.33	2595
INF	2329	1.892	3.61	−6.00	20.44
RI	2329	3.916	2.927	−3.852	13.347

It is shown that the average longer debt maturity (DML) of the Asian companies is 0.510, and shorter debt maturity is 0.499. It is evident that the firms on average have a slightly higher amount of long-term debt. The deviations within the sample are considerable (standard deviation = 0.29). The result indicates that mainly companies wanted longer maturity in their debt maturity structure, which could be due to avoiding liquidity risk and underdeveloped bond market in Asia. Control variables also show some differences in the debt maturity structure of the Asian firms. In particular, the standard deviation is too much high in the interest coverage ratio (IR) = 177.4, and in the domestic stock market (SM) = 367.7. This could be due to firms being selected from heterogeneous markets from highly developed markets like Korea, Japan to less developed such as Indonesia and India etc.

Table 4 displays the mean of the shorter debt maturity and the longer debt maturity of the sample with respect to each credit rating scale. The higher-rated firms show mixed evidence for debt maturity structure. At AA+ rating with 1 coding number shows more short-term debts 0.53 (SM), and at code 1, and 2 with AA, AA− credit rating scales, long-term debts are higher in the debt maturity structure of firms, 0.542, 0.542, respectively. The average short-term debts are high at the top rating scales A+, A, A–. Moreover, at the lowest rating scale from BB+ to B–, firms show high short-term debt as compared to long-term debts, while BBB+, BBB, BBB– category of firms have the highest average longer debt maturity. The distribution of average short-term debt and long-term debt ratios provides initial evidence of being consistent with the theory of Diamond (1991), and with the intended hypotheses that suggested a non-linear association of credit rating scales and the debt maturity structure of Asian firms.

Table 4. Mean of shorter and longer debt maturity at each rating scale.

ICR	Variable	N	Mean	Std Dev	Minimum	Maximum
1 (AA+)	DMS	67	0.537	0.28	0.0034	0.98
	DML	67	0.462	0.285	0.016	0.996
2 (AA)	DMS	90	0.457	0.25	0.008	0.9817
	DML	90	0.542	0.25	0.018	0.991
3 (AA−)	DMS	90	0.457	0.257	0.008	0.981
	DML	90	0.544	0.257	0.018	0.991
4 (A+)	DMS	318	0.544	0.285	0.003	0.999
	DML	318	0.455	0.283	0.0002	0.996
5 (A)	DMS	110	0.515	0.272	0.0112	0.999
	DML	110	0.484	0.270	0.0006	0.9887
6 (A−)	DMS	345	0.566	0.294	0.0046	0.999
	DML	345	0.432	0.295	0.0003	0.995
7 (BBB+)	DMS	524	0.422	0.28	0.000	0.999
	DML	524	0.574	0.28	0.000	0.999
8 (BBB)	DMS	277	0.418	0.29	0.002	0.999
	DML	277	0.581	0.299	0.000	0.997
9 (BBB−)	DMS	134	0.376	0.264	0.00395	0.998
	DML	134	0.622	0.265	0.0016	0.996
10 (BB+)	DMS	105	0.574	0.266	0.0031	0.999
	DML	105	0.439	0.272	0.0004	0.996
11 (BB)	DMS	50	0.506	0.278	0.018	0.999
	DML	50	0.493	0.278	0.0004	0.981
12 (BB−)	DMS	70	0.573	0.3305	0.007	0.99
	DML	70	0.4250	0.330	0.001	0.992
13 (B+)	DMS	37	0.562	0.304	0.018	0.982
	DML	37	0.438	0.301	0.017	0.963
14 (B)	DMS	24	0.741	0.226	0.112	0.964
	DML	24	0.258	0.226	0.035	0.887
15 (B−)	DMS	82	0.779	0.243	0.096	0.9977
	DML	82	0.218	0.242	0.002	0.9031

Figure 2 illustrates the maturity structure of debt (DML) of the Asian firms with respect to each rating scale (ICR). Consistent with the results in Table 3, the maturity structure of debt shows a non-linear association with credit-rating scales.

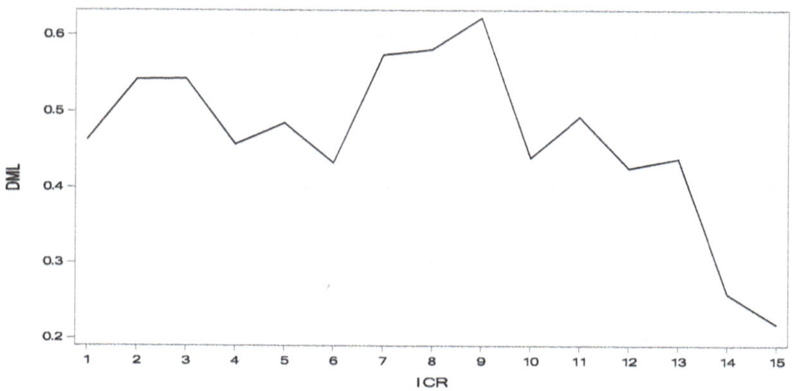

Figure 2. Longer debt maturity and individual credit rating.

Proc Panel was used for pooled OLS, FE and GMM estimations, and Proc Genmod was used for the GLM technique in SAS programming.

Table 5 shows the findings of pooled OLS and generalized linear model (GLM). The individual credit rating ICR and its square ICR^2 both are significant at a coefficient estimate of 0.039 *** and −0.0031 *** in the GLM. Results of pooled OLS also show that each credit rating (ICR) and its square ICR^2 are significantly related to debt maturity structure (DML) at a coefficient estimate of 0.0392 *** and −0.0030 *** respectively. Moreover, a negative sign with ICR^2 shows that with increasing rating scales longer debt maturity is decreasing. Results indicate that the longer-term debt maturity structure of firms in Asia varies with their credit ratings.

Table 5. Influence of rating scales on the debt maturity structure.

	Generalized Linear Model (GLM)		Pooled OLS	
Parameter	Estimate	Wald Chi-Square	Estimate	*t* Value
Intercept	0.2622	(42.36) ***	0.262247	(6.48) ***
ICR	0.0392	(29.45) ***	0.039222	(5.40) ***
ICR2	−0.0031	(48.79) ***	−0.00306	(−6.95) ***
IR	−0.0001	(4.90) **	−0.00007	(−2.20) ***
AR	−0.0199	(6.45) **	−0.01991	(−2.53) ***
FAR	0.0006	(7.02) ***	0.000618	(2.64) ***
LIR	−0.0115	(9.08) ***	−0.01149	(−3.00) ***
PR	0.0005	0.33	0.000492	0.57
SIZ	0.0008	(2.32) *	0.000834	(1.52) *
BMD	0.1341	(20.55) ***	0.134066	(4.51) ***
CGD	0.1466	(23.03) ***	0.146582	(4.78) ***
CSD	0.2753	(51.34) ***	0.275252	(7.13) ***
INDSD	0.1453	(25.24) ***	0.145308	(5.00) ***
TECD	0.1531	(25.08) ***	0.153106	(4.98) ***
TELD	0.1894	(36.00) ***	0.189438	(5.97) ***
UTILD	0.3308	(88.55) ***	0.330808	(9.37) ***
OGD	0.3191	(61.67) ***	0.319068	(7.82) ***
HCD	0.0149	0.04	0.014868	0.20
GD	−0.0034	(3.34) *	−0.00338	(−1.82) **
SM	−0.0001	(42.96) ***	−0.00011	(−6.52) ***
INF	0.0076	(11.66) ***	0.007584	(3.40) ***
RI	0.0090	(12.79) ***	0.00897	(3.56) ***
Scale	0.2752		R^2	0.13

Note: Values in parenthesis are Wald chi-square and *t*-values. ***, ** and * indicates that value is statistically significant at 1%, 5% and 10% level of significance, respectively.

It is evident that there is a non-linear association of credit rating scale with debt maturity structure of Asian firms. The coefficient estimates show that the debt maturity ratio increases by 3.9 percentage points with the exacerbation of each credit rating levels, but this rise has a declining rate of 0.31 percentage points with every squared individual credit rating level in both GLM and pooled OLS. The findings of the study supported the formulated hypothesis that "There is a non-linear (inverted U-shaped) relationship between rating scales and debt maturity choices by assuming liquidity risk, with other factors being steady". It is also evident that at each rating scale the behavior of firm toward debt maturity choices is different and consideration of liquidity risk at different rating scale induces non-linear inverted u-shaped relationship between credit ratings and maturity choices of debt.

High-rated firms possess shorter maturity as compared to mid-level rating firms due to lower concerns about liquidity risk. Low-rated firms, even when they are prone to high liquidity risk, have shorter maturity. This is because of limited accessibility to the long-term debt market. This is an important piece of evidence and it has practical implications for the optimization of the debt maturity structure of Asian firms. The evidence is also supported by Diamond (1991) and is consistent with the U.S.-based studies (Barclay and Smith 1995; Mark Hoven Stohs 2002) and U.K. based studies (Naeem 2012).

Liquidity (LIR), shows a negative and significant relationship with longer debt maturity structure with coefficient estimates of −0.011***, and it is approximately the same in both the estimation techniques. The findings clearly show that when there is higher liquidity ratio, firms are inclined toward shorter debt financing into the firm's financial structure. When there is a lower liquidity ratio or a higher rollover risk, then firms will prefer long-term debt financing in their debt maturity structure. Results also indicate that among the firm's factors liquidity has larger and significant Wald-chi square (9.08) in GLM and (−3.0) in pooled OLS as compared to the firm's other variables.

Interest coverage ratio (IR) and total assets turnover ratio (AR) show a negative and significant relationship with a longer debt maturity structure by both GLM and pooled OLS estimations. The tangibility ratio (FAR), shows a positive and significant relationship with longer debt maturity. Size (SIZ) shows a positive and less significant association with debt maturity structure. Profitability ratio (PR), shows a positive but insignificant relationship with the longer debt maturity structure.

Macroeconomic factors show mixed evidence in the current study. GDP growth (GD), shows negative and less significant association with a longer debt maturity of companies. Domestic stock market (SM,) shows a negative and significant relationship with longer debt maturity ratios. Inflation (INF), and real interest ratios (RI) show positive and significant association with longer debt maturity structure by both GLM and pooled OLS estimations.

All industrial dummies show a positive and significant relationship with longer debt maturity structure of Asian firms except the healthcare industry, which shows a positive and insignificant relationship with the longer debt maturity structure of Asian firms. It is evident that it is mainly industries in Asia that have longer debt maturity structure. This could be one of the reasons for avoiding liquidity or rollover risk in their corporate financial decisions.

Robust Check by Other Estimation Techniques

Table 6 shows the impact of each rating scale on the debt maturity structure by the fixed effect method (FE), heteroskedastic consistent variance (HCV), and generalized method of moment (GMM). The evidence is consistent with the findings of the generalized linear model (GLM) and pooled OLS estimations.

Longer debt maturity shows a positive and significant relationship with each rating scale at 0.0692 ***, 0.03922 ***, 0.22130 *** coefficient estimates respectively by all three estimation techniques. Moreover, ICR^2 shows a negative and significant relationship with longer debt maturity structure at −0.0045 ***, −0.003 ***, and −0.012 *** respectively, by fixed effect (FE), heteroskedastic consistent variance (HCV) and generalized method of moment (GMM). It is evident that the impact of each rating scale on the debt maturity structure is non-linear and inverted U-shaped. FAR and SM are used as an exogenous instrument. The Sargan test statistic 50.67 (PR = 0.168) shows that the selected instrumental variables are valid and does not show any over-identification problem in the GMM estimation. All variables jointly explain 13% variation within the debt maturity structure by the heteroskedastic consistent variance (HCV) estimation. R^2 by fixed effect (FE) increased and explains 48% variation in debt maturity structure by all variables. Control variables show mixed evidence. Liquidity (LIR) shows a negative and significant relationship with longer debt maturity structure by HCV and GMM estimations but shows a positive and insignificant relationship with longer debt maturity structure by the fixed effect (FE) model.

Table 6. Credit ratings and maturity structure of debt.

Variable	Fixed Effect	Heteroskedastic Consistent Variance	Generalized Method of Moment (GMM)
	DML	DML	DML
Intercept	0.174178 (2.17) **	0.26225 (6.96) ***	−0.18285 (−0.51)
ICR	0.069224 (7.37) ***	0.03922 (5.59) ***	0.221305 (11.60) ***
ICR^2	−0.00452 (−7.97) ***	−0.00306 (−7.35) ***	−0.01239 (−14.09) ***
IR	−0.00004 (−1.43)	−7.3E−05 (−1.72) *	0.000027 −0.19
AR	−0.01381 (−1.01)	−0.01991 (−2.34) **	−0.07291 (−1.55) *
FAR	0.000677 (2.79) ***	0.000618 (3.06) ***	−0.00007 (−0.35)
LIR	0.004518 −1.11	−0.01149 (−2.63) ***	−0.02113 (−2.89) ***
PR	−0.00072 (−0.81)	0.000492 −0.61	−0.00261 (−11.63) ***
SIZ	0.000076 −0.15	0.000834 (3.80) ***	0.038683 (9.23) ***
BMD	0	0.13407 (5.07) ***	−0.51494 (−1.40)
CGD	−40.4352 0	0.14658 (5.44) ***	−0.85954 (−2.05) **
CSD	38.55667 0	0.27525 (8.02) ***	0.831662 −1.49
INDSD	0.499514 (2.19) **	0.14531 (5.77) ***	−0.13095 (−0.36)
TECD	0	0.15311 (5.31) ***	−0.17543 (−0.46)
TELD	77.86987 0	0.18944 (6.27) ***	−0.866 (−1.93) **
UTILD	0.635812 (1.96) **	0.33081 (10.21) ***	−1.20083 (−2.23) **
OGD	44.49687 0	0.31907 (9.24) ***	−0.43596 (−0.98)
HCD	230.6575 0	0.01487 −0.16	12.02196 −0.47
GD	−0.00016 (−0.05)	−0.00338 (−1.79)	0.003053 (3.28) ***
SM	−0.00002 (−0.53)	−0.00011 (−5.85) ***	0.000065 (3,27) ***
INF	0.001257 −0.35	0.00758 (3.19) ***	−0.01216 (−2.20) **
RI	0.005664 (1.59) *	0.00897 (3.39) ***	−0.00561 (−1.24)
R^2	0.48	0.13	
Sargan test			50.67 −0.1687
ARtest(m1) (m2)			−1.83 −0.067 −0.17 −0.864

Note: Values in parenthesis are t-values. ***, ** and * indicates that value is statistically significant at 1%, 5% and 10% level of significance, respectively.

5. Conclusions

The purpose of the study is to examine the impact of each rating scale on debt maturity structure. The study proposed a conceptual framework of credit ratings (ICR) and debt maturity structure (DML) with control variables such as firms' factors, industry dummies, and macroeconomic variables. The study also empirically tested Diamond's liquidity hypothesis, which gives the theoretical basis for two variables DMT and ICR. Estimation techniques such as the generalized linear model (GLM), pooled OLS, fixed effect (FE), heteroskedastic consistent variance (HCV) and generalized method of moment (GMM) were used. The findings of the study indicate that high-rated firms show mixed evidence and have slightly more short-term debt, but long-term debts are also not too low that can be due to less information asymmetry which decreases the liquidity risk and easy access to financial markets. Low-rated firms face high refinancing risk due to the deterioration in credit ratings and consequently face restricted access to long-term debt markets, and so they have short-term debt in their debt maturity structure. Only mid-rated firms prefer more long-term debt because they have an option for long-term debt maturity and they also have a certain amount of liquidity risk, which stops them from increasing shorter maturity in their debt maturity structures. Results also indicate that maximum industry dummies show a positive and significant association with the longer debt maturity structure of Asian companies. Among financial variables of firms, liquidity shows a significant and negative association with longer debt maturity structure. Macroeconomic factors also show a substantial effect on the debt maturity structure of Asian companies.

The findings of the study have answered the main research question and proved the hypothesis that there is a non-monotonic relationship between the credit-rating scales and debt maturity choices of Asian firms. The evidence is also supported by Diamond's (1991) theoretical framework and is consistent with U.S.-based studies (Barclay and Smith 1995; Mark Hoven Stohs 2002) and U.K. based studies (Naeem 2012), Moreover, the importance of credit ratings in the financial structure is also supported by previous studies (Bedendo and Siming 2016; Daniels et al. 2010; Gul and Goodwin 2010; Lütkebohmert et al. 2017; Naeem 2012). The study also reveals that credit rating has a substantial effect on the optimization of debt maturity structure of Asian companies.

Credit ratings should be considered as a key determinant for making financing decisions. Credit rating agency assigns credit rating codes after analyzing internal and external factors of firms that help to reduce information asymmetry. Findings also suggested that credit ratings have significant explanatory power for debt maturity structure and gives unique insight to capture the behavior of firms toward debt financing choices by considering the cost and benefits of credit ratings such as, liquidity risk, creditworthiness of firms, the loyalty of customers and suppliers, restriction to enter into debt market, costly covenants, access to commercial paper market etc.

This study is useful for chief financial officers (CFOs) in firms wishing to make optimal financing decisions. Regulatory bodies and policymakers can benefit by considering credit ratings as a regulatory tool in financial market development and should monitor and regulate credit-rating agencies for transparent credit-rating outcomes.

Like most research studies, this study also has some limitations. This study has a limited number of rated Asian firms from Standard and Poor's rating agency. Thus, it cannot investigate the impact on a broader range of data. Future studies on the debt maturity structure may also employ different financial and macroeconomic ratios. Different rating categories and rating indexes can also be implied in future research. Data from local and other international rating agencies can also be used for further research.

Author Contributions: F.S. wrote the paper and M.Z. supervised and edited the paper.

Conflicts of Interest: The authors declare no conflict of interest.

References

Antoniou, Antonios, Yilmaz Guney, and Krishna Paudyal. 2006. The Determinants of Debt Maturity Structure: Evidence from France, Germany and UK. *European Financial Management* 12: 161–94. [CrossRef]

Antoniou, Antonios, Yilmaz Guney, and Krishna Paudyal. 2008. The Determinants of Capital Structure: Capital Market-Oriented versus Bank-Oriented Institutions. *Journal of Financial and Quantitative Analysis* 43: 59–92. [CrossRef]

Ataullah, Ali, Andrew Vivian, and Bin Xu. 2018. Time-varying managerial overconfidence and corporate debt maturity structure. *European Journal of Finance* 24: 157–81. [CrossRef]

Bancel, Franck, and Usha R. Mittoo. 2004. The Determinants of Capital Structure Choice: A Survey of European Firms. *Financial Management* 33: 103–32. [CrossRef]

Barclay, Michael J., and Clifford W. Smith Jr. 1995. The Maturity Structure of Corporate Debt. *The Journal of Finance* 50: 609–31. [CrossRef]

Bedendo, Mascia, and Linus Siming. 2016. Debt structure and credit ratings. Working Paper. Available online: ftp://ftp.repec.org/opt/ReDIF/RePEc/baf/papers/cbafwp1622.pdf (accessed on 20 January 2018).

Bolton, Patrick, Xavier Freixas, and Joel Shapiro. 2012. The credit ratings game. *Journal of Finance* 67: 85–112. [CrossRef]

Brick, Ivan E., and S. Abraham Ravid. 1985. On the Relevance of Debt Maturity Structure. *The Journal of Finance* 40: 1423–37. [CrossRef]

Bruche, Max, and Anatoli Segura. 2015. Debt maturity and the liquidity of secondary debt markets. *Journal of Financial Economics* 124: 599–613. [CrossRef]

Cantor, Richard. 2004. An introduction to recent research on credit ratings. *Journal of Banking and Finance* 28: 2565–73. [CrossRef]

The Credit Rating Controversy. 2015. *CFR Backgrounders*. pp. 1–5. Available online: http://www.cfr.org/financial-crises/credit-rating-controversy/p22328 (accessed on 20 January 2018).

Chava, Sudheer, Rohan Ganduri, and Chayawat Ornthanalai. 2014. Are Credit Ratings Still Relevant? Working Paper. Available online: https://doi.org/10.2139/ssrn.2023998 (accessed on 20 January 2018).

Chen, Hui, Yu Xu, and Jun Yang. 2013. *Systematic Risk, Debt Maturity, and the Term Structure of Credit Spreads*. Working Paper No. 18367; Cambridge, MA, USA: National Bureau of Economic Research.

Cheng, Hang. 2014. Determinants of Capital Structure in Asian Firms: New Evidence on the Role of Firm-Level Factors, Industry Characteristics, and Institutions. Ph.D. dissertation, University of Leicester, Leicester, UK. unpublished.

Chong, Byung, In Deokand Hwang, and Young Sang Kim. 2015. Credit ratings and short-term debt financing: An empirical analysis of listed firms in Korea. *Asia-Pacific Journal of Financial Studies* 44: 88–128. [CrossRef]

Dang, Viet A., and Hieu V. Phan. 2016. CEO inside debt and corporate debt maturity structure. *Journal of Banking and Finance* 70: 38–54. [CrossRef]

Daniels, Kenneth, Demissew Diro Ejara, and Jayaraman Vijayakumar. 2010. Debt maturity, credit risk, and information asymmetry: The case of municipal bonds. *Financial Review* 45: 603–26. [CrossRef]

Debortoli, Davide, Ricardo Nunes, and Pierre Yared. 2017. Optimal time-consistent government debt maturity. *Quarterly Journal of Economics* 132: 55–102. [CrossRef]

Deesomsak, Rataporn, Krishna Paudyal, and Gioia Pescetto. 2004. The determinants of capital structure: Evidence from the Asia Pacific region. *Journal of Multinational Financial Management* 14: 387–405. [CrossRef]

De Haan, Ed. 2017. The financial crisis and corporate credit ratings. *Accounting Review* 9: 161–89. [CrossRef]

Diamond, Douglas W. 1991. Debt Maturity Structure and Liquidity Risk. *Quarterly Journal of Economics* 106: 709–37. [CrossRef]

Dimitrov, Valentinand, Darius Palia, and Leo Tang. 2015. Impact of the Dodd-Frank act on credit ratings. *Journal of Financial Economics* 115: 505–20. [CrossRef]

Efing, Matthias, and Harald Hau. 2015. Structured debt ratings: Evidence on conflicts of interest. *Journal of Financial Economics* 116: 46–60. [CrossRef]

Fan, Joseph P.H., Sheridan Titman, and Garry Twite. 2012. An International Comparison of Capital Structure and Debt Maturity Choices. *Journal of Financial and Quantitative Analysis* 47: 23–56. [CrossRef]

Flannery, Mark J. 1986. Asymmetric Information and Risky Debt Maturity Choice. *The Journal of Finance* 41: 19–37. [CrossRef]

Fox, John. 2008. Generalized Linear Models. *Applied Regression Analysis and Generalized Linear Models* 135: 379–424. [CrossRef]

Fracassi, Cesare, Stefan Petry, and Geoffrey Tate. 2016. Does rating analyst subjectivity affect corporate debt pricing? *Journal of Financial Economics* 120: 514–38. [CrossRef]

Gopalan, Radhakrishnan, Fenghua Song, and Vijay Yerramilli. 2014. Debt Maturity Structure and Credit Quality. *Journal of Financial and Quantitative Analysis* 49: 817–42. [CrossRef]

Graham, John R., and Campbell R. Harvey. 2000. The Theory and Practice of Corporate Finance: Evidence from the Field. Available online: http://ecsocman.hse.ru/data/030/124/1231/Empirich_issled_po_byudzh_i_dr_Graham2000.pdf (accessed on 20 January 2018).

Guedes, Jose, and Tim Opler. 1996. The Determinants of the Maturity of Corporate Debt Issues. *The Journal of Finance* 51: 1809–33. [CrossRef]

Gul, Ferdinand A., and John Goodwin. 2010. Short-Term debt maturity structures, credit ratings, and the pricing of audit services. *Accounting Review* 85: 877–909. [CrossRef]

He, Zhiguo, and Konstantin Milbradt. 2016. Dynamic Debt Maturity. *Review of Financial Studies* 29: 2677–736. [CrossRef]

He, Zhiguo, and Wei Xiong. 2012. Rollover Risk and Credit Risk. *Journal of Finance* 67: 391–430. [CrossRef]

He, Xue Zhong, Eva Lütkebohmert, and Yajun Xiao. 2017. Rollover risk and credit risk under time-varying margin. *Quantitative Finance* 17: 455–69. [CrossRef]

Jensen, Michael C., and William H. Meckling. 1976. Theory of the firm: Managerial behavior, agency costs, and ownership structure. *Journal of Financial Economics* 3: 305. [CrossRef]

Jõeveer, Karin. 2013. Firm, country and macroeconomic determinants of capital structure: Evidence from transition economies. *Journal of Comparative Economics* 41: 294–308. [CrossRef]

Katper, Naveeda K., Aziman Madun, Karim Bux Syed, and Muhammad Nawaz Tunio. 2017. Determinants of debt maturity structure in Shariah and non-Shariah firms in Pakistan: A comparative study. *Journal of Applied Economic Sciences* 12: 1210–25.

Kedia, Simi, Shivaram Rajgopal, and Xing Alex Zhou. 2017. Large shareholders and credit ratings. *Journal of Financial Economics* 124: 632–53. [CrossRef]

Khurana, Inder K., and Changjiang Wang. 2015. Debt maturity structure and accounting conservatism. *Journal of Business Finance and Accounting* 42: 167–203. [CrossRef]

Kisgen, Darren J. 2006. Credit ratings and capital structure. *The Journal of Finance* 61: 1035–72. [CrossRef]

Kisgen, Darren J. 2009. Do firms target credit ratings or leverage levels? *Journal of Financial and Quantitative Analysis* 44: 1323–44. [CrossRef]

Lok, Stephen, and Scott Richardson. 2011. Credit markets and financial information. *Review of Accounting Studies* 16: 487–500. [CrossRef]

Lu, Yang Cheng, Yu Chen Wei, and Tsang Yao Chang. 2015. The effects and applicability of financial media reports on corporate default ratings. *International Review of Economics and Finance* 36: 69–87. [CrossRef]

Lütkebohmert, Eva, Daniel Oeltz, and Yajun Xiao. 2017. Endogenous Credit Spreads and Optimal Debt Financing Structure in the Presence of Liquidity Risk. *European Financial Management* 23: 55–86. [CrossRef]

Martins, Henrique C., Eduardo Schiehll, and Paulo R. S. Terra. 2017. Country-level governance quality, ownership concentration, and debt maturity: A comparative study of Brazil and Chile. *Corporate Governance: An International Review* 25: 236–54. [CrossRef]

Mian, Atif, and João A.C. Santos. 2017. Liquidity risk and maturity management over the credit cycle. *Journal of Financial Economics* 127: 264–84. [CrossRef]

Mittoo, Usha R., and Zhou Zhang. 2008. The capital structure of multinational corporations: Canadian versus U.S. evidence. *Journal of Corporate Finance* 14: 706–20. [CrossRef]

Modigliani, Franco, and Merton H. Miller. 1958. The Cost of Capital, Corporation Finance and the Theory of Investment. *American Economic Review* 48: 261–97. [CrossRef]

Morris, James R. 1976. On Corporate Debt Maturity Strategies. *Journal of Finance* 31: 29–37. [CrossRef]

Myers, Stewart C. 1977. Determinants of corporate structure. *Journal of Financial Economics* 5: 147–75. [CrossRef]

Myers, Stewart C., and Nicholas S. Majluf. 1984. Corporate financing and investmentdecisions when firms have information that investors do not have. *Journal of Financial Economics* 13: 187–221. [CrossRef]

Naeem, Shammyla. 2012. Financial Structure of UK Firms: The Influence of Credit Rating. Ph.D. thesis, University of Glasgow, Glasgow, UK; p. 371.

Öztekin, Özde, and Mark J. Flannery. 2012. Institutional determinants of capital structure adjustment speeds. *Journal of Financial Economics* 103: 88–112. [CrossRef]
Parise, Gianpaolo. 2017. Threat of entry and debt maturity: Evidence from airlines. *Journal of Financial Economics* 127: 226–47. [CrossRef]
Faiza Sajjad, Muhammad Zakaria. 2018. Credit Rating as a Mechanism for Capital Structure Optimization: Empirical Evidence from Panel Data Analysis. *International Journal of Financial Studies* 6: 13. [CrossRef]
CScherr, Frederick, and Heather M. Hulburt. 2001. The debt maturity structure of small firms. *Financial Management* 30: 85–111. [CrossRef]
Stiglitz, Joseph E. 1988. Why Financial Structure Matters. *Journal of Economic Perspectives* 2: 121–26. [CrossRef]
Mark Hoven Stohs, David C. Mauer. 2002. The Determinants of Corporate Debt Maturity Structure. *Journal of Business* 69: 279–312. [CrossRef]
Valta, Philip. 2016. Strategic Default, Debt Structure, and Stock Returns. *Journal of Financial and Quantitative Analysis* 51: 1–33. [CrossRef]
Wang, Haiping, and Jing Zhang. 2017. Fair value accounting and corporate debt structure. *Advances in Accounting* 37: 46–57. [CrossRef]
Wojewodzki, Michal, Winnie P.H. Poon, and Jianfu Shen. 2017. The role of credit ratings on capital structure and its speed of adjustment: An international study. *European Journal of Finance* 24: 735–60. [CrossRef]
Wulff, Shaun S. 2007. SAS for Mixed Models. *The American Statistician* 61: 184–85. [CrossRef]

MDPI
St. Alban-Anlage 66
4052 Basel
Switzerland
Tel. +41 61 683 77 34
Fax +41 61 302 89 18
www.mdpi.com

Journal of Risk and Financial Management Editorial Office
E-mail: jrfm@mdpi.com
www.mdpi.com/journal/jrfm

www.ingramcontent.com/pod-product-compliance
Lightning Source LLC
Chambersburg PA
CBHW041754220926
51847CB00014B/199
* 9 7 8 3 0 3 9 2 1 6 2 4 6 *